LITERATURE AND HUMANITARIAN REFORM IN THE CIVIL WAR ERA

PHILANTHROPIC STUDIES

Robert L. Payton and Dwight F. Burlingame,
GENERAL EDITORS

LITERATURE AND HUMANITARIAN REFORM IN THE CIVIL WAR ERA

Gregory Eiselein

Indiana
University
Press

BLOOMINGTON AND INDIANAPOLIS

Excerpts from "Isolation" by Tony J. Giordano from *Unending Dialogue: Voices from an AIDS Poetry Workshop* by Rachel Hadas. Copyright © 1991 by Tony J. Giordano. Reprinted by permission of Faber and Faber, Inc.

A version of Chapter 5, "Whitman and the Humanitarian Possibilities of Lilacs," appeared in *Prospects* 18 (1993). Copyright © 1993 Cambridge University Press. Reprinted with the permission of Cambridge University Press.

The paper used in this publication meets the minimum requirements of American National Standard for Information Sciences—Permanence of Paper for Printed Library Materials, ANSI Z39.48-1984.

Manufactured in the United States of America

Library of Congress Cataloging-in-Publication Data

Eiselein, Gregory, date
    Literature and humanitarian reform in the Civil War era / Gregory Eiselein.
        p.   cm. — (Philanthropic studies)
    Includes index.
    ISBN 0-253-33042-4 (alk. paper)
    1. American literature—19th century—History and criticism. 2. United States—History—Civil War, 1861–1865—Literature and the war. 3. United States—History—Civil War, 1861–1865—Civilian relief. 4. Authors, American—19th century—Political and social views. 5. Literature and society—United States—History—19th century. 6. Social problems—United States—History—19th century. 7. Charities—United States—History—19th century. 8. Social problems in literature.   I. Title.   II. Series.
    PS217.C58E38   1996
    810.9'358—dc20   95-33576

1   2   3   4   5   01   00   99   98   97   96

To my loving parents,
Kathy Scholes and Jim Eiselein

CONTENTS

ILLUSTRATIONS

PREFACE

Philanthropy lives on because the opportunity to realize it has been missed. Perhaps the notion that philanthropy could be made real and thus come to an end is strange. To most, philanthropy, like the poor, will always be with us. But, at moments in the past and now in our own age, a few others have tried to imagine a philanthropy that would succeed so well as to eliminate the inequalities that divide the needy from the well-off. Realizing philanthropy, according to these committed but eccentric humanitarians, would entail perhaps not the end of all suffering (a truly utopian thought) but at least the end of the hierarchical distinction between powerful persons who bestow assistance and weaker persons who merely receive it (persons sometimes thought of as "patients"). Reciprocity and self-empowerment would replace charitable paternalism. The subject of this book is humanitarian writer-activists who urged this eccentric benevolence. (And by "eccentric benevolence" I mean philanthropy that deviates from established forms of benevolence by offering assistance in a way that dismantles the disparity in power separating humanitarian agents from humanitarian patients.)

Although its historical focus is expressly the Civil War era, the book begins and ends in our own era—the age of AIDS. By joining analyses of neglected portions of the cultural history of philanthropy to the exigencies and innovations in contemporary philanthropy, I illuminate the significance of alternative approaches to humanitarianism for our own era. Hence, this is a work of connected criticism, combining historical analysis of literature and culture with thoughts on present avenues for humanitarian action. The belief that theory and criticism should be actively linked to prosocial practices will, I hope, become a central principle of philanthropic studies. As a contribution to philanthropic studies, I want to show that academic critical inquiry into philanthropy can and must be persuasively and productively connected to contemporary philanthropic action.

In the chapters that follow, I track eccentric conceptions of patient/agent relations in the humanitarian works of Harriet Wilson, John Brown, Harriet Jacobs, Louisa May Alcott, Walt Whitman, and Henry Thoreau among others. In the introduction, I introduce the critical and theoretical assumptions that underpin my project, and I clarify a few key concepts—such as "eccentric," "patient" and "agent," "philanthropy" and "humanitarianism"—using an analysis of Wilson's *Our Nig*. This first chapter also explains how upheavals in Civil War–era philanthropy spurred the creation of eccentric humanitarianism. As conflicts over slavery escalated prior to the Civil War, as the romantic reform ideal collapsed, and as war-related suffering grew in disturbing and unprecedented proportions, the complex struggles around humanitarianism intensified. A crisis erupted. And the crisis sent humanitarians looking for new and sometimes eccentric approaches to suffering and care.

As I illustrate in chapter 2 ("Dangerous Philanthropy"), the responses to John Brown's raid on Harpers Ferry were indicative of this crisis in humanitarianism and representative of the concerns that troubled this humanitarianism in flux. Chapter 3 ("Harriet Jacobs and the Subversion of Style") reveals the ways that *Incidents in the Life of a Slave Girl* deployed sentimental conventions to argue for an equitable relation between paternalistic white abolitionists and African Americans. "Suffering beyond Description," the fourth chapter, looks at Civil War efforts to care for the wounded and the patient-centered approaches developed by Walt Whitman and Louisa May Alcott. In chapter 5 ("Whitman and the Humanitarian Possibilities of Lilacs") I demonstrate how Whitman's postwar poetry reshaped mourning conventions to create a less coercive consolation. The sixth chapter ("Eccentric Benevolence and Its Limits") illuminates some of the dilemmas facing humanitarianism after the war, dilemmas created by dominant prewar and postwar models of philanthropy. Thoreau's perspective on philanthropy, though limited by the very eccentricity of his thinking, offered humanitarians a path through these dilemmas, a path not taken.

The concluding chapter reconsiders the problems and possibilities in nineteenth-century benevolence by moving the discussion to a late-twentieth-century context, the humanitarian and literary responses to AIDS. Like the humanitarians I examine, like any author, I am writing from a specific place at a specific moment in history. New suffering, new crises, new dangers, new forms of coercion, and new forms of resistance have determined the writing of this book, and the afterword is an explicit acknowledgment that historical writing is inevitably about the present.

I am deeply appreciative of all the support I received while writing this book. The University of Iowa and an Alumni Dissertation Fellowship Travel Award provided assistance to begin research on this book. A fellowship from the Indiana University Center on Philanthropy on behalf of the Lilly Endowment and other donors enabled me to continue work on it. My colleagues in the Department of English and the Program in Cultural Studies have made Kansas State University a productive and inspiring place to work as I finished it.

The generosity, thoughtfulness, and talk of a number of people made this book possible. I want to thank those who were and are a part of the Manhattan AIDS Project and The Iowa Center for AIDS Resources and Education, including Deb Tiemens, Javier, Donald, and especially the late David Ellingsworth who taught me what this book was really about. I would like also to thank the students in my Literature and AIDS course and my Literature and Culture of the Civil War–Reconstruction Era course for their enthusiastic interest and thoughtful discussions. Friends and colleagues in a variety of fields—American Studies, Cultural Studies, English, History, Philanthropic Studies, and Women's Studies—offered critical, constructive, stimulating responses to earlier versions of this project: Alice

Adams, Anne Bartlett, Linda Brigham, Dwight Burlingame, Nancy Cervetti, Ken Cmiel, Kathleen Diffley, Wayne Franklin, Lawrence Friedman, Michael Meyer, Dee Morris, Anne Phillips, Larry Rodgers, Jane Schultz, Leslie Schwalm, Albert Stone, and Craig Stroupe. Their generosity has enlivened and sustained me and my work. It is a special pleasure for me to acknowledge the steady encouragement and support of Ed Folsom, my teacher, whose limitless supply of discerning insight, reassurance, and faith enabled me to write precisely the book I was hoping to write.

LITERATURE AND
HUMANITARIAN
REFORM IN THE
CIVIL WAR ERA

ONE

AN INTRODUCTION TO
ECCENTRIC BENEVOLENCE

The unusual needs to be commented upon. . . .
ANNE SEXTON[1]

Memory at a Moment of Danger

A political problem and an epidemiological nightmare, AIDS is also a humanitarian crisis. The promise of a scientific solution to the spread of HIV looks as far away as ever: no cure, no magic bullet seems imminent. The realization that "AIDS is not a transitory phenomenon" has led David L. Kirp, among others, to call for a "refocusing on the human factor" in the fight against AIDS. Kirp writes, "If nature, tamed [that is, science], is not going to provide a solution, at least not for some time, then nurture—how we care for ourselves and for one another—is where we must look again."[2] This turn to "nurture" (medical, nursing, preventive, humanitarian care) is not meant to divert attention from HIV/AIDS or delay scientific research. Instead, it is the recognition that caregiving is currently our most reasonable source for hope in dealing with AIDS. But the provision of care for people living with AIDS remains grievously inadequate. In the United States, the unjust distribution of healthcare, the victim bashing, and the indifference to and abuse of people with AIDS highlight our society's present inability to offer decent, responsible humanitarian care.

Because writing this book on humanitarianism in the Civil War era has coincided with and, indeed, emerged out of our current crisis, I have thought continually about the relationship of humanitarianisms past and present. I have been concerned with how a history of humanitarianism might participate, however modestly, in changing contemporary humanitarian thought and practice, in making the provision of care more humane. Traditional, realist historiography, purporting to give an objective account of what really happened, cannot and has not often intended to play a transformative role in society. Orthodox historical methods tend to produce explanations and justifications for the "what is," the status quo, and thus almost always serve conservative rather than transformative ends.[3] In his "Theses on the Philosophy of History," Walter Benjamin criticizes conventional historiography for its "empathy with the victor," insisting that such empathy benefits the current state of society and those who hold power in it. "[A]ll rulers are the heirs of those who conquered before them," he writes.[4] Thus, a traditional, realist historiography could never change contemporary humanitarian practice, but would instead justify and defend humanitarianism in its present form.

If historical writing aims to participate in, rather than suppress, changes in humanitarian thought and practice, then it must, to use Benjamin's words, "brush history against the grain" (257). Under the pressure of the contemporary crisis, wanting to do more than interpret philanthropy and hoping in fact to change it, this book has sought out an alternative to traditional, realist historiography—a way to brush history against the grain. Rather than study the victors (what succeeded in the history of philanthropy), I have deliberately focused on what failed in humanitarianism's past, on the losers, the nondominant, the marginal, the unusual, the eccentric. Here, at the eccentric, is where historical knowledge might produce social change. Eccentric historiography provides an awareness of alternative ways of being and doing and helping. Such an awareness reminds us that social forms like philanthropy can and do change, and that the present state of society is by no means something inevitable or natural. Moreover, some alternatives may serve as useful models for present action.

According to Benjamin, once again, "To articulate the past historically does not mean to recognize it 'the way it really was' (Ranke). It means to seize hold of a memory as it flashes up at a moment of danger" (255). In this present moment of danger, the AIDS catastrophe and the attendant crisis in humanitarian care, my historical study attempts to seize hold of a memory of a past catastrophe, the Civil War, and its philanthropic crisis. This memory does not claim to be neutral knowledge. It's a perspective on history shaped by and shaped for the present danger. It is adrenaline to carry us through the present danger.

Humanitarianism in Crisis

In the years leading up to the Civil War, the United States witnessed a fairly widespread breakdown in humanitarian thought and action conventionally conceived. On August 25, 1859, the New York Times registered its deep dissatisfaction with philanthropy in an editorial on "Reform Schools and Houses of Reformation." During that summer, inmates at two Massachusetts reform schools had torched their institutions. Four days after the second arson (apparently a copycat crime of the first), the Times called for a reexamination of the "theory" and "practical operation" of humanitarian reform. Like numerous humanitarians, the *Times* felt that the usual modes of philanthropy were inadequate, out of date, ineffective, and even harmful. Humanitarians needed new approaches to philanthropic reform, new practices and new theories. The significance of the reform school fires was clear to the *Times* editorialists: "'moral suasion' was too exclusively relied on, and the distrusted 'restraint' too scrupulously avoided." Hoping for reform through enlightenment of individual sensibilities and seeking spiritual as well as political changes, antebellum humanitarians in the North had assiduously devoted themselves to the possibilities of "moral suasion." Yet, here at the end of the 1850s, the *Times* had come to see moral suasion as weak and naive, and insisted instead upon an idea that would dominate philanthropic enterprises for years to come: discipline. In reform institutions, declared the editorial, "there must be strict discipline." Dismissing the "sentimental" philanthropy that had animated reform projects for decades, the writer concluded: "All sentimental and amiable argument to show that they [reform school boys] are the victims of unfortunate circumstances is a positive injury, and tends only to sour and madden them towards society, not to renovate their character or improve them."[5] Moral suasion in humanitarianism was fading; an era of philanthropic discipline was emerging.

"Reform Schools and Houses of Reformation" appeared at a moment when the dominant model for humanitarian work was shifting in the North. In the years prior to the Civil War, as philanthropists were gradually abandoning the sentimental or romantic notion of a glorious moral reformation of the American people, humanitarianism began to undergo dramatic changes in its "theory" and "practical operation," its discourse, systems, and practices. No longer would moral suasion, education, sentiment, private conscience, and perfectionism remain the dominant themes; instead, the 1850s and 1860s launched a movement toward new ideals: discipline, order, science, centralization, efficiency, action, and state institutionalism. Although most nineteenth-century humanitarian enterprises contained a mix of sentiment and discipline, moral suasion and efficiency, an important change in the mix happened around the time of the Civil War.[6]

The reasons for the shift in philanthropic thought and action are inseparable from the Civil War itself. The persistence of slavery, the principal cause of the war, had frustrated activists and ignited numerous calls for change. In the 1850s, as the promise of romantic reform remained dishearteningly unfulfilled, and as knowledge of continued unjust suffering became popularized through texts like *Uncle Tom's Cabin,* antislavery humanitarians turned to electoral politics early in the decade and then, at decade's end, to more dramatic and untried strategies: John Brown's raid on Harpers Ferry was perhaps the boldest of these attempts to alter the direction of antislavery humanitarianism.

The enormous suffering created by the war itself—the sweeping dislocation and the casualties so numerous as to have been previously inconceivable—also transformed the thinking and practices of humanitarians, moving them to imagine humanitarian work of a comparable magnitude. The stupendous scale of the suffering created a sense of crisis and put intense pressure on humanitarians to move toward an approach that could account for and manage such large-scale pain. Thus, humanitarianism began to move toward large, bureaucratic, state-run, "incorporated" institutions—like the United States Sanitary Commission. While suffering of such unprecedented magnitude produced a willingness to experiment with new approaches to relief work, the military, the war's central institution, also played a key role in both instigating and regulating change within philanthropy during the 1860s. Humanitarians adopted the military's passion for organization, efficiency, mechanization, and large scale, while also absorbing its language of duty and discipline.

The changes in humanitarianism were, of course, only part of larger transformations throughout society and culture in the North. The creation of national markets, the industrialization and economic growth, the extension of railroads and westward migration that characterized the 1850s and 1860s no doubt expanded humanitarians' sense of scope and mission. The wartime move toward centralization and the widespread nineteenth-century trend toward professionalization shaped changes in the organization and management of humanitarian enterprises, just as rapid technological change forced humanitarian workers to rethink their means and methods. Although this period became for humanitarians a time of desperate innovation and difficult flux rather than consolidation or routine, benevolent work (like other aspects of society and culture in the United States) was headed for an era of "incorporation," to use Alan Trachtenberg's capacious term. The economic and demographic pressures that were shaping what Trachtenberg calls "the emergence of a changed, more tightly structured society with new hierarchies of control" had just begun to alter the course of humanitarianism.[7]

In the midst of this transformation, between the decline of antebellum humanitarianism and the full emergence of a disciplined and incorporated postbellum philanthropy, a crisis erupted. The frustrations that led to the war ignited the crisis, and the overwhelming suffering produced by the war fueled it. Humanitarians of all sorts had begun to see conventional ways of helping and thinking about help as woefully inadequate to the suffering around them. Moral suasion didn't seem to work. The rhetoric of romantic reform seemed unconvincing, while the unproven and not yet appealing ideology of discipline and efficiency lacked purchase. Humanitarianism was in crisis.

As a set of cultural signs and political practices, humanitarianism was throughout the nineteenth century a site of struggle and change. Dominant modes of humanitarianism worked to stabilize this flux and normalize their own theories and procedures; but in a time of social crisis, such normalizing and stabilizing became difficult when not impossible. In the 1850s and 1860s, the complex struggles within and around humanitarian work became more apparent and escalated in intensity. As the romantic ideal collapsed, humanitarian writers and activists began searching for new approaches to the suffering of others, new styles of humanitarianism, alternative modes for benevolent work. Multiple contending possibilities opened up in humanitarianism, making the historical moment rich with diverse, inventive, and unconventional conceptions of benevolence.

The focus of this book is not the shift from the predominant antebellum paradigm to the predominant postbellum paradigm, but rather the other possibilities that developed in the interval. I do not track the major changes in humanitarianism in the North, changes like those registered by the *New York Times* editorial. Instead, my aim is to investigate humanitarian works that never properly belonged to the philanthropic mainstream, humanitarian works that originated and flourished in this crisis.[8] As the agony of the enslaved re-presented itself to Northern readers with a moving new intensity and as Americans faced the suffering caused by the war, humanitarians were forced to develop new practices for dealing with suffering and new ways of understanding pain and the amelioration of pain. Sharpened by the realization that moral suasion could not end slavery and that romantic reform had failed to transform society, this pressure to invent new approaches gave remarkable rise to "eccentric" humanitarianism—humanitarian visions that stood apart from dominant models.

To the study of this transformative crisis in philanthropy and to philanthropic studies in general, I want to introduce the notion of "eccentric" benevolence. The term "eccentric" indicates here not so much idiosyncrasy or whimsy as that which veers from the center. It designates the way in which certain humanitarian ideas, texts, and practices deviated from but also maintained an appreciable relation to conventional philanthropy. Never exactly inside or outside dominant paradigms, eccentric benevolence stood at the edge of what is called "humanitarian." Its relation to dominant humanitarian discourses was one of disconnection as well as connection. Some of these eccentric, unorthodox humanitarian texts criticized established humanitarianism for being coercive. They suggested that what had allowed mainstream humanitarianism to become coercive was its conventional disregard for the ideas, feelings, and circumstances of those who received humanitarian care. More to the point, some of these alternative philanthropic visions hoped to create a less coercive humanitarianism by redressing the traditional power imbalance between the "patients" of humanitarianism (the sufferers, the persons needing help) and the humanitarian "agents" (those who do the helping).[9] I use the term "eccentric" to refer to precisely these culturally marginal humanitarian works that sought to make humanitarianism less coercive by making it more patient-centered.

Harriet Wilson's Humanitarian Work

Copyrighted on August 18, 1859, a week before the *New York Times* editorial on humanitarian reform, Harriet Wilson's autobiographical novel, *Our Nig,* is an illustrative example of the eccentric benevolence that flourished during (and because of) this crisis.[10]

Our Nig's main character, its themes, and its most overt function make the novel unmistakably humanitarian, and aspects of this humanitarianism are identifiably sentimental. Like Ellen from *The Wide, Wide World* (1850) or Gerty from *The Lamplighter* (1854), *Our Nig*'s protagonist, Frado, is a mistreated orphan, just as her mother is an orphan. The representation of a female hero as an orphan is a commonplace of sentimental fiction. By giving the audience a plucky and tenderhearted orphan heroine who struggles against the villainous Mrs. Bellmont and endures the abuse of a heartless world, *Our Nig* (like other sentimental-humanitarian novels) invites identification with the heroine and teaches readers to sympathize with the abused and the friendless. Because Frado is unmistakably autobiographical (even the third-person narration is sometimes dropped, as in the chapter titles "Mag Smith, My Mother" [5] or "A New Home for Me" [24]), the conventions of sentimental writing that invite identification with Frado also encourage readers to sympathize with the author and become participants in the novel's most overt aim—the search for humanitarian assistance.[11] As Wilson's Preface and the documents in the novel's Appendix attest, the book was written explicitly as an appeal for aid:

> [Wilson's] health is again falling, and she has felt herself obliged to resort to another method of procuring her bread—that of writing an Autobiography. (Appendix 137)

> Deserted by kindred, disabled by failing health, I am forced to some experiment which shall aid me in maintaining myself and child. (Preface 3)

Wilson directs this appeal to "my colored brethren" (3), the free black community in the North. Her hope is that they are willing to assist the author—a single, African American mother who has an illness and a disability, but no money and no family to fall back on.

Although *Our Nig* emerges from a sentimental cultural context, the novel's humanitarianism is not entirely typical of sentimental philanthropy. Indeed, in a number of ways, the book is eccentric to the conventions and ideals of romantic humanitarianism. Wilson's novel is, first of all, a sentimental humanitarian text that critiques sentimental humanitarianism. Although *Our Nig,* like the traditional antebellum humanitarian text, encourages philanthropic action by constructing sympathy between characters and between characters and readers, Wilson's text also draws attention to sympathy's failure. In the novel's final chapter, Frado meets and falls in love with a man who claims to be a fugitive slave. She marries him because she believes they share a similar, though unspoken, experience of "enslavement" and "oppression" (127). Wilson writes, "There was a silent sympathy which Frado felt attracted her, and she opened her heart to the presence of love" (127). Unfortunately, these feelings of "silent sympathy" utterly betray her: Frado and her husband share no such sympathetic bond; her husband was never a slave, only a fraud, one of the "professed fugitives from slavery" (126); and, with this "disclosure," he abandons Frado (128). Although the novel is not exactly a treatise against sympathy (the story ends by appealing directly to the "gentle reader" for "sympathy and aid" [130]), *Our Nig* does dramatically call into question the wisdom of trusting "sympathy."

Similarly, *Our Nig* is rather wary of orphan sheltering. Within sentimental literary humanitarianism, orphan sheltering is among the most admirable of humanitarian works. In Maria Susanna Cummins's *The Lamplighter,* for instance, Trueman Flint (the lamplighter who takes in the orphaned Gerty) represents all that is noble about those who rescue orphans: he is instinctively protective, caring, kind, sympathetic. "Great tears" well up in his eyes as he sits beside Gerty who "in a voice of fear" talks in her sleep. True's benevolence is admirable, and, ultimately, he will be rewarded for his selfless concern: "the Lord will bless and reward your kindness to that poor child," says the church sexton.[12] *Our Nig,* however, presents readers with a different picture of orphan protectors. In chapter 3, Mrs. Bellmont decides to take in the orphaned Frado and says:

> If I could make her do my work in a few years, I would keep her. I have so much trouble with girls I hire, I am almost persuaded if I have one to train up in my way from a child, I shall be able to keep them awhile. I am tired of changing every few months. (26)

Mrs. Bellmont practices orphan sheltering, not because she feels moved by the orphan's plight, but because she wants someone to do the housework. As Mrs. Bellmont's philanthropy confines and disempowers Frado, as it forces Frado to work without pay, orphan sheltering becomes a type of slavery in *Our Nig.* Thus, instead of using it primarily to introduce a benevolent ideal, as in *The Lamplighter,* Wilson deploys orphan rescuing to critique benevolence, the self-serving motivations that inspire it, and the coercive consequences for those helped.

Our Nig's relationship to New England's most famous antebellum philanthropic project, the antislavery movement, is likewise eccentric. Besides exposing fraud within the movement by identifying her no-account husband as only a "professed" fugitive slave (126), Wilson condemns racism among white abolitionists and her mistreatment at the hands of "professed abolitionists, who didn't want slaves at the South, nor niggers in their own houses, North. Faugh! to lodge one; to eat with one; to admit one through the front door; to sit next to one; awful!" (129). The novel's language generates a skeptical attitude toward the putatively benevolent abolitionists (by inserting and repeating the adjective "professed" so as to evoke a distinction between benevolent professions and benevolent action), and it ridicules their racism (by mimicking in broken, inarticulate prose the racist thinking of those who insincerely profess sympathy with African Americans). Wilson's skeptical view of abolitionist philanthropy begins in the Preface where, in explaining the incomplete nature of her story, she derisively quips: "I have purposely omitted what would most provoke shame in our good anti-slavery friends" (3). There was, apparently, a good deal of antislavery "shame" left unreported.[13]

While it is clear that Wilson partially rejects the sentimental humanitarian model, she is even more suspicious of disciplinary-institutional philanthropy. As an antebellum novel, *Our Nig* is largely silent about this mode of philanthropy that had not yet achieved cultural dominance. Yet, the novel finds the nascent forms of this type of philanthropy—the proto-institutional hospices for the chronically ill and the county farm for the indigent poor—cruel and intolerable. In chapter 11, for example, Frado is removed to a home where two older women care for the sick and collect public money for doing so. The novel represents the women as greedy, impatient, and ill-suited to caring for the sick. During her stay, Frado hopes to perfect her sewing so that she can help herself, earn some money, and escape the confines of public charity. Yet, before she can save more than a few dollars, one of the managers at the hospice uses Frado's sewing in bed as grounds for having her removed as an "imposter" (123). Bereft of support and now acutely ill, Frado feels the tyrannical hold that these "benevolent" women have over her life. The experience returns Frado to her "old resolution": to avoid the help of philanthropic souls, "to take care of herself, to cast off the unpleasant charities of the public" (124). In *Our Nig,* institutional philanthropy is something to be "cast off" (124), something to be "rescued" from (128). Hence, Wilson does not reject the dominant cultural form as a way to embrace this emerging form: her view is clearly eccentric to both of these mainstream forms of philanthropy.

Wilson does not, of course, disavow humanitarianism altogether; what she rejects is the domination of benevolent agents. *Our Nig* is a humanitarian novel that criticizes coercive humanitarianism and distances itself from accepted philanthropic ideals and practices. Yet, the most fascinating aspect of *Our Nig's* eccentricity is not its critique of conventional humanitarianism, but its enactment of a patient-centered humanitarianism. Nineteenth-century books about humanitarianism were usually authored by well-off middle-class folks who wanted to comfort and observe supposedly helpless, suffering others.[14] The autobiographical *Our Nig,* however, voices the ideas, stories, and plans of a woman who struggles against disability and disease, who suffers because of poverty and patriarchy, who carries the physical and psychical wounds inflicted by racism and humanitarianism. The body that suffers becomes in *Our Nig* the voice that directs help. In presenting *Our Nig* as an act of self-help, Wilson undercuts the othering hierarchy that structures benevolent discourse—the opposition between powerful humanitarian agents and helpless humanitarian patients. In *Our Nig,* the governing center for philanthropic activity is the person who suffers.

In writing a book in search of aid for her son and herself, Wilson intends, in turn, to help other black people, to alleviate some of their suffering just as she asks them to ease her pain. She offers her life story as a means to critique social ills that plagued all free blacks: white racism in the North, abolitionist hypocrisy, and the abuse and domination that, from her point of view, typically play a role in philanthropic acts. For Wilson, this kind of narrativized social critique might spur further examination of these problems and inspire action for change. Such a relationship between the author-patient and humanitarian readers in the black community eliminates the hierarchy separating patients and agents; paternalism and coercion are replaced by exchange and reciprocity. *Our Nig* moves away from a charity characterized by dependence and a domineering philanthropic agent and toward, in the words of John Ernest, "a more active system of exchange, based on mutual dependence and devoted to communal development." This shift is mirrored by the marriage of Mag (an impoverished and ostracized fallen white woman, Frado's mother) and Jim (Frado's African American father). As Ernest notes:

> Jim's efforts to help Mag (and himself) begin with pity. This pity leads to genuine reciprocity, however, for Mag surrenders her hope to reenter the circle of cultural

respectability, and Jim not only gets what he wants but also commits himself to give what he can.[15]

It is this belief that humanitarian action might be founded upon "genuine reciprocity" rather than the vulnerability and dependence of the person needing help that makes *Our Nig* both an example of a patient-centered philanthropy and an unconventional sentimental-humanitarian narrative.

In writing *Our Nig*, Wilson aimed to help herself and by doing so engage in cultural work that would alter conventional ways of helping and, at the very least, call into question conventional benevolence by using her own example to show the harm it could do. Yet, Wilson did not write *Our Nig* to advocate an end to humanitarian action. Indeed, the novel does the opposite: it makes a direct appeal for humanitarian assistance. But, as (a) humanitarian work, *Our Nig* is "eccentric": patient-centered, atypical, experimental, unconventional in several ways, unprecedented in some respects, and marginalized from mainstream humanitarian discourse.

It is important to add that, in 1859, the very form of Wilson's humanitarian work made it an eccentric text. With traditional avenues of assistance either closed or unacceptable to her, Wilson was "forced to some experiment" (3), and hit upon novel writing as a mode of humanitarian self-help. The experiment produced an unprecedented literary event: the first novel published by a black person in the United States. Thus, Wilson's text was atypical, an anomalous fragment within the literary and humanitarian discourse of the 1850s. Despite the novel's eccentric position in these literary and humanitarian discourses, *Our Nig* was necessarily a product of mid-nineteenth-century U.S. culture. It emerged from a specific cultural milieu where self-help was generally valued, where sentimental fiction argued the causes of humanitarian reform movements, and where African Americans used life stories to fight racism in the North and slavery and racism in the South. Before Wilson, African Americans had written poems, lectures, and autobiographies that agitated for humanitarian social reform, and a few had written novels published in England. Although this novel was an unprecedented literary and humanitarian occasion, *Our Nig* had both literary and humanitarian cultural precedents.

In other words, *Our Nig* absorbed and borrowed from literary-philanthropic culture in the North, while also resisting and criticizing aspects of that culture. To call *Our Nig* an "eccentric" text is not, then, to pretend that it arose out of thin air, nor to deny the social-historical determination of the novel within its cultural milieu. Instead, it is to suggest that cultural milieus are not homogeneous, that cultural milieus allow for innovation based upon already existing discourses and practices. *Our Nig* was a product of its culture as well as a text that took up an eccentric position within that culture.

Writing Histories of Benevolence

In contemporary discussions of humanitarian reform, eccentric texts like Wilson's *Our Nig* remain as marginal as they were in nineteenth-century humanitarianism. And what I am calling "eccentric benevolence" has never been given much of a place in the cultural and intellectual history of philanthropy. Such neglect is not, of course, incomprehensible. History is (usually) written by the victors, not the losers. The *New York Times'* call for discipline helped shape a trend that, because of its sweeping impact on humanitarian practice, received a great deal of historical attention in the twentieth century. Wilson's critique of philanthropy and her attendant move toward a patient-centered self-help were, on the other hand, ignored, forgotten for over 120 years.[16]

Such neglect is not necessarily justified, however. It is mostly the result of prevailing approaches to writing the history of humanitarianism and not the result of an intrinsic lack of historical significance or contemporary relevance within these eccentric humanitarian works. As I demonstrate in the chapters that follow, eccentric benevolence provides a remarkably illuminating critical vantage on the midcentury's transformative crisis, a vantage that opens up the complex struggles within and around humanitarianism in the Civil War era. Yet, as a brief survey of the historiography of benevolence illustrates, twentieth-century histories rarely allocate space for an analysis of eccentric humanitarian work. They often homogenize the complexity of humanitarian movements and motivations and focus attention on prominent white, middle- and upper-class reformers and the rationales they articulated for the reform projects they directed. Such approaches too readily dismiss reformers, projects, motivations, and discourses that stand outside the mainstream.

In writing a history of humanitarianism, historians take as an object of study a set of persons who like to help, who indeed ache to help those who suffer.[17] Historians have often praised benevolent work as altruistic, compassionate, noble. According to some scholars, the explosion of Anglo-American philanthropic activity in the eighteenth and nineteenth centuries was the result of "a new sensitiveness to human need" or "a new sensitiveness to human suffering." In his highly respected *English Philanthropy 1660–1960,* for example, David Owen has characterized the growth of charitable work, hospitals, and infirmaries in the late-eighteenth century by citing and endorsing John Wesley's view: "benevolence and compassion toward all forms of human woe have increased in a manner not known before from the earliest ages of the world." In histories like Owen's, humanitarian work is an expression of innate human qualities, and the growth of humanitarian work marks a step forward in the moral progress of humans. Robert Bremner's account of Civil War philanthropy, *The Public Good: Philanthropy and Welfare in the Civil War Era,* has attempted to counter skeptical antihumanist histories of reform by claiming that there is no reason to doubt that "altruism is a part of human nature." Earlier this century, F. J. Klingberg voiced a similar but less cautious belief in the altruistic capacities of human beings and spoke confidently of the British campaign against slavery as a victory of disinterested human benevolence against self-interest. For Russel B. Nye, humanitarian reform was "a movement in which rich and poor, cultured and uneducated, radical and conservative joined alike" in "a planned, rational, pragmatic effort . . . to realize for once and all the innate capabilities of mankind." Participating in the liberal-humanist assumptions of scholars like Owen, Bremner, Klingberg, and Nye, the neo-abolitionist historians of the 1960s celebrated the altruistic, "human," moral, and egalitarian achievements of the previous century's antislavery activists.[18]

Humanist historians like these often use the words of humanitarians to explain the history of humanitarian movements, sometimes citing the reformers' own explanations without submitting those explanations to a historicized, critical analysis. The humanitarian rhetoric of Wesley becomes for Owen the substantiation of the historical reality of benevolence. Relying on the professions of reformers as evidence for moral progress, humanist historians risk ignoring the consequences of reform and the patients' perspectives on reform. Such a method produces a celebratory but one-sided account of humanitarianism. Humanist perspectives tend also to lack historical explanatory power. By invoking "ordinary humanitarianism" or "the instinctive response of the humanitarian to the suffering of others" as historical explanations, historians tell us a great deal about the reformers' (and historians') faith in the innate benevolence of human beings but little about the historical and cultural conditions that shape humanitarian activity.[19]

This progressivist or humanist perspective has been increasingly under attack, due in large part to the ascendancy of "social control" historiography.[20] Social control interpretations begin with a skepticism similar to Jacques Lacan's psychoanalytic generalization about humanitarians: "we place no trust in altruistic feeling, we who lay bare the aggressivity that underlies the activity of the philanthropist, the idealist, the pedagogue, and even the reformer."[21] Armed with suspicion, these historians have carefully scrutinized philanthropy, demonstrating that humanitarian works are typically a part of rather ordinary attempts to control the difficult, the different, the out-of-order. To these historians, descriptions of progressive developments in humankind's moral sensibility or explanations of humanitarian action that refer to the unselfishness of reformers have seemed vague, ingenuous, useless. Accordingly, late-twentieth-century histories of humanitarianism are often stories of aggressive philanthropic efforts to direct behavior, exact obligations, stabilize society, and control the thinking, values, and activities of certain groups.[22]

Michel Foucault, for example, reads changes within nineteenth-century legal and penal systems not as humanitarian reforms but as sinister advancements in social control apparatuses. Nothing resembling a new humanitarian sensibility or "a new sensitiveness to human suffering" materialized in the eighteenth and nineteenth centuries. According to Foucault, the legal and penal apparatuses learned "not to punish less, but to punish better." Thus, he remarks in *Discipline and Punish*: "The conjecture that saw the birth of reform is not, therefore, that of a new sensibility, but that of another policy with regard to illegalities."[23]

Such arguments intelligently complicate our understanding of humanitarianism. But, if pushed to their logical extremes, they force us to yield to one of two options: (1) abandon the entire notion of humanitarianism as merely the masking of an insidious will to power; or, more unsatisfactorily, (2) fall back on the humanist view that humanitarians have somehow renounced their will to dominate and have thus been able to make transcendentally moral choices leading to inherently right action. I am deeply dissatisfied with both extremes.[24] The first is cynical and forecloses the possibility of humane action or ameliorative social change. A history of philanthropy that could justify a refusal to help others on the grounds that such helping might be oppressive is as useless as a history that ignores the inequalities and suffering created by philanthropic practices. The second extreme, the humanist view, is naive and rather mystifying in its appeal to a transcendental realm. In its admiration for the philanthropists' self-certifyingly good intentions, it overlooks the experiences of patients who found humanitarianism coercive, restraining, and humiliating. Neither extreme seems particularly useful to those who actually practice philanthropy. The humanist perspective can discourage critical self-reflection, while the social control view seems paralyzing in its skepticism about the value of organized attempts to alleviate human suffering.

Moreover, neither the social control position nor the notion of philanthropy as unselfish moral action can explain the complexity, diversity, or idiosyncrasy of benevolent work. Both positions divide too neatly humanitarian culture into two camps: the helpers, the powerful agents of humanitarian action, and the helped, the passive, usually helpless or victimized patients. Although humanist and social control perspectives theorize power and the patient/agent opposition in a variety of ways, these historians rarely recognize the agency of patients. Humanist versions of benevolence tend to see power as dangerous when used improperly or immorally, but power in the hands of moral, altruistic humanitarian agents can produce positive benefits for patients.[25] For many social control historians, humanitarian agents exist as formidable, conservative, relatively homogeneous, self-interested groups of persons, usually from the dominant classes, who use benevolence as a means to maintain power over their society and those whom they would help.[26] In Foucault's work, the exercise of domination over humanitarian patients is the effect of a particular system of truth. The agent of humanitarianism is not any individual or group of individuals; instead, agency is located in a specific set of discourses and practices, which taken together count as truth for a particular historical moment. Patients do not exist prior to the emergence of a truth discourse that creates subjects as patients, and power does not so much dominate as it creates and constitutes subjectivity through discourse. Power, then, is not something ruling-class humanitarians can hold over patients—although, to be sure, patients are subjected by humanitarianism.[27]

Despite their differing conceptions of power, these accounts generally represent humanitarian action flowing in one direction only, from agents to passive and malleable patients.[28] While it accords well with the views of many nineteenth-century humanitarians, the patient/agent distinction does not consider or account for the works and the agency of patients like Harriet Wilson. Attention to such activity disrupts the usual idea of the direction and source of humanitarian action and hence challenges both humanist and social control historiography. The focus on the agency of dominant humanitarians (or dominant humanitarianisms) and the reliance on their discourses as the principal source for historical evidence have produced accounts that ignore marginal, local, counterhegemonic, eccentric, patient-directed humanitarian projects. Likewise, homogenizing perspectives in which humanitarians are either self-evidently altruistic or surreptitiously self-interested tend to generate one-dimensional pictures of the complex interactions among conflicting organizations, individuals, discourses, and practices. Although my goal cannot be to render the whole of this complexity "the way it really was," I will introduce to the historical debate on philanthropy and culture some instances of eccentric humanitarianism, instances that complicate and problematize previous interpretations of nineteenth-century humanitarian culture in the North.

Eccentricity and Culture

This book's aim is to encourage attention to unconventional, patient-centered philanthropic practices by giving an account of the place of eccentric humanitarian works within Civil War–era philanthropy. Because interpreting (or even finding) instances of eccentric benevolence involves careful attention to the diversity and complexity of humanitarian activity, I conceptualize humanitarianism as a heterogeneous field of contending discourses, practices, ideologies, and actions. Understanding *Our Nig's* place within humanitarian culture requires a notion of culture that allows for heterogeneity, change, the unexpected, and subversion of the conventional—a notion that can explain how diverse types of oppositional agency are constructed *within* culture. Thus, I have rejected the view of philanthropy as one-directional action, just as I have rejected perspectives that tend to ignore the social and ideological variations among humanitarian works.

Fortunately, within what is sometimes called the "new cultural history" and, perhaps more importantly, within recent feminist histories of reform, I have found valuable guides to my own inquiry into nineteenth-century humanitarian culture. Moving away from the constraints of humanist and social control historiography, historians such as Lori Ginzberg, Mary Ryan, and Barbara Leslie Epstein have demonstrated how the study of reform activity within its social and cultural context can produce a multilayered understanding of how philanthropy functions within culture and how social power circulates through philanthropic practices. Linda Gordon's *Heroes of Their Own Lives* has shown, moreover, that writing a more useful and more complicated history of benevolent work requires, first of all, an explicit, careful attention to those who sought out or found themselves the recipients of humanitarian assistance.[29]

Following the example of these historians as well as various cultural critics from Antonio Gramsci to Raymond Williams to Judith Butler and bell hooks, I see culture as complex, contradictory, uneven, and at multiple points susceptible to revision, intervention, and improvisation.[30] I do not doubt that certain ideologies and practices assume a dominant or hegemonic place in culture over and against competing ideologies and practices. Certainly, counterhegemonic practices and countercultural ideologies are limited by and shaped in relation to the dominant culture. While the dominant culture attempts to normalize the anomalous and to quell crises, it often does so unsuccessfully or incompletely. Since such dominance is always incomplete, always in process, and often in crisis, oppositional and eccentric cultural practices question, challenge, shape, and reshape the dominant.

It is my initial assumption, then, that neither domination nor resistance are total, consistent, or historically invariable. Both cultural hegemony and counter-hegemonic incursions in all their forms are the provisional products of a culture that is fluid and uneven and more fluid and uneven in times of social crisis. That the conventions and contingencies of culture and history determine the style and direction of oppositional interventions makes such interventions no less opposi-tional. To show how these eccentric projects were determined by the very historical and cultural formations that they contested does not prove that culture is a uniform monolith that admits only noncontradictory parts. Instead, I contend, a reading of a work in its cultural context can reveal the cultural sources of resistance, the expansive and contradictory nature of culture, and the combina-tions of historical traditions and historical accidents that spark improvisatory transformation and allow for eccentric thought and practice.

Arguments which conclude that humanitarianism functions only as social control or insist that since a novel is undeniably a part of culture it must inevitably reproduce or exemplify its culture's regime of truth/power would have to explain a text like *Our Nig* as either a tale of victimization or an unconscious and marvelously duped vehicle for the reproduction of dominant ideology. Such readings suggest a totalizing picture of power and culture that miscorresponds to the diverse struggles in and around humanitarianism in 1859, a picture that erases eccentricity. Such readings reify the patient/agent hierarchy and (like conventional humanitarianisms) perpetuate the notion that patients had no power and no agency.

Throughout this study, the patient/agent axis is the principal structure along which I conduct my analysis of nineteenth-century humanitarianism. I do so not to further universalize or naturalize such an opposition but to present the relationship between helper and helped as a social relationship subject to change. Seeking to excite pity and action in readers, conventional humanitarian texts represented those who suffered as abject, helpless victims who needed and craved the aid of humanitarians. Fashioning some people (such as implied readers) as agents and others as patients, humanitarian literature constructed a power imbal-ance that separated the agents (the helpers, the position of privilege, strength, knowledge) from the patients (the helpless, the position of marginality, weakness, powerlessness). Despite its pervasive, structuring presence in humanitarian dis-course, the agent/patient hierarchy did not work to expedite or channel the amelioration of suffering in the most efficient or most humane way possible; likewise, it was not a reflection of the natural or inevitable inequality separating those who suffered from those who worked to reduce suffering. Instead, con-nected as it was to other inequalities in society—inequalities constructed from differences like race and class but also health, social status, and physical ability—this hierarchical power relation authorized the agent of humanitarianism to assume a benevolent-but-paternalistic attitude toward the patient. The agent/

patient hierarchy worked to empower those who could assert themselves as knowledgeable agents and to (morally) sanction the agents' schemes, whatever they might be, regardless of how the targets of such schemes felt, regardless of the coercive, humiliating, or disempowering consequences of such schemes for those in the patient role.

While the patient/agent relationship is my primary focus, I also discuss other aspects of social identity, such as gender, class, sexuality, social status, health, physical ability, and race. Since such differences played integral roles in the ideological construction of patients and agents in nineteenth-century humanitarian discourse, I devote a great deal of attention to these differences, especially the ideological function of "race." Although I do not treat race, gender, class, sexuality, social status, health, or physical ability in any systematic way, these categories shape my entire discussion, and at times I foreground certain categories of difference in order to advance my central argument about patients and agents. My project is about social inequality and the ideologies that structure othering categories and othered identities, but more specifically it is an investigation of the relationship between a privileged class (who would proffer aid) and those who suffer.

The agent/patient hierarchy in conventional humanitarianism often obscured the ideas, feelings, and experiences of those designated patients. Eccentric ventures, on the other hand, were deeply involved with the patients' ideas about suffering, comfort, and care. Most of the eccentric projects I examine were authored by persons who had lived as patients and felt prompted by that experience to rethink humanitarianism: Harriet Wilson, for example, or Harriet Jacobs as a former slave in the antislavery movement, Louisa May Alcott as a temporary patient in an army hospital, Walt Whitman as consoler and mourner in the postwar United States. Each of these eccentric humanitarians—whether a patient, a former patient, or a nonpatient—had considered and reconsidered patients' views and the relationships between patients and agents. As humanitarians, they wondered: how should humanitarians help, regard, represent, or speak for those being helped? As humanitarians, they criticized conventional modes of humanitarianism without ever relinquishing the central goal of humanitarianism—the reduction and elimination of suffering.

I call these humanitarians "eccentric" as a way of locating them in their cultural-historical context. "Eccentric" is a relational term. It marks humanitarian discourses and practices in terms of their relationship to mainstream philanthropy. Though less coercive than conventional philanthropy, this patient-centered philanthropy was consistently marginalized and ignored by dominant humanitarians. Still, to avoid confusion, I do not use "eccentric" to refer to all marginalized forms of humanitarianism. The humanitarians I examine theorized or urged a less coercive relationship among agents and patients, but many nonmainstream humanitarians did not. Clara Barton's work in the war, for example, often veered from the more accepted modes of nursing, yet the innovations she advocated and practiced were not about redefining the agent/patient hierarchy.[31] Thus, to distinguish among the diverse forms of humanitarianism generated by the midcentury crisis in philanthropy and to clarify a distinct and underexamined aspect of the cultural history of philanthropy in the North, I reserve the term "eccentric" for humanitarian projects that deviated from the mainstream by advocating less-coercive, patient-led approaches to care—approaches that put the ideas, attitudes, insights, and needs of patients at the governing center of philanthropic action. Like Michel de Certeau, I am interested in "the ingenious ways in which the weak make use of the strong."[32] In theorizing the relationship of patient-centered projects ("the weak") to mainstream humanitarianism ("the strong"), I use the term eccentric to describe that relationship.

To reconstruct eccentric philanthropic thought and practice, I examine most carefully humanitarian *activists* who produced *writing* that exemplifies a committed but counterhegemonic engagement with philanthropy. I devote my principal attention to figures like Whitman (a poet *and* a nurse) and Jacobs (an antislavery activist and relief worker *and* an autobiographer). Because these writers never conceived of eccentric benevolence as an organizational plan, because eccentric benevolence was never in fact a single movement, but rather a cluster of nonidentical traversals and contraversions of conventional humanitarianism, I turn to reconstructive, contextual analysis of texts by nonmainstream author-activists to illustrate patient-led philanthropy's ephemeral, discontinuous emergence during the Civil War era. In this study of humanitarians who played dual roles as activists and authors, whose writings were a form of humanitarian action, I pay careful attention to language and representation. My look at the role of language entails close readings of selected eccentric humanitarian works combined with analytical surveys of key dimensions of nineteenth-century humanitarian discourse and practice. My project, then, is both an historical account of marginalized philanthropic projects during the Civil War era (an account that seeks to "brush history against the grain") and a rhetorical analysis of humanitarian texts in their cultural contexts. I do not intend to give a full account of philanthropy in this period; hence, I do not rely primarily on the discourses that constituted dominant forms of benevolence. When I do incorporate these dominant discourses, I critically and contextually juxtapose them to nondominant philanthropic discourses and the perspectives of patients. My approach to the cultural history of philanthropy is to read fragments of its past by closely examining eccentric humanitarian texts and acts, the contexts in which they were formed, and the social world they attempted to reform.

TWO

DANGEROUS PHILANTHROPY

His life is in the body of the living.
When they hanged him the first time, his image leaped
into the blackened air.

MURIEL RUKEYSER, "THE SOUL AND BODY OF JOHN BROWN"[1]

Plans for a New Approach

Like Harriet Wilson, Shields Green had grown frustrated with conventional humanitarianism. On the day after Wilson copyrighted *Our Nig,* Green, a former slave living in Rochester, traveled with Frederick Douglass to Chambersburg, Pennsylvania, to meet with John Brown. During that weekend, August 19-21, 1859, Brown laid out a plan to raid the federal arsenal at Harpers Ferry, incite an insurrection among slaves in Virginia and nearby Maryland, and thus commence a revolution that would end slavery. Brown wanted to rouse the nation because, according to Douglass, "it seemed to him that something startling was just what the nation needed." In the past, many women and men in the antislavery movements had emphasized "moral suasion" and other peaceful means in their fight against slavery. Dissatisfied with these older and apparently ineffective modes of humanitarian work, Brown was proposing an eccentric approach—an approach that relied on a direct, violent strike against slaveholding states and on the combined efforts of slaves and their humanitarian allies from the North. Thinking the plan impractical, Douglass returned to Rochester. Green, ready for a change, decided to go with the old man.[2]

Less than two months later, Brown and his Provisional Army (five African American recruits and sixteen whites) loaded a wagon with pikes, shouldered their rifles, and descended upon Harpers Ferry. During the opening moments of the attack, the raiders enjoyed spectacular success as they secured the armory and arsenal buildings. Captain Brown then ordered a small party into the surrounding countryside to take a few hostages and start the liberation of slaves. Brown hoped that news of the raid would spread rapidly, triggering a massive rebellion among slaves and adding new strength to his campaign. Unfortunately for Brown and his soldiers, white citizens in and around Harpers Ferry and a contingent of marines led by Colonel Robert E. Lee responded most quickly to the news. Townspeople and local impromptu militias surrounded the raiders assembled inside the armory's fire-engine house and began a counterattack, firing at Brown's army and, after the rain started, congregating at the Galt House saloon for liquor and loud, angry talk. The next morning, the marines stormed the engine house, killing or capturing the remaining raiders. Brown's wild and unprecedented plan to end slavery had failed, and Brown along with Green and five other followers were jailed and, six weeks later, hanged.[3]

The raid on Harpers Ferry and Green's decision to join Brown were departures from abolitionism-as-usual—symptoms of the larger discontent within the antislavery movements and within philanthropy in general. Amid this discontent, Brown's dangerous philanthropy quickly became a significant, contested, and revealing cultural symbol. The sensation of Brown's alternative philanthropy sparked interpretive struggle in humanitarian thought, and the appropriations and interpretations of Brown that followed Harpers Ferry illustrate the conflict and instability that characterized humanitarianism on the eve of the Civil War.

Harpers Ferry and the responses to it aggravated the instability of this humanitarianism already in a process of change. As uncertainty grew and the pressure for change intensified in the wake of Brown's raid, humanitarians faced troubling questions about their methods and principles: Should humanitarians countenance the use of nonhumanitarian means, like violence or war, to achieve humanitarian ends, such as the abolition of slavery? Was it possible to effect humanitarian social change through justice, tolerance, or love rather than zeal, coercion, or righteous violence? What was the value of philanthropic intentions, and how were they connected to or disconnected from philanthropic actions? What were the most effective or most desirable ways to bring about meaningful reductions of suffering in or caused by the social world? How should humanitarians "help," treat, regard, represent, work with, and speak for those being helped?

The ways that philanthropic discourse after Harpers Ferry handled questions like these in the representation of John Brown revealed both a yearning for new approaches to benevolent work and the fissures in antebellum humanitarianism created by such yearning. Northern philanthropic discourses readily constructed Brown as a humanitarian figure. Yet, the contradictory, ambivalent, uncertain appropriations of John Brown—more than any other individual, icon, or idea— was indicative of a crisis in humanitarian thought. In their attempts to use images of Brown to resolve the dilemmas facing antebellum philanthropy, humanitarian writers left a picture of a transformative crisis—a crisis characterized by the desire for a new humanitarian action coupled with a countervailing hesitation to abandon older modes of benevolent work.

This crisis readied a space for eccentric benevolence. As the speeches of leaders and the letters of the rank and file demonstrate, many black abolitionists unhesitatingly admired Brown. More than gratitude, however, their admiration purposefully produced a discursive version of Brown identified with an alternative approach to humanitarian work. Their "John Brown" humanitarianism redefined philanthropy as militant political action and dismantled the hierarchy separating agents (the helpers, the abolitionists, white people) from the supposedly power-less patients (those being helped, slaves, African Americans). Yet, while African Americans used Brown to promote an eccentric benevolence, many white humani-tarians—ambivalent about Harpers Ferry and anxious about the rapid and uncertain changes in philanthropy—reappropriated Brown to reinforce conven-tional philanthropic ideology.

A Philanthropic Icon

During this transformative moment, John Brown became a widely recognized symbol of humanitarian work. In her play *Ossawattomie Brown; or, The Insurrection at Harpers' Ferry,* first presented at New York City's Bowery Theater on December 16, 1859, Mrs. J. C. Swayze fabricated a self-sacrificing Brown, a well-intentioned humanitarian who nobly declares in the Virginia prison scene of the final act:

> Whatever is represented to the contrary, believe me, our sole object was to free the slaves, from motives of philanthropy. We look upon ourselves as workers in a great and good cause to which we have sacrificed our lives.[4]

Although such a marvelously self-righteous proclamation might appear to have an ironic design, Swayze never aimed to deride Brown with irony. Attempting instead to persuade her New York audience to accept and admire Brown's pious humani-tarianism, she introduced an intelligent, honest but skeptical "New York Reporter" who vouches for the sincerity and admirability of Brown's motives. "However I may condemn that cause, or the means taken to uphold it," says the astute reporter, "I can but admire the man, who, *thinking it right,* sacrifices all to it as you have done" (25). Given credibility in *Ossawattomie Brown* by an "objective" character, this notion of personal sacrifice would become central to Brown iconography.

Poets too cast the old man as a great humanitarian by bestowing on him a Christ-like altruism. Franklin Sanborn made it clear that "the faithful martyr" had "[n]o selfish purpose." Bronson Alcott emphasized the "self-sacrifice" of Brown, and William Ellery Channing celebrated Brown as one "who lived—to die, / As he lived to act,—for the oppressed, the weak." Drained of "selfish purpose," Brown was commemorated in these poems as a humanitarian, as one who lived, acted, and died to help those who suffered. For many antislavery humanitarians, it was Brown's decision to help enslaved black people, and not simply his altruistic sacrifice in and of itself, which ennobled his action. The poetry columns of the *Liberator* were filled with verses that sang, for instance, "He dared to live and die

/ For Afric's sable race" or "His life was spent for others' good . . . / He periled every thing most dear / To liberate the slave."[5]

In his short story "Excalibur" (1860), Moncure Conway illustrated how Brown's philanthropy grew out of his faithful adherence to dictums from the Bible. As "[t]his old man" led his life according to the golden rule and the divine imperative to "Remember those who are in bonds as bound with them," Brown became the model humanitarian: "old John Brown lived what he knew: he fed the hungry, clothed the naked, and ministered to the afflicted."[6]

While representations produced by the literati enhanced the old man's reputation in the North, John Brown, in brilliant displays of self-fashioning, played a crucial role in the manufacture of himself as a humanitarian. With widely published letters and statements following Harpers Ferry, Brown molded his self-representation into a symbol for humanitarian meanings. Immediately after his capture, in an interview with Virginia senator James M. Mason, Ohio representative Clement L. Vallandigham, newspaper reporters, and bystanders, a wounded and supine Brown managed to turn a criminal interrogation into a pulpit for philanthropic ideals. Interested in possible motivations for such an astonishing venture, the interrogators fired questions like "How do you justify your acts?" at the disheveled old man. Despite his matted hair and blood-covered clothes, Brown seized this opportunity to preach, explaining with eloquence, emotion, and a dash of self-righteousness the principles upon which he acted:

> Upon the golden rule. I pity the poor in bondage that have none to help them; that is why I am here; not to gratify any personal animosity, revenge or vindictive spirit. It is my sympathy with the oppressed and the wronged, that are as good as you and as precious in the sight of God.[7]

Hence, when writers presented Brown as a noble humanitarian who lived according to the golden rule, they were not simply projecting their own ideals onto a factional character but also repeating what Brown had said about himself. In response to charges that he was a criminal, Brown styled himself a golden-rule comforter of the oppressed well before Northern humanitarians used a similar Brown for their own purposes.

Like John Brown figures found in the texts of humanitarian writers, Brown's own autobiographical character disclaimed violent intentions, any "incendiary" or "ruffian" aims. Brown's John Brown also maintained a self-sacrificing disposition, announcing, for instance, "We expect no reward, except the satisfaction of endeavoring to do for those in distress and greatly oppressed, as we would be done by." Moreover, he encouraged his addressees to do the same, to help others: "I charge you all never in your trials to forget the griefs 'of the poor that cry, and of those that have none to help them.'"[8] Partly as a result of these vigorous efforts to fashion himself as a humanitarian figure—efforts which indicate Brown's willingness and skill at deploying self-representation in the service of the antislavery cause—Brown became a meaningful albeit controversial icon within humanitarianism.

Crime and Benevolence

In a Thanksgiving Day sermon delivered about a month after Harpers Ferry, George B. Cheever proposed his own interpretation of Brown. A resolute and sometimes obnoxious antislavery minister from New York and author of *God Against Slavery* (1857), Cheever (much like John Brown) saw radical abolitionism as an expression of conservative, Bible-based religious principles.[9] Although he had no doubts about the righteousness of Brown's actions, Cheever had become interested in the nation's confusion about Brown. In his sermon, Cheever declared:

> It is wonderful to behold the eyes of the whole nation turned upon one old man, condemned to die upon the gallows for an action which multitudes of men stand in doubt whether to pronounce a great crime or one of the most heroic, disinterested, virtuous, noble deeds of obedience to God and benevolence to man, recorded in the century. There he is, in modern Egypt, a greater riddle, a greater Sphinx for men's opinions, than ancient Egypt ever saw.[10]

Perplexed by this "one old man," the uncertain "multitudes" were, in Cheever's assessment, unable to decide whether the raid was "a great crime" or an extraordinary act of pious humanitarianism. Crime and benevolence are vastly different types of action. Thus, he found the nation's indecision about Brown "wonderful"— that is, strange and amazing.

As his amazement suggests, Cheever tries to remain outside the uncertainty of his fellow citizens. His rhetoric works to convey surety and clarity by grounding its pronouncements in "fixed principles" and "the one infallible standard of God's Word" (170). Harpers Ferry is, according to Cheever's sermon, God's strategy for calling "us anew to the consideration of our own duty, and of the means by which we may avoid God's judgments, and redeem our country from a wickedness that threatens to consume us" (149). In this reading of Harpers Ferry, God planned to use Brown as a way to bring the entire nation to repentance for its complicity in the sin of slavery. Cheever tries to avoid the culture's post–Harpers Ferry bewilderment by talking with certainty about the raid as an element in a sacred design to unnerve proslavery Southerners and complacent Northerners.

What Cheever admires most about Brown is his uncompromising adherence to divine principle. As "one of those rare instances of men . . . who act out a conviction of duty" (158), Cheever's Brown epitomizes the Christian activist ideal—the militant holy warrior who shuns "any temporary expediency or compromise," "every act of yielding," and "every silent submission" as "a sinful betrayal of principle" (171). Because this stern devotion to righteous principle is so self-evidently a virtue in Cheever's sermon, Brown becomes a marvelous example of how all Christians ought to regard sin, slavery, and "the victims of oppression" (160). And, for Cheever, only racist discrimination can account for the nation's confusion about Brown and his attack on slavery. Explains Cheever:

Now, remember that if the *color* had been *white,* and the victims of oppression your relatives, neighbors, or neighbors' descendants, you would have made no question of the virtue, righteousness, and nobleness of John Brown's attempt. You would not have set the determination of the quality of his act upon the probability of success. You would have said he was so much the greater, truer, more disinterested hero for going forth in an undertaking so grand, though, to human appearance, hopeless, yet trusting in God. (160)

In an apparently "hopeless" situation, Brown's intentions—which depend not upon human estimations but upon faith in God—become purer, making Brown a "greater, truer, more disinterested hero." But, while Cheever sees the "justice, heroism, [and] piety" of Brown's intentions, America's racist blindness condemns "John Brown's movement" as "treason," "murder," and "a wicked act" (158).

Cheever extols not only Brown's pious, deeply principled intentions, but also the object of those intentions—his desire to end the suffering of the enslaved, even though their "*color*" was not "*white.*" Struggling on behalf of an oppressed people, Brown becomes heroically altruistic and devout because he practiced God's law regarding the duty of believers toward the "race of strangers," Cheever's metaphor for persons of African descent living in the United States (142-43). Showing us a hero who overcomes the race prejudices of his nation, Cheever quotes the old man saying ironically, "'I am yet too young to be able to understand that God is any respecter of persons'" (159). Cheever's egalitarian Brown acts according to sacred, nonprejudiced principles to help the poor, the despised, the suffering: he is the model of humanitarian, antiracist intentions put into action.

Throughout this sermon Cheever uses Brown to prompt his listeners to engage in humanitarian acts. He presents Brown as the ideal to which we aspire, the role model whom we follow while we labor for benevolence and justice. Brown and his example of action remind us of "our own duty," "[o]ur duty as Christians and our duty as politicians" (149). Hence, moving toward the "what shall be done" part of his sermon, Cheever says: "John Brown is the crystallization into action of maxims which all would act upon, if the enslaved and injured . . . *were whites*" (158). Brown as the paragon of humanitarian action represents the direction which "all" would take, if race prejudice had not so thoroughly distorted Americans' conception of moral duty to "the enslaved and injured" of all races. Having abandoned unhumanitarian and un-Christian prejudice, Brown acts. Cheever tries to persuade his congregation to act as well, by arguing in the conditional that if the enslaved were white, "[y]ou would not only contribute money and arms to any party who would undertake to do this [free the slaves], but you would yourselves take arms" (159). Cheever extends this call to action/call to arms by preemptively rebutting the argument for nonviolence: "if I excused myself on the plea that I could not do it but by producing violence and death, you would say that by such a refusal I was myself guilty of the continuance of a system of infinite cruelty and robbery" (160). Moreover, in imagery with a penchant for picturing bombs exploding at "the heart of the South" (see 154, 159), Cheever's language often disavows nonviolence. Thus, using Brown as a model for decisive and violent righteous action, the sermon moves toward a thundering "Go thou, and do likewise!" (160).

Cheever found Brown a compelling symbol around which to build this call to militant, Christian action against the institution of slavery, because Brown symbolized what one New York paper contemptuously called "Practical Abolitionism." Cheever did not, of course, criticize the efforts of practical abolitionists, "men of action in the Abolitionist ranks [who] take their leaders at their word." He admired them. Cheever saw Brown as a portent of the impending violence to be visited on an impenitent South and a symbol of humanitarian religious principles translated into practical action. While other white abolitionists, like William Lloyd Garrison and Samuel Joseph May, continued to preach "moral suasion," John Brown devised an elaborate plan for liberating slaves and attacking slaveholders. As was often reported in the North before and after Harpers Ferry, Brown had grown tired of eloquent abolitionists preaching moral suasion. "Talking is a national institution; but it does no good for the slave," Brown had exclaimed. At the New England Anti-Slavery Convention in May 1859, he observed fractiously: "These men are all talk: what is needed is action—action!" According to Brown, talk (eloquence, representation, signification) had become an inadequate substition for action, a practical, probably violent *doing* that would free slaves.[11]

Interestingly enough, however, Cheever cannot ultimately counsel John Brown–like action and instead retreats to what he as a preacher knew best—talk. "A most remarkable thing it is," Cheever's sermon declares,

> that just at this juncture, God should have shot John Brown out of the cannon of his providence right into the bosom of that vested interest [slavery]; shot him as a bomb against it, scattering all the theories of politicians to the winds, and setting all men to a new discussion. . . . There is no stopping this discussion, when it pleases God that it should come. (154)

In the confident, combative, militant rhetoric of Cheever's interpretation, Brown serves as God's catalyst for starting "a new discussion" about slavery. That this sermon imagines Harpers Ferry as the opening gesture in a discussion betrays perhaps Cheever's own confusion about the significance of Brown. Despite his candid admiration for the Captain, despite his rhetoric about action and violence, Cheever avoids any direct call to violent action to free slaves, never once urging action as Brown understood it. The principal themes and moral of his sermon revolve instead around the notion of talk—signification, representation, texts and the interpretation of texts, words, discussions.

Ardently prophesying "public mass meetings" where "[a]ll the questions involved, of right and wrong, ought to be thoroughly, fervently discussed in every aspect, in every place" (149), Cheever presents Brown as the instigator of a great national "discussion" on "questions" about slavery. Now that Brown has opened the discussion, Cheever admonishes the antislavery forces to know their weapons well:

> Our instruments of aggression and of conquest against this sin are grand and mighty: the Word of God, rightly interpreted, and the Constitution of our country, rightly interpreted. (149)

In the conflict between the slave power and the antislavery forces, Cheever believes that victory depends on the proper interpretation of two texts. Slavery has prevailed only because the Bible and the U.S. Constitution have been wickedly misinterpreted:

> The perversions of the Word of God and of the Constitution of our country are the great stratagems by which the defenders of Slavery have enthroned it as a legitimate power. (163)

The consequences of such immoral exegetical errors and the toleration of such distorted misreadings are, for Cheever, dire: "if in either [the Bible or Constitution] the perversion is suffered to become law, then we are lost" (149). Thus, Cheever urges the righteous to take up the arsenal of antislavery hermeneutics against the wicked slaveholders and their "perversions" of the Bible and Constitution. He pleads with his audience:

> These charters of our Freedom, the Constitution and the Bible, must be rescued from such perversion. We are bound to resist Slavery every where,—first, with the truth of God, which is irresistible, overruling, overriding, and sweeping down every thing before it; and, second, with all the constitutional, legal, and moral appliances which God has put in our power. We are bound to make the most of every weapon and every advantage. . . . We are bound to interpret the Constitution in behalf of Freedom and against Slavery. (163)

In the aftermath of Harpers Ferry and the discourse about "practical abolitionism," it seems remarkable that a strong Brown partisan like Cheever would see right interpretation of the U.S. Constitution and the Word of God as the most important and powerful "weapon" made available by God "to resist slavery." Nevertheless, Cheever appears convinced that correct application of the word, whether the Bible or the Constitution, will abolish the wicked institution. "If God's Word had been applied to this iniquity of Slavery forty years ago," he insists, "the whole system would by this day have gone out of existence" (175).

Sharing Brown's deep faith in the Bible as well as his defense of the Constitution (against the nonresistants' condemnation of the Constitution for its complicity with slavery[12]), Cheever hopes to accomplish with words and interpretations what Brown had planned to accomplish with revolvers, rifles, and pikes. Yet, by emphasizing the text, Cheever ignores Brown's weariness with talk as a means for abolishing slavery. At the same time, however, Cheever's figuration indicates a zealous though never explicit endorsement of action, militancy, and battle—the John Brown method—in and through language. He encourages his congregation to wield "the letter of the Constitution" against "the spirit of Slavery" (151) and to enter this conflict on God's side by "fighting the battle with His Word" (174). Extending his confidence in the power of words, the preacher transforms Brown, the self-proclaimed man of action, into a text: "He is God's handwriting on the wall of Slavery" (157).

The contradictions here, both logical and figurative, are exquisite. The sermon praises Brown, who criticized proponents of talk. Then, in a maneuver that seems unintentionally oxymoronic, the sermon advocates talk as the solution to slavery and appropriates Brown's activism to be the symbol of this linguistic approach to abolitionism, merging in metaphor Brown and text: "He is God's handwriting." Considered in the context of his lavish admiration for Brown and his condescending attitude toward the "multitudes" confused by Harpers Ferry, Cheever's return to talk reveals a deep, never-acknowledged ambivalence about Brown's actions. Cheever's figurative language and spirited defense of action guided by high moral principles indicate the profound inspiration Cheever took in Brown's example. Yet, Cheever's reiterative insistence on the importance of discourse, discussion, texts, and right interpretation takes Cheever away from the John Brown method and returns him to a position much closer to Garrisonian moral suasion.

Cheever interests me not because he wrongly put faith in the power of words, not because he hoped slavery would be resolved by talk instead of blood, and not simply because he simultaneously admired and shrank from Brown. Rather, what makes Cheever's rhetoric so significant and revealing is its unsuccessful attempt to erase the ambivalence that structures it. Cheever never qualifies his admiration and yet advocates an approach to the antislavery crusade that ignores Brown's strong criticism of that approach. Despite his attempt to sermonize in a way that would help his bewildered congregation understand the significance and benevolence of Brown's deeds, this sermon—ambivalent yet unable to acknowledge or erase the traces of such ambivalence—is not removed from the confusion it identifies. Cheever's sermon is symptomatic of that confusion.

"God Makes Him the Text"

As the confusion in Cheever's sermon indicates, Brown's distinction between talk and action introduced a problem to humanitarian thought. For decades, abolitionists had considered their talk to be action. They wrote speeches, drafted petitions, and printed newspapers not to enjoy the pleasure of texts for their own sake, but to incite action, to use language to reshape society. The hope was always that antislavery speech would *act* to end slavery and racism. In Brown iconography, however, talk could now symbolize inaction. By wanting to give "abolition theories a thoroughly practical shape," declaring moral suasion "hopeless," and privileging "action" over "talk," Brown represented a rejection of moral suasion and a search for a more "practical abolitionism," a more effective humanitarianism.[13] In the aftermath of Harpers Ferry, a number of activists joined Brown in demanding action and disdaining talk. No one actually wanted to give up talk, however, and nearly every antislavery advocate continued to use it as an indispensable way to incite action. Moreover, few were prepared to pursue the type of action that Brown had demonstrated in northern Virginia. The debate about talk and action was never actually about which was the more effective strategy for causing the humanitarian changes the abolitionists sought. Instead, talk had come to symbolize an older, ineffective method of antislavery work; action meant a new, more productive approach to the same end. Yet, as the post–Harpers Ferry valorization of action demonstrates, few reformers had a clear or coherent notion of what precisely this new approach ought to be.

Losing faith in older approaches to antislavery work, many reformers in the 1850s had worried about the efficacy of benevolent action, but few took decisive steps toward rethinking philanthropic methods, means, and ends. Most abolitionists remained committed to moral suasion.[14] After Harpers Ferry, however, grumblings about the inefficacy of humanitarian endeavors erupted into dramatic calls for action and practical abolitionism. In one such call the Reverend Edwin M. Wheelock noted the important change in antislavery humanitarianism after Brown:

> Like the Swiss valleys, the first clash of arms brings down the avalanche. From the martyrdom of John Brown dates a new era of the anti-slavery cause. To moral agitation will now be added physical. To argument, action. The dispensation of doctrine will be superseded by the higher dispensation of facts.[15]

No longer shackled to the feeble tactics of "moral agitation," "argument," and "doctrine," abolitionists would turn to the John Brown method—"physical" agitation, "action," "facts." The "new" antislavery humanitarianism would supplant talk and become "action."

In "A Plea for Captain John Brown" (1859), a lecture delivered in Concord just twelve days after Brown's capture, Henry Thoreau ardently voiced his approval of practical humanitarianism. Scorning older approaches that had failed to liberate slaves, he advocated a Captain Brown philanthropy:

> I shall not be forward to think him mistaken in his method who quickest succeeds to liberate the slave. I speak for the slave when I say, that I prefer the philanthropy of Captain Brown to that philanthropy which neither shoots me nor liberates me.[16]

According to Thoreau, the best philanthropic method is the most expedient one, the one that "quickest succeeds" in its mission. While speaking rather presumptuously for "the slave," he suggests that even death is preferable to a philanthropy which can only talk about emancipating the enslaved and not accomplish it.

In a similar defense of a new, dangerous philanthropy over and against methods that had failed to free slaves, James Redpath devoted most of his Preface to *Echoes of Harper's Ferry* (1860) to a rebuke of Henry Ward Beecher, who had refused to endorse Brown. According to Redpath:

> Agitation is good when it ultimates in action: but not otherwise. Sarcasm, wit, denunciation, and eloquence, are excellent preparatives for pikes, swords, rifles, and revolvers; but, of themselves, they yet never liberated a Slave Nation in this world, and they never will. . . . The Beechers of our age are only useful in proportion as they prepare the way for the John Browns. When they try to oppose the progress of actors, the preachers are to be summarily kicked out of the way. . . . I thus introduce the name of Mr. Beecher, because, more than any other man I know, he embodies the average prejudice of the Northern States; and

is the ablest and most eloquent exponent of that hypocritical cant which *talks* of sympathy for the Slave, and, at the same time, extinguishes all effective attempts to help him.[17]

The proponents of talk are "useful" only as preparation for the new form of practical antislavery action that can and will liberate the slaves. Antislavery activists were now repeating what Brown had told the New England Anti-Slavery Convention: "talk . . . will never set the slave free." To realize their humanitarian ends, abolitionists needed "action-action!"[18] After a decade of increasingly frustrating recognition of the limits of romantic reform, antislavery proponents like Redpath and Thoreau were eager to embrace Brown as the embodiment of a new humanitarian action and equally eager to disparage the older models and methods.

Despite this posturing about action, Redpath and Thoreau (like Rev. Wheelock and Rev. Cheever) never engaged in any Harpers Ferry–like assaults on slavery. Although he preferred "the philanthropy of Captain Brown," Thoreau neither purchased pikes to distribute to slaves nor organized guerrilla bands to raid the plantations and arsenals of slaveholders. Instead, he wrote and delivered public addresses that praised Brown and condemned slavery. Despite his impatience with mere talk of sympathy for slaves, despite his low regard for "agitation," "[s]arcasm, wit, denunciation, and eloquence," Redpath spent most of his time after Harpers Ferry working on books. In what John McKivigan has called "a two-year period of feverish literary production," Redpath authored a biography of Brown and edited *Echoes of Harper's Ferry,* a large collection of verbal responses to Brown's raid.[19]

Thus, if we can imagine momentarily a message that could exist apart from its medium, the message of these texts seemed explicitly to privilege action over talk, to conceive of talk as something not like action but more like inaction. The medium, the texts themselves, however, attested to a continuing faith in language as a form of action—and this, of course, became part of the message. Indeed, despite his insistence on action in "A Plea for Captain John Brown," Thoreau quoted Brown at length throughout the last eight paragraphs. He concluded this lecture by letting Brown's words—not his actions—speak for themselves. Redpath and Thoreau used language to incite antislavery action, just as nonresistants like Garrison and Lydia Maria Child had used language to incite antislavery action. Hence, the debate was never really about talk versus action. What differed was the type of action imagined, not the use of talk. Those who opposed talk wanted a new type of antislavery action. Whereas nonresistants like Child held to their long-standing "peace principles," Redpath (like Brown) wanted to see a massive insurrection of slaves aided and armed by abolitionists.[20]

What this controversy over talk and action reveals, then, is not how some abolitionists wanted to do away with writing and speech as modes of humanitarian work, but how a system of humanitarian discourses and practices registered the pressure for change. As a committed nonresistant whom Brown had categorized not among "men of action" but among "men who have the gift of eloquence,"

Wendell Phillips struggled with the tension between an older humanitarianism distinguished by its dedication to moral suasion and the emerging pressures for more effective means of opposing slavery and more practical approaches to the suffering of the oppressed. Following Harpers Ferry, Phillips joined Redpath and others in the celebration of action. In "The Puritan Principle and John Brown" (1859), Phillips praised Brown as a person who "did not stop to ask what the majority thought, or what forms were, but *acted.*" In an earlier speech on Brown, "The Lesson of the Hour" (1859), Phillips announced:

> I think the lesson of the hour is insurrection. (Sensation.) Insurrection of thought precedes the insurrection of arms. The last twenty years have been an insurrection of thought.[21]

Like Wheelock's prediction that "To moral agitation will now be added physical" and Redpath's judgment that "Agitation is good when it ultimates in action," Phillips's oration positions abolitionism's "insurrection of thought," its agitation of the nation's moral conscience, as the natural and necessary basis for Brown's "insurrection of arms."

But, like Cheever, Phillips is in no way prepared to follow the John Brown method, despite the rhetoric about insurrection and his unqualified canonizing praise for Brown. In his last written testimony, a sentence handed to a guard shortly before his execution, Brown prophesied that "the crimes of this *guilty, land: will* never be purged *away*; but with Blood." Six days later, at Brown's burial, Phillips asserts precisely the opposite: "I do not believe slavery will go down in blood. Ours is the age of thought. Hearts are stronger than swords."[22] Brown pronounces moral suasion "hopeless," but Phillips affirms an unwavering commitment to it in "The Lesson of the Hour": "I believe in moral suasion. The age of bullets is over. The age of ideas is come" (269). His devotion to a humanitarianism founded upon "hearts," upon moral suasion, "public opinion, literature, education" (270) is so strong that he retreats completely from the rhetoric of insurrection used to open his address. Reasoning that Virginia is not a legitimate government, Phillips decides in the middle of this address to stop suggesting that Brown advocated insurrection. Phillips recants:

> I said that the lesson of the hour was insurrection. I ought not to apply that word to John Brown of Osawatomie, for there was no insurrection in his case. It is a great mistake to call him an insurgent. (271)

For clever rhetorical reasons and sound moral ones, Phillips takes the focus away from Brown's relatively minor violence at Harpers Ferry and shifts it to Virginia and that state's pervasive, unrelenting violence against black people. While the violence of slavery was without question far more dangerous and damaging than any raid the old man could put together, this shift in emphasis counters Redpath's version of Brown and obscures Brown's own advocacy of armed insurrection. Phillips begins with the notion that the insurrection of thought would have to be followed by a Brown-like insurrection of arms; however, by the middle of the oration, he no longer acknowledges any need for physical, violent antislavery insurrection. Indeed, to call Brown an "insurgent" is, Phillips concludes, "a great mistake."

"The Lesson of the Hour" opens with a widely recognized version of Brown—Redpath's Brown associated with the specter of violent, open resistance to the Southern slave power. But Phillips wants so desperately to make the nineteenth century into an "age of ideas" and not an "age of bullets" that he finally drains his representation of Brown of any violent aims. Brown becomes—as in Cheever's sermon—a "text." To accomplish this moral suasionist transformation of Brown from "insurgent" to "text," Phillips invokes a divine author:

> God makes him the text, and all he asks of our comparatively cowardly lips is to preach the sermon, and to say to the American people that, whether that old man succeeded in a worldly sense or not, he stood a representative of law, of government, of right, of justice, of religion. (276)

God's purpose for John Brown is semiotic. Brown signifies. Representing ideals such as "justice" and "religion," he is a text for preaching, reading, edification, and interpretation. According to Phillips, it is this status as "text" that matters and not Brown's successes or failures "in a worldly sense." Brown's physical or worldly action is irrelevant when compared to his significance (his signification) as a kind of divine talk about "right," "justice," and so on.

Phillips hopes in this address to embrace Brown as a symbol of a revitalized antislavery humanitarianism pledged to practical action and to hang on to the abolitionist ideals that inspired his work and life for over two decades. Yet, because Brown—especially Brown as figured in the work of writer-activists like Redpath—constitutes a strong challenge to those ideals, Phillips cannot do both without considerable contradiction. Hence, Phillips leaves a portrait of Brown that advocates "action" and insurrection and then disavows such dangerous philanthropy by recasting the insurgent himself into a species of "talk"—that is, the old method of humanitarian action that the insurgent had renounced. Such contradictions were not, of course, peculiar to Phillips. Instead, what emerges again and again in humanitarian discourse about John Brown is a fresh and committed desire for action coupled with a countervailing reluctance to forgo the older modes of romantic humanitarianism and a fear of where such action would lead. This wish to move simultaneously in apparently opposite directions is emblematic of the uncertain flux in post–Harpers Ferry humanitarianism.

Nevertheless, it was in Phillips's uncertain, contradiction-filled attempt to make the self-styled man of action into a text that Phillips came to his understanding of the paradoxical significance of Brown. Because he refused to criticize Brown while still holding to a humanitarianism founded upon moral suasion and nonviolence, Phillips in his eulogization of the "martyr" arrived at this evaluation of Brown's efforts: "His words,—they are stronger even than his rifles" ("Burial of John Brown" 293). This interpretation of Brown's significance elides, again, Brown's criticism of antislavery humanitarianism: because "words" were doing nothing to free slaves, some type of action with rifles, revolvers, and pikes was necessary. Nonetheless, Phillips's observation that Brown's "words" (his "talk," his self-representation) did more to free the slaves than his "rifles" (his ineffectual venture at liberating slaves in northern Virginia) was deeply accurate. While the raid at Harpers Ferry was by itself a failure, the symbolic value of such a raid— combined with Brown's eloquent letters and statements from prison, his humani- tarian self-fashioning, and the vigorous martyr-making efforts of Northern hu- manitarians—had an important influence on the events that accelerated the movement toward disunion, civil war, and the emancipation of the enslaved. Like Herman Melville's *meteor of the war,*" John Brown as "Portent," as sign, incited action far bloodier than any slave insurrection, action far bloodier in fact than anyone could have imagined.[23]

The Bloody Hand and Loving Heart

And blood was the issue that worried these humanitarians. In their tussles about talk versus action, activists faced trying questions about violence, coercion, and the use of non-humanitarian means in the service of humanitarian ends. The questions were familiar, but a disturbingly new context demanded new answers. For decades most abolitionist leaders had maintained nonviolence as a consistent, necessary cornerstone of their antislavery work, even while some activists, par- ticularly black abolitionists, were calling into question the value and legitimacy of such a reliance on nonviolence. Harpers Ferry, however, sparked new, widespread, and vigorous arguments about the role of violence.[24] John Brown—the humanitar- ian martyr-saint of the abolitionist movement—not only verbally advocated the use of violence but actually carried wagonloads of pikes and boxes filled with rifles to Virginia to start the war on slavery. Moreover, Brown's role in the infamous 1856 Pottawatomie Massacre, his instigation of the slaying of five proslavery settlers during the Kansas-Missouri border war known as Bleeding Kansas, did not tally with the image of Brown as a humanitarian.[25] Hence, the nonresistants faced a dilemma. Should they abandon their principled stand against violence and embrace Brown as a powerful icon of antislavery action? Or should they rebuke Brown and the John Brown method in the maintenance of nonresistance? Neither option appealed to most abolitionists. So, rethinking their positions on nonvio- lence and attempting to use the image of Brown in whatever way possible, antislavery writers negotiated a variety of discursive paths through this dilemma. Like the ambivalence that structured the addresses of Cheever and Phillips, the treatment of violence in Brown iconography reveals the pressures on humanitarian discourse on the eve of the Civil War—pressures demanding improvisation on dominant forms and discourses, pressures creating a space for eccentric designs.

John Greenleaf Whittier's "Brown of Osawatomie" exemplifies a typical negotiation of this dilemma. As a Quaker pacifist who held as ardently and inflexibly to his antislavery beliefs as Brown did to his own, Whittier could never condone Brown's actions. Deeply anguished by Harpers Ferry and the enthusiasm for Brown within antislavery circles, Whittier saw Brown's raid not as the beginning of the war against slavery but as a troublesome crisis for antislavery humanitarianism. In a letter calling Brown "brave but, methinks, sadly misguided," Whittier wrote to Child:

> We feel deeply (who does not?) for the noble-hearted, self-sacrificing old man. But as friends of peace, as well as believers in the Sermon on the Mount, we dare not lend *any* countenance to such attempts as that at Harper's Ferry.
>
> I hope, in our admiration of the noble traits of John Brown's character, we shall be careful how we encourage a repetition of his rash and ill-judged movement. Thou and I believe in "a more excellent way." . . . God is now putting our non-resistance principles to a severe test. I hope we shall not give the lie to our life-long professions. . . . we must be true to our settled convictions. . . . My heart is too heavy and sorrowful. I cannot write now, and can only *wait,* with fervent prayer that the cause we love may receive no detriment.[26]

Rather than sensing an opportunity to capitalize on the martyrdom of Brown for the greater good of the antislavery cause, Whittier sees Brown's "rash and ill-judged movement" as an obstinate liability to the cause. Brown precipitates a crisis not in the Union but in antislavery humanitarianism itself whose "non-resistance principles," "life-long professions," and "settled convictions" are now being severely tested. At the same time, Whittier seems willing to acknowledge "the noble traits of Brown's character," describing him as "brave," "noble-hearted, self-sacrificing."

While Whittier could never, of course, accept the proslavery excoriations of Brown, neither could he approve of the antislavery movement's canonization of a militant who advocated killing as a justifiable instrument for Christian-humanitarian social change. The result was genuine anguish over the raid, the interpretation of the raid within antislavery circles, and his own inability to formulate a nonresistant response to Brown's violent antislavery endeavor. In a letter to his friend, Elizabeth Lloyd Howell, he wrote:

> I have been quite ill, and am still troubled with pain in my side and head, but am better, and hope to be able to get about and do something. I have not been able to write for weeks beyond a mere note or brief letter. This sad affair at Harper's Ferry has pained and troubled me exceedingly. . . . I made several attempts last week to write out my thoughts on the subject, but was compelled to give over from sheer inability to exert mind or body. It seemed to me that nobody said precisely the right thing, and that I could and must say it.

As this letter indicates, Whittier experienced Harpers Ferry as a personal crisis: the pain and inability to write haunted him for weeks. The letter to Howell goes on to mention the "great relief" Whittier found in Henry Ward Beecher's interpretation of Harpers Ferry. Beecher disapproved of "the folly of the bloody foray," but declared that Brown's "soul was noble."[27] This was exactly the direction Whittier took when he did eventually write about Brown in his well-known poem "Brown of Osawatomie."

Whittier's poem constructs Brown through a series of binary oppositions:

"folly"/"generous purpose," "raid of midnight terror"/"thought which underlies," "outlaw's pride of daring"/"Christian's sacrifice," "Might"/"Right," "Hate"/"Love." In the third stanza, Whittier writes:

> Without, the rash and bloody hand
>> Within, the loving heart.
> That kiss, from all its guilty means
>> Redeemed the good intent.[28]

By identifying and applauding Brown's noble qualities such as his "loving heart" while contraposing them to his failings such as his "bloody hand," the poem praises Brown's "good intent" and condemns his "guilty means." This good-intention-but-bad-action perspective allowed Whittier and other humanitarians to work their way through their uneasiness about Brown, embracing him as the martyr of antislavery humanitarianism while disapproving of the actions that made him such a martyr.

Child took substantially the same position. As a nonresistant she declared, "such violent attempts to right wrong are both injudicious and evil." Despite Brown's "evil" actions, Child praised him: "Deeply as I regret the whole affair, I cannot help honoring the brave old man." She voiced the same view in a letter to Brown himself: "Believing in peace principles, I cannot sympathize with the method you chose to advance the cause of freedom. But I honor your generous intentions." Unitarian minister James Freeman Clarke also condemned Brown's actions and praised his intentions, suggesting incorrectly that everyone in the North and the South shared his perspective:

> His whole course has been so convincingly conscientious, manly, truthful, and heroic, that his enemies have been compelled to honor him. For the first time within our memory, the whole North and South seem to be united in one opinion and one sentiment—the opinion that this attempt of Brown was unwise and unwarranted—the sentiment of respect for the man himself, as a Hero.

Although he was deeply mistaken in supposing that the South felt "compelled to honor" Brown "as a Hero," such an inaccurate observation does perhaps reveal how satisfying Clarke found the Beecher-Whittier-Child interpretation of Brown, how appealing the good-intention-but-bad-action view must have been to humanitarians committed to abolitionism as well as peace.[29]

Such an interpretation depends on a distinction between intention (motive, purpose) and action (method, means) and the appreciation of intention as the more accurate indicator of moral value. And Clarke, for example, asserted just such a distinction: "The only thing of much worth in life is the spirit in which a man acts. Not what we do, but the *motive* of the action, is the great thing."[30] While this separation of intention and action was certainly useful rhetorically and psychologically to humanitarians who wanted, despite their aversion to violence, to admire Brown, this distinction ignored the fact that Brown certainly *intended* to use violence. It is difficult to imagine how the hundreds of rifles, revolvers, and pikes that Brown took to the South could have indicated anything other than violent intentions. By separating Brown's intention to free slaves ("the good intent" so admired by these abolitionists) from his intention to free slaves by injuring, shooting, stabbing, and killing those who might prevent such a liberation ("the method" so deplored), these humanitarians sought to marginalize or at least compartmentalize the dimension of Brown's intentions which most disturbed them. With violence safely relegated to the realm of bad method and thus not recognized as central to Brown's intentions at Harpers Ferry, they were free to laud Brown's generous purpose, his motive.

The move was thoroughly contradictory, but it allowed these humanitarians to admire in Brown precisely what they admired in themselves: the philanthropic desire to end slavery, "[n]ot what we do, but the *motive* of the action." By bracketing the violent nature of Brown's intentions, they could emphasize their own ideals as refracted through Brown and represent him as a martyr to their cause. That a stalwart pacifist like Whittier would have felt so compelled to make sense of Brown suggests how very acute the pressure was to rearticulate an older humanitarianism within the context of these new demands for action.

Other humanitarians took a different approach to the disquieting fact of their saint's want of peace principles. Instead of bracketing Brown's method as a way to admire his goals as Whittier had done, they tried to ignore, forget, dismiss, and deny utterly Brown's violent intentions at Harpers Ferry as well as his violent past. Although both Thoreau and Redpath knew of the Pottawatomie Massacre, Thoreau chose to ignore and Redpath denied Brown's involvement in the 1856 slaying of five slavery men in Kansas. The antislavery press also disassociated Brown from these brutal executions. One magazine wrote:

> The Browns suffered cruelly in the border warfare, several of John's sons being slain or wounded. It is not true, however, that John Brown or his sons ever inflicted retaliatory injury on the border ruffians.[31]

Stories of surprise midnight murders with broadswords could not help in the construction of an antislavery saint, so these pro-Brown writers obliterated the connection between Brown and the unarmed men who died at Pottawatomie.

Some humanitarian writers claimed that Brown at Harpers Ferry had attempted only a nonviolent intervention against slavery. "He did not intend an insurrection," swore Clarke, "but only an escape of fugitives."[32] In the third act of *Ossawattomie Brown,* Swayze gave the title character a speech in which he tells his raiders:

> This is no lawless outbreak—we are not here to murder and to rob. God knows I have no thirst for blood. Those weapons are for self-defense—to guard the passage of our rescued band to shores of greater safety. . . . We are not here for purposes of blood and riot. (18)

Attributing nonviolent motives to Brown seemed crucial to the picture of the martyr that some humanitarians were trying to create. This emphasis on nonviolence was thoroughly consistent with humanitarian principles like peace, moral suasion, and nonresistance; but the image of Brown pursuing a nonviolent venture did not, could not, concur with all of the widely published evidence to the contrary. After Harpers Ferry, newspapers were filled with stories about Brown, his men and his conspirators, and his plan to foment a slave insurrection. The *New York Times* published Brown's plans for a sweeping war against slavery throughout the South. Even Garrison's *Liberator* published reports about "the large stores of arms, ammunition, &c., found among the effects of the insurgents," including:

> 200 revolvers
> 200 Sharp's rifles, and
> 1000 spears.[33]

Such widely reported evidence undercut every attempt to construct a nonviolent Brown.

Yet humanitarian writers like Swayze and Clarke persisted, aided by their beloved soon-to-be martyr himself, who shortly *after* his capture began disowning his intention to use deadly force. On the day of his capture, Brown said:

> Yesterday I could have killed whom I chose; but I had no desire to kill any person, and would not have killed a man had they not tried to kill me and my men. I could have sacked and burned the town, but did not; I have treated the persons whom I took as hostages kindly.

At his trial, in a bid to reinforce the representation of himself as a nonviolent antislavery humanitarian, Brown lied: "I never did intend murder or treason, or the destruction of property, or to excite or incite the slaves to rebellion, or to make insurrection."[34] The image of a nonviolent Brown who intended no slave insurrection was not widely credible, but Brown's sympathizers like Swayze and Clarke produced and promoted this image because just as it saved Northern humanitarians from some political embarrassment, it also comfortably masked the growing crisis in antislavery humanitarianism. Instead of challenging antebellum humanitarian principles, this version of Brown embodied those principles.

While some humanitarian interpretations erased or de-emphasized Brown's violent intentions, an approach apparently sanctioned by Brown himself after his capture, others evaded the issue of violence in ways not endorsed by Brown. The violence at Harpers Ferry was for many sympathetic and nonsympathetic writers the result of madness. They portrayed Brown as a lunatic "goaded to insanity by wrongs inflicted upon him by Pro-Slavery ruffians in Kansas." Even in the twentieth century, those interested in Brown have been preoccupied with questions about his supposed madness.[35] Was he genuinely insane or not? Was he a madman or a singularly lucid and realistic abolitionist? The fixation on establishing the fact of Brown's insanity avoids the more interesting and important questions about the rhetorical-political effect of declaring Brown mad. What was the value of such "madness" to those who created images of "mad John Brown"? How did the representation of Brown's madness function?

Although he often referred to the influence of his terrible experiences in Kansas on his decision to attack Harpers Ferry, Brown explicitly and strongly rejected all arguments that presented him as insane. He not only felt that the charges were untrue, but also realized that an insanity plea obscured the ideals and the cause that he sought to advance by going to Harpers Ferry and dying as a martyr. If the public interpreted Harpers Ferry as simply the "crazy freak" of one man and not as a sign of righteous protest àgainst slavery, then Brown's efforts to hasten the bloody demise of slavery could be neutralized.[36]

His sympathizers did not, of course, reject the cause Brown sought to advance at Harpers Ferry, yet several read his actions as insanity. Ralph Waldo Emerson saw him as both a hero and a lunatic, describing Brown as "the rarest of heroes" in one sentence and "crazy" in the next. The Reverend Leonard Bacon surmised that Brown's turn to violence at Harpers Ferry was the result of proslavery violence in Kansas. He wrote:

> The recent outbreak at Harper's Ferry has a palpable connection with the attempt to establish slavery in Kansas by mingled fraud and violence. It was in Kansas that John Brown, excited to a frenzy of fanaticism by the murder and torture of his children and by the outrages perpetrated all around him, learned to fight against slavery, and learned to dare great things.[37]

Citing proslavery violence in Kansas as the cause of Brown's "fanaticism," Bacon used Brown's "madness" as a vehicle for blaming the South for the violence at Harpers Ferry. For Julia Ward Howe, the personal experience of violence was a perfectly understandable cause of madness. Howe recounted:

> [Brown] one day saw two of his sons shot by the Border Ruffians (as the Missourians of the border were called), without trial or mercy. Some people thought that this dreadful sight had maddened his brain, as well it might.[38]

These representations of Brown's madness moved the responsibility for the Harpers Ferry violence from Brown to the proslavery forces who incited retaliation by murdering and torturing Brown's sons. These interpretations did not condone Brown's violence, but instead condemned the underlying cause of that violence, proslavery rowdies. This interpretation constructed sympathy for Brown, the victim of proslavery ruffianism, but it also dismissed the possibility that Brown, wanting an end to the brutality and immorality of slavery, saw a violent, direct attack as the only effective option—a possibility that would have suggested that dominant humanitarian ideals were outdated or inconsistent with the exigencies of the antislavery fight in 1859.

Other humanitarians proposed that Brown's mania had something more than an earthly or psychological origin. Although he did not overlook the influence of Bleeding Kansas, Moncure Conway hinted also at a sacred source of Brown's madness:

> A divine madness seized upon him; as it is written, "Oppression maketh a wise man mad"—but whether such madness be not wisdom of God, which is foolishness with men, we are not all calm enough to judge now.

While Conway's Brown is no less insane than Bacon's Brown or the Brown of the popular press, Conway suggests without deciding definitively that Brown's madness is of a holy nature. Brown's insane actions might be "divine" inspiration or simply the result of the "Oppression" he faced in Kansas; his "madness" might be the "wisdom of God," but no one in this crisis is "calm enough to judge now." Departing from most explanations of Brown's mental state, Conway's notion of a "divine madness" holds in view a judgment of insanity (the mad John Brown) alongside a glorification of a holy John Brown (the martyr-saint). Rather than railing against charges of insanity in order to make Brown a martyr-saint as Thoreau did, or declaring Brown mad in order to feel sympathy for him while dismissing his actions as Bacon did, Conway invented "divine madness."[39] The conceit reveres Brown, while it distances him from responsibility for the violent events at Harpers Ferry.

Swayze, who constructed a Brown professing nonviolent motives, also used the image of the mad John Brown to shunt aside bothersome questions about violence in the service of humanitarian ends. Like Bacon and Howe, Swayze saw in Brown "a madness that has grown out of his misfortunes" in Kansas (15). In a scene at the end of Act II where Julia, Brown's fictional daughter-in-law, and Mr. Cook talk about the old man, Swayze brings together these competing versions of Brown—the mad John Brown and the nonviolent John Brown. At the beginning of the scene we learn that Mr. Cook is the real mastermind of the Harpers Ferry raid. Cook and others want to press "the old man Brown" into service as "the most fit leader of the undertaking" (15). "Mr. Cook" is supposed to be John E. Cook, one of Brown's officers at Harpers Ferry. Although Swayze cast "Mr. Cook" as the driving intellectual force behind the Harpers Ferry plans, John E. Cook was initially reluctant to participate in a raid on Virginia. Only after an argument with Brown and the encouragement of the other recruits did Cook agree to join Brown.[40] By transferring the initiative for the plan from Brown to Cook, the play makes Brown less culpable for any violent wrongdoing at Harpers Ferry. Swayze's "Ossawattomie Brown" becomes their moral leader and continues to voice humanitarian ideals, but—as the presence of Cook works to indicate—this nonviolent Brown is not guilty of actually devising "The Insurrection at Harpers' Ferry."

In this same scene, Julia pleads with Mr. Cook to release Brown from such service. Explaining why and how Brown is ill-equipped to lead the daring scheme, she says:

> His mind has been so tired with suffering, I fear 'tis overbalanced. I need not tell you there are some men that sink under great trials hopelessly and at once, and others whose minds will bend beneath the storm, to rise, crooked, deformed perhaps, but not extinguished. Is it not so with him? under his great trials, his mind has warped and cramped until he can see nothing but through the glass of revenge, and lives but to redress his wrongs. . . . is it just or generous to choose him for this purpose? Is it not fostering a madness that has grown out of his misfortunes? (15)

Julia's presentation of Brown's violent motives ("madness," "revenge") differs from Brown's own version of his nonviolent motives in this play ("motives of philanthropy" [25], no vengeful desire for "blood" [18]). But, because Swayze makes both Julia and Brown noble and reliable characters, the playwright gives the audience no way to decide which are Brown's true motives: she keeps both sets of motives in play. Yet the audience does not necessarily experience these disparate accounts of Brown as a conflict because both work to explain his extraordinary and confusing action in terms familiar to the world of domestic melodrama. Julia's explanation: Brown acts, perhaps violently but understandably, out of a heartfelt hurt about wrongs inflicted unjustly on his family. Brown's explanation: Brown acts sympathetically (and nonviolently) from a bourgeois desire to help the less fortunate. Hence, the play explains Brown's violent motives in terms of "madness that has grown out of his misfortunes," while it continues to work to deny those violent intentions by having the hero disavow them and by transferring them to Mr. Cook. Crafting both mad and nonviolent versions of Brown, the play uses these representations of Brown to beg the questions about violence and humanitarianism raised by Harpers Ferry.

Still, up until the very last scene in the play, the violence and strife associated with Brown haunt this melodrama which cannot finally deploy any image of Brown to restore peace. The John Brown of this play remains a disturbing obstacle to harmony in the bourgeois domestic world and to unity between the North and South. Swayze ultimately restores peace only by severing Brown from any blood relation to those who remain. Throughout the play, the lovers, Alice and Ralph, are separated by Ralph's father who will not agree to a "union" between his son and the daughter of the "mad" John Brown, "a wild fanatic" (21). The "union" between the play's young lovers—like the union between the North and South—is threatened by Brown and his ties to Alice/the North. Yet, in a deus ex machina solution to the Brown problem, the play's closing scene disassociates Alice—and the North—from any blood relationship to the "mad" (and now dead) John Brown. Julia produces surprise evidence that Alice was Brown's *adopted* daughter, and the "union" moves unproblematically forward (27). Wishful thinking in 1859.

Although numerous humanitarian writers tried to sidestep, reinterpret, and deny troubling questions about violence posed by Brown's raid, some antislavery activists had abandoned the path of moral suasion prior to Harpers Ferry; some changed their views only after the raid. In the rancorous political atmosphere of the 1850s, abolitionists like Thomas Wentworth Higginson and Theodore Parker became energetic advocates for the use of force in the antislavery cause as well as firm, albeit sometimes unenlightened, supporters of Brown's activities. Thus, when he spoke of the enslaved's "*natural right to kill every one who seeks to prevent his enjoyment of liberty*" and "*natural duty*" to "*actually kill all those who seek to prevent his enjoyment of liberty*," Parker surprised few readers: he was only elaborating a previously held belief. Likewise, Frederick Douglass's advocacy of violence in the fight against slavery predates Harpers Ferry. His conversations with John Brown in 1847 convinced him that "peaceful abolition" was impossible. While he shocked Sojourner Truth with his "sanguinary doctrine" in 1847, Douglass shocked no one in 1859.[41]

Before Harpers Ferry, Brown had persuaded only a few abolitionists to his position. After the raid, his influence on the antislavery humanitarians' commitment to peace principles was marked. His actions prompted nonresistants like Whittier to rethink their long-held beliefs, and forced others—Garrison is a good example—to make serious departures from their peace platforms. Immediately after Harpers Ferry, Garrison condemned the raid as "misguided, wild, and apparently insane." Two months later Garrison had turned to criticizing Whittier's principled, nonresistant response to Brown and to wishing "Success to every slave insurrection at the South." Although Garrison never completely rejected moral suasion and nonresistance, his response to Brown acknowledged the limits of such tactics in the fight against slavery in a sinful world. After Harpers Ferry, in ways similar to Garrison, most abolitionists were changing their notions about the use and legitimacy of force. By the time Beauregard opened fire on Fort Sumter, most antislavery humanitarians had relinquished their commitments to moral suasion, nonviolence, and peace. "Even non-resistant principles gave way," Ednah Dow Cheney wrote about this moment in the crisis, remembering only Samuel May's abiding commitment to nonresistance. As Cheney and other antislavery humanitarians realized, May had become the exception and not the rule.[42]

African Americans and Representations of John Brown

Less anxious about the violence of the John Brown method, African Americans generally admired and appreciated Brown's efforts at Harpers Ferry. Following Brown's execution, Harriet Tubman, the legendary "General" of abolitionism, declared: "It's cla'r to me that it wasn't John Brown hung on that gallows—it was God in him." Unlike her white colleagues, Tubman identified the forces working "in" Brown as divine, not to justify a presumed madness, but to acknowledge without qualification the righteousness of Brown's unconventional humanitarianism. Similarly, in Simcoe, Ontario, Harvey Jackson printed a broadside that read in part: "we should do our duty,—show the world that we appreciate such noble and philanthropic actions."[43] As Jackson's public declaration begins to suggest, black responses to Brown's "philanthropic actions" were more than heartfelt thankfulness. Within humanitarian discourse, this appreciation and admiration served a deliberate rhetorical purpose, shaping a discursive version of Brown associated with an eccentric approach to helping others. Departing from established abolitionist principles, this John Brown humanitarianism—the product of black abolitionist representations of Brown—dismantled the hierarchy separating humanitarian from supposedly "helpless" slave and redefined philanthropy as direct and, when necessary, violent action.

Compared to their white coworkers, African American abolitionists felt far less queasy about Brown's willingness to use violence. "I am prepared to endorse John Brown's course fully," announced the Reverend J. Sella Martin, a Baptist minister and former slave. Despite the ambivalence of white abolitionists, despite the confusion noted (and enacted) by Cheever, Martin unhesitatingly supported the John Brown method over a nonviolent strategy or equivocating middle position. Explained Martin:

> I know that there is some quibbling, some querulousness, some fear, in reference
> to an out-and-out endorsement of his course. Men of peace principles object to
> it, in consequence of their religious conviction. . . . but I am prepared . . . in the
> light of all human history, to approve of the *means*; in the light of all Christian
> principle, to approve of the *end*.

Absent from Martin's discourse was uncertainty about how much and for what
purpose abolitionists should celebrate Brown. Martin expressed no ambivalence
about the morality of violence or Brown's use of violence. In fact, Martin was so far
removed from white abolitionist handwringing about violent means that his only
criticism centered on Brown's reluctance to use the John Brown method, reasoning
that "[i]n not shedding blood" more deliberately, "he left the slaves uncertain how
to act." If philanthropy were going to be useful, it would have to be practical,
realistic, dangerous. Thus, Martin saw no incongruity between the humanitarian
end and Brown's means. Tired of a conventional abolitionism that they judged
ineffective, black abolitionists demanded a new approach to antislavery work, an
approach that would, in the words of lawyer and antislavery lecturer John S. Rock,
end slavery "peaceably if it can, forcibly if it must." As the editor of the *Weekly
Anglo-African,* George Lawrence, Jr., put it: "We want Nat Turner—not speeches;
Denmark Vesey—not resolutions; John Brown—not meetings."[44]

While black abolitionists like Martin, Rock, and Lawrence used their praise
for Brown to argue for armed struggle, others linked Brown to an egalitarian ideal.
In a letter to Mary Brown, a group of black women from New York called John
Brown "our honored and dearly-loved brother," referring to him repeatedly as
"brother" or "beloved brother." By admiring him as a brother, these sisters
constructed an egalitarian affiliation between themselves and Brown; they used a
domestic rhetoric to align Brown with themselves, fashioning him as a familial
equal rather than a superior or benefactor. Drawing on a different but still
egalitarian rhetoric, a group of African Americans in Detroit called the Brown
family "our special friends." Another group in Chicago wrote to Brown:

> We certainly have great reasons, as well as intense desires, to assure you that we
> deeply sympathize with you and your beloved family. Not only do we sympa-
> thize in tears and prayers with *you* and *them* but we *will* do so in a more tangible
> form, by contributing material aid to help those of your family. . . . How could we
> be so ungrateful as to do less for one who has suffered, bled, and now ready to
> die for the cause?

Presenting their relationship to Brown as one marked by sympathy and gratitude,
these Chicagoans engaged in humanitarian consoling and philanthropic giving as
acts of reciprocation: they would consider it "ungrateful" for them "to do less."
Brown, the daring agent of humanitarian change, becomes in this letter the
patient, the recipient of help; African Americans—the patients of the "cause"—are
the agents. Yet, this philanthropy did not simply or permanently reverse the
positions of the agent and patient, but instead made these positions fluid, creating

a flexible and democratic helping praxis in which all philanthropic actors operate as both agents and patients. Whether representing Brown as a "brother," "friend," or participant in a reciprocal helping relationship, these texts produced and affirmed a connection between African Americans and Brown—an alliance that earned Brown a reputation among African Americans as one who "had divested himself of color prejudice" and devoted himself absolutely to the antislavery crusade. "His zeal in the cause of my race was far greater than mine," remembered Frederick Douglass, "it was the burning sun to my taper light." As Brown became a sign for an eccentric humanitarianism committed to racial equality and a revolutionary approach to antislavery work, the admiration of Brown became a useful rhetorical tool.[45]

Representations of Brown played a strikingly different role in white philanthropic discourse. Anxious and ambivalent about the consequences of Harpers Ferry, many white humanitarians were drawn to images of Brown that reinforced conventional humanitarian ideology. In a newspaper account of the execution of Brown, Henry S. Olcott, a correspondent for Horace Greeley's *New York Tribune*, invented one of the most popular of these images—the fable about John Brown being led to his execution and pausing to kiss a black infant. The newspaper reported:

> As he stepped out of the door a black woman, with her little child in arms, stood near his way. . . . His thoughts at the moment none can know except as his acts interpret them. He stopped for a moment in his course, stooped over, and with the tenderness of one whose love is as broad as the brotherhood of man, kissed it affectionately.[46]

Although Olcott's account had no relation to what happened in Charlestown on December 2, 1859—because of the rumors of an abolitionist plot to free Brown, only military personnel were allowed anywhere near the prisoner as he moved from the jail to the gallows—this story did function as a (mis)interpretation of Brown's fantasy of what he would have liked to have happened at his hanging. In a letter written just three days before his execution, Brown told Mary Stearns:

> I have asked to be spared from having any weak or hypocritical prayers made over me when I am publicly murdered, and that my only religious attendants be poor little dirty, ragged, bareheaded, and barefooted slave boys and girls, led by some old gray-headed slave mother.[47]

The representations of this imagined event, whether derived from Brown's daydream or Olcott's fabricated newspaper account, performed a significant role in the creation of a "John Brown" attractive to white humanitarians.

In "Brown of Osawatomie," Whittier used this incident to undo Brown's militancy. The poem begins by repeating Olcott's apocryphal story about Brown kissing the enslaved mother's child. The second and third stanzas read:

John Brown of Osawatomie,
    They led him out to die;
And, lo!—a poor slave-mother
    With her little child pressed nigh.
Then the bold, blue eye grew tender,
    And the old, harsh face grew mild,
As he stooped between the jeering ranks
    And kissed the negro's child!

The shadows of his stormy life
    That moment fell apart;
Without, the rash and bloody hand,
    Within, the loving heart.
That kiss, from all its guilty means,
    Redeemed the good intent,
And round the grisly fighter's hair
    The Martyr's aureole bent!

As discussed earlier, Whittier used this poem to work through his hatred of Brown's "guilty means" and his admiration of the antislavery "intent." In these stanzas, the Quaker poet presents the "kiss" as the act that redeems Brown from his sinful use of violence, erasing his militancy and thereby confirming his status as an abolitionist saint. The kiss transforms Brown from a "grisly fighter" into a kind Christian. On a theological level, the poem enacts this transformation through a metaphysics of forgiveness in which a single symbolic act of atonement (in this case, a kiss) can stand in for a multitude of sins. On a formal level, the poem soothes antislavery anxiety and ambivalence by deploying sentimental domestic imagery to create this kinder, gentler John Brown and, rhythmically, by relying on an adaptation of the popular and familiar Common Meter. To contain the challenge posed by John Brown abolitionism, Whittier packages his anxiety-producing subject in rhythms, images, and religious beliefs that were as comforting as they were familiar.

The poem uses representations of African Americans to construct a kinder image of Brown, while it evades the strong black abolitionist critique of antislavery humanitarianism—a critique located in very different images of Brown. Built upon the good-intention-but-bad-action interpretation of Harpers Ferry, "Brown of Osawatomie" displaces the centrality of violence in Brown's plans. A stern rejection of the inadequacy of nonviolent antislavery action, Harpers Ferry—especially as it was read by African Americans—represented a deep fatigue with older humanitarian discourses and practices. By marginalizing the fact of Brown's violent actions and intentions, Whittier and other humanitarians eluded the criticism that such a turn to violence entailed. This version of Brown allowed abolitionists like Whittier to understand Brown in terms of their own humanitarian ideology, and it worked to alleviate anxiety about what Brown and African American abolitionists had come to see as imperative—the role of injuring and killing to end slavery.

The image of Brown pausing to kiss the slave mother's child also appealed to William Ellery Channing who used it to counter a different aspect of the African American version of John Brown. Unlike black abolitionists who saw an egalitarian philanthropic alliance between Brown and African Americans, Channing refigured that relationship in his representation of Brown. Following the "wounded dying saint" as he walked to the gallows, the poet says:

> And as he went,
> A poor devoted slave, a mother stood,
> One of the race that Christ came down to love,
> Bearing upon her breast an infant slave,—
> There, by the prison-gate, his blessing craved.
> Softly, with angel voice, he blessed her there,—
> One of his children, for whose good he lived,
> His mind on heaven, his heart still loving earth![48]

Like other white renditions of this scene (see, for instance, Thomas S. Noble's painting *John Brown's Blessing* [Figure 2.1]), Channing's Brown blesses the slave mother and her child. In his own daydreaming of a similar scene, however, Brown imagined that the children and the slave mother would bless him. In Brown's wish

Figure 2.1. Thomas S. Noble, *John Brown's Blessing*,
1867. Courtesy Kansas State Historical Society.

he indicated that the power for any religious blessing would reside with these African Americans and not with a traditional minister who could manage only "weak or hypocritical prayers." Channing's poem reverses the direction of the blessing, investing such religious power in Brown and not the slaves. While working to emphasize Brown's peaceful and religious attributes, such a reversal also reestablishes the conventional philanthropic distinction between the godly and empowered white abolitionist "helper" and the supposedly "helpless" slave. Whereas black abolitionists and Brown had configured the relation between Brown-the-humanitarian and oppressed slaves in a less paternalistic manner, Channing used the image of Brown and the slave mother with child to return readers to white abolitionism's more orthodox conception of the patient/agent relationship.

In his 1860 oil painting, *John Brown on His Way to Execution* (Figure 2.2), Louis Ransom also perpetuated the conventional hierarchy between the patient and the powerful white humanitarian agent. With eyes directed at the mother and child below him, Brown towers over the other figures, some of whom Ransom has made strangely diminutive. Brown's noticeably imposing stature, his static hands-in-pocket posture in the midst of the agitated activity of the seven other figures, and, of course, the radiant halo behind his head all suggest Brown's moral

Figure 2.2. Louis Ransom, *John Brown on His Way to Execution*, 1860. Courtesy Kansas State Historical Society.

preeminence and certainly his dominance within the humanitarian dyad. The composition emphasizes Brown's goodness, his power to bless, his position as agent. This return to a conventional understanding of the structure of humanitarian help permitted these white humanitarian writers and painters to evade the challenge of John Brown humanitarianism. Instead of considering the egalitarian relation between agent and patient suggested by African American representations of John Brown, these white humanitarians portrayed Brown as an exaggerated version of their own collective ego-ideal, as the benevolent but dominant white humanitarian agent. The symbol of a radical, egalitarian philanthropy had become—in these conventional rewritings—an image of humanitarian paternalism.

Another conventional humanitarian strategy for countering a racially egalitarian philanthropy was to avoid, or at least de-emphasize, the issue of race altogether. Ransom gestures toward this type of evasion by presenting the oppressed slave mother as a European figure from classical art: indications of racial difference are fairly erased. In *The Life, Trial, and Execution of Capt. John Brown* (1859), Robert M. De Witt avoids a confrontation with the problem of Brown's alliance with African Americans by claiming that personal wrongs suffered in Kansas, and not antiracist politics, prompted Brown to wage war on slavery.[49] Also emphasizing the magnitude of personal wrongs endured by the Brown family, Swayze's three-act melodrama rarely addresses slavery or race issues. Despite the manifest subject of the play, despite its settings in North Elba, a primarily African American community, despite its attention to Brown and his raiders (just under one-fourth of Brown's recruits were black), *Ossawattomie Brown* has, astonishingly enough, no black roles. By moving African Americans and/or their Africanness out of the picture, white Americans could overlook Brown's alliance with African Americans and thereby avoid the anxiety created by the incursion of racial difference and racial equality into the realm of humanitarianism.

Representations of Brown's relation to African Americans create a contradictory, if not confusing, collage portrait of Brown-as-humanitarian. In the production of these very different images, Brown's own mercurial self-fashioning played a substantive role. When addressing a primarily white audience, as in the interview with Mason and Vallandigham or in his final trial speech, Brown speaks about pure humanitarian aims based on principles like the golden rule, de-emphasizes the role of violence in his plans, and talks as the powerful but benevolent humanitarian agent who pities a powerless people, the patients for whom he has a disinterested regard.[50]

In his texts written for a primarily black audience—"Sambo's Mistakes" and "Words of Advice," for example—Brown is far more militant, calling for organized, armed, courageous action.[51] In these texts Brown dispenses unending advice in a critical, sometimes impatient, always bossy fashion, preaching against "errors" like "silly novels," "tobacco," or the willingness "to ape the follies and extravagances of their white neighbors, and to indulge in idle show, in ease, and in luxury." His criticism of whites resembles contempt, when, for example, he says, "the Dough-faced Statesmen of the North . . . think themselves highly honored if they may be allowed to lick up the spittle of a Southerner." His criticism of African Americans, on the other hand, comes in the form of practical, if sometimes moralistic, guidance about everything from conducting a meeting to lassoing slave catchers to creating "a tumult in the court-room" as a diversionary maneuver to effect the escape of a slave.

Brown also undoes the agent/patient hierarchy in these texts directed at black audiences, representing himself not as the white humanitarian agent with superior goodness and knowledge but as a comrade in arms. In "Sambo's Mistakes" he adopts the persona of an African American sharing wisdom with "others of my colored brethren" about personal mistakes—self-criticism in hindsight shared with those who might learn from it. (Oates points out that Brown is in this article consciously or unconsciously self-critical, "for some of the mistakes Brown described were clearly his own.") Brown's appropriation of a black identity as a position from which to lecture against the wrongs he saw within the black activist community is certainly suspect. His speaking not only for others but also as other is a rhetorical gesture that, in a manner typical of coercive humanitarianism, disregards the sufferings, histories, and identities of African Americans while ostensibly working to end that suffering. Nevertheless, there is also an eccentric dimension to this text: an indentification that drives Brown to struggle for justice and humane social change and permits him to regard African Americans as his equals. Recognizing this eccentric quality, Benjamin Quarles reads "Sambo's Mistakes" as a sign of Brown's lack of color prejudice and his egalitarian antiracism. Quarles argues: "Always treating blacks on a peer basis, Brown did not ignore their faults as one might condescendingly gloss over the shortcomings of those assumed to be one's inferiors."[52]

Another part of the explanation of these contradictory images of Brown must focus on the structure of humanitarianism and the difficulties associated with forgetting or altering long-lived structures, habits, and conventions, particularly when those structures, habits, and conventions are regarded as benevolent, moral, kind, good. The racialist beliefs of white antislavery humanitarians shaped their interpretations of Brown, interpretations that often contradicted African American representations of Brown and Brown's own self-representation. In his *Roving Editor* (1859) Dedication addressed to Brown, Redpath wrote: "You are willing to recognize the negro as a brother, however inferior in intellectual endowments."[53] Redpath catches some inkling of Brown's egalitarian affinity with black struggle against slavery and also misses it completely, as his racialist beliefs prevent him from acknowledging Brown's unwillingness to see African Americans as inferior.

Yet, in this moment of profound change in humanitarianism, a number of structures, ideals, and practices were called into question. Experimentation became easier and more common during this search for new, hopefully more adequate, approaches to ways of helping, and the pressure for change became more palpable. Many white humanitarians continued to hold to romantic humanitarian ideals, hierarchic philanthropic structures, and racialist ways of seeing. African Americans, however, had less invested in these status quo mainstays of philanthropy. Many black abolitionists experienced the 1850s as a decade of setbacks: the Compromise of 1850, including its more stringent Fugitive Slave Law, the 1854 Kansas-Nebraska Act repealing the Missouri Compromise's ban on slavery north of 36° 30', and the Supreme Court's Dred Scott decision that denied African Americans rights as citizens. In 1830 abolitionism offered hope to African Americans; slaves were "taught to hope for deliverance" as Thomas Hamilton put it in an editorial for the *Weekly Anglo-African*. Yet, in 1859 slavery was still flourishing, seemingly strengthened by proslavery judicial and legislative victories. The antislavery movements had not made war on slavery, but had instead, Hamilton argued, acted as slavery's "great safety valve; the escape pipe through which the dangerous element incident to slavery found vent." Hence, many African Americans were ready to abandon conventional abolitionism, slavery's "great safety valve," and to foster instead the "dangerous element"—which African Americans like Hamilton identified with Nat Turner, Denmark Vesey, and John Brown.[54]

Harriet Jacobs's "John Brown"

As these various, competing, and internally contradictory images of John Brown indicate, humanitarianism after Harpers Ferry had fallen into a crisis, and this instability within philanthropy fueled the demand for eccentric modes of humanitarian work. Still, even while some humanitarians (mostly African American) used images of Brown to champion the development of eccentric approaches, many others (mostly white) appropriated John Brown to resist eccentric changes in antislavery humanitarianism.

This struggle within humanitarian discourse, over the dead body and soul of John Brown, was similar to the struggle Harriet Jacobs had with her white editor, Lydia Maria Child. During the editing of her autobiography, *Incidents in the Life of a Slave Girl* (1861), Jacobs was denied the opportunity to make use of John Brown in her advancement of a patient-centered alternative to conventional humanitarianism. While editing *Incidents,* Child asked Jacobs to omit the final chapter on Brown, suggesting that "It does not naturally come into your story, and the M.S. is already too long. Nothing can be so appropriate to end with, as the death of your grandmother."[55]

Bruce Mills has argued that Child's editorial revisions worked benignly toward shaping a narrative that "was aimed at a higher reason and thus was designed to nurture a more lasting reform." No one should assume, however, that Jacobs preferred the editorial changes or that she wanted to emphasize "eternal values," "higher values," "spiritual laws," or "higher reason" over temporal action and politics. In fact, Child's editorial control over *Incidents*—her attempt to mold *Incidents* into "a *story*" that would "promote nonviolent reform more effectively by appealing to eternal values rather than to passions engendered by contemporary events"—might be seen as an act of coercive humanitarianism, an example of a humanitarian agent not listening to the patient being "helped" while ostensibly working to help that patient.[56]

Because of Child's deletion and the lack of an extant manuscript text, no one knows what Jacobs wrote about Brown. We do know that Jacobs felt uneasy about Child's editing and that she probably held a different perspective on Brown than Child did. While happy to have Child edit and promote her manuscript, Jacobs also thought that the editorial process should have been collaborative and not unilateral as it appears to have been. "I know that Mrs. Child will strive to do the best she can," wrote Jacobs in a letter to Amy Post, "but I ought to have been there that we could have consulted together, and compared our views." Jacobs respected Child, calling her elsewhere "a whole souled Woman," and never apparently blamed Child for the lack of an opportunity to edit together. Work-related obligations kept Jacobs from meeting with Child. Still, her letter—written after Child had made the editorial changes—indicates a dissatisfaction about her separation from the editing decisions and perhaps those decisions in themselves. A writer skilled in the use of irony and indirection, Jacobs quipped: "Although I know that hers are superior to mine yet we could have worked her great Ideas and my small ones together." Such a dissatisfaction after the fact suggests that Jacobs was not entirely pleased with Child's revisions.[57]

Moreover, with reference to John Brown, there are grounds for supposing that Jacobs might have strongly disagreed with Child's spoken and unspoken rationale for the deletion of the final chapter. While Mills has assumed correctly that Child wished to mold *Incidents* so as to promote "a higher reason," Jacobs showed no indication that she wrote her narrative in order to express such "eternal values." Hoping to effect social changes in this world—to struggle with others to combat an especially brutal form of oppression—Jacobs wrote *Incidents* for reasons that are unmistakably political. In her Preface she clearly states that she wants "to convince the people of the Free States what Slavery really is" (2). Thus, despite whatever ideal meaning Child desired for *Incidents,* Jacobs saw the book as a political intervention against slavery, against contemporary social injustices, not as an aesthetic or religious or domestic meditation about "a higher reason."

Furthermore, it is doubtful that Jacobs shared Child's "regret" about Harpers Ferry or her judgment that "violent attempts to right wrong are both injudicious and evil."[58] African American antislavery activists admiringly and sympathetically embraced John Brown without the handwringing about ends, means, actions, and intentions that characterized the response of white abolitionists like Child. There is no reason to think that Jacobs would have rejected this approach to Brown in order to adopt the more confused impressions of whites. Moreover, it seems unlikely that Jacobs would have held as tenaciously as Child, Whittier, Phillips, and company to nonviolence as a suitable or productive method for opposing slavery. There is no evidence to suggest that in the late 1850s Jacobs favored the nonviolent path, in opposition to the leading tendencies of black abolitionists like her brother, John S. Jacobs, who announced to an 1859 meeting of African American Bostonians, "My colored brethren, if you have not swords, I say to you, sell your garments and buy one."[59] In fact, Harriet Jacobs's use of ironic commentary on the Nat Turner insurrection to ridicule white misconceptions about the contentment of the enslaved (*Incidents* 63) and her heroic portrayal of the defiant Uncle Benjamin's use of physical force to resist a whipping and to make an attempted escape (*Incidents* 17-26) suggest that Jacobs felt no qualms about the use of violence in the fight against slavery. While many white abolitionists revered nonresistance as a Christian and principled response to slavery (as in Harriet Beecher Stowe's portrayal of the Christ-like Uncle Tom), Jacobs ends her chapter on Uncle Benjamin with a statement that seems to call enslaved peoples to resist just as Uncle Benjamin resists: "He that is *willing* to be a slave, let him be a slave" (26).

Since we know that Jacobs disliked the editorial process and since we can reasonably assume that there might have been a genuine difference of opinion about the substance and effect of the John Brown chapter, I have difficulty seeing Child's deletion as a benign editorial decision making the story a better, more compact and coherent narrative. Instead, motivated not by any conscious racist dislike for Jacobs but probably by her own powerfully ambivalent feelings about Brown (her professed "love" for Brown and her deep longing to "nurse" his wounds combined with her principled condemnation of the John Brown method), and empowered by the structures of antislavery humanitarianism itself which placed her in a position of control over Jacobs, Child through her editing silenced a portion of Jacobs's message about antislavery humanitarianism and John Brown.[60]

Such acts of coercive humanitarianism—acts putatively intended to help patients of humanitarianism but which actually hinder, constrain, or regulate those being helped—were common in antislavery and not, of course, particular to Child. And Jacobs, perhaps as clearly as anyone in the antislavery movement, understood the nature and consequences of coercive humanitarianism. In the late 1850s, while continuing to struggle against slavery alongside her white coworkers, Jacobs also sensed an opportunity to make a fresh intervention into humanitarianism itself. Although she had lost her opportunity to comment directly on Brown and his role in the crisis in antislavery humanitarianism, Jacobs nevertheless used that crisis, this moment of turbulent flux in humanitarianism's self-conception, to suggest a new model for humanitarianism: an eccentric humanitarianism that would redress power imbalances like the one she endured while trying to get her book edited and published. *Incidents* is testimony to her ability to oppose coercive humanitarianism while working subversively within its boundaries.

THREE

HARRIET JACOBS AND
THE SUBVERSION OF STYLE

*Construction is not opposed to agency; it is the necessary scene of agency, the very
terms in which agency is articulated and becomes culturally intelligible.*

JUDITH BUTLER[1]

Jeremiah Durham Asks Some Questions

In chapter 31 of *Incidents in the Life of a Slave Girl* (1861), Linda Brent,
sunburned and barely able to walk, steps out of a rowboat and onto a wooden dock
in Philadelphia. Meeting the Reverend Jeremiah Durham, a minister who worked
with other African Americans on the Philadelphia Vigilant Committee to assist
fugitive slaves, she encounters for the first time an antislavery humanitarian from
the North.[2] Mr. Durham invites her to stay with his family, eat with them, rest and
recuperate. Shortly after her arrival, he begins to question Linda about her age, her
situation as a never-married woman with two children, and other events in her life.
Mr. Durham ends the interview, which Linda describes as "painful," with a genteel
apology that explains his altruistic reasons for quizzing her ("Excuse me, if I have
tried your feelings. . . . I wanted to understand your situation in order to know
whether I could be of any service to you"), a condescending pat on the back ("Your
straight-forward answers do you credit"), and, of course, some well-meaning,
paternal advice spoken in the imperative ("don't answer every body so openly. It
might give some heartless people a pretext for treating you with contempt" [160]).
His use of the word "contempt" throws Linda on the defensive, prompting her to
respond by mentioning God's mercy, her intentions "to be a good mother" (161),
and her own suffering—allusions that a minister and humanitarian would recognize and respect. Perhaps noticing her uneasiness, perhaps not, Mr. Durham closes

their conversation with a bit of condescending reassurance and some high-toned, Christian, do-good advice again in the imperative voice: "Place your trust in God, and be governed by good principles, and you will not fail to find friends" (161).

Besides being the first humanitarian Linda meets in the North, Mr. Durham interests me not because his behavior is shocking or unusual for a humanitarian (it isn't), but because Jacobs calls attention to him in this passage. She appreciates his efforts on her behalf, just as she acknowledges and appreciates all the women and men who help "Linda" in *Incidents*. Equally important to the characterization of Mr. Durham, however, are the descriptions of how his questions caused Linda to suffer, how his words "burned me like coals of fire," "made an indelible impression upon me," and "brought up great shadows from the mournful past" (161).

Mr. Durham's questions raise an interesting question: Why does Jacobs focus our attention on Mr. Durham, representing him as a kind but tactless, charitable but condescending antislavery activist? She does not insinuate an attack on Mr. Durham. Although pain is the result of his questions and advice, he does not intend to cause Linda pain. Sincere in his desire to help Linda, he intends exactly the opposite. The portrayal of Mr. Durham is not an attack, but rather a vignette of someone who can in some (but not all) respects typify the antislavery humanitarians of the North. This is one section of Jacobs's larger picture of antislavery humanitarianism.

In addition to taking a stand against slavery and racism, Jacobs writes *Incidents* in order to examine, critique, rethink, and reformulate antislavery humanitarianism itself. What makes *Incidents* a rather uncommon document of antislavery humanitarianism is not, however, its criticism of the movement per se; antislavery activists were indeed famous for criticizing each other. *Incidents* is remarkable, instead, for the subversive style of its critique and for its movement toward a new, eccentric mode of humanitarianism, one that would avoid the coercive, patronizing, sometimes cruel aspects of conventional humanitarianism, one that would seek to redress the power imbalance between the agent and the patient.

Although I will maintain that Jacobs's text is an uncommon, indeed exceptional, document from a heterogeneous antislavery movement, *Incidents* is still a product of that movement, a product of the discourses of that movement and the discourses of the nineteenth century in general. I will not argue that Jacobs somehow got outside of her historical situation to critique and rethink antislavery humanitarianism; rather I see her text as a consequence of that situation. Nevertheless, because the discourses that shaped antislavery humanitarianism were multiple and contradictory, and because she imperfectly absorbed these discourses, and because she had access to certain discourses outside the mainstream of antislavery humanitarianism (including black abolitionism and African American modes of language use), Jacobs's discursive venture into antislavery humanitarianism resulted in a "subversive repetition" of conventional humanitarianism.[3] Furthermore, her bifurcated position as an agent of humanitarianism and a patient of humanitarianism (a fugitive slave, the object of antislavery efforts, one of the persons being "helped") gave her a split perspective on the meaning and effect of humanitarianism. Traces of this split are present in her writing.

In what follows in this chapter, I examine the subversive style of Jacobs's critique of antislavery humanitarianism (in the section titled "Subverting Texts"), her use of such a style in the formation of an eccentric humanitarianism (in "Jacobs's Humanitarian Work"), and her practice of this reimagined philanthropy during the Civil War (in this chapter's final section). Before considering Jacobs's response to antislavery humanitarianism, however, I first want to survey the coercive features of antislavery discourse. While I do not dispute the integrity of these humanitarians' intentions, and though I am skeptical of efforts to reduce their humanitarianism to a screen for a sinister bourgeois or racist conspiracy, my examination of antislavery discourse takes careful notice of the "humanitarian" efforts to supervise and control the attitudes, actions, and lives of its patients.

The Rhetoric of Helping Others

Rationalizing and reproducing the agent/patient hierarchy, antislavery humanitarian rhetoric tried to promulgate and naturalize controlling relationships. Antislavery discourse constructed subservient roles for black people and then justified and naturalized those roles. Antislavery discourse also had a didactic function that entailed persuading black people to adopt the values and beliefs of the North's white middle class. While never entirely successful in its "social control" designs, this discourse used benevolent, racialist, and paternalist rhetoric along with the language and ideology of sympathy and self-help to promote coercive designs.

The various schemes of white philanthropists to colonize American blacks in Liberia, the West Indies, Central America, and elsewhere are an obvious example of the coercive nature of antislavery humanitarianism.[4] In an 1824 letter to Jared Sparks, Thomas Jefferson saw African colonization as a "humane" and "justifiable" project, benefiting whites and blacks. Yet, to advocate forced emigration (what he called "the getting rid of them") as the humanitarian alternative to forced labor is clearly an example of coercive humanitarianism.[5]

To promote and argue for their ideas, colonizationists (like Jefferson) deployed various types of benevolent rhetoric. Abraham Lincoln constructed his plan on a piece of altruistic rhetoric aimed at showing black people the beneficence of colonization. In an 1862 "Address on Colonization to a Committee of Colored Men," he coaxingly insisted:

> you ought to do something to help those who are not so fortunate as yourselves. . . . For the sake of your race you should sacrifice something of your present comfort for the purpose of being as grand in that respect as the white people. It is a cheering thought throughout life that something can be done to ameliorate the condition of those who have been subject to the hard usage of the world.[6]

His argument was a model humanitarian appeal: because you are "so fortunate," you should put the suffering of others before your own selfish concerns and help those who suffer. What I find incongruous yet typically coercive about Lincoln's position is that he asked black people—those who endured the pain of racism and slavery (the patients of antislavery humanitarianism)—to endure a different type of pain (a massive expatriation) as the means to a humanitarian end (the elimination of slavery).

Harriet Beecher Stowe also pictured colonization as the avenue for the betterment of African Americans. Her presentation of colonization in *Uncle Tom's Cabin* (1852) revolves around the imagined domestic fulfillment of a black family on the far away shores of Africa. Through the incredible reunion of George Harris's family and their immigration to Africa, Stowe envisions a future happiness for black people and simultaneously soothes the consciences and eases the anxieties of her white readers in the North. Even Cassy's lost son and Topsy eventually head to Africa. The fantasy is one of happiness, domestic unity, and noble, Christian work in not-yet civilized Africa. Although Stowe's novel was famously popular with white readers throughout the world, *Uncle Tom's Cabin* was less well-received by black abolitionists trying to combat colonization sentiment and win social and human rights in the North.[7]

In Stowe's novel, Lincoln's speech, and Jefferson's letter, as in most colonizationist discourse, benevolent rhetoric is used to assert some command over black lives, to urge their separation from whites and their transplantation to a colony. Colonization rhetoric was made even more coercive by its disregard for the situation, opinions, and feelings of African Americans. Discussing the spread of colonization sentiment, Theodore S. Wright, a black minister from New York, said:

> The slaveholder and the pro-slavery man, the man of expanded views, the man who loved the poor and oppressed of every hue and clime, all united in this feeling and principle of expatriation. But, sir, there were hundreds of thousands of men in the land, who never could sympathize in this feeling; I mean those who were to be removed. The people of color were broken-hearted.

Beyond the fact that few blacks wanted to (be forced to) move, Wright and other black abolitionists had other important reasons for opposing colonization. Such schemes were notoriously unfeasible. Moreover, as it became more and more "popular to say the people of color must be removed," Wright continued, "[w]e saw indications that coercive measures would be resorted to. . . . Maryland passed laws to force out the colored people. It was deemed proper to make them go, whether they would or not." Hence, many blacks began to suspect that the colonization societies were not part of any antislavery philanthropy but rather a proslavery plot, in David Walker's words, "a plan got up, by a gang of slave-holders to select the free people of colour from among the slaves, that our more miserable brethren may be better secured in ignorance and wretchedness, to work their farms and dig their mines, and thus go on enriching the Christians with their blood and groans." Colonization efforts incited black protest and provoked black abolitionists to distrust the obtuse determination of humanitarians: "Why will the American Colonization Society persist in its deceptive efforts?" asked George Downing. "*We are not going to Africa! ! !*" Nevertheless, the Society and others proceeded with their efforts, rarely soliciting the views of those who would be repatriated. The coercive designs of such schemes, indifferent as they were to the well-being of black people, and Northern black protest convinced only a few white activists to question the colonizationists' ends and means.[8]

Another key factor in the construction of coercive humanitarianism was unquestionably the racialist rhetoric and representations that sustained racism inside and outside the antislavery movement.[9] These representations emerged from the widespread belief, in antislavery humanitarianism as elsewhere, that black people were "inferior" because of their "race." Hence, when a radical abolitionist like James Redpath called "the negro" "a brother, however inferior in intellectual endowments," he was reinforcing the notion that black people were "inferior," even while combating slavery and attempting to acknowledge the humanity of black people.[10]

A variety of interrelated racialist discourses dominated nineteenth-century American society, and antislavery rhetoric often participated in these discourses. An important component in this set of fluid, shifting racialisms was what Ronald T. Takaki has named the "child/savage" ideology, which negatively characterized blacks as "naturally" immature, lazy, unintelligent, drunken, criminal, and licentious. When the emphasis fell on their supposedly "savage" nature, writers often depicted blacks as animals, cannibals, or debased humans.[11] In references designed to reveal the cruelty and idiocy of such assumptions, Jacobs illustrated how these notions pervaded the mentality of slaveholders. "Women are considered of no value," Jacobs wrote, "unless they continually increase their owner's stock. They are put on a par with animals" (49).[12]

The influence of the child/savage ideology notwithstanding, the "negative" aspects of child/savage representations did not hold the same appeal to Northern humanitarians as did the clustering of representations and beliefs that George Fredrickson has called "romantic racialism." The ideas and images of romantic racialism were significantly shaped by historians such as William H. Prescott, Francis Parkman, and John Lothrop Motley, who narrated rousing tales of the struggles between various races or peoples and described the characteristics that inhered to each national group or race, depicting with ethnocentric pride the particularly superior qualities of the Anglo-Saxon race. Although importantly linked to the widespread "child/savage" ideology, romantic racialism emphasized the "child" rather than the "savage," depicting in supposedly flattering terms the childlike loyalty, spirituality, gentleness, docility, patience, forgiveness, and affection of blacks.[13]

In *Uncle Tom's Cabin* Stowe's stereotyped representations of black people proceeded from a racialist understanding of black people as simple and childlike. "Quiet and peaceable in his disposition" (304) and "perfectly submissive" (342), Tom with his "religious patience" (304) and "his strong faith in Almighty, eternal love" (341) epitomizes romantic racialism's ideal black person, illustrating in pious terms how blacks were (perhaps more than whites) naturally suited to the practice of Christian virtue. Stowe, interested in the characteristics and supposedly "indigenous talent[s] of the African race" (179), paused at various moments in her novel to give readers some of the particulars of the racialist doctrine from which her characters were made:

> The negro, it must be remembered, is an exotic of the most gorgeous and superb countries of the world, and he has, deep in his heart, a passion for all that is splendid, rich, fanciful; a passion which, rudely indulged by an untrained taste, draws on them the ridicule of the colder and more correct white race. (141)

Stowe was not alone in her beliefs about an African "nature," but shared these racialist ideas with most of her (white, New England) society. Many of her opinions about race and character are derived from her reading of antislavery literature; and many of Jacobs's readers would have found themselves in agreement with Stowe's representations of black people.[14]

Examples of black people who did not conform to these childlike images did not dissuade white antislavery activists from their attachment to romantic racialism. In *Uncle Tom's Cabin,* Stowe depicts George Harris as an intelligent, skeptical person who aggressively pursues freedom—someone quite unlike the docile, childlike, Christian Uncle Tom. Yet, she understands the contrast between the two characters in strictly racialist terms: George is part white, a "mulatto" (10), whereas Tom is "full glossy black" with "truly African features" (18). Elizabeth Cady Stanton made use of such racialist distinctions from antislavery fiction in her perception of her abolitionist coworker, Frederick Douglass. Although he was never docile, obedient, and childlike, his independence, ambition, and refusal to accommodate the representations of racialist discourse posed no real threat to her racialist thinking, because, in her words:

> a few drops of Saxon blood gave our Frederick Douglass such a clear perception of his humanity, his inalienable rights, as to enable him, with the slaveholder's Bible, the slaveholder's constitution, a southern public sentiment and education laid heavy on his shoulders, to stand upright and walk forth in search of freedom.[15]

Although Stanton was trying to praise Douglass in this passage, the racialist implications of attributing his search for freedom to his "Saxon blood" threatened to reenslave Douglass and other African Americans with a different set of chains, rhetorical ones. By allowing humanitarians to *know* in a particular way the "nature" of blacks, racialist representations provided humanitarians with justification for their paternalistic, controlling attitudes toward black people.

Even the more encouraging, less discriminatory antislavery humanitarians produced a rhetoric marked by paternalism, generously giving well-intentioned advice and instruction and treating blacks with benevolent condescension. In a letter to the black abolitionist Sarah Douglass, Angelina Grimké, a forthright opponent of racism within the antislavery movement, told Douglass and black women in general:

> You, my dear Sisters, hav a work to do in rooting out this wicked feeling [racial prejudice], as well as we. You *must be willing* to come in amongst us, tho' it *may be* your feelings *may* be wounded by the "putting forth of the finger," the

avoidance of a seat by you, or the glancing of the eye. To suffer these things is the sacrifice which is calld for at *your hands,* & I earnestly desire that you may be willing to bear these mortifications with christian meekness, gentleness & love.[16]

Although she displays a sensitive awareness to the subtle forms of racist behavior among whites and remains unequivocal in her opposition to racism, Grimké is also assigning Douglass duties in the struggle against the racism of white people. Knowing well that in urging Douglass to confront directly the prejudice of whites she is also asking her to suffer personal distress from the contempt of white women, Grimké uses the rhetoric of Christian self-sacrifice (a popular device in humanitarian discourse) to convince Douglass to endure this pain for the moral betterment of white women. Setting aside the incongruity of using humanitarian rhetoric to ask an oppressed people to suffer further as a means to a humanitarian end (the same coercive incongruity appears in Lincoln's "Address on Colonization"), we detect nonetheless an ordering about—a paternalistic, instructive tone—in Grimké's letter.[17]

More than just unwanted advice, however, antislavery paternalism often emerged in the form of direct control over the lives and labors of patients. During the Civil War, the Pennsylvania Abolition Society worked to "help" war refugees by shipping them North and turning these Southern slaves into Northern servants. Exemplifying coercive humanitarianism's combination of philanthropic intention with imperious action, a white Northerner sent a detailed request to the Society:

I would like to have a coulored Girl from 12 to 14 years of age of rather dark coulor of sprightly appearance, one that would be well calculated for general housework in the country.[18]

The Society received a number of similar offers to help these contrabands, particularly those who could milk a cow, cook, wash, and iron.

In their desire to help the "downtrodden" blacks and in their tendency to treat these patients of antislavery humanitarianism as if they were children, antislavery activists were simply taking on what Lawrence J. Friedman calls "the formalized role that white evangelical middle-class missionary reformers assumed toward all 'debased' and 'deprived' lower classes." Although Friedman does not inaccurately characterize the majority of antislavery reformers, such paternalism was not limited to whites, or necessarily the middle class, the evangelical, or the missionary. Paternalism as a formalized role appropriately characterizes the posture Mr. Durham (who is black) takes in relationship to Linda Brent, for instance. Garrison's working-class upbringing did not prevent him from insisting that the antislavery cause was so complex that it had "transcended the ability of the sufferers from American slavery and prejudice, as a class, to keep pace with it, or to perceive what are its demands, or to understand the philosophy of its operation." And the Brahmin elite within Boston abolitionism often treated all those in the lower classes (white or black) with aristocratic condescension. Paternalism was endemic to conventional humanitarianism. Nevertheless, as Friedman correctly suggests, paternalism resided pervasively and clearly in the white leadership of the antislavery movement.[19]

Among the most common and most patronizing gestures in antislavery humanitarianism were the calls to self-help. From a host of articles in the *Liberator* to Lincoln's public addresses, white antislavery discourse produced numerous exhortations to blacks to uplift themselves by devoting themselves to the virtues of self-reliance. In these texts self-help usually signified the adoption of certain values associated with the middle class: respectable displays of religious devotion, self-discipline, thrift, cleanliness, individualism, humanitarian benevolence, industry, sobriety, tidiness, good manners, etc.[20] A key source of these admonitions to self-help was the misapprehension among whites that blacks were somehow unable or unwilling to help themselves. Stowe was exasperated by and confused about what she perceived as an unwillingness or incapacity among African Americans to help themselves. Alluding to a school construction project in Rochester, Stowe complained:

> I see, by F. Douglas's paper that the poor foolish folk are murmuring & repining still about an industrial school—of all vague unbased fabrics of a vision this floating idea of a colored industrial school is the most illusive. If they want one why dont they have one. . . . Will they *ever* learn to walk?

Yet, for many antislavery folk, getting blacks (Stowe's "poor foolish folk") "to walk" meant teaching them white middle-class values. Demonstrating faith in self-reliance, Sarah Grimké urged blacks to help themselves: "However zealously the abolitionists may preach, even if all of them consistently practise what they preach, they cannot do one hundredth part so much as you can do for yourselves." But, for Grimké, self-help entailed the taking up of certain values and practices, such as "neat and orderly habits, . . . the desire for education, . . . sobriety, decorum, industry, neat appearance, and desire for improvement." Grimké and other white philanthropists defined self-help by these lists of virtues, these guides to living. And sometimes they used coercively worded warnings to persuade blacks to adopt these self-help regimens. A writer for the *Liberator* insisted: "if they are not willing to make these exertions, they must give up forever all idea of being considered the equals of the rest of the human species."[21] Thus, within this rhetoric of self-help, we find a rather explicit attempt to control the behavior of black people: a well-intentioned and unsurprising but nonetheless coercive bid to pressure African Americans to adopt white, middle-class habits and values.

Another rhetorical move, what I will call "altruizm," seemed less coercive; but altruizm often disguised coercive designs. Altruizm designates an imaginative/psychological process in which a person intensely and sympathetically identifies himself or herself with an "other," another person, or another group. This imaginative transformation of oneself into another might involve pretending to be someone else, yearning to be another certain person, or strongly identifying with a person or group, a representation of a person or group, a character in a book, etc. I derive my term from the verb "altruize," which means to change into someone else.[22] Whereas altruistic persons so prize the welfare of others that they can, in principle, set aside their own interests in the pursuit of a greater good, humanitarians who altruize undergo such an intense affective-imaginative internalization of the welfare of others that the distinction between self-interest (what "I" need and want) and others' welfare (what "they" need and want) is erased.

A distinct example of altruizm comes from Whitman's "Song of Myself" where the poet announces:

> I am the man, I suffer'd, I was there. [. . .]
> I am the hounded slave, I wince at the bite of the dogs,
> Hell and despair are upon me, crack and again crack the marksmen, [. . .]
> Agonies are one of my changes of garments,
> I do not ask the wounded person how he feels, I myself become the wounded
>   person.[23]

What the speaker in this passage rejects is the notion that he merely sympathizes with a slave or other suffering person. Instead, the poem insists, he altruizes: "I am the man, I suffer'd, I was there. . . . I am the hounded slave." Whitman's aim here is to expand sympathy, feeling, pain beyond the ordinary boundaries of the self, to incorporate into the self an altruistic concern for others so large as to confuse or eliminate any distinction between self and other. Thus, he enacts in poetry a paradigmatic example of what I call "altruizm."

Stowe's *Uncle Tom's Cabin,* however, locates altruizm in the reader, not in the speaker or narrator. As Eliza flees the Shelby plantation after learning that her son was to be sold, Stowe pauses to address the reader, whom she imagines is, like Eliza, a mother:

> If it were *your* Harry, mother, or your Willie, that were going to be torn from you
> by a brutal trader, to-morrow morning,—if you had seen the man, and heard that
> the papers were signed and delivered, and you had only from twelve o'clock till
> morning to make good your escape,—how fast could *you* walk? How many miles
> could you make in those few brief hours, with the darling at your bosom,—the
> little sleepy head on your shoulder,—the small, soft arms trustingly holding on
> to your neck? (43-44)

By repeating "you" or "your" eleven times in this short passage, Stowe actively encourages her readers to identify themselves with the heroine and her situation. The author enables her readers to see a common identity between themselves and Eliza by pointing to what she hopes is a shared experience: motherhood. Following Eliza through her adventures and hoping that she will escape, readers are encouraged to feel sympathy with Eliza and to imagine themselves in her place. Although most of her readers were white, Stowe wanted them to identify not with the white slavers who want to capture Eliza and sell her son, but with Eliza the slave mother. Other examples of altruizm might include Garrison's exhortations to "feel" the suffering of the slaves, or Lydia Maria Child's request to be "buried in some ground belonging to the colored people . . . among her brethren and sisters of dark complexion."[24]

Although the altruizm in these examples might seem a benign, to some extent necessary, part of philanthropy, altruizm was a feature of a coercive humanitarianism when the pain of the patient ("the hounded slave") became merely a site for the agent of humanitarianism (such as Whitman's "I") to experience the vicarious pleasure of suffering unjustly inflicted pain. If, in the process of altruizm, knowledge of the pain of the enslaved was simply absorbed into the affective lives of white humanitarians, the suffering of slaves could then become, rather than a spur to humane, political action, a diversionary discursive site where whites could at their imaginative will relieve guilt about racist violence and domination, envisage themselves as martyrs, feel aggression against imagined enemies, or indulge in self-pity.

I am not arguing that intense sympathetic identifications across racial boundaries were or are inappropriate, nor am I attempting to decry the pleasures of imagined transformations of identity. I do want to suggest, however, that altruizm always threatened to deter humanitarians of a dominant group from acknowledging the position of privilege they occupied in the maintenance of an oppressive (in this case, racist) social structure by giving them a way to identify themselves with the oppressed rather than confront the ways in which they might function as oppressors. Although the process of altruizm could begin in a desire to see an end to the oppression and suffering of others, as the suffering of others receded from memory replaced by an imagined sense of one's own suffering ("I am the one who suffers"), the humanitarian risked complicity in the maintenance of oppression by slipping into a kind of amnesic denial of the patient's pain. Moreover, advocating altruizm as a practice of the (white humanitarian) self inevitably participated in the reduction of the experiences, stories, and representations of black people to tractable discursive sites or icons where ideological, cultural, and personal meaning could be fashioned by whites. Thus, rather than lending a voice to suffering, altruizm could lead to a continued silencing.

To give a brief account of the ways humanitarian rhetoric served various coercive purposes is to tell only a part of the story. While necessarily a part of the material world, rhetoric is not identical to the material realm that it claims to depict and hopes to mold. While paternalistic rhetoric was certainly related to the controlling practices of humanitarians, and while racialist representations cannot be disassociated from the racist mistreatment of black people, such signs of coercion are not proof that the patients of antislavery humanitarianism were in fact always controlled and coerced. The rhetoric of conventional humanitarianism suggests that agents held certain controlling designs. And patients were often mistreated by a humanitarianism that purported to help them. Yet, to read the discourse of dominant agents without knowing how the patients of humanitarianism resisted such coercion and reformulated humanitarianism itself is to get only one side of a multifaceted story.

Subverting Texts: Distrust and the Discursive Context of Jacobs's Style

The paternalistic, coercive aspects of antislavery humanitarianism triggered conflict and distrust between white and black Americans in the movement. For Jacobs, a writer-activist who hoped to change the coercive nature of antislavery and end the subservient position of African Americans in the movement, this climate of conflict and distrust became the discursive context that shaped her writing style. To understand her rhetorical choices and discursive strategies is to appreciate, first of all, the distrust that pervaded black-white communication in Jacobs's cultural milieu.

Resenting the constant exhortations to adopt certain values and accept racially proscribed roles within the movement, a writer for *Frederick Douglass' Paper* told white abolitionists that they had to do more than admonish "colored people to merely be good and honest and not think too highly of themselves, and hence get out of their place."[25] Similarly frustrated by the subordination of black people within the movement and specifically angered by the exclusion of black speakers from an abolitionist "*sympathy* meeting," Agnes Mary Grant confronted her friend Wendell Phillips in a letter:

> *Why is it that White men* are for ever making speeches & self gloryfying themselves & these men with their bursting hearts & grand utterances are kept in the background in this so falsely called Free North, as much socially and politically proscribed almost as their enslaved Brethren? . . . there are some who would like to hear the Black men speak about what it is presumed they are well fitted to speak viz. their own wants & their own wrongs.[26]

Many African Americans believed that they were "well fitted" to speak against slavery, some insisting that African Americans were better qualified to lead the movement and speak for the enslaved. In a letter to the editor of the *New York Tribune* written eight years before the publication of *Incidents,* Jacobs announced, "in *Uncle Tom's Cabin* she [Stowe] has not told the half. Would that I had one spark from her storage house of genius and talent I would tell you of my own sufferings."[27] Jacobs's implication was clear: Stowe did not (could not) tell the whole story of the suffering of slaves; she did not even tell half; and, perhaps, better suited to the task of narrating the suffering of slaves was a former slave.

Sensing as did Jacobs that whites did not adequately understand slavery or black life in the United States, Frederick Douglass continually encouraged African Americans to take up for themselves the fight to end slavery and racism. He urged them to see the antislavery struggle as their own battle, insisting that they "*do their own thinking.*" After years of conflict with the Garrisonians, Douglass remained embarrassed and annoyed by "the guidance, example, control and direction of what are called the men of the superior race," particularly white control of the antislavery movement. "Even in the management of the anti-slavery cause itself," he exclaimed, "it is considered preposterous for a colored man to assume anything more than to follow the guidance of those superiors." The white leadership often tended toward religious, ideological abstraction in its announced intentions, often not realizing how intertwined slavery and racism were as a problem, while black activists sought a more practical abolitionist crusade focused on abolishing slavery, expanding civil and human rights, and improving the material conditions of black life.[28]

Despite instances of biracial cooperation, the coercive aspects of antislavery humanitarianism combined with the feeling among blacks that most whites were ill-prepared to understand or speak about the suffering of free and enslaved black people led to confrontations and to a rise in black-led antislavery organizations. The antislavery efforts of African Americans often intensified the conflicts between whites and blacks. In a discussion of the tendency among whites to castigate blacks who departed from the strictures of the white leadership, Douglass revealed his own abiding wariness of whites in the movement. According to Douglass, white abolitionist "friends" usually treated independent black activists in a patronizing, fair-weather manner:

> those who pretend to be their friends measure their place and gauge their ideas and pat them on the back, but if they step beyond that narrow place, those friends become villifiers and enemies.[29]

His suspicions about white humanitarians reflected a pervasive, lingering mutual distrust between antislavery whites and blacks.

Distrust, of course, characterized black-white relations inside and outside of the antislavery crusade. William Whipper, a leader in the national negro conventions movement and editor of the *National Reformer,* observed:

> The national prejudice has so complexionally separated the interest of the people of this nation that when those of opposite complexions meet each other, it is for the most part impossible, generally speaking, to divine their real meaning and intent.[30]

Such racial distrust not only thwarted candid, rational exchange, it also shaped a particular kind of exchange, since, as Whipper, Douglass, Jacobs, and others realized, the façades that blacks and whites put up when talking with each other did not come down in antislavery meetings. Thus, in texts directed to white or partially white audiences, African American writers often used various masks or artifices. Jacobs, for instance, adopted the pseudonym Linda Brent as a way to shield herself. According to Robert Stepto, this "discourse of distrust" that includes distrusting writers as well as unreliable readers has assumed a variety of forms in African American writing.[31]

Unlike Douglass, however, who adopts as his motto "Trust no man,"[32] Jacobs appears at times to disregard Douglass's warning and to avoid this African American discourse of distrust, asserting instead that "It is always better to trust than to doubt" (*Incidents* 109). On the other hand, she speaks elsewhere about "how difficult it was to trust a white man" (158), how her heart "was freezing into a cheerless distrust of all my fellow beings" (190), and how "my experiences in slavery had filled me with distrust" (34). Moreover, she assumes that her readers do not trust her. At the beginning of chapter 29, for example, she writes, "I hardly expect that the reader will credit me, when I affirm that I lived in that little dismal hole . . . for nearly seven years" (148). Her distrust of readers is also the motivation for the occasional asides that remind readers of the accuracy of her story: "Reader, I draw no imaginary pictures of southern homes. I am telling you the plain truth" (35). The mutual distrust in *Incidents*—Jacobs's distrust of her readers, the readers' distrust of a former slave as narrator—further confirms the pervasive presence of distrust in the African

American literary tradition, in the antislavery movement, and in biracial communication in general. It also provides us with an important key to understanding Jacobs's
rhetorical choices in *Incidents* and the discursive/cultural context of those choices. To
make a connection with her distrustful audience, Jacobs had to authenticate her
narrative voice and craft a style that could persuasively communicate the difficult
and unfamiliar in a language that seemed familiar and comprehensible.[33]

    While at times she seems to address women and men, white people and black
people, antislavery activists as well as the "unconverted," Jacobs's ideal implied
reader is a Northern white woman, presumably middle class, who has benevolent
inclinations. Tending to see this audience as something of a problem, she begins
Incidents, somewhat defensively, with a statement on the veracity of her text:
"Reader, be assured this narrative is no fiction. I am aware that some of my
adventures may seem incredible; but they are, nevertheless, strictly true" (1).
Apparently such assertions were warranted. Although opening prefaces or letters
attesting to the truthfulness of the text were an established convention in slave
narratives, *Incidents'* four supplementary, truth-verifying documents (Jacobs's
Preface, Child's Introduction, and two statements in the Appendix by Amy Post
and George W. Lowther) underscore the author's and publisher's concern about
the audience's perception of the text's credibility.[34] Jacobs is remarkably attentive
to the suspicions of her readers, sensing that they are inclined to disbelieve the
testimony of a black woman who might (they think) exaggerate "the wrongs
inflicted by Slavery" or write her experiences "in order to attract attention" to
herself (1). While defending herself in advance against these accusations, Jacobs
remains skeptical in this Preface of the ability of her white audience to come to an
understanding of the sufferings of African Americans. "Only by experience," she
explains, "can any one realize how deep, and dark, and foul is that pit of
abominations" (2). This appeal to the immediacy of (her own) experience serves
a purpose similar to that of the supplementary documents: it forestalls criticism by
establishing the author as the most reliable narrator. How could her white
audience have any genuine experience of the horrors of slavery? None could, of
course, actually encounter slavery as a slave does. Thus, Jacobs turns her status as
a former slave, originally a cause for reader distrust, into the most reliable position
from which to know and speak the truth of slavery. Later in the book, Jacobs
implicitly reaffirms the adequacy and accuracy of her perspective, when she calls
into question the eyewitness accounts of white visitors to the South. According to
Jacobs, when a Northerner visits the South,

> The southerner invites him to talk with these slaves. He asks them if they want
> to be free, and they say, "O, no, massa." This is sufficient to satisfy him. . . . What
> does *he* know of the half-starved wretches toiling from dawn till dark on the
> plantations? of mothers shrieking for their children, torn from their arms by
> slave traders? of young girls dragged down into moral filth? of pools of blood
> around the whipping post? of hounds trained to tear human flesh? of men
> screwed into cotton gins to die? The slaveholder showed him none of these
> things, and the slaves dared not tell of them if he had asked them. (74)

Thus, quite unlike slaves and former slaves, white Northerners, never having the opportunity to observe the true horrors of slavery, are less reliable sources for knowledge about slavery.

While establishing the reliability of her narrative voice, Jacobs also constructs a style that will reach and convince her somewhat unreceptive, mostly white readership. Because her readers are unreliable (they distrust her, they are largely ignorant of slavery and black life in the United States, they carry with them racist and sexist stereotypes about black women), and because she wants to be persuasive in her arguments while attempting to criticize the attitudes and assumptions that sustain coercive humanitarianism in the antislavery movement, ideological racism in the North, and the machinery of slavery in the South, Jacobs crafts an autobiography suited to her unreliable readers. By blending, revising, and borrowing from discourses familiar to her readers (sentimental domestic fiction, male slave narratives, social reform speeches and tracts), that is by attempting to greet them in their language, Jacobs gains access to an audience otherwise inaccessible, unreliable, distrustful. These various discourses create the "self" of *Incidents* for a particular audience.[35]

In the process of writing "herself," Jacobs inevitably participates in the ideological precepts circulating in those discourses, including especially notions of self-reliance, domesticity, individualism, and humanitarianism. Yet, in the process of repeating such precepts, she also revises, subverts, and critiques them. Jacobs fabricates a subtly but profoundly subversive text that seeks to accomplish its rhetorical work by discursively undermining certain social norms and stereotypes, displacing conventional ways of seeing and knowing, and inappropriately deploying popular literary conventions. Many of this text's subversions are mere happy reversals of readerly expectations, such as the "kind-hearted" jailer who lets Linda into the jail at midnight to visit her brother (21). Linda's clever use of the racist, anti-emancipation *New York Herald* is another such happy inversion; gathering information about New York from a copy of the newspaper, she concocts letters purporting to originate from the North as a way to further confuse Dr. Flint (her former master) about her whereabouts after her escape; "and, for once, the paper that systematically abuses the colored people, was made to render them a service" (128). Nonetheless, other reversals, such as her suggestion that New York is inappropriately called a free state (193), overturn the expectations of her Northern readers with perhaps less cheer.

Another feature of *Incidents'* unsettling style is its repeated upsetting of racist stereotypes. Instead of "the stupidity of the African race" (172), readers find a sassy, keenly intelligent Linda and three generations of African American women (the Grandmother, Linda, Ellen) who outwit and outmaneuver white men. In chapter 12, refusing to use characterizations of black people as uneducated, illiterate, criminal, drunken, abject, pitiable, witless, and coarse, Jacobs assigns precisely these qualities to a band of marauding whites; she depicts herself, her grandmother, and others in her community as polite, respectable, quietly religious, literate, astute, and law abiding (63-67).

Related to this reversal of stereotypes is Jacobs's use of subversive repetition, the calling up of an assumption or representation from popular discourse (a ubiquitous notion, a common theme, a stock character, etc.) in a way that duplicates that assumption or representation with a slight but signal and subversive difference. In chapter 10, for instance, when Linda begins her love affair with Mr. Sands, Jacobs invokes a common theme from literature about the antebellum South: miscegenation. In Jacobs's story, however, the biracial encounter takes neither of its usual forms, the romance involving mistaken racial identity or the rape by a lecherous master. Instead, we find the repetition of this theme with a subversive difference: the black woman chooses her white lover (54–55). Her account of the slave trader (a conventional villain in antislavery writing) who helps free a slave is another subversive repetition (105–107).

Jacobs's subversive style finds its diction, syntax, and structure in the discursive possibilities available to her as a mid-nineteenth-century writer. In addition to the popular literary genres from which she borrows, these possibilities include the modes of language use and models of rhetorical strategy manifest in African American writing and speaking. In his brilliant exploration of the relationship between black vernacular traditions and African American literature, *The Signifying Monkey,* Henry Louis Gates, Jr., has used the term "Signifyin(g)" to designate an associated cluster of these modalities of language and rhetoric. Signifyin(g) is, according to Gates, "a pervasive mode of language use," that is synonymous with figuration and is associated with black people who "named the term and invented its rituals."[36] Claudia Mitchell-Kernan has succinctly defined Signifyin(g) as "a way of encoding messages or meanings which involves, in most cases, an element of indirection," while Geneva Smitherman has emphasized that this "mode of discourse" often depends on the "introduction of the semantically or logically unexpected."[37]

Jacobs's own knowledge of Signifyin(g) doubtless began with her upbringing in a black community and her experiences as a slave. As a technique of survival and resistance in the South, slaves used a secret, double-voiced method of communication. In his *Narrative and Writings of Andrew Jackson, of Kentucky* (1847), Andrew Jackson explained that slaves "have a means of communication with each other, altogether unknown to their masters, or to the people of the free states," while in *Iola Leroy* (1892) Frances Harper illustrated the uses of Signifyin(g) conversation as a way for slaves to surreptitiously spread news about an advancing Union Army.[38] This indirect form of communication, called "sig'fication" by one ex-slave, was widespread among slaves.[39] While *Incidents* (like the narratives of Harper, Jackson, and others) illustrates and enacts Signifyin(g), Jacobs also defends the slaves' use of indirection as a means of resistance. "Who can blame slaves for being cunning?" she asks. "They are constantly compelled to resort to it. It is the only weapon of the weak and oppressed against the strength of their tyrants" (100–101).

Jacobs deploys her Signifyin(g) style to serve multiple purposes in *Incidents.* When, for example, Jacobs uses animal metaphors to describe her master and other whites, she Signifies upon and criticizes the pervasive presence of animal metaphors in "child/savage" rhetoric. In chapter 7, after a free black carpenter proposes marriage to Linda, Dr. Flint jealously and racistly refers to the young man as a puppy (39), adding "if I catch him lurking about my premises, I will shoot him as soon as I would a dog" (40). In a response that criticizes Flint while parodying his use of racist animal metaphors, Jacobs describes Flint as a "tiger" (39) and an "animal" (40). Later in the book Flint springs upon Linda "like a wolf" (59), speaks to her "in a hissing tone" like a snake (59), and tries to deceive her like an "old fox" (172). Jacobs's subversive, parodic reversal of these racist animal metaphors corresponds roughly to what Gates calls "motivated Signifying," a type of imitative, mocking critique which "functions to redress an imbalance of power" in language.

Jacobs also uses her subversive, Signifyin(g) style as a way to make *Incidents* accessible to her largely white and largely unreliable audience. Such a rhetorical intention is closer to unmotivated Signifyin(g); "unmotivated" does not imply, as Gates says, "the absence of a profound intention but the absence of a negative critique," and therefore it corresponds roughly to pastiche.[40] Using a rhetorically expedient pastiche, Jacobs duplicates well-known cultural representations and puts them to service as avenues upon which her unreliable readers can gain access to and be persuaded by her critique of humanitarianism. When, for example, she presents Linda's daughter, Ellen, as a pious, tearful, forgiving, long-suffering, innocent, perceptive, and sensitive little girl who likes to read, Jacobs re-presents a type of character that her readers already know and love: the child heroine of the century's most popular books. Ellen is fashioned from the same literary mold as Eva from *Uncle Tom's Cabin* (the best-selling book of the century), Gerty from Maria Susanna Cummins's *The Lamplighter* (the 1854 blockbuster), and Ellen from the country's first best-seller, *The Wide, Wide World* (1851) by Susan Warner. Because Ellen so resembles Ellen and these other child heroines, she becomes a character with whom Jacobs's readers are already familiar, a character that they can recognize, relate to, sympathize with, and understand. By introducing this senti-mental heroine figure as a device for talking in her audience's language, Jacobs facilitates a type of "unmotivated" communication between the text and her readers.

Ellen also allows Jacobs indirectly to critique coercive humanitarianism. Like the woman who sought to help a former slave girl by making her into a maid "well calculated for general housework," a white couple in the North (Mr. and Mrs. Hobbs) arrange for Ellen to "be well taken care of" (138) and trained as a "little waiting maid" (142), thus fusing supposed charity with a type of Northern slavery. But because Ellen, who in the North is "[w]ithout a mother's love to shelter her from the storms of life" (139), suffers so unjustly under the putatively benevolent but cruelly paternalistic "care" of Mr. and Mrs. Hobbs, Ellen becomes a *recogniz-able* symbol of black pain under Northern paternalism. By fashioning Ellen as a child heroine of popular sentimental literature, Jacobs allows her readers to see Ellen's pain and also its relationship to the peculiar blend of enslavement and charity in humanitarianism.

Jacobs's Humanitarian Work

Jacobs's writing style, this fascinating cluster of borrowed rhetorics and subverted discourses, was crafted for a specific type of cultural work: the creation and dissemination of an eccentric mode of humanitarianism. Her subversive style allowed her to assail the language and structure of coercive humanitarianism and at the same time persuade her antislavery colleagues to rethink the nature of humanitarian work. Established upon a power disparity between patients and agents, conventional humanitarianism was unable, despite its moral idealism and benevolent intentions, to overcome this inherently oppressive relation. Jacobs keenly felt the paternalistic, controlling, even demeaning ways in which the antislavery movement treated its patients. Yet, rather than reject humanitarianism altogether, Jacobs sought to redress this power relation within humanitarianism conventionally conceived.

Jacobs moves toward eccentric humanitarianism by (1) disabling the blinding altruizm and moralistic rhetoric that supported status quo humanitarian ideas and practice, and (2) attacking the racism and paternalism that structured patient/agent relations within antislavery philanthropy. These two moves emerge from her subversive style—a style that entails the discourse of distrust, the unsettling of racist stereotypes, subversive repetition, and motivated and unmotivated Signifyin(g). This carefully crafted style allows Jacobs to do a number of eccentric things: thwart readerly identifications, treat dominant ideologies (religious, humanitarian, domestic, self-help) in a critical or ironic manner, use sentimental literary conventions in unconventional ways, and represent black women as agents. Furthermore, Jacobs's style prepares the rhetorical ground for her most fundamental subversion of conventional philanthropy, the dismantling of the patient/agent hierarchy.

For many African Americans one of the most insulting aspects of antislavery humanitarianism was the assumption among white leaders that they understood slavery, racism, and the political challenges facing the antislavery crusade better than those who actually suffered under slavery and racism. Such an assumption could be emotionally deepened by altruizm, the rather myopic but intense sympathetic identification encouraged in antislavery literature. When used as a means for ignoring racism within the movement, disregarding what African Americans had to say about their own suffering, or dismissing the efforts of black abolitionists, this discursive taking over of the suffering of slaves and free blacks worked to maintain status quo inequalities within the movement. Black abolitionists responded to white attempts to colonize their suffering with a type of "you have never known" discourse. Theodore Wright, for example, told his white colleagues, "You have never felt the oppression of the slave. You have never known what it is to have a master, or to see your parents and children in slavery."[41]

In her attack on antislavery humanitarianism and its propensity for altruizm, Jacobs utilizes this "you have never known" discourse to change the ways in which her white humanitarian readers identify with "the hounded slave." Unlike Stowe, for example, who actively encourages altruizm, or Whitman, who legitimates it by grandiosely enacting it, Jacobs encourages her white readers to distance themselves from the particular suffering of enslaved black women. She wants her white readers not to identify their experiences with those of black women, but to contrast those experiences:

> O, you happy free women, contrast *your* New Year's day with that of the poor bond-woman! With you it is a pleasant season, and the light of the day is blessed.

> . . . But to the slave mother New Year's Day comes laden with peculiar sorrows.
> She sits on her cold cabin floor, watching the children who may be torn from her
> the next morning; and often does she wish that she and they might die before the
> day dawns. (16)

Whereas Stowe emphasizes the identity of relation between the reader and the
slave mother, Jacobs underscores the differences. Refusing to let white readers
identify with her black heroines, she says, "Reader, if you have never been a slave,
you cannot imagine the acute sensation of suffering at my heart" (196). Similarly,
she writes:

> You never knew what it is to be a slave; to be entirely unprotected by law or
> custom; to have the laws reduce you to the condition of a chattel, entirely subject
> to the will of another. You never exhausted your ingenuity in avoiding the snares,
> and eluding the power of a hated tyrant; you never shuddered at the sound of his
> footsteps. (55)

With the thrice-insistent "you never," she reminds readers that they cannot know
the experience of being a slave. Although one of the aims of *Incidents* is to give
white readers (through a readerly engagement with the narrative) some knowledge of slavery, Jacobs doubts her readers' abilities to imagine what it feels like to
be a slave. She interrupts her narrative to remind them that they are not the
heroines of this book (though it is pleasurable to identify with a text's heroic
characters) and that even an imagined identification of themselves with Linda, the
text's autobiographical heroine, is difficult, if not impossible. This refused identification upsets the expectations of readers and leaves them distanced from the text.

Jacobs does not, however, eliminate all possibilities for identifying with the
text's characters. Instead, she suggests two ways for white Northerners to read
themselves in relation to the text. She indirectly suggests a connection between the
white North and the jealous mistress of the plantation. Allegorically, the master is
the white South who rapes and exploits the black woman (slaves), while the
mistress (the white North) grows jealous of the black woman because she is
splitting up the union between master and mistress, South and North. Hence, the
mistress (the white North) does nothing to protect the slave from the master's
cruelties.[42] More directly, she compares Northerners to bloodhounds: "when
victims make their escape from this wild beast of Slavery, northerners consent to
act the part of bloodhounds, and hunt the poor fugitive back into his den" (35–
36). Two chapters later, she tells us that the "bloodhounds of the north" (humans)
are "scarcely less cruel" than the "bloodhounds of the South" (dogs) (44). Jacobs
positions Northerners to see themselves not as oppressed slave heroines, but as the
ignorant and obedient accomplices of Southern slavers.

Prevented from identifying themselves with Linda and her struggles, white
readers cannot escape an unsettling look at themselves as participants in the
oppression of black people by pretending in the reading process to be the
oppressed rather than the oppressor. Jacobs establishes here a relationship not of
identity between her readers and herself but rather one of alterity. Writing in a

humanitarian genre that so prized sympathy, her deliberate thwarting of reader-character identification is disturbing.[43] Still, these refused identifications are neither an all-out assault on the potential for sympathy in humanitarian writing nor a suggestion that white people (because of their "whiteness") lack the capacity to read and understand and appreciate African American writing. Instead, the assertion of alterity is more specifically a tactic within her larger attempt to dismantle the agent/patient power disparity. By refusing the altruizm that Stowe and other white humanitarians perform, Jacobs prompts her readers to examine their own complicity in racism, slavery, and the marginalization of African Americans within the antislavery movement.

In her attempt to reveal the blindnesses of coercive humanitarianism, Jacobs further unsettles readers by calling into question the Christian rhetoric used to represent humanitarian aims. Whereas *Uncle Tom's Cabin's* vision of the destiny of African Americans centers on the colonization of Liberia and the conversion of Africans to Christianity, Jacobs (describing herself as "indignant" toward such schemes[44]) opposes colonization and focuses her reader's attention instead on the hypocrisy of the Christian church in the United States. More concerned with the un-Christian character of American slaveholders than with the unconverted souls in Africa, Jacobs writes:

> They send the Bible to heathen abroad, and neglect the heathen at home. I am glad the missionaries go out to the dark corners of the earth; but I ask them not to overlook the dark corners at home. Talk to American slaveholders as you talk to savages in Africa. Tell *them* it is wrong to traffic in men. Tell them it is sinful to sell their own children, and atrocious to violate their own daughters. (73)

Although she would no doubt maintain that the slaveowner's rape of his slave daughter is more reprehensible than sanctimonious sermonizing about "savages," Jacobs's implication here is that the two acts are not unrelated. Self-righteously proclaiming its desire to convert the Africans, the church ignores, and thus implicitly condones, the savage treatment of African Americans. Without immediately passing judgment on whether the clergy is self-serving or merely self-deluded, she does indicate their lack of humanitarian feeling:

> Are doctors of divinity blind, or are they hypocrites? I suppose some are the one, and some are the other; but I think if they felt the interest in the poor and the lowly, that they ought to feel, they would not be so *easily* blinded. (73)

Jacobs's attack on the hypocrisy of the church challenges the self-certifyingly good intentions of Christians by pointing to their culpability in the maintenance of slavery. Such an attack was, of course, an important element in black abolitionist rhetoric. As the *New York Sun* reported, for example:

> *Frederick Douglass* said that after an anxious and careful investigation into causes of the continuance of slavery in the land, he found that it was caused by too much religion. The people were too reverential God-ward to be honest man-ward. . . .

The Episcopalians, the Presbyterians, the Universalists, the Unitarians, the Methodists, are all in connexion with and abettors of slavery. The American church is a brotherhood of thieves.[45]

Yet, in addition to "too much religion," slavery was also being sustained, as Jacobs points out, by a more general rhetoric of moral benevolence. This humanitarian rhetoric, an important tool in the antislavery crusade, was also deployed by proslavery advocates, including Mississippi Senator Albert Gallatin Brown. Although she knew that he had witnessed the cruelty of slavery, Jacobs, galled by his hypocritical use of the rhetoric of moral benevolence, documents how "he stood up in the Congress of the United States, and declared that slavery was 'a great moral, social, and political blessing; a blessing to the master, and a blessing to the slave!'" (122). By juxtaposing Brown's words with her own eyewitness accounts of the cruel treatment of slave women, Jacobs unmasks the hypocrisy, the lie, in Brown's words.

Still, she does not limit her critique to the absurd cant of a proslavery politician, but also reveals other baleful uses of a humanitarian rhetoric inflected with domestic sentiments. Throughout the autobiography Linda is explicit about what she most wants in her life: freedom and a home for herself and her children. Thus, no reader should overlook the irony of Dr. Flint's offer to fulfill precisely those two aspirations. Mustering up his most benevolent demeanor, Flint tells her:

Linda, you desire freedom for yourself and your children, and you can obtain it only through me. If you agree to what I am about to propose, you and they shall be free. There must be no communication of any kind between you and their father. I will procure a cottage, where you and the children can live together. Your labor shall be light, such as sewing for my family. Think what is offered you, Linda—a home and freedom! (83)

Linda fully realizes that his offer of freedom and domestic happiness is a "snare" (84), and she rejects him. But, in the process, Jacobs reveals the ways in which supposedly benevolent proposals contain sinister consequences. Likewise, when her "friend and mistress" Emily Flint Dodge (Dr. Flint's daughter) writes to Linda and invites her ever so kindly to return home to the South, Linda tells us, "Of course I did not write to return thanks for this cordial invitation. I felt insulted to be thought stupid enough to be caught by such professions" (187).

This unmasking of altruizm and benevolent rhetoric allows Jacobs to push beyond the usual justifications sustaining coercive humanitarianism and to counter racism and paternalism, the twin ideologies most oppressive to the patients of antislavery humanitarianism. Several times in her book, Jacobs directly attacks racism in the North, reminding her humanitarian readers that racism contaminates the North as much as the South and that Northern racism like Southern racism functions in the preservation of slavery. After her brief stay with Mr. Durham, Linda encounters Northern racism when she is unable to buy a first-class train ticket. Moving to a more "disagreeable" car, the narrator says:

This was the first chill to my enthusiasm about the Free States. Colored people were allowed to ride in a filthy box, behind white people, at the south, but they were not required to pay for the privilege. It made me sad to find how the north aped the customs of slavery. (162-63)

This disappointment about having to live with racism in the North becomes an important theme in the last eleven chapters of *Incidents*. Ellen is mistreated, virtually reenslaved, within the Hobbs household. During his first day in the North, Linda's son, Benjamin, is sorely mistaken in supposing that "free boys can get along here at the north as well as white boys" (173). And, in her chapter on "Prejudice against Color," Linda talks of the ubiquitous presence of racism in the North: "every where I found the same manifestations of that cruel prejudice, which so discourages the feelings, and represses the energies of the colored people" (176). But, rather than despair over what is clearly a heartsickening disappointment, the narrator critiques and encourages action against this "cruel prejudice." She launches a spirited attack against the Fugitive Slave Law (190–94), refuses to call the North "*free* soil" (193), and incites black workers ("colored servants" like herself) to fight racist oppression: "I was resolved to stand up for my rights. . . . Let every colored man and woman do this, and eventually we shall cease to be trampled under foot by our oppressors" (177).

In her attempt to undermine the foundations of coercive humanitarianism, Jacobs struggles against not only racist prejudice but also the racialist assumptions that shaped antislavery humanitarianism. Many antislavery humanitarians saw the romantic racialism of writers like Stowe as a sympathetic way of understanding black people. Working to create an eccentric, alternative approach to antislavery humanitarianism, *Incidents* confronts and contradicts these racialist assumptions by revising the stereotyped, romantic racialist representations of black women, especially as those representations appear in *Uncle Tom's Cabin*. For example, although Aunt Chloe from *Uncle Tom's Cabin* and Aunt Martha from *Incidents* both spend their days and nights in the kitchen baking cakes and cookies, Chloe has neither the strength to face down white people nor the independence and outspokenness that readers find in Martha. Both Linda Brent and Stowe's Cassy hide in a garret while waiting to escape, and both have children by white fathers; Linda, however, manages to elude her master and chooses to have her children by a different white man. Moreover, Linda is not (like Cassy) a hardened soul, worn out from years of victimization; despite the ordeals of slave life, Linda represents herself as an agent rather than a victim. In the youngest generation, Ellen in no way resembles Topsy: Ellen is, instead, a subversive repetition of Eva. Rather than repeat the dominant, stereotyped images of black women (even though Stowe and others found those images useful in the fight against slavery), Jacobs rewrites those images as a means for opposing the racialism that sustained coercive humanitarianism.

Though dedicated to overturning dominant cultural assumptions about black women, Jacobs's portrayal of Linda and her grandmother as determined, strong-minded, self-reliant, outspoken opponents of racist and sexist oppression was not without cultural precedents. These representations were not unparalleled originals, but neither were they uncritical, co-opted parts of a white supremacist, patriarchal culture. The oppositional capacity of "Linda" and "Martha" as representations had definite cultural sources, such as the sentimental discourses upon which Jacobs Signifies and, importantly, the popular images of determined, strong-minded, self-reliant, outspoken black women (free born, slave, or ex-slave) in antebellum African American culture: Sojourner Truth challenging her white audience with "A'n't I a woman?"; Maria W. Stewart urging her audience to fight "Prejudice, ignorance, and poverty"; Harriet Tubman planning and executing the escape of runaway slaves; in Douglass's *My Bondage and My Freedom,* the indomitable Nelly "sternly resisting" the overseer's attempt to flog her; and Ellen Craft telling her husband how they will escape and urging him not to be a "coward."[46] As representations in Northern culture, "Linda" and "Martha" bore a strong family resemblance to their oppressed sisters.

As an oppositional text, *Incidents* takes aim at racism and also paternalism, the well-intentioned but imperious attempt to control the patients of antislavery humanitarianism. Building from her interrogation of altruizm and benevolent rhetoric, Jacobs asks white readers to consider the ways in which their paternalistic humanitarian actions might interfere with black freedom and happiness. In the conclusion to *Incidents,* for example, Jacobs writes about Mrs. Bruce's offer of "freedom," while at the same time subtly insinuating a critique of the paternalistic ways in which humanitarian-minded whites impart "freedom" to black people. Although freedom and home are Linda's explicit goals, she reminds us that her story cannot end happily with the realization of her dream:

> Reader, my story ends with freedom; not in the usual way, with marriage. I and my children are now free! We are as free from the power of slaveholders as are the white people of the north; and though that, according to my ideas, is not saying a great deal, it is a vast improvement in *my* condition. The dream of my life is not yet realized. I do not sit with my children in a home of my own. (201)

Linda is explicit about how her story ends—with some type of freedom but not a home.

Nevertheless, in her explanation of how her "freedom" was obtained and why she does not yet have a home of her own, Linda indirectly criticizes the obstacles that prevent her from finding freedom and a home. Although she thanks Mrs. Bruce "who has bestowed the inestimable boon of freedom on me and my children" (201), Linda also resents being bought (without her permission and against her wishes) by Mrs. Bruce; "being sold from one owner to another seemed too much like slavery" (199). Nevertheless, Mrs. Bruce completes the purchase and writes Linda to tell her that "the money for your freedom has been paid" (199–200). Mrs. Bruce adds, in the imperative voice, "Come home" (200). Earlier in the narrative, the Flint family writes to Linda to say the same thing, "Come home" (171). Linda can barely contain her anger at being transferred from one type of servitude in the South to a different type in the North:

> So I was *sold* at last! A human being *sold* in the free city of New York! The bill of

sale is on record, and future generations will learn from it that women were articles of traffic in New York, late in the nineteenth century of the Christian religion. It may hereafter prove a useful document to antiquaries, who are seeking to measure the progress of civilization in the United States. (200)

The "freedom" Mrs. Bruce buys for Linda is a major impediment to Linda's dream of freedom and a home. After the sale Linda finds herself divinely directed to stay with and work for Mrs. Bruce:

> God so orders circumstances as to *keep* me with my friend Mrs. Bruce. Love, duty, gratitude, also *bind* me to her side. It is a privilege to *serve* her who pities my oppressed people. (201, emphasis added)

Because of Mrs. Bruce's purchase, "circumstances" will "keep" and "bind" Linda to Mrs. Bruce in order to "serve" her. Linda's diction seems to betray her dissatisfaction about the obligation into which Mrs. Bruce has just pulled her. Linda argues earlier in the chapter against having herself purchased:

> The more my mind had become enlightened, the more difficult it was for me to consider myself an article of property; and to pay money to those who had so grievously oppressed me seemed like taking from my sufferings the glory of triumph. (199)

When we compare this declaration to Linda's situation as Mrs. Bruce's servant, Linda's statement about her "Friend" (201) seems ironic or, at the very least, ambivalent.[47]

Jacobs's relationship with Cornelia Grinnell Willis, the second Mrs. Bruce of *Incidents,* was in fact never quite friendly. In letters to Amy Post, Jacobs depicts a mistress/servant relationship between herself and Willis. Although she was eager to write her autobiography (without having Willis know anything about it), Jacobs had "but a little time to think and write." To give herself more time to work on her book, Jacobs had to make a deal with Willis: "I would give her Louisa['s] services through the winter if she would allow me my winter evenings to myself."[48] Evidently, Willis kept her very busy.

While Mrs. Bruce's intention to help Linda is by no means as sinister as Dr. Flint's offer of "a home and freedom," the discouraged tone in this last chapter prompts the reader to recognize that service to a white woman from the North is what *keeps* Linda from securing her happy ending. Certainly Jacobs objects to neither Mrs. Bruce's good intentions nor the end of Linda's anxiety about the possibility of being returned to slavery. Instead, in her subtle, subversive style, Jacobs is taking exception to what her black abolitionist colleagues had been protesting for years: the paternalistic manner in which white struggle for black freedom spawned "humanitarian" attempts to keep black people in their place.

Supposing that African Americans were more or less helpless, humanitarian paternalism encouraged African Americans to accept their place in society and the fatherly advice of white abolitionists. Ironically enough, antislavery humanitarians often pushed this advice wrapped in a rhetoric of self-help. Annoyed by the condescension in these efforts, African Americans resisted this philanthropic control and replied with an alternate version of self-help.[49] In an 1849 "Self-Help" speech to black New Yorkers, Frederick Douglass said: "Our white friends may do much for us, but we must do much for ourselves. . . . We must elevate ourselves by our own efforts." While such statements bear a resemblance to the exhortations of whites, the context of enunciation is changed: encouragement from a member of one's own group is different from encouragement from someone belonging to a group manifestly more privileged than one's own. Although he was at times an ardent proponent of certain mainstream middle-class values (such as the virtue of hard work), Douglass did not in this lecture recommend the adoption of middle-class values as the road to self-reliance, but instead pressed blacks to actively seize the equality withheld from them. Thus, for example, rather than promote respectable displays of religious devotion, Douglass, as might be expected, attacked the church for encouraging apathy among black people, for preaching the "absurd notion" that "people [should] wait for God to help them."[50]

Douglass's version of self-help also included a critique of conventional white philanthropy and the defensive paternalism of the white-led antislavery movement. "The Abolitionists did not act rightly," claimed Douglass, "they attempted to support, to bear up, the colored people, and looked upon any other method as an impeachment of their cause." For Douglass the struggle for African American liberty and equality required more than the help and pity of white humanitarians. He demanded their "respect," not merely their "sympathy." He called for self-determination and for a black-led antislavery movement, designating this struggle "our battle; no one else can fight it for us, and with God's help we must fight it ourselves."[51] Although his self-help philosophy undoubtedly drew from other self-help discourses (including Emersonian notions of self-reliance, perfectionism, laissez-faire liberalism, and Benjamin Franklin–like images of self-made men), Douglass did not use self-help to exhort blacks to follow white philanthropists and their middle-class definitions of self-reliance; instead he deployed it as a vehicle for inspiring black political action and criticizing the paternalism of white abolitionists.

Nevertheless, the utilization of the rhetoric of self-help and self-reliance posed a dilemma for black antislavery activists. By advocating self-help within the antislavery movement were they discouraging white folks from taking action against slavery and racism? Would whites think that because African Americans were insisting on helping themselves, whites had no role in dismantling slavery or racism? Did black rhetoric about self-reliance provide whites with justification for abandoning humanitarian work? On the other hand, to stop arguing for the necessity of black-led efforts to help black people seemed to invite the continued paternalistic domination of whites in the antislavery movement. By suspending their emphasis on the "special mission" of African Americans in the movement, "a mission which none but themselves could perform,"[52] would black abolitionists be encouraging whites to carry on with their advice about how to behave?

Drawing upon various nineteenth-century notions of self-reliance, the rhetoric of humanitarianism, and the language of popular novels, Jacobs's negotiation of this self-help dilemma in Incidents allows her to call into question the paternalism of the antislavery movement and to suggest a reformulation of the patient/agent relationship within humanitarianism. Unflinching in her critique of racism in its various Northern manifestations and skeptical at times of the well-intentioned efforts of benevolently minded whites (such as Mrs. Bruce), Jacobs does not, however, discourage whites from speaking out against slavery or taking action to end racism. She writes *Incidents* "to arouse the women of the North to a realizing sense of the condition" of enslaved women in the South (1). Moreover, the continued refusal among Northerners to take action to end slavery elicits from her a wondering disbelief: "In view of these things, why are ye silent, ye free men and women of the north? Why do your tongues falter in maintenance of the right?" (29–30). The biblical diction here only reinforces Jacobs's suggestion that Northerners have a moral/religious obligation to stand against slavery.

Nevertheless, diverging from the norm within antislavery discourse, Jacobs does not base her appeal on an image of the slave woman as helpless victim—a patient requiring the aid of wiser, more powerful humanitarians. Instead, she represents Linda as a resolute agent, someone who can act to make something happen, someone who can match her cunning against her master's cunning and win. Conventional antislavery discourse, by contrast, emphasized the powerlessness of slaves ("They can't take care of themselves," *The New England Anti-Slavery Almanac* wrote in 1841) and the helplessness of black people in general ("Will they *ever* learn to walk?" Stowe asked).[53] Even in most black abolitionist literature, such as the male-authored slave narratives, slave women were represented as helpless, powerless, exploited; what Frances Foster calls "the image of the slave woman as sexual victim" was widespread in the autobiographies of African American men.[54] Although Jacobs uses words like "victim" from the conventional abolitionist vocabulary, her narrative belies that vocabulary and shows us a woman empowered to resist and to take care of herself and her family. Despite the multiple oppressions which confront her, Jacobs announces to her white readers that she is neither a victim nor a patient.

The foremost sign of Linda's status as an agent who can make things happen is her use of language. As Joanne Braxton has pointed out, Linda uses "sass" as a linguistic weapon of self-defense. Though it often brought on physical abuse, sass—speaking as an equal to a superior, back talk, talking back—was one of the ways for black women to struggle against white domination.[55] In *Incidents*, Linda back talks Flint as a way to fend off his verbal, sexual, and physical aggressions. After she answers his questions about her desire to marry a free-born carpenter, Flint explodes: "He sprang upon me like a tiger, and gave me a stunning blow. It was the first time he had ever struck me; and fear did not enable me to control my anger" (39). So she sasses him: "You have struck me for answering you honestly. How I despise you" (39). Here, as in other scenes, Linda's talking back causes Flint to pause: "There was a silence for some minutes" (39). Her willingness to stand openly against him and speak to him as an equal arrests (temporarily) his attack on her, because it contradicts the customary ways in which slave women behave in the presence of slaveowners. Her sassiness linguistically undoes the slave/master relationship and momentarily confuses Flint. To restore the old order, Flint tries to clarify for Linda the rules which he thinks ought to govern their relationship: "Do you know that I have a right to do as I like with you,—that I can kill you, if I please?" (39). She meets his threats with still more sassiness: "You have tried to kill me, and I wish you had; but you have no right to do as you like with me" (39).

Later in the book, Linda learns to use the indirection of Signifyin(g) to defend herself and to undo Flint. When he learns that she is pregnant, Flint demands to know if Linda loves the father of her child:

> "Do you love him?" said he, in a hissing tone.
> "I am thankful that I do not despise him," I replied.
> He raised his hand to strike me; but it fell again. (59)

Linda's Signifyin(g) circumlocution distracts him, cloaks a clear answer to his question, and reminds him indirectly that she does despise him (as she tells him in chapter 7). He sits down "with lips tightly compressed" and admits his bewilderment: "I don't know what it is that keeps me from killing you" (59).[56]

The day after his church confirmation, Flint returns to "his usual talk" (74), his use of "foul words" and "unclean images" (27), language which gave Linda "no indication that he had 'renounced the devil and his works'"(74). Thus, the author introduces the exchange between Linda and Flint with this motivated repetition of Flint's confirmation oath in order to highlight the hypocrisy of his conversion. Linda responds to his "usual talk" by reminding him "that he had just joined the Church" (74). Not feeling the point of her words, Flint says, "It was proper for me to do so," (74) and encourages Linda to join the church. "There are enough sinners in it already" (75), she replies with derisive innuendo. Apparently unaware that by sinner she means him, he says, "You can do what I require; and if you are faithful to me, you will be as virtuous as my wife" (75). Linda, unwilling to submit to what he requires, reminds him "that the Bible didn't say so." (75). Finally, catching the sense of her indirection or, perhaps, just growing frustrated with her lack of submissiveness, Flint loses control and explodes into strident declarations of his power as master: "What right have you, who are my negro, to talk to me about what you would like, and what you wouldn't like? I am your master, and you shall obey me" (75). Despite his assertions, Linda's linguistic agency challenges his (moral) authority over her and lays bare the contradictions within his own religious thinking.

The "verbal jousts" between Linda and Flint are not, however, the only passages in which we find such subversive linguistic agency, the language of the trickster, Signifyin(g), and sassiness.[57] When a patrol of white men finds one of Linda's letters in a search of her grandmother's house, the captain demands to see the rest of her letters and wants to know, "Who writes to you? half free niggers?" (65–66). Linda retorts, "O, no; most of my letters are from white people. Some request me to burn them after they are read, and some I destroy without reading" (66). The mockery and unexpectedness of Linda's reply end his call for her letters: "An exclamation of surprise from some of the company put a stop to our conversation" (66).

In addition to sassy or slippery language, Linda also engages in misleading acts to evade, disarm, or confuse her foes, especially Flint. She pretends to be illiterate to avoid reading Flint's notes. Taking a secret lover as part of a plot to enrage Flint to sell her, Linda conceals her pregnancy and the identity of Mr. Sands, her white lover. She disguises herself as a sailor to run away; hides herself in Snaky Swamp, a neighbor's house, and then, for seven years, in a garret above her grandmother's shed; and dupes Flint into thinking she has escaped to the North, by arranging to have letters sent postmarked from New York. Even after her arrival in the North, Linda retains her masks, including the veil that she wears in public. Thus, just as Jacobs use indirection and the language of indirection to persuade her readers, Linda also uses these tools to gain a degree of control in her life.

All of these subversive acts, verbal and nonverbal, testify to Linda's status as an agent and to, more generally, the possibility for an oppositional agency located in the lives and languages of black women. As Linda overturns Flint's expectations and as Jacobs overturns her readers' expectations about who black women are and how they should act, Jacobs represents black women not as powerless victims and mere patients, but as formidable agents. She undoes the agent/patient hierarchy within humanitarianism by demonstrating how Linda (the slave woman/patient) helps herself, how she becomes "a self-liberated liberator."[58]

Incidents is a document from an era of humanitarianism in crisis. Entering that flux, Incidents urges Northerners to take a stand against slavery and racism and to change the very structure of their humanitarianism. Her tactic is subversion. She handles conventions in an unconventional manner for specific rhetorical purposes. She works within culturally available discourses so as to exploit the contradictions within and between them and, hence, register a perspective that opposes or contradicts the dominant direction of certain cultural formations. While Jacobs's mode of subversion helps me to understand how oppositional agency is a part of culture, Jacobs's subversive style, her sub-versions of other styles, demonstrates her confidence in the value of language in the reform of humanitarian work. Unlike John Brown who distrusted language and always favored action over talk, Jacobs uses language to reconstruct humanitarian work—to oppose conventional philanthropy and advocate a less racist and less paternalistic humanitarianism. She hopes for a humanitarianism less repressive in its actions, less blind to the needs of its patients, and more responsive to the ideas and feelings of those being helped.

The War Refugees

In 1862, about a half year before Louisa May Alcott arrived in the city, Jacobs suspended her antislavery speaking efforts and traveled to Washington, D.C., to organize humanitarian relief efforts for the war refugees entering the capital. After working among the contrabands and witnessing the poverty, hunger, home-lessness, and disease caused by years of slavery and the start of a devastating war, Jacobs wrote an open letter to Garrison's Liberator. Appealing to these readers in a rhetoric familiar to them, she emphasized their moral obligation to the freed-people: "You have helped to make them what they are. . . . You owe it to them." Jacobs's letter also revealed her continuing sensitivity to the dignity and desires of those being helped, including their wish "to do all they could to help themselves."[59] Thus, while encouraging philanthropists to lend a hand, she did not overlook the freedpeople's aspiration to become agents in this humanitarian work.

In a letter printed in an 1864 issue of the *National Anti-Slavery Standard,* Jacobs reasserted the freedpeople's desire for independence and self-government: "they are willing to earn their own way, and generally capable of it." Always aware of her audience, Jacobs represented this desire in terms of "self reliance," a notion heartily embraced by white middle-class readers in the North.[60] Yet, the use of a familiar and appealing rhetoric was not mere pandering to readers' tastes. Jacobs was attempting to win additional political and financial support for the freed-people, their immediate material needs, and their continuing efforts to establish a self-determining community. She was also aiming to register a condemnation of the racist and paternalistic mistreatment of the freedpeople at the hands of Northerners. Such a project required both a language that would be discursively available to such an audience and a rhetorical tact that would not alienate Northern white readers disinclined to hear negative reports of their brave soldiers and their noble humanitarians. In an 1863 letter to the *Liberator,* she described and deplored how, despite "their kindness, and ever-ready service," the freedpeople "often receive insults, and sometimes beatings" from Union soldiers. Her criticism of such racist abuse was preceded by a description of the Northern army as "deliverers" and followed up with reassuring remarks about her sympathy for the soldiers and her pride in Colonel Robert Shaw, the white commander of the first regiment of black soldiers in the war.[61]

Remaining in the D.C. area until the end of the war, she continued her humanitarian efforts by raising money, nursing the sick, distributing food and clothing, and working to create a community life in Freedmen's Village. In 1864, after white "missionary" school teachers tried "to take charge of the school" the black community had built, Jacobs stepped in and insisted that the freedpeople decide the mission and administration of the school, since, in her words, "the time had come when it was their privilege to have something to say." Although one of the black trustees "said he would be proud to have the [white] ladies teach in their school," he and the rest of the community were affronted that "the white people had made all the arrangements without consulting them." Eventually, after a meeting to settle the matter, the black community secured its claim to the school and installed Louisa Jacobs (Harriet's daughter, "Ellen" from *Incidents*) and her friend, Miss Lawton, as instructors. "I do not object to white teachers," Jacobs went on to write, "but I think it has a good effect upon these people to convince them their own race can do something for their elevation. It inspires them with confidence to help each other."[62]

This belief that the patients of humanitarianism could become the agents in their own labors and lives, though importantly linked to the work of other African Americans, distinguished Jacobs's efforts from conventional benevolence. Emerging at a time when conventional forms of benevolence were changing in rapid and uncertain ways, Jacobs's subversive repetition of philanthropy, in her relief work and in *Incidents*, both heralds and enacts the promise of eccentric humanitarianism, the possibility of help without control.

FOUR

SUFFERING BEYOND DESCRIPTION

Pain—has an Element of Blank—
EMILY DICKINSON[1]

Action of a Kind Hitherto Unknown

"The suffering here beggars all description," Cornelia Hancock told her mother. Earlier that month Hancock, a nurse serving in a field hospital at Fredericksburg, had written the same thing to her sister Ellen:

> On arriving here the scenes beggared all description and these two men [Detmold and Vanderpool], eminent as they are in their profession, were paralyzed by what they saw. Rain had poured in through the bullet-riddled roofs of the churches until our wounded lay in pools of water made bloody by their seriously wounded condition. On these scenes Dr. Detmold and Dr. Vanderpool gazed in horror and seemed not to know where to take hold.

This suffering which "beggars all description"—a scene of pain so extraordinary that it ravages linguistic faculties—attests to what Elaine Scarry has called "the referential instability of the hurt body" and to Walt Whitman's insistence that the real war could never be represented in a book. But, according to Hancock, witnessing such agony produced more than a breakdown of language or crisis in representation: it also created a failure in humanitarian action. Not knowing how to act, the paralyzed doctors stared on aghast, while the pain-racked wounded bled into expanding circles of crimsoning rain water.[2]

The magnitude of suffering brought on by the Civil War stunned everyone at first. These two doctors, Vanderpool and Detmold, had not yet realized the extent to which this war was different, how these battles could generate dead and wounded in unprecedented numbers and in unprecedented ways. When she met these New York physicians, Hancock had already been initiated into the horrors of this war. At Gettysburg, she "saw for the first time what war meant." After her first encounter with "the sufferings of the wounded," "the desolation of the bereft," and the war's "other horrors," Hancock tried to describe what she had seen:

> Hundreds of desperately wounded men were stretched out on boards laid across the high-backed pews as closely as they could be packed together. The boards were covered with straw. Thus elevated, these poor sufferers' faces, white and drawn with pain, were almost on a level with my own. I seemed to stand breast-high in a sea of anguish. . . . So appalling was the number of the wounded as yet unsuccored, so helpless seemed the few who were battling against tremendous odds to save life, and so overwhelming was the demand for any kind of aid that could be given quickly, that one's senses were benumbed by the awful responsibility that fell to the living. Action of a kind hitherto unknown and unheard of was needed here.

Awash in this "sea of anguish," Hancock realized that the "appalling," unprecedented magnitude of this suffering would require new practices for dealing with pain and the mitigation of pain, new ways of providing humanitarian care. "Action of a kind hitherto unknown." Suffering beyond description necessitated a humanitarian care that had not yet been described.[3]

Hancock's recognition of the need for new approaches to benevolent work was not unique in this era of dramatic changes in humanitarianism. Many tried to adapt by improvising on older humanitarian practices and traditional values; others resisted established methods and pursued modern, large-scale, scientific means. In part because of these different approaches, this moment of change, this searching around for action of a kind hitherto unknown, generated considerable philanthropic giving and caring. According to Linus Pierpont Brockett, "neither in ancient nor modern times, has there been so vast an outpouring of a nation's wealth for the care, the comfort, and the physical and moral welfare of those who have fought the nation's battles or been the sufferers from its condition of war."[4] Humanitarians provided an extraordinary amount of care, performing countless operations, producing miles of bandages, and pouring millions of glasses of lemonade.

These nineteenth-century physicians, nurses, and volunteers saw their healing and caring vocations as forms of humanitarian work. Echoing Henry J. Bigelow's definition of "medical science" as the field that "approaches so nearly that of philanthropy," prominent New York surgeon Alexander H. Stevens told the American Medical Association that "Our profession . . . is the link that unites Science and Philanthropy."[5] Most of them also held to a hierarchical view of the difference between helpless patients and powerful humanitarian agents. And their humanitarian works sometimes seemed patronizing, paternalistic, humiliating, and even mean, according to some observers, mostly soldiers and refugees but also nurses and volunteers. All the care and innovation in this period notwithstanding, the humanitarianism of Civil War medical and relief workers, like most nineteenth-century benevolence, could at times visit its own peculiar, usually unintentional suffering on patients.

In response to this war-related suffering attended by humanitarian care and humanitarian coercion, Louisa May Alcott and Walt Whitman attempted to reformulate dominant ideas about humanitarianism and the relationship between patients and agents. The Civil War texts of these two writers turned nurses turned writers revealed the limits of sanctioned approaches to suffering and tried to propose instead "action of a kind hitherto unknown." Although Alcott and Whitman supplied no programmatic blueprint for the renovation of medical-humanitarian care, their texts provided a critical examination of the patient/agent relation, illuminated the overlooked issue of power in this dynamic, and suggested the need for an eccentric humanitarian practice.

Two Commissions

During the war humanitarians hotly debated a variety of approaches to the care of the sick and wounded. No consensus approach ever emerged. No single ideological position ever governed the entirety of benevolent acts. The conflicts between the Christian Commission and the United States Sanitary Commission, for example, illustrate not only the complexity of the ideological-rhetorical divisions but also, chronologically, the Civil War–era paradigm shift within humanitarianism.[6]

Early in the war, a number of bourgeois women and men, including an important contingent of New York professionals, pressed for the formation of a council that would organize disease prevention and sanitary inspection in hospitals and camps and provide some general relief for soldiers. What began with an impromptu meeting of fifty or sixty women at the New York Infirmary for Women on April 25, 1861, evolved into the United States Sanitary Commission, an organization that George Fredrickson has called "the largest, most powerful, and most highly organized philanthropic activity that had ever been seen in America." Hancock called it "a gigantic machine."[7]

The immense, unprecedented size of the commission was in part the result of the organizational energies of its leaders, upper-class elites who had a passion for fund-raising, order, and a kind of scientific professionalism removed from the sympathetic feeling characteristic of antebellum humanitarianism. These aristocrats and professionals, patricians like George Templeton Strong, the conservative New York lawyer who served as the organization's treasurer, created a commission whose governance was "central, federal, national." The surly but tireless executive secretary of the commission, Frederick Law Olmsted, a self-confessed "growler," demanded a "system of centralization and absolute subordination."[8]

Sanitarians prized discipline, organization, and efficiency. Fond of praising "the most beneficent results" of "discipline," commission member and commission historian Charles J. Stillé urged the implementation of an exacting discipline in the Union armies. Deploying machine imagery, he claimed that the common soldier quickly and cheerfully learned that "true military discipline was not only essential to his efficiency but to his safety, and indeed to his very existence, as part of this vast human machine." Mary A. Livermore, another Sanitarian, blamed the common soldier's "misery" on the lack of "efficient military discipline."[9]

The Commission advocated not only "a stern and rigorous discipline" for the army, but also a *disciplining* of popular humanitarian feeling in general. Lecturing on aid to the soldiers, Sanitary President Henry Bellows argued that "however ardent and warm the heart, its pulsations . . . must be regulated by order and method." The Commission envisioned its work as "methodizing and reducing to practical service the already active but undirected benevolence of the people." Making use of machinery imagery (as in Stillé and Hancock), Katharine Prescott Wormeley saw "undirected benevolence" as a positive danger to the efficient, mechanical operation of humanitarian relief:

> [T]he government needed the Commission to protect it against the vast tide of home-feelings and the ardor of a people pouring down upon it in indiscriminate benevolence, and clogging the machinery, already too limited, through which alone a real good to the soldier could be applied.

Throughout her letters written from commission headquarters during McClellan's 1862 peninsular campaign, Wormeley criticized "home-feelings," "ardor," and other passions associated with the antebellum model for humanitarian work. She forthrightly disavowed emotion and endorsed mechanistic efficiency. "No one must come here who cannot put away all feeling," explained Wormeley. "Do all you can, and be a machine,—that's the way to act; the only way."[10]

Those who did not put away feeling and perform as a machine (those humanitarians who did not function as a cog within the Sanitary Commission) became the object of Commission reproach. Complaining about the Army Medical Bureau, Stillé wrote, "Its members were, doubtless, it was said, good men, but they were sentimentalists." He objected to "excitable philanthropists" and relief workers whom he described as "humane and zealous, but irresponsible persons." In the same vein, Strong belittled Superintendent of Female Nurses Dorothea Dix (who was thought by many to be "endowed with warm feelings and great kindness of heart") and denigrated generally the members of the Christian Commission. "They were an ugly-looking set, mostly of the Maw-worm and Chadband type. Some were unctuous to behold, and others vinegary; a bad lot." Thus, emotion, the heart of philanthropic reform and privileged sign of humanitarian sympathy in the antebellum period, was refigured in Sanitarian discourse as irresponsible, impractical, inefficient, and unattractive.[11]

But not everyone thought or spoke as the Sanitarians. Supported by evangelical organizations and local Protestant churches, the Christian Commission worked within an older humanitarian ideology, and it encouraged the sentimentalism deplored by the Sanitarians. Setting itself against the Sanitary's large, impersonal, centralized structure as well as its mechanistic and scientific rhetoric, the Christian

Commission wanted, in the words of its *Second Annual Report,* to "enhance the value of both gifts and services by kind words to the soldier as *a man,* not a machine." An 1862 circular of "INSTRUCTIONS" to "Delegates of the Christian Commission," considered "personal conversation and prayer with individuals" among "the chief means by which the delegate can benefit the men of the hospital." Material relief was only a minor component of a greater spiritual mission. In *The War and the Christian Commission* (1865), Andrew B. Cross explained, "Continuing to make the body comfortable, might be called a small part of the work." The more important work was spreading "the consolation of the gospel to all who are in sorrow and trouble, who are sick, wounded or dying." In the benevolent rhetoric of the Christian Commission, religious instruction, individual kindnesses, and personal feeling as well as material relief were all essential to humanitarian care.[12]

Sometime Christian Commission delegate Walt Whitman, while at odds with the commission's evangelical views, warmly concurred with the emphasis on individual heartfelt ministrations. In his numerous hospital notebooks, one of which contained an "Instructions to Delegates of the Christian Commission" circular, and in his autobiographical *Specimen Days* (1882), Whitman held that such personal, emotional caring did more to heal soldiers than medical science. In an 1863 notebook, he scribbled:

> and bending over the hospital cots, in those vast collections of decent born American soldiers, mostly young men fagged out with fevers or wounds, is [?] not afraid to cheer copiously the homesick youth, & vivify the feeble, with the firm-pressing kisses of his lips, often perhaps more real benefit to them than drugs or surgery.

The entry reveals Whitman's distance from Christian Commission discourse. His passionate attachment to the bodies of these "young men fagged out with fevers," his desire to "bend . . . over the hospital cots" and intrepidly bestow curative "firm-pressing kisses of his lips," was different from the commission's proselytizing attachment to soldiers' souls, its desire "to instruct, cheer, and win them to Christ." Nevertheless, Whitman and the Christians shared a discourse that privileged "warm . . . sympathy," "cheer," "personal conversation," "kindness," and "affection above all things." Warm, benevolent impulses were, in the writings of Whitman and his missionary comrades, the foundation of humanitarian practice.[13]

The issue of pay, a recurrent and contentious subject in philanthropic debates, also divided humanitarians in the Sanitary from those in the Christian Commission. While the Sanitary paid some of its benevolent workers, the Christian Commission and its part-time delegate-poet disparaged paid humanitarians and claimed that volunteer efforts were more disinterested, more genuinely benevolent. Whitman complained to his mother:

> As to the Sanitary Commission & the like, I am sick of them all, & would not accept any of their berths—you ought to see the way the men as they lie helpless in bed turn away their faces from the sight of these Agents, Chaplains &c. (*hirelings* as Elias Hicks would call them—they seem to me always a set of foxes

& wolves)—they get well paid, & are always incompetent & disagreeable—As I told you before the only good fellows I have met are the Christian Commissioners—they go everywhere & receive no pay.

The issue of pay was never his only reason for disliking the Sanitary Commission: he also knew that the soldiers loathed the Sanitary, and he believed its agents were "incompetent & disagreeable." But, for Whitman, volunteerism separated the "good fellows," the antebellum-oriented Christian Commissioners, from the "*hirelings*." Although it did in fact pay many of its delegates, some handsomely, the Christian Commission esteemed unpaid humanitarian works and criticized professional agents.[14]

Examining the conflict between the Sanitary Commission and the Christian Commission reveals part of the depth and scope of the disagreements among humanitarians in the early 1860s. The two commissions represented different social constituencies within the middle class: the Christian Commission appealed to the religious bourgeoisie and its provincial networks of ministers and church-goers, whereas the North's scientific-professional-intellectual elite ran the Sanitary.[15] The Christians treated suffering as an individual experience, and the Sanitary developed a large-scale, bureaucratic response suited to the magnitude of suffering. Quite unlike the Christian Commission's grassroots organization, the Sanitary's vast but centralized structure heralded an emerging trend toward what Alan Trachtenberg has called "incorporation."[16] The two organizations fashioned differing ideological justifications for their work, promoted conflicting values, advocated dissimilar humanitarian practices, and used different benevolent rhetorics. The rift between the two groups—the Christian Commission's appeal to religious and sentimental values associated with antebellum benevolence, the Sanitarians' advocacy of a disciplined philanthropic machine characteristic of the postromantic era—illustrates the paradigm shift within humanitarianism, the drift in benevolent thought and the dissension within benevolent discourses.

Humanitarianisms

Nevertheless, just as it would be innaccurate to see the era's philanthropic acts emanating from a single ideology, so too should we resist the urge to reduce Civil War benevolence to a binary contest between a residual humanitarianism represented by one organization and an emergent humanitarianism represented by its foe. However useful the Sanitary-Christian opposition for pointing to the dominant tendencies within the ideological-rhetorical struggles among Civil War humanitarians, neither side used a wholly consistent rhetoric or operated from a coherent ideological site. Neither side acted from noncontradictory motives. Values identified with the antebellum period, like sentimentalism, sometimes played a role in Sanitary Commission rhetoric and humanitarian rhetoric in general after 1861, though indeed a smaller role. Likewise, the Christian Commission was never a pure product of a monolithic romantic humanitarianism, but rather a heterogeneous amalgam of mostly antebellum ideals, rhetorics, and practices.

The Sanitary Commission's fiercest disputes were never with pious Christian Commission delegates but with bureaucrats and doctors in the Army Medical Bureau and the philanthropists who formed an autonomous organization in St. Louis called the Western Sanitary Commission. The imperious Strong wanted to "declare war against the Medical Bureau" and compel "the schismatic St. Louis Sanitary Commission" to acknowledge his organization's "authority derived from the War Department." Still, the maverick Western Sanitary Commission and the Medical Bureau were only two more players in the growing web of controversy over the control and organization of benevolence during the war. Numerous local and state soldiers' aid societies also challenged Olmsted's dream of a "system of centralization and absolute subordination," as did the throng of nurses under the supervision of the distinguished but uncooperative Dorothea Dix.[17]

Famous for her vigilance, energy, and zealous devotion to common soldiers, Mary Ann "Mother" Bickerdyke always performed her humanitarian labors on her own terms, violating military regulations when it suited her, discharging irresponsible doctors when they bothered her, and using Sanitary Commission stores while ignoring its agents. Even General Sherman avoided confrontations with Mother Bickerdyke, saying, "She ranks me." Clara Barton's highly individualized humanitarian style drew criticism from Dix, the Medical Bureau, and the Sanitary Commission. Objecting to the institutionalized approach to suffering and frowning upon amateur battlefield nursing (including pious relief workers who used soldiers' traumas as an opportunity to talk about the "Physician of the Soul"), the maverick Barton never quite fit into any of the dominant models for benevolent action. Seeming to move simultaneously in different directions, she possessed "a profound suspicion of all organizations," and yet craved some official authority and then, after the war, founded the largest of humanitarian organizations, the American Red Cross. She was deeply moved by the pain of individual soldiers but was also calm, bright, and unperturbed when faced with a battle's aggregate carnage.[18]

Working-class philanthropy also eluded easy assimilation to either of the dominant models. In *The Philanthropic Results of War in America* (1864), Brockett recorded approvingly the generous acts of workers in New York and Philadelphia:

> The spontaneous instincts of patriotism among the working classes in the vicinity of the landings, in both cities, exhibited itself in hastening to the cars with food from their own scanty stores to appease the hunger of these famishing citizen soldiers.

> The citizens of the vicinity, a large portion of them mechanics, laboring by day in the busy manufactories of that vicinity, were greatly distressed at witnessing this suffering, and resolved, though with very small available means, to erect near the station house a hospital for the temporary accomodation of the sick and wounded soldiers. . . . One poor Irishman wheeled a half-worn stove to the new hospital. "He had nothing else to give," he said, "and must do something for the sogers."

The quaintness of working-class folk spontaneously engaged in humanitarian works, including the construction of a hospital, despite their "scanty stores" and "very small available means," apparently moved the narrator of these passages. He deepened the quaintness and condescension of the second passage by having the noble but "poor Irishman" who ingenuously felt he "must do something for the sogers" speak in dialect that marks his exclusion from the usual philanthropic classes. Later in his narrative, however, in a section on the New York City draft riots, Brockett offered a much different view of the urban Irish working class, calling it "the most degraded portion of the population." Brockett's inconsistent perspective on the working class was an important part of the wonder in his representation of this population's humanitarian efforts. He wrote:

> The feeling of sympathy and patriotism which has actuated the masses of the people, manifested itself in numberless instances of thoughtfulness and tenderness, even from classes, among whom it was hardly to be looked for.

A surprised Brockett seemed uncertain about how to treat working-class humanitarian sympathy: after all, "it was hardly to be looked for" among these classes, the "most degraded portion of the population." The contradictions, astonishment, and condescension in Brockett's representation of working-class benevolence suggest the problems (inconsistency and middle-class hauteur) bourgeois humanitarians had understanding the infiltration of the lower classes into an activity considered the domain of the middle and upper classes.[19]

Just as the Sanitary-Christian binary does not absorb or exhaust the multitude of cultural practices and beliefs considered "humanitarian" in this period, this opposition is also unable to illuminate the surfeit of public and private motivations for engaging in humanitarian work. Religious duty (Christian), the desire for a more efficient management of the war (Sanitary), and patriotism (both) were only a portion of the heterogeneous collection of discursive rationales for this organized compassion. Moreover, organizational justifications for such work, whether from the Sanitations, the Christians, or some other group or leader, could scarcely account for the numerous individual desires and motivations that fed this burst of philanthropic energy.

Using language that voiced nonaltruistic motivations and desire-filled yearnings, humanitarians often noted that charitable acts most help the humanitarian agent. Discussing midcentury philanthropy with Whitman, Horace Traubel asserted, "My arguement with doers of good deeds is, that its best effect is upon them & not upon the persons for whom they do good." Whitman agreed, and in doing so surprised none of his listeners. During the war Whitman rarely attempted to disguise the often sad pleasure he took in tending these "handsome" young men. "I have comfort in ministering to them," wrote Whitman, explaining in clear terms his personal reasons for going around the hospitals, "especially to their thirst for real friendship."[20]

Numerous other "doers of good deeds" also ached to help others and spoke of their wish to love and comfort patients. Esther Hill Hawks, for example, a white doctor from New England serving in Florida and the Sea Islands, recorded in her diary "an ever increasing yearning in the heart for some object . . . on which to lavish strong pure heart love." "I have longed for this, prayed for it with all the passionate entreaty of a desolate nature," she wrote, "I *do* need something to love." Caring for the sick and wounded brought fulfillment to many humanitarians. "I admit painfulness; but no one can tell how sweet it is to be the drop of comfort to so much agony," Wormeley explained to her mother. The avoidance of personal pain as much as the search for humanitarian pleasures motivated care providers. The strain of the war sent many noncombatants, including Annie K. Kyle, into benevolent service. Telling a doctor that "I must have constant occupation or I will lose my mind," Kyle became a wound-dresser. And in this humanitarian work she apparently found what she needed: "my grief and sorrow were forgotten in administering to the wants of the sick."[21]

By identifying these humanitarians with nonofficial motives, I am not suggesting that the rhetoric of the Sanitary and Christian Commissions played no role in inducing men and women into benevolent service, nor am I arguing that humanitarians acted only from ulterior motives (though certainly not all motives were known or knowable). No single, isolated motive prompted humanitarians to care for the sick and wounded: they were moved to action by multiple, sometimes conflicting motivations, many of which surpassed those sanctioned by the two predominant models.

Louisa May Alcott, for example, expressed in her public and private writings multiple motives for becoming a nurse. Before Sumter, Alcott yearned for the adventure and excitement associated with a war on slavery. In an 1859 journal entry she wrote: "Great State Encampment here. Town full of soldiers, with military fuss and feathers. I like a camp, and long for a war, to see how it all seems. I can't fight, but I can nurse." As a woman barred from serving in the military, she settled on nursing as a socially sanctioned alternative. A year and a half later, Alcott was still longing to see the war and still frustrated that a male-dominated social order prevented her from enlisting. "I've often longed to see a war," she told herself, "and now I have my wish. I long to be a man; but as I can't fight, I will content myself with working for those who can." Alcott's decision to enter benevolent service was from the beginning knotted up with other wishes ("to see a war," "to be a man"). But nursing could never quite give her what she wanted. In the midst of her nursing labors, she would still write: "That way the fighting lies, & I long to follow." From the very beginning, nursing seemed a poor substitute, cold comfort, something to content herself with because her most-wished-for desires were unobtainable.[22]

This type of ulterior, complex, and unconventionally gendered motivation did not typically have a place in the representation of female humanitarian desire in the period's philanthropic discourses. In *The Ideal of Womanhood* (1857), for example, Lizzie R. Torrey readily identified true humanitarian feeling with a specifically female nature: "woman is everywhere recognized as the natural friend of the unfortunate." Throughout her text, Torrey linked womanhood to benevolence, the "desire of others' good, of relieving distress," and to humanitarian consolation: "Women are true consolers of the human race—their ears are never closed to the voice of suffering."[23] As a nurse, Alcott did listen to the voice of suffering—yet her reasons for doing so were not apparently part of her feminine nature. In *Hospital Sketches* (1863), Alcott's autobiographical persona, Tribulation Periwinkle, is motivated to care for the wounded in part by an unfeminine fascination with the morbid. "Having a taste for 'ghastliness,'" she admits with all the humor and non-conforming spunk of Jo March, "I had rather longed for the wounded to arrive" (32). When she admits to conventionally gendered motives, such as "a philanthropic desire to serve the race" (40), her ironic tone tends to undercut the purity and piety of such motives. Moreover, like Whitman, both Alcott in her journal and Trib in *Hospital Sketches* show how the desire to give and receive affection functioned as a motivation for nursing.[24] Alcott never had a lone motive for becoming a nurse; she always had several that were knotted up with other wishes. And these clusters of motives both participated in and exceeded available dominant philanthropic rhetorics.

Alcott was not unique in her struggle with a plethora of nonofficial motives. All humanitarians, I assume, acted from a complicated knot of known and unknown, publicly sanctioned and privately held motives. Even when their beliefs and motivations only partially conformed to organizational ideals, benevolent workers still enlisted to care for the sick and wounded. Hancock, for example, often had mixed feelings about the humanitarian organizations with which she worked, saying in one instance, "The Sanitary Commission is flooded with delegates and some of them of a very inferior character, then again some of the noblest souls that ever drew breath." Despite her occasionally critical view, she continued to receive supplies from them and insist, "The Sanitary are great friends of mine."[25]

The loving and desiring humanitarian rhetoric of Whitman never quite fit with the moralizing rhetoric of the Christian Commission. Although the Christians hoped to use their humanitarian role to deliver short religious talks to wounded soldiers, "to speak words of comfort to their souls, pointing them to Jesus Christ, the Saviour of Sinners," Whitman would never have considered proselytizing. When given an opportunity to profess some conventional Christian belief—when, for example, a wounded believer asked the poet if he "enjoyed religion"—Whitman always and gently asserted his heterodox views, "probably not my dear, in the way you mean." Despite the differences between the Christians and Whitman, and despite his claim to be "a hospital missionary after my own style," he proudly accepted from them a commission and thought them "good fellows."[26]

Alcott, a part-time fund-raiser for the Sanitary Commission, sometimes had her Tribulation Periwinkle resolve to discard sentiment in accordance with Sanitary values.[27] Soon after her arrival at Hurly-burly House (Georgetown's Union Hotel Hospital), Trib tells us, "I corked up my feelings, and returned to the path of duty" (34). Yet, when she describes the deathbed of John, a beloved patient, Trib sentimentally evokes her own "heart ache" and John's "emotion at the thought of such a sudden sundering of all the dear home ties." She narrates the moving good-bye of Ned and John, notes the comforting "presence of human sympathy" that "lightened that hard hour" for John, and describes the "lovely expression which so often beautifies dead faces" (62-64). Although Alcott was a supporter of the Sanitary Commission, her Tribulation Periwinkle can only partially subscribe to its postbellum values and often prefers an antebellum sympathy.

Moreover, the distinctions between the Sanitarians and the Christians, between a scientific philanthropic ideal and a sentimental one, should not be conceived as rigid. Both organizations used suffering as a type of moral capital for justifying their actions.[28] Most humanitarianisms exploited the rhetoric of domestic ideology to broaden their popular appeal, win popular recognition, and raise funds. And widely different organizations and discourses often turned to similar icons, images, and slogans. Florence Nightingale, for example, operated as a legitimizing signifier within the rhetorics of most Civil War humanitarian organizations, even though these Florence Nightingales differed widely. The male commissioners of the Sanitary used Nightingale as a sign of the necessity for "plenary authority" and "unlimited power" in efficiently providing and scientifically administering care for the sick and wounded. A much different Nightingale—the self-sacrificing "Lady with a Lamp" whose noble deeds represent "Heroic Womanhood," as in Henry Wadsworth Longfellow's popular "Santa Filomena"—inspired hundreds of women to enter nursing during the war.[29]

Just as certain icons, such as Florence Nightingale, circulated among various humanitarian discourses, certain values permeated these diverse humanitarianisms, emerging from the sentimental ideal as readily as from the scientific one. The Christian Commission, for instance, sometimes championed the notion of authority and respect for authority, one of the Sanitary's policy cornerstones. The Christian Commission advised its delegates to "hold themselves subject to orders, and place themselves under orders" when coordinating aid for soldiers. "Officers are supreme in the field, and Surgeons in the hospital."[30] Convinced of the need to control humanitarian feelings with its oft-professed government-derived authority, the Sanitary Commmission always advocated the virtue of such authority. Yet, when explaining the need for disciplining benevolent sentiment to *North American Review* readers, some of whom may have been quite attached to the role of sympathy in humanitarian work, Sanitary President Bellows described the commission's tasks in a rhetoric that balances and blends an antebellum devotion to feeling and a decidedly postbellum desire to order feeling. He wrote:

> Between these two important and indispensable interests, home feeling, and governmental responsibility and method, the Sanitary Commission steered its delicate and difficult way. It assigned to itself the task, requiring constant tact, of *directing,* without weakening or cooling, the warm and copious stream of popular *beneficence* toward the army.[31]

This passage indicates that, however certain of the necessity for scientifically managed humanitarian care, Bellows would not abandon rhetoric that pictured humanitarianism emanating from the heart. Instead of attempting to eradicate sentimental beneficence, the Sanitary would insist that *directing beneficence* was its principal mission.

Directing Beneficence

The Sanitary Commission was hardly the only agent seeking to direct humanitarian feeling. Despite separate histories, contrasting rhetorics, and different approaches, most humanitarianisms shared this desire for directing beneficence. By "directing beneficence," I am suggesting two intertwined ideas: (1) the organization and regulation of humanitarian work in the society, and (2) the construction of a humanitarian work that could guide or control the patients of humanitarianism and society in general. Humanitarians like the Sanitarians and others wanted not only to regulate benevolent care in their society, but also create a type of care that would regulate their society. While battling with each other for political control of benevolent service during the war, humanitarians also struggled over how patients would be cared for and how such humanitarian care would be used to shape society. Hence, it is not ironic that "care" meant (as it still does) both supervision or controlling custody over someone as well as medical-humanitarian attention.

In the nineteenth century, directing beneficence usually entailed control of the environment in which suffering and disease occurred, including not only the immediate physical surroundings of patients, but also their behavior, and even the values of society in general. One of the most important changes in medical care that materialized during the Civil War was the assiduous attention to hygienics. Influenced by Florence Nightingale and the experience of the British Sanitary Commission in the Crimea, Civil War humanitarian discourse rarely separated hygienics from the need for establishing a type of (moral) order in which disease and suffering could not thrive. In this medical world before modern germ theory, the emphasis fell on a preventive medicine that saw disease caused by disorder, impure air, uncleanliness, dank atmosphere, and other bad environments. According to such an etiology, the role of the nurse-doctor-humanitarian was to create and maintain a proper environment for healing and for health. Working with such assumptions, various sorts of care providers, especially those from the Sanitary Commission, emphasized the need for cleanliness, proper drainage, good ventilation, fresh bedding, clean water supplies, and order in hospitals and camps. Yet, this desire for order almost always embraced more than the need for clean water and adequate ventilation. To prevent the spread of venereal disease, for example, a Sanitary Commission monograph demanded that:

> Every soldier who contracts venereal disease, should be required to give the name and address of the woman who infected him; and if, upon examination, she be found diseased, her removal from the neighborhood should be enforced by the military authority.

This medical text emphasized not the cure but the need to control the moral environment, by military force if necessary.[32]

This concern for the moral environment often overlapped with humanitarians' interest in the moral character or spiritual well-being of soldiers. "The soldier has a soul as well as a body," argued Brockett, "a soul to be blighted and polluted by the vices of camp, or to be kept pure and holy." With such rationales, many humanitarians argued that relief organizations should care for souls as well as bodies, discourage immorality as well as disease. The *Armory Square Hospital Gazette,* a newspaper written for hospitalized soldiers, contained articles that attacked "Malingering," to cite one vice loathed by these hospital humanitarians, "the artifice of feigning sickness or lameness in order to procure a discharge." In "A Sad Story" the newspaper warned against "the 'enemy of the camp'—death-dealing liquor" by narrating a melodramatic tale about an eighteen-year-old patient who dies at the hospital after a binge. While condemning the *"use of intoxicating drinks"* in general, humanitarians had varied approaches for dealing with the problem. The *Armory Square Hospital Gazette* encouraged temperance meetings, while continuing to catalog the deleterious effects of alcohol. Hannah Ropes, Alcott's nursing supervisor, took a different approach. When "the noisiest" of a group of patients "wild with liquor" returned to the hospital, she gave him a dose of cider vinegar and ordered him to say his prayers and fall asleep.[33]

This humanitarian will to control the (moral) behavior of patients often moved beyond advice, warnings, and disapprobation of certain vices. Some humanitarian agents used their office to persuade patients to acquiesce to conventional religious beliefs. The Reverend William W. Lyle, for example, used patients' suffering as an opportunity to preach to them about "the ever-living and ever-loving Physician of souls." Talking to a dying patient who "seemed to quiver under the power of some untold agony," Lyle suggested that they pray and read the Bible together. Lyle apparently mistook the patient's "untold agony," seeing it as a sign of spiritual crisis and not as an indication of the painfulness of a gangrened bullet wound. When the patient, weak and in excruciating pain, declined the offer, Lyle persisted, telling the patient that he ought to "pray for pardon through the Savior's blood." Finally, after several more offers, the patient incompletely stammered "I don't! I don't!" Not one to give up easily, Lyle persevered "with the intention of making yet another effort to point the dying one to Christ." The patient does not speak again.[34] Preoccupied with his patient's welfare in the hereafter (despite the patient's indication that he'd prefer not to listen to Lyle's ideas about the hereafter), Lyle offered no mitigation of the patient's earthly suffering and only exacerbated a dying person's agonies. Lyle's humanitarianism might have alleviated psychological or spiritual suffering in patients who were believers. For those wounded who did not share Lyle's beliefs, however, his religious philanthropy must have seemed coercive and unwelcome, perhaps even sadistic.

Pushy ministers were not, however, the only humanitarians who hoped to modify the moral beliefs of patients. Neither the Sanitary Commission nor the Christian Commission wanted to limit its work to the mitigation of physical suffering. Each organization instead envisioned for itself a role of national scope, a role that would allow it to reshape the behavior, values, and beliefs of their patients and ultimately the entire nation. Although such goals might seem grand, the Christians and the Sanitarians never balked. With pride in the expansive work of the Christian Commission, Andrew Cross wrote:

> Continuing to make comfortable the body, might be called a small part of the work. . . . [Our delegates have] labored as volunteer chaplains to our soldiers in the army. Seeing that our men are furnished with the word of God, bringing them tracts, religious papers. Throwing around them the influences and restraints of the Gospel, as at home. We believe good has been done which will appear after many days. When this war is over and the army returns home it will not be to curse, defile and pollute the communities into which they shall go. We look for the influence of the Gospel to exercise such a sanctifying power that they will go loving liberty, loving their country, loving their God, loving order and law.[35]

Not the body, but the soul of these soldiers was the object of such benevolence. The Christian Commission threw around "the influences and restraints of the Gospel" not only to convert soldiers or restrain them from vices that would "defile and pollute the communities into which they shall go," but also to teach them devotion to "liberty" (which in this context did not mean personal freedom but rather a national ideal), "country," "God," "order and law." Having distributed religious tracts, instructed soldiers in the "influences and restraints" of Christian belief, and taught them love of God and country, law and order, the Christians expected that their humanitarian work would do more than inspire fond memories of a comforter during a time of physical pain; they planned to leave an enduring influence on the values and loyalties of the thousands whom they helped during the war.

The Sanitary Commission also yearned to play a major role in the shaping of American values, behaviors, and beliefs. Although the Sanitary with its "scientific" aims tended to eschew the Christian Commission's pious evangelical rhetoric, both commissions shared similar middle-class patriotic and benevolent ideals. Yet, the Sanitarians never focused exclusively or even primarily on soldiers as the site for imparting their values and beliefs, but instead sought to instruct the entire population, military and civilian. At the end of *The United States Sanitary Commission: A Sketch of its Purposes and its Work* (1863), Katharine Prescott Wormeley argued that the Sanitary's work always went beyond providing humanitarian aid. "The Sanitary Commission is a great teacher," she announced. "It has within it the means for a national education of ideas as well as instincts." That the Sanitary wanted others to share their values (order, discipline, and efficiency) was not surprising. Instead it was the depth and scope of this project, this desire to shape American values, which seemed awesome. The Sanitarians wanted to form and reform not only ideas but also instincts. Their vision was not individual, selective, or local but always inclusive, expansive, and national. "[G]uiding the national instincts; showing the value of order, and the dignity of work," the Sanitary "sprang from the nation" in order to teach and mold the nation in its own image, Wormeley sang.[36]

Humanitarian justifications for these varied and often coercive efforts to direct benevolence usually rested on a shared set of presuppositions. Typically humanitarians supposed that some type of higher law or essential truth sanctioned their practices, that patients were basically unable to help or speak for themselves, or that patients had somehow called the humanitarians into action. All of these notions worked to naturalize what was perhaps the most fundamental assumption—the distinction between agents and patients.

Humanitarianism often appealed to fixed meanings or inalterable laws to justify bids to articulate or regulate values, actions, and beliefs. Christians like Rev. Lyle or Andrew Cross, for example, spoke of the Gospel (and its claim to impart eternal verities as well as its command to love thy neighbor) to explain and defend their humanitarian actions, especially when those actions moved beyond mitigation of physical pain and into the teaching of Christian beliefs and conversion of patients. The Sanitarians, on the other hand, relied on patriotic and scientific truths as the basis for their directing beneficence. In a different way, women sometimes used domestic ideology and maternal metaphors to justify their work as nurses during the war. Even when these women's desires were professional rather than maternal, women nurses could deploy conventional, essentialist truths about feminine nature and motherhood to defend their resolution to enter humanitarian service in a society anxious and skeptical about the propriety of women working outside the domestic sphere. Regardless of their motivations, middle-class women could and often did turn to domestic ideology as a sanction for their nursing . Although the difficulties and exigencies of the war often forced humanitarians to rethink cherished ideals, humanitarians also made important use, sometimes tactically and sometimes in earnest, of conventionally espoused higher laws as the justification for their actions.[37]

Like appeals to higher truths, conventional humanitarian representations of patients worked to justify directing beneficence. Doctors, nurses, and relief workers usually portrayed patients as children or helpless infants. Although many wounded soldiers were indeed boys (there were more than 10,000 soldiers under the age of eighteen in the Union army[38]), the infantalizing language in humanitarian discourse was hardly used to distinguish adults from minors. The references to soldier-patients of all ages as "boys" or "my boys" or "our boys" were countless. Hannah Ropes described soldiers in her care as "weak, as helpless babes" who "sank upon us to care for them." Emily Parson's patients were her "forty-five children," while Alcott affectionately called her patients "my big babies." With less affection and a greater sense of power over the black adults whom she helped, Hawks thought of her patients as "ignorat [sic] unformed children." Since the culture considered them persons-to-be-cared-for, patients and children shared a similar status; doctors, nurses, and relief workers assumed parental roles. And these humanitarian "parents" would speak with satisfaction about their benevolent power over these helpless "children." Patients who behaved as autonomous adults, however, rather than as beloved children were seen as difficult to manage. "I may as well confess that I like the patients very much better before they are able to be dressed and walk out," wrote Ropes in her diary. But, even when patients were "up and dressed," and hence less helpless than infants, Ropes would still represent them as children by giving them juvenile names such as "Naughty Duane" and writing about their "pranks" and "mischief."[39]

As children, patients in humanitarian discourse were, for the most part, seen and not heard. Many of the Civil War wounded were in fact remarkably quiet. As Gerald F. Linderman has shown in his examination of Civil War beliefs about courage, "Pain expressed . . . was weakness revealed. . . . Hospital courage meant staying calm and not complaining, even to the point of death."[40] Hospital workers fostered and favored this type of quiet courage, and soldiers struggled, sometimes successfully, to perform it. Although humanitarian writers often read such silence as courage, they also used observations of speechlessness to construct images of patients as helpless and childlike. In *Hospital Life in the Army of the Potomac* (1866), William Howell Reed contentedly remembered:

> Men of roughest exterior, who had faced death in every form, who were grim and fearless in battle, and who had seemed utterly destitute of the finer sensibilities, when lying in pain, would become as quiet, and gentle, and subdued as children.[41]

Reed transformed the soldiers' courageous suffering (that is, suffering in silence, without complaint) into an image of patients as unadult and powerless.

Representations of speechless patients did not, however, always serve humanitarian parentalism. In one of his *New York Times* articles, "The Great Army of the Sick" (1863), Whitman also observed nonspeaking patients:

> Reader, how can I describe to you the mute appealing look that rolls and moves from many a manly eye, from many a sick cot, following you as you walk slowly down one of these wards? To see these, and to be incapable of responding to them . . . is enough to make one's heart crack.[42]

Unlike Reed's "subdued" children, "the mute appealing look" of the wounded soldiers in this passage had something to say, as did many of the silent voices in Whitman's writings. As "you" the "reader" walk between the beds, the sick follow you, calling and appealing to you. Silence is not an indication that patients should be cared for as children. Instead, in Whitman's account, you feel anguish, feel "one's heart crack," at the impossibility of communication created by sickness. Whitman located inability or helplessness not so much in patients as in "you" (the humanitarian) who is "incapable of responding to them."

As important as images of silent patients were representations of patients' talk. Because the wounded often vocalized sound without meaning ("inarticulate cries"[43]) or no sound at all in humanitarian discourse, accounts of patients' referential language are revealing. What did patients say, according to humanitarians? Different careproviders heard and recorded different words, pleadings, voices, cries. In an 1862 letter to her mother, Nurse Ropes, a mother of four children, wrote about a confused patient suffering intense pain whom she comforted after he awoke screaming "Mother! Mother! Mother!" Mary Livermore, author of "Woman and the War," an article that argued that "[o]nly women can understand the fierce struggle and exquisite suffering this sacrifice involves," would also hear injured soldiers cry out "Mother! Mother! Mother!" Women nurses often reported hearing patients call for their mothers; and sometimes soldiers referred to these nurses as "mother" or, as Ropes remembered, "good mother." The Rev. Lyle also recalled that injured and dying soldiers often murmured "Mother! Home!" Such calls were, according to Lyle's careful ranking, "second only to the blessed names 'Jesus!'"[44]

Sanitary Commission worker Wormeley, a far less pious and less sentimental humanitarian than Lyle, did not hear the wounded cry out for Jesus, home, or mother. Instead, this scientifically minded professional reported that the injured and sick men "seldom groan, except when their wounds are being dressed, and then their cries are agonizing: 'Oh doctor, doctor!' in such heartrending tones." Reed noted in a chapter on the Sanitary Commission that "Men blessed it with their dying breath." It would seem that those who worked with the Sanitary Commission tended not to hear cries for Jesus and home but instead pleas for the doctor and blessings for the Sanitary. In *The War and the Christian Commission,* however, readers were told how injured soldiers blessed the Christian Commission. Bishop McIlvaine recalled the response of the wounded to the Christians:

> And how the poor sufferers welcomed them—how they appreciated their work—how they thanked them! In how many cases did I hear them say "We should have been dead by this time but for the christian commission men."[45]

Mothers turned nurses heard patients call for mother. Ministers heard cries for Jesus. Christians and Sanitarians heard the wounded gratefully praise their commissions.

These voices were, we might assume, precisely what each careprovider remembered patients saying: most people tend to listen more carefully when they hear themselves being hailed or blessed. Still, the transcribing of patient voices was not typically an attempt to learn how patients thought and felt. Apparently very few humanitarians ever considered consulting patients as a way to improve the quality and nature of care. Instead, humanitarian writers tended to use patients' voices as endorsements of their own particular humanitarian project. As patients called agents into benevolent action, patient voices were made to authorize or legitimate an array of attempts at directing beneficence. Humanitarianism, no matter how coercive, would seem less so if those being helped had asked to be taken care of.

Patients: "how every body seems to try to pick upon them"

Undoubtedly soldiers appreciated those who removed them from the battlefield, operated on their injuries, nursed their wounds, and comforted them while they healed. Benton H. Wilson, for example, wrote to Whitman: "your kindness to me while in the hospital will never be forgotten by me." Whitman received numerous similar letters from soldiers and their families. While being transported in a hospital ship, Allen Morgan Geer, a wounded soldier from Illinois, recorded in his diary that "2 ladies belonging to the sanitary commission were very kind indeed to the sick & wounded going home." Later in his diary, he called the

Christian Commission "a glorious humane institution" and insisted that "its conductors deserve the gratitude of every American soldier."[46]

Although soldiers often felt enormous gratitude toward those who worked to relieve their pain, patients continued to suffer, sometimes despite the efforts of humanitarians *and also sometimes because of those efforts.* While the pain from a bullet in the lungs was certainly different from the torment of Rev. Lyle's invitations to pray, humanitarianism itself, according to the accounts of sick and wounded soldiers, often produced its own kinds of suffering.

In an 1862 letter to his father, a soldier offered a patient's perspective on a Sanitary Commission hospital at Fortress Monroe, Virginia:

> For neglect, incapacity, bullying of patients, starvation, and a hundred other meannesses that my indignant pen refuses to write, this hospital goes ahead of anything this side of creation.[47]

Outraged that an institution pledged to the mitigation of suffering would mete out its own brand of anguish on patients, Private Cox, the author of this letter, expressed feelings similar to those of other soldiers and even some humanitarians. The "meannesses" that he specifically mentioned were a mere fraction of the problem with hospitals and humanitarians during the war.[48] Yet, from his soldier-patient perspective, "meannesses" like "neglect, incapacity, bullying of patients, [and] starvation" were the most appalling and unforgettable.

One of the most common complaints was directed against what Cox called "neglect." In fact, accounts of negligent or indifferent physicians became so widespread that surgeons at the Armory Square Hospital responded with their own stories about caring and sensitive doctors. In "A Narrow Chance" readers of the *Armory Square Hospital Gazette* were told:

> The sad stories which are sometimes told of neglectful surgeons are extremely depressing to the friends of the soldier at home. As an offset to these pictures, . . . we will tell you of things which faithful surgeons in our army—and there are many such—sometimes do for the soldier. As nearly as we can, we will give this instance in the words of the surgeon who related it.

Quoting doctors verbatim, the article insists that doctors worked hard and that their efforts were greatly appreciated by patients. "He seemed very grateful to me," said one doctor, "I assure you." Physicians' testimony notwithstanding, doctors ignored patients, and soldiers continued to languish without medical treatment. Searching the ward for doctors, hoping to find someone to examine the neglected patients with whom he sat, Whitman constantly worried that soldiers had no proper medical attention.[49]

Because Civil War hospitals were always understaffed, neglect was perhaps inevitable. Soldiers, however, often felt that neglect was more than a staffing problem. William E. Vandemark, a wounded soldier and comrade of Whitman, provided his own analysis of this situation: "the doctors here are meen for they have no feeling to a man." Neglect plagued the hospitals, according to the

wounded soldiers, because some doctors and philanthropists were never especially concerned with soldiers as patients. In a letter to his father about the death
of a friend, Edward Edes wrote, "He never received humane treatment from the
docters & I believe they thought no more of his death than they would of a sheep."
One soldier remarked, "The blamed Sanitary & Christian will not help a fellow
unless he has shoulder straps," while a Tennessee Unionist observed in his diary,
"Our Regimental doctor has no more respect for sick soldiers than I would have for
a good dog . . . no not near so much, for if my dog were sick or wounded I would
spend some little time in relieving him." Fiercely criticizing "one head surgeon,
who cares no more for a private than for a dog," Nurse Ropes also thought doctors
showed a notable lack of humane concern for common soldiers.[50]

Part of the problem was nonmalicious ineptitude, what Whitman called
"incompetency" and Private Cox called "incapacity." Faced with a deluge of sick
and wounded soldiers, the nation needed doctors and was often obliged to hire
inexperienced or unqualified physicians. Ropes complained in her diary of a new,
young head surgeon who "was ignorant of hospital routine, ignorant of life outside
of the practice in a country town, in an interior state, a weak man with good
intentions." While many of these doctors hoped to help, their "good intentions" in
no way spared them from the contempt of soldiers, officers, and visitors dismayed
by their incompetence. "[W]ith our present surgeon," wrote E. G. Abbott to his
father in Massachusetts, "I see no prospect of good medical attendance in case of
sickness. He is a jackass—a fool—and an ignorant man—three-quarters of the
sickness could have been prevented by a good physician." Whitman had a more
positive opinion of doctors ("I never ceas'd to find the best men, and the hardest
and most disinterested workers, among the surgeons in the hospitals"), but he also
noted the exceptions, surgeons who were "very incompetent and airish." In
Specimen Days Whitman noted a host of other problems as well:

> serious deficiencies, wastes, sad want of system, in the commissions, contribu-
> tions, and in all the voluntary, and a great part of the governmental nursing,
> edibles, medicines, stores &c. . . . Whatever puffing accounts there may be in the
> papers of the North, this is the actual fact. No thorough previous preparation, no
> system, no foresight, no genius. Always plenty of stores, no doubt, but never
> where they are needed, and never the proper application. Of all harrowing
> experiences, none is greater than that of the days following a heavy battle. Scores,
> hundreds of the noblest men on earth, uncomplaining, lie helpless, mangled,
> faint, alone, and so bleed to death, or die from exhaustion, either actually
> untouch'd at all or merely the laying of them down and leaving them, when there
> ought to be means provided to save them.

It was not a lack of "warm sympathy," but a "sad want of system" that generated this
suffering. Although he remained critical of the callous machinery of the Sanitary
Commission, Whitman here acknowledged what the Sanitarians had preached
from the start of the war—the need for a "system." Nevertheless, he was outraged
that despite humanitarianism's rave press in the North and these organizations'
considerable cache of medical and relief supplies, wounded soldiers died simply

because of some bungling incompetence in the management and distribution of food and medicine.[51]

While problems such as inadequate food, incompetence, and neglect caused usually nonintentional harm (the result of humanitarians' inability to do something), part of the suffering inflicted upon patients by humanitarians was deliberate abuse. Because of the desperate need for staff, hospitals often conscripted patients to work as orderlies, especially the war's black refugees, the contrabands, who were impressed into "a sort of second hand slavery."[52] The "bullying of patients" also included prying "donations" "[b]y hook or crook" from the wounded to fund gifts for doctors and philanthropists and even outright stealing from sick and dying soldiers. Whitman noted that "every body seems to try to pick upon them." And Ropes described in detail the extraordinary physical abuse which patients suffered at the hands of hospital workers, including a steward who "struck a boy with a chisel and put him in the guard house."[53]

In *Embattled Courage,* Linderman describes how a wounded Union soldier thought to be a coward, for intentionally shooting himself in the foot, receives a brutal and excessive amputation of his leg. In this particular historical situation, in this specific cultural context, the operation—though violent and even cruel—was understood to be a lesson, for the wounded soldier and the other soldiers observing, in the iniquity of cowardice and the consequences awaiting the coward. For Linderman, this incident described by Frank Wilkeson, a private from New York, indicates how courage (and, thus, contempt for cowardice) stood at the center of a constellation of Civil War–era values that enabled soldiers to fight in and make meaning of the war.[54] Wilkeson's account might also suggest how humanitarian abuse could emerge from an agent/patient hierarchy that authorized and even encouraged agents like the surgeons to prescribe such hard lessons in the importance of values like courage.

Particularly abusive were white medical officers treating black soldier-patients. White physicians serving in the United States Colored Troops were often underqualified, neglectful, incompetent, and always overworked. Yet, as Joseph T. Glatthaar has argued, the sometimes brutal mistreatment of black patients by white doctors was "inexplicable on any grounds other than racism." A surgeon in Texas "bucked and gagged" a critically ill black soldier for alleged malingering. His patient died the following day. Another doctor kicked a patient who had left his tent to relieve himself. That patient died later the same night. Racism, combined with already difficult working conditions and miserably inadequate medical facilities and provisions, reinforced the power disparity between careproviders and patients. Such a hierarchy was the source of daily abuses as well as the disproportionate mortality suffered by black patients.[55]

While enduring such abuse as well as neglect, incompetence, and lack of food, patients also suffered what Private Cox called "a hundred other meannesses." Among the most annoying of these meannesses was the pity of benevolent volunteers looking to sympathize. An Indiana soldier, William D. F. Landon, having experienced their collective pity, described in detail the "wordy sympathizers" who plagued the hospitals:

the male portion of these "drones" are generally composed of broken-down, short-winded, long-faced, seedy preachers of all denominations. They walk solemnly up and down the wards, between the couches of patient sufferers; first casting their cadaverous looks and ghostly shadow upon all, and then, after a *whispered* consultation with the surgeon of the ward, offer to pray; do so, and retire, without having *smiled* on a single soldier or dropped a word of comfort or cheer. The females . . . go gawking through the wards, peeping into every curtained couch, seldom exchanging a word with the occupant, but (as they invariably "hunt in couples") giving vent to their pent up "pheelinks" in heart-rending (?) outbursts of "Oh, my Savior!" "Phoebe, do look here!" "Only see what a horrid wound!" "Goodness, gracious, how terrible war is!" "my! my!! my!!! Oh, let's go—I can't stand it any longer!" And as they near the door, perhaps these dear creatures will wind up with an audible—"Heavens! what a smell! Worse than fried onions!"[56]

While his satirical caricature of these do-gooders presumably aimed to adjust the power imbalance between "gawking" agents and silent patients, Landon also showed how humiliating sympathy could be. Though "wordy" (they drone on with prayers, whisper with surgeons, and exclaim in astonishment at all the hospital's sights and smells), these "sympathizers" avoided talking with patients. The lack of dialogue created a distance that sustained the typically coercive relation between the silent patients and the peering agents who, instead of talking with and listening to the wounded, objectified them, turned them into things to be looked at. Landon's language presented these humanitarians as voyeurs who cast cadaverous looks and gawked and peeped and begged their hunting partners to look upon and see and take lurid pleasure in the horrid wounds. In his letter, Landon attempted to turn the voyeurs into objects of mocking representation; but in the hospital, these gazes functioned as reminders of the structure of authority that subdued patients.

Such voyeurism was only one of "a hundred other meannesses." In fact, "[e]verything seems to be done to aggravate the wounded," wrote Hancock from a hospital at Gettysburg. Still, not all humanitarians overlooked that oppression. The multitude of "sins committed upon soldiers and contrabands" infuriated Hancock, just as the "laziness, heartlessness, gouging, and incompetency" that seemed "more or less prevalent" in the hospitals angered Whitman. Patients also understood, perhaps most acutely, the ways in which their benefactors ignored, mistreated, controlled, abused, and spoke for them. "[T]he Relief association may be a verry nice thing, *but I cant see it,*" wrote the recovering Lewis Brown to Whitman.[57]

While corresponding with and talking intimately with wounded soldiers like Brown, Whitman also failed to see the merit of such organizations. In an 1864 letter to his mother, Whitman wrote:

I feel lately as though I must have some intermission, I feel well & hearty enough, & was never better, but my feelings are kept in a painful condition a great part of the time—things get worse & worse, as to the amount & sufferings of the sick, & as I have said before, those who have to do with them are getting more & more

callous & indifferent—Mother, when I see the common soldiers, what they go
through, & how every body seems to try to pick upon them, & what humbug
there is over them every how, even the dying soldier's money stolen from his body
by some scoundrel attendant, or from some sick ones, even from under his head,
which is a common thing—& then the agony I see every day, I get almost
frightened at the world.[58]

Listening to soldiers like Brown who couldn't see how humanitarians were
helping, watching humanitarians who were growing "more & more callous &
indifferent," Whitman began to actively question Civil War humanitarianism. The
agony produced daily by the war stimulated proliferation and innovation in
humanitarian discourses and practices; yet the new attempts at directing benevolence like their predecessors often created their own agonies. Patients and self-
critical humanitarians like Whitman were never asking for an end to humanitarianism; they did not want the wounded to be left alone on the battlefield or ignored
in the hospital. They did, however, yearn for a different kind of humanitarianism,
one less distressing to patients and less controlling in its aims. Despite the diversity
and innovation within Civil War humanitarianism, it seemed that "action of a kind
hitherto unknown" was still required and that a less coercive humanitarian project
would have to start not with biblical tracts or plans for centralizing humanitarian
authority but with a reconsideration of the position of the patient.

Being a Nurse, Being a Patient

Soon after her arrival at Hurly-burly House, Alcott's Tribulation Periwinkle
realizes that the suffering produced by this war would require a new kind of
humanitarian action. In *Hospital Sketches* Trib wants "something to do" (9),
presumably something to feed her penchant for "ghastliness" (32). But, when she
first encounters the wounded from Fredericksburg and the "sight of several
stretchers, each with its legless, armless, or desperately wounded occupant" (34),
Nurse Periwinkle gets more ghastliness than she bargained for: "my ardor experienced a sudden chill, and I indulged in a most unpatriotic wish that I was safe at
home again" (32–33). While astonishment was hardly an unusual first reaction to
Civil War casualties (medical professionals like Drs. Detmold and Vanderpool
were paralyzed by their first encounter with crowds of war wounded), Trib's
"sudden chill" is only her initial realization that the suffering is far beyond what she
imagined. Moreover, the care she witnesses is not exactly what she expects either.
She speaks with outrage, for example, at the rather common practice of compelling patients to work as hospital attendants (74). Mentioning to her publisher,
James Redpath, some other "samples of humbug which so disgust Nurse P.," Alcott
the author complained about "the sanctified nurse who sung hymns & prayed
violently while stealing the men's watches and money" as well as "the much
esteemed lady whose devout countenance was abominated by the boys though the
Chaplain approved of her till it was found that her exhortations ceased when the
patients had made their wills in her favor."[59]

Yet, more than her anger at the often abusive ways of Civil War benevolence, it is Trib's experience as a patient that enables her to see the gap separating patients from careproviders; and it is this experience that prompts her to begin imagining an eccentric humanitarianism. In chapter 5 of *Hospital Sketches*, Nurse Periwinkle grows sick and joins the hospital's "bouquet of patients"(66). As a patient she never endures intentional abuse. She is never forced to work while ill; doctors and nurses do not generally overlook her; no surgeon saws off her leg to teach her a lesson about courage; no one ever clobbers her with a chisel. In fact, she says, "Every one was very kind" (83). While overworked nurses and attendants try to make her comfortable during her painful and fatiguing illness, the doctors, while not neglectful or intentionally mean, do apparently make the situation worse. In Trib's words:

> The doctors paid daily visits, tapped at my lungs to see if pneumonia was within, left doses without names, and went away, leaving me as ignorant, and much more uncomfortable than when they came. Hours began to get confused; people looked odd; queer faces haunted the room, and the nights were one long fight with weariness and pain. Letters from home grew anxious; the doctors lifted their eyebrows, and nodded ominously. (83)

Although Alcott never accused these doctors of deliberate mistreatment, the physicians at the Union Hotel Hospital did in fact exacerbate physiologically Alcott's worsening health. Diagnosing her illness as a case of typhoid pneumonia, they prescribed ever-increasing doses of calomel, a mercury-laden medicine used to treat a variety of ailments. While such emetics were common in eighteenth- and nineteenth-century medical practices (which advised "heroic" purgings of the body to starve diseases), calomel debilitated numerous patients like Alcott who developed nasty cases of mercury poisoning that led to hair loss, swollen tongues, weakness, pain, restlessness, delirium, and other disorders. Alcott suffered through the remainder of her life with an illness that sapped her energy and slowly destroyed her body.[60]

But Tribulation Periwinkle never makes any direct connection between the "doses without names" and the delirium, nightmares, confusion, weakness, and hair loss that followed. She doesn't imagine that the cure is debilitating her faster than the disease, and she generally admires the doctors she knows. Still, their bedside manner disturbs Trib. Her doctors prescribe medicines without telling her what they contain, what they do, or even what they are called. The facial expressions of physicians seem knowing, superior, ominous; yet the doctors leave her "ignorant," never informing her of her condition or treatment. Their visits actually make Trib "much more uncomfortable"—physiologically using "doses without names" (calomel), and psychologically or emotionally by treating her as a patient. Following medical convention, they assume that she is helpless, childlike, ignorant, and therefore unable to understand her illness, speak for herself, or make decisions for herself. Finally, without the patient's consent, the hospital staff peremptorily sends for her father to escort her back to Massachusetts. Although Trib dutifully answers "Yes, father" to his order to "Come home" (84), Alcott recorded a somewhat different response in her journal:

> Was amazed to see father enter my room that morning, having been telegraphed
> to by order of Mrs Ropes without asking leave. I was very ~~mad~~ angry at first,
> though glad to see him.[61]

However cheered she was by her father's visit, Alcott was also peeved by his and
Hannah Ropes's conspiring to return her to Concord; she was mad that no one
asked her about her own wishes; she was angry about being treated like a patient.

But Alcott, like Tribulation Periwinkle or Jo March, tried eventually to focus
on the positive features of a bad episode. She wrote in her journal:

> I hope . . . that the Washington experience may do me lasting good. To go very
> near death teaches one to value life, & this winter will always be a very
> memorable one to me.[62]

And Trib, of course, also puts an affirmative spin on the ordeal:

> I shall never regret the going, though a sharp tussle with typhoid, ten dollars, and
> a wig, are all the visible results of the experiment; for one may live and learn
> much in a month. A good fit of illness proves the value of health; real danger tries
> one's mettle; and self-sacrifice sweetens character. . . . though a hospital is a
> rough school, its lessons are both stern and salutary. (84)

According to these passages, a formidable and difficult situation is also an
opportunity to learn.

By enduring the ordeal of being a patient, Trib learns in *Hospital Sketches* how
to be a nurse, or how better to be a nurse. While ill, Trib says:

> I was learning that one of the best methods of fitting oneself to be a nurse in a
> hospital, is to be a patient there. For then only can one wholly realize what the
> men suffer and sigh for; how acts of kindness touch and win; how much or little
> we are to those about us. (83)

Being a patient becomes for Trib a way to learn how to be a careprovider, since *only*
by experiencing the suffering of a patient can anyone understand what patients
feel or how they see their worlds. This experientially based identification with
patients is the beginning of a patient-centered approach to humanitarian care. By
the end of *Hospital Sketches,* being a nurse requires more than a yearning to do
something or a sympathy constructed from good intentions. Being a fit, capable
humanitarian agent means remembering what it feels like to suffer and knowing
how patients might perceive their situations and their helpers.

Thus, even while protesting the conscription of patients into service as
hospital attendants, *Hospital Sketches* argues that former patients make the best
careproviders. What she objects to is the coercive manner in which patients were
forced into hospital work; she never doubts the ability of patients to become
understanding careproviders. Indeed, the transformation of patients into agents
seems an indispensable component of this less coercive humanitarian care. In texts
written after her nursing experience, Alcott's humanitarian characters are often
former patients. In *Work* (1873), Christie Devon explains her qualifications to Mrs.

Carrol, "a stately woman" who wants to hire a nurse-companion for her infirm daughter, by telling her:

> I think I can promise to be patient, willing, and cheerful. My own experience of illness has taught me how to sympathize with others and love to lighten pain.[63]

Likewise, in "A Hospital Christmas" (1864), the altruistic Big Ben, a sympathetic and diligent humanitarian agent working in a crowd of growlers and whiners, is an ex-patient turned hospital attendant. A creator and admirer of multiply gendered heroes (like the "boyish" Jo March of *Little Women* [1868] and the feminized John from *Hospital Sketches* who kisses tenderly as a woman [63]), Alcott gives Big Ben the attributes of her humanitarian ideal: "Patient, strong, and tender, he seemed to combine many of the best traits of both man and woman."[64] The widespread use of soldiers as attendants was a more or less spontaneous response to the unanticipated magnitude of suffering caused by the Civil War, an improvised attempt to find a new type of humanitarian action suited to a new situation. Alcott saw the coercive nature of this impressment and entered her "protest against employing convalescents as attendants" (74). But, she also saw the potential: patients helping patients.

Beyond Sympathetic Identification

A compassionate volunteer like Big Ben and a tender kisser like John, Whitman shared Alcott's commitment to a patient-centered caring praxis founded on sympathetic identification with the sufferer. When he began his work in the hospitals, Whitman had never been critically ill, wounded, or hospitalized. He hadn't yet experienced being a patient, the important foundation of Alcott's approach, although he would later become seriously ill. In the spring of 1864 Whitman was forced to return to Brooklyn after, as he told Lewis Brown, "having too deeply imbibed poison into my system from the hospitals." A contemporary diagnosis of his symptoms would also suggest a hospital-related sickness, probably a combination of hypertension, post-traumatic stress disorder, and (like Alcott) mercury poisoning from calomel treatments. Like Alcott, Whitman would never quite recover from his wartime sickness.[65]

Yet, before suffering as a sick patient, Whitman had tried to imagine and practice a patient-centered humanitarianism. This humanitarian praxis was not based on lived experience, but on a critical appraisal of conventional humanitarianism and on altruizm, the intense sympathetic identification that required an imaginative transformation of oneself into another.

Whitman's experience in the Civil War hospitals made him deeply and openly critical of the arrogance, negligence, and indifference that could, at times, attend conventional humanitarianism. He publicly criticized benevolent organizations, editorializing in the *New York Times* against the incompetence, capriciousness, and needlessly strict discipline of these groups. Privately, he felt disgust, telling his mother that he was "sick of them all," especially the Sanitary Commission. While he liked the more personable Christian Commissioners, Whitman could never approve of their proselytizing. Indeed, Whitman's willingness to encourage soldiers in their religious hopes (when asked, he read to them from the Bible and talked to them about their beliefs) and his concomitant refusal to attach religious tutelage to his offer of humanitarian care made him the antithesis of dogmatic and insistent religious philanthropists like Rev. Lyle. He disdained attempts to use humanitarian assistance as a means for advocating religious beliefs. Undoubtedly the coercive and hierarchical nature of conventional humanitarianism contradicted his own democratic aspirations for the United States. Moreover, his hospital visits with soldiers profoundly shaped his particular view of the humanitarian enterprise. As a volunteer, Whitman devoted his time to soldier-patients, distributing gifts, writing letters for them, reading to them, perhaps washing and dressing the wound of a particularly admiring or beloved soldier, but mostly just sitting and talking with them. While talking with patients and listening to their take on humanitarianism or perusing their opinions in the letters they sent him, Whitman saw humanitarianism from the perspective of those who were being helped and hurt by it. His most powerful motivation for engaging in this type of benevolent work was his attraction to and affection for these young men, and Whitman accepted their perceptions, rather than those of bourgeois philanthropists. Instead of conforming to one of the dominant philanthropic models, Whitman pursued an eccentric course, becoming what he called "a hospital missionary after my own style," a style informed by the experiences and perspectives of patients.[66]

But Whitman's patient-centered humanitarianism pushed beyond an intellectual appreciation for the soldiers' views; it also entailed altruizm. Writing about his hospital visits to his "darlings & gossips" in New York, he mentioned his attempts to imagine what it felt like to be one of the thousands of soldiers "languishing" in the Washington hospitals: "I sometimes put myself in fancy in the cot, with typhoid, or under the knife." For years, in fact, using the transformative possibilities and identificatory plentitude associated with paradigmatic substitution (metaphor) in poetic language, Whitman had spoken with awesome confidence in such expanded sympathies. In "Song of Myself" the speaker declares, "I do not ask the wounded person how he feels, I myself become the wounded person." Though not yet a patient himself, he did strive to become "in fancy" the wounded person. Such altruizm intensified his determination to criticize coercive humanitarianism and deepened his commitment to an eccentric, patient-centered care.[67]

In *Drum-Taps* (1865) Whitman tried to represent this patient-centered humanitarian praxis in verse. Throughout the second half of the war, he had intended to publish a book about his observations of and work in the military hospitals, "something," he told Alcott's publisher James Redpath, "considerably beyond mere hospital sketches." Thinking it would "do good to make the public more familiar with the interiors of these establishments," with the "sights seen day after day in the Hospitals," Whitman wanted to present his case for the reform of humanitarian-medical care: "I have much to say of the hospitals, the immense national hospitals—in them too most radical changes of premises are demanded."

Although he never had an opportunity during the war to publish this book about the "radical changes" needed (Redpath thought it would cost too much), he did voice his concerns in letters and newspaper articles.[68] And in the condensed poetic language of "The Dresser," later called "The Wound-Dresser," he dramatized the patient-centered caring praxis that he thought the situation demanded. But, in illustrating this style of benevolent work, Whitman came face to face with the difficulties of a humanitarianism built on altruizm.

"The Dresser" is in many ways Whitman's ideal humanitarian—tender, compassionate, steady, devoted to his patients. This humanitarian's patient-centered approach to care emerges gradually during the first half of the poem. When asked in stanza 1 about his memories of the war ("What stays with you latest and deepest?"), the poem's speaker declines the chance to talk about his adventures as a soldier and instead remembers "my wounded," describing his cleaning and dressing of their injuries.[69] Even though the wounds are "so sickening, so offensive" and his chores "sad" and difficult, the speaker perseveres in this work for his soldiers: "Straight and swift to my wounded I go. . . . I onward go. . . . On, on I go. . . . I am faithful, I do not give out." The repeated insistence on going forward and not giving out suggest the physically and emotionally demanding nature of his job. With his "hinged knees and steady hand," the dresser performs his work in a manner that is outwardly mechanical, dispassionate, and methodical: he moves carefully and calculatedly from patient to patient ("not one do I miss"); and though each pull and each scrub causes pain ("the pangs are sharp, yet unavoidable"), he changes their bandages without external show of feeling. Yet this unemotional bedside manner while dressing wounds is not the cold, scientific (Whitman would say "disagreeable") professionalism of a Sanitarian, but rather, like the "pangs" of the injured, a "sharp, yet unavoidable" necessity—a work-related demand that forces him to mask his ardent love for these young men and makes that love all the more poignant. "These and more I dress with impassive hand," says the speaker, "(yet deep in my breast a fire, a burning flame.)" Even though his affection is restrained when his "impassive hand" changes bandages, the dresser expresses his loving devotion with a "soothing hand," just as his wounded express their love with embraces and kisses:

> The hurt and wounded I pacify with soothing hand,
> I sit by the restless all the dark night—some are so young;
> Some suffer so much—I recall the experience sweet and sad;
> (Many a soldier's loving arms about this neck have cross'd and rested,
> Many a soldier's kiss dwells on these bearded lips.)

Neither interest in the religious salvation of his patients nor philanthropic selflessness motivate this speaker. Instead, he cares for these soldiers because he loves them and they return that love.[70] Thus, it is not only an appreciation of patients' concerns nor only a profound identification with these young men that drives the patient-centered, eccentric, a-institutional benevolence represented in "The Dresser." It's also love.

Which is not to say that intense sympathetic identification plays no role in this poem's humanitarianism. As he moves among the cots, the wound-dresser and a patient exchange a look:

> One turns to me his appealing eyes—(poor boy! I never knew you,
> Yet I think I could not refuse this moment to die for you, if that would save you.)

The speaker's sympathy is conspicuous; he would altruize (transform himself into another person) and die in the patient's place, "if that would save you." Yet, in striking contrast to the humanitarian voice in "Song of Myself," which confidently and effortlessly declares its altruizm, the speaker of these lines cannot altruize, cannot put himself in the place of the patient (despite his willingness to do so), cannot, it seems, ultimately help the soldier. Sympathetic identification, even in its most intense form, fails this humanitarian threading his way among the cots.

Like his wound-dresser, Whitman felt an intense personal anguish at confronting the limits of such sympathetic identification. Although he understood early during the war that altruizm was an incomplete response to this suffering, Whitman was nonetheless deeply distressed by the inadequacy of such sympathy and by the feelings of powerlessness that such a realization stirred within him. As he told his mother, "To see such things & not be able to help them is awful—I feel almost ashamed of being so well & whole." He described the inability to help (that is, extend sympathy in a way that reduces suffering) as "awful" and characterized the failure of altruizm in terms of shame—a shame generated by the gap between the injured and suffering bodies and his own "well & whole" body.[71]

Moreover, in the figurative language of "The Dresser" and in its representation of patients, Whitman embodies this failure. Whereas the altruizm in "Song of Myself" depends upon the fullness often associated with metaphor (the paradigmatic substitution of one thing for another, the poet becomes the wounded person), the figurative language of "The Dresser" is staggeringly metonymic, suggesting fragmentation and indeed the impossibility of any fullness. In "The Dresser," readers cannot readily find any wounded *person* with whom to identify or altruize. Instead, among the rows of cots, we face: "The crush'd head," the "poor crazed hand," "The neck," "the stump of the arm," "the perforated shoulder," "the foot with the bullet wound," "The fractur'd thigh, the knee, the wound in the abdomen." As Kerry Larson has noted, in the poem's "gothic magnification of detail" we do not meet "fallen sons and comrades" but instead a litany of injured body parts.[72]

While modeling the difficulty of identifying one's own experience (the reader's or humanitarian's) with the suffering of the wounded, this syntagmatic substitution of wound for person also plays a key role in Whitman's representation of patients. Metonymy's linguistic function is reduction, and in "The Dresser" patients are known by and reduced to their wounds.[73] This metonymic representation divests patients of their personhood in the poem. Whitman's depiction of patients as silent also suggests a truncation of their language, identity, and power. The dying patient (for whom the empathetic, altruizing speaker would die) cannot express his concerns or even talk, but instead can only turn "his appealing eyes" mutely toward the wound-dresser. The patient's *"appealing* eyes" (like "the mute appealing look" in his "The Great Army of the Sick" article) implies a type of semiotic recourse; and the wound-dresser's skill at reading faces, his careful attention to patients and their body language, enables him to recognize this attempt to communicate. Still, much to the poet's dismay, the suffering patient of "The Dresser," like the patient in conventional humanitarian discourse, has no voice.

Hence, "The Dresser" both represents a humanitarian caring praxis founded on sympathetic identification and recognizes and repeats the limits and failures of such a humanitarianism. Readers encounter a speaker who ardently wishes to altruize, but also the impossibility of altruizm. Whitman embodies in the wound-dresser an extraordinary sympathy for patients, and then reveals the enfeebled nature of such sympathy in the face of profound, shattering, and indescribable pain. No matter how sincere or heartfelt the intentions, this sympathy can neither save patients from death nor restore their fragmented, reduced bodies to whole-ness. This altruizing, patient-centered care neither empowers patients nor gives them a voice.

In "A March in the Ranks Hard-Prest, and the Road Unknown," Whitman further explores the relative meaninglessness and impotence of individual acts of other-directed compassion.[74] The poem begins in "darkness" along a "road un-known," where there is "A march in the ranks hard-prest." There are yet no persons who do the marching—just a march. In fact much of the action in this poem, especially at the opening and closing of the poem, occurs without human agency intending, willing, or directing the action. There is no army officer who gives orders, but instead we hear only about "the orders given." The poem closes with these lines:

> . . . and I speed forth to the darkness,
> Resuming, marching, ever in darkness marching, on in the ranks,
> The unknown road still marching.

The speaker begins "marching," but is quickly swallowed up into the "darkness marching." Who is performing the action now? The soldier-speaker (a human agent)? Or the darkness (an impersonal and unknown force)? Finally, the speaker seems to have vanished, leaving readers with "The unknown road still marching." Whitman uses these dislocated participles to suggest that in this unknown darkness actions like "marching" happen apart from the will or control of the human agents in the poem.

With this implied powerlessness framing the poem, the speaker comes upon "an impromptu hospital" inside a church filled with crowds of undescribed wounded. Whereas metonymic description in "The Dresser" tends to strip patients of personal identity, the lack of description in "A March in the Ranks" obstructs seeing or knowing the wounded as persons, as individuals, as humans with whom one could identify and sympathize. They become instead abstract, depersonalized "groups of forms" or "Faces, varieties, postures beyond description" or "the crowd of the bloody forms." Whitman had originally written "crowd of the bloody forms of soldiers," but deleted the last prepositional phrase to emphasize the abstract and impersonal "forms" rather than bring any attention to the wounded as "soldiers"— that is, as persons.[75] Amid these "vaguely" seen "crowds," the speaker recognizes "distinctly" one person and commits a humanitarian act. Writes Whitman:

> At my feet more distinctly, a soldier, a mere lad, in danger of bleeding to death,
>   (he is shot in the abdomen;)
> I staunch the blood temporarily, (the youngster's face is white as a lily).

Perhaps identifying with this fellow soldier, the speaker attempts to help. Yet, even though "staunch," an irregular spelling of the homophonic verb "stanch," suggests firmness and lasting devotion, the speaker's act is only momentary and ultimately futile.[76] As readers later learn in the brief line and a half in which the patient mutely responds, the speaker's compassionate gesture cannot help, save, or rescue this "mere lad." The speaker says, "I bend to the dying lad—his eyes open—a half-smile gives he me; / Then the eyes close, calmly close." The patient's dying expression—an ambiguous "half-smile" that suggests gratitude, perhaps comfort at the sight of a comrade caring for him, but also relief at the approach of death and the end of suffering—brings together momentarily the patient and agent, the wounded lad and the speaker, just as the subject and object of the phrase are brought side by side in the rhymed pair "he me." Still, as the soldier closes his eyes in death, the speaker's humanitarian act is finally unavailing, inconsequential, despite his other-directed compassion and obvious sympathy.

Timothy Sweet has used a discussion of this poem to illustrate how Whitman "thematizes the potential unrepresentability of the war." For Sweet, "the scene of 'postures beyond description' . . . threatens the possibility of representation."[77] While this is undoubtedly, perhaps even tautologically, true, a scene of suffering beyond description produces more than a breakdown in representation. In "A March in the Ranks" and in Cornelia Hancock's attempt to describe the church-hospital packed with wounded after Gettysburg—examples that not only evoke similar settings but also emphasize the unrepresentable nature of the suffering witnessed—humanitarian action itself fails. In Hancock's account, the two doctors, paralyzed with horror, are unable to act. In Whitman's poem, the soldier-speaker acts but only in vain: the humanitarian action has no material benefit or consequence for the patient. While the crisis in representation and the crisis in action are not unrelated, and while it is certainly alarming to imagine pain so widespread and so intense that it devastates the linguistic abilities of patients as well as humanitarian agents as well as poets, suffering that renders all previously conceived humanitarian action useless is also deeply, deeply harrowing.

It is not, however, only suffering in itself or by itself that produces the failure in "A March in the Ranks." The context in which suffering and humanitarian care happen is also very important. Echoing the individual speaker-soldier's temporary emergence from "the ranks hard-prest," this poem is about the circumstances that press in around, determine, and limit individual acts. The humanitarian's act (lines 11 and 12) and the patient's response (lines 22 and 23a) are submerged within a larger humanitarian scene, the hospital (lines 7–23a), which is situated inside a church (a remnant of another benevolent institution). The entire scene is in turn framed by the army marching (lines 1–6 and 23b–25), an army which emerges from the darkness and returns to the darkness. The darkness represents the war, the origin and purpose of the army and the broader context in which suffering is created and humanitarian care needed. Whitman's recognition of the failure of humanitarianism is not condemnation of humanitarianism in itself. Using shadows and light, he sketches where he sees glimmers of hope: the opening and closing of the poem are engulfed in darkness; the hospital is "dim-lighted," and thus a partial relief from the darkness; and the humanitarian act itself is illuminated at least well enough to permit the speaker to see the young man's face, his smile, and his eyes. The blame for this suffering and this failure of humanitarian action lies ultimately within the larger context, the darkness and the war. Eventually swallowing the entire scene into darkness, war and the power relations that shape war render this speaker's act of compassion useless. Although Whitman offers his culture no analysis of that "darkness" in "A March in the Ranks," he does encourage readers to look beyond humanitarianism and to locate the limits and failures of benevolence in the social-political contexts that determine suffering and compassion.

Patients and Power

In her recently rediscovered "A Nurse's Story" (1865–66), an anonymously published thriller written during the year of the war's end and serialized in *Frank Leslie's Chimney Corner,* Alcott also acknowledges that sympathetic identification with or sympathetic regard for patients is an inadequate remedy to the failures and wrongs in humanitarianism.[78] But, rather than look to the broader social-political contexts, she explores the structure of the caring relationship itself, particularly the power disparity between patients and agents. In this story told by Kate Snow, a gentle and understanding nurse who cares for the insane Elinor Carruth and later joins forces with Dr. Harry Carruth (hear "careth") to treat other "lunatics," Alcott shows us that humanitarian care—no matter how altruistic or sympathetic or compassionate—is first of all a practice of power.

Although Madeleine B. Stern has pointed to Alcott's pre–Civil War experience nursing a temporarily insane friend as "the factual basis" for this thriller, the most troubling and absorbing concerns in "A Nurse's Story" are not antebellum, nor are they primarily based on Alcott's experiences with this unnamed young friend in 1860.[79] The language of "A Nurse's Story" identifies it as a postwar text. While the story is never about soldiers or fighting battles, the text erupts with the diction of war and peacemaking: we read of taking prisoners, standing guard, routing the enemy, leaving the field, signing a truce, ratifying the peace treaty, and so on (see 59, 93). In chapter 7, to his vanquished half brother, Robert Steele, who is filled with "rebellious emotion," the victorious and "conciliatory" Harry says in his kindest reconstruction rhetoric: "Here's my hand, brother; do not let us be enemies" (104–105).

While the text's language incorporates the discourses surrounding the nation's internecine struggle and its attempts at reconciliation, Alcott makes rather deliberate use of her personal Civil War and postwar experiences in the creation of this postbellum serial. Stern's linking this thriller to Alcott's 1860 nursing experience is plausible enough, but such an experience is only one of the several memories and events in Alcott's life that find themselves replayed in this tale. Alcott's work in the Union Hotel Hospital in 1862–63 undoubtedly shaped her thinking about nursing, about how to control and soothe patients and how to represent nurses and their patients. Moreover, in 1865, the year she wrote "A Nurse's Story," Alcott worked as a private nurse for Carrie Pratt, her sister-in-law, and later for Anna Weld, the daughter of a Boston shipping merchant, and translated these experiences into material for a story. Like Elinor in "A Nurse's Story," Anna Weld was a "fidgety," melancholic "nervous invalid" and, for Alcott, a rather difficult patient to control: "hers is a very hard case to manage & needs the patience & wisdom of an angel."[80]

Still, Alcott's autobiographical sources for "A Nurse's Story" were not limited to these *nursing* experiences. Just as *Hospital Sketches* narrates Tribulation Periwinkle's (Alcott's) adventures as a nurse and then a patient, "A Nurse's Story" draws also from Alcott's experiences *as a patient*. In chapter 1, for example, Kate Snow sedates the restless Elinor by laying hands on the patient, staring at her with fixed eyes, and then magnetizing her. Counting hypnosis among her nursing "powers," Kate declares, "I magnetized her, and she will sleep for hours, unless I awake her" (39). Alcott the nurse never used hypnosis or magnetism as therapy; she never "magnetized" (hypnotized) John of *Hospital Sketches,* Carrie Pratt, Anna Weld, or any of her other patients. Alcott *the patient,* on the other hand, did have experience with such nursing remedies. During Alcott's 1863 bout with mercury poisoning and pneumonia, a Concord mesmerist named Mrs. Bliss visited the Alcott household, laid hands on the patient, and "magnetized" her.[81] My point is not simply that Alcott introduced autobiographical elements into her fiction, but rather that portions or episodes of Alcott's experiences as a nurse *and as a patient* are reconstructed and transformed in the intertwined lives of Kate Snow *and* Elinor Carruth. Readers hear the author's autobiographical voice in the nurse's story and in the patient's story.[82]

This tale's gothic style also marks it as a patient's story. Critics have linked Alcott's anonymously or pseudonymously published sensation stories to the fevered dreams that she endured during her 1863 tussle with mercury poisoning and pneumonia, to, as Alcott put it, "the strange fancies that haunted me." According to these critics, her ordeal as a patient provided her with "motifs," themes, characters, settings, "emblems," and images for dozens of thrillers like "A Nurse's Story"—these expressions of the dark side of her "double literary life."[83] While she weaves the patient's nightmares into her sensation fiction, Alcott also writes about the humanitarian's sympathy: Kate Snow is a gentle, well-intentioned nurse who listens sympathetically and cares deeply for those whom she pities.

Never completely a moralizing domestic story nor only "a blood & thunder tale" of "the lurid style," "A Nurse's Story" draws from both parts of Alcott's double literary life, making use of humanitarian rhetoric and a sensational style tied to her own nightmares as a patient. "A Nurse's Story" is about being the sympathetic humanitarian and fearing the sympathetic humanitarian. It explores the desire to control and the fear of being controlled. In the process, Alcott reveals the limits of humanitarianism, showing readers something to be scared of.[84]

Dramatizing various struggles for control, "A Nurse's Story" is a story about power. Early in the serial, Mrs. Carruth (the mother of Elinor, Harry, Amy, and Augustine) hires Kate as a nurse because of her ability to control the mentally ill. Mrs. Carruth tells Kate, "I learned from Mrs. Hamilton that you have had some experience in the care of the insane, and have peculiar power over them" (31). When explaining to Elinor her reasons for becoming a nurse, Kate herself refers to this "peculiar power" over the insane: "I preferred this, for I like to nurse the sick, because I find I have the power of making them comfortable" (35). While she does like to nurse the sick, Kate also seems to quietly enjoy power for its own sake, smiling "involuntarily" at thoughts of her own power (89).

Examples of this power are scattered throughout the tale. When the mad Elinor in a fit of desperate anxiety becomes "wild," Kate subdues her with a benevolent power, explaining:

> Many women would have trembled and called for help, I should have done so had not pity conquered fear; I forgot myself, I only thought of this poor girl so hopeless, helpless, and afflicted; I went to her and put my arms about her as tenderly as if she had been my sister; I did not speak, but held her close, feeling that I could control her by gentleness alone. (45)

Controlling Elinor "by gentleness alone," Kate is, according to this self-description, a sympathetic and self-sacrificing nurse, a benevolent user of her power over the insane patient. In Kate's humanitarian ethic, "if you have power use it magnanimously" (72). And, if readers accept her as reliable narrator, Kate is magnanimous in the exercise of humanitarian power. With a calm and solicitous demeanor, she is full of pity and sympathy for those who are weak, ill, and in pain. Offering her support whenever and wherever it is needed, Kate "helps" not only Elinor but also importantly Harry, Mrs. Carruth, and even the tale's villain, the "all-powerful" (54) Robert Steele. Selflessly devoted to her patients, Kate listens to them and tries to make them comfortable and secure, saying "it makes me glad to do my best for those who need all the help and tenderness their fellow beings can bestow upon them" (31). Such benevolence earns her the warm esteem of patients like Elinor, who declares, "You are a good nurse, Kate" (37).

To calm "insane" patients, Kate calls upon other powers. She hypnotizes them (39), sings to them (38), and tells stories (46). At times she successfully persuades them to behave in accordance with societal standards: expecting patients to "behave with propriety" is for Kate a compelling way to win the "obedience" of patients (35). "You are very kind," says the increasingly docile Elinor, "and I'll try to prove my gratitude by being quiet and obedient" (36).

Kate's ability to read faces and expressions is a key source of her power as a humanitarian. "I am quick at reading faces," Kate tells her readers (30). Like Whitman's wound-dresser who reads the "appealing eyes" of the speechless patient, Kate reads and interprets carefully the eyes, faces, looks, and expressions of her patients. She diagnoses Elinor's "wild and woeful" nature by looking into her eyes (34). When Elinor wants to enlist Kate's help in stopping the wedding of Amy Carruth who might then bequeath the family's hereditary madness to a new generation, Kate listens carefully to Elinor's imploring eyes. "Her eyes pleaded more eloquently than her tongue," says Kate as she consents to help her beloved patient (63). Examining the eyes and faces of other characters as well, Kate peeks into their souls and ascertains at a glance, for example, Mrs. Carruth's melancholy (30) or Amy's "cold, shallow, selfish nature" (47). Yet, in her struggle to free the Carruths from Steele's sway over the family, she demonstrates most convincingly the formidable power of her expertise in reading expressions. By paying careful attention to his eyes, Kate knows when Steele is angry (51), sincere (73), or in love (71, 73, 94–95). Eventually she uses the knowledge of Steele's love for her—plus some information obtained accidentally and duplicitously from Marie Grahn, Steele's slighted former love—to dupe him and to release the Carruths from their fear of Steele. "I did deceive you for a day, that these injured people might obtain the means of righting themselves," Kate admits to the conquered Steele. "Chance put this power into my hands, and I freely used it" (104).

Kate joins her talent for reading faces with a cautious guarding of her own face. Like the voyeuristic humanitarians whom William Landon described, Kate delights in and derives power from looking without being looked at. Remarkably aware of the ways in which her eyes and expressions might unconsciously disclose her inner thoughts and feelings, Kate always knows when her own face is being read by another: "A question rose to my lips but did not pass them, yet my face must have betrayed me" (43; see also 58, 95). When she does allow her face to be studied for silent clues—when, for example, she permits Mrs. Carruth, a skilled reader of faces (see 90), to scan her countenance—Kate looks back. "[H]er eyes searched my face with a wistfulness that was pathetic" (79), says Kate, demonstrating that although Mrs. Carruth's eyes are doing the searching in this sentence, Kate is the one reading expressions for their unspoken import and observing Mrs. Carruth's silent "wistfulness." At other instances, when the success of her task depends on cloaking her thoughts, feelings, or identity, Kate carefully shields her face from any would-be interpreter. While trying to learn more about the mysterious Steele, Kate finds herself a bit captivated. She remarks, "It was impossible to resist the charm of his manners and conversation, when he chose to exert their fascination; but while I enjoyed this, I guarded my own face and words, and studied him with daily increasing interest" (54). Gratified by looking ("[I] found a curious pleasure in watching him" [66]) but aware that her attraction to him might make her vulnerable, an open book, Kate hides her own face while continuing to examine his. Indeed Steele is quite conscious that her face is both enchanting and deceiving, telling her that she has "a face that would beguile a saint" (70). Elsewhere, while talking to an inquisitive Mrs. Carruth, Kate uses a veil to conceal her blushing attraction to Steele (81); and again a veiled Kate exploits her hidden face to gather secrets from Marie (83–87). In the penultimate chapter, after Steele confesses his wrongs and sincerely declares his love, Kate—feeling slightly shamed by her betrayal of Steele—again hides her expression from "the steady fire of the eyes fast fixed on mine." Not yet able to admit her guile, Kate admits to readers, "Words deserted me, and I covered up my face" (103).

This penchant for looking without being looked at is wedded to Kate's final source of power: deception. Deception and power are invariably fused in Alcott's sensation fiction. Moreover, as Ann Douglas has argued, Alcott often treats deception as a form of women's power. According to Douglas:

> For Louisa May Alcott, deception can be a means for women to infiltrate a closed world and get some of what they want from it. And, if nothing else, deception allows women to manipulate and make excitingly perilous their one culturally sanctioned area of expertise: the creation and display of emotion.[85]

In "A Nurse's Story," both Kate and the male villain, Steele, practice deceit, but the heroine's keen intellect allows her to outwit, outdeceive, and ultimately subdue her foe. Candid about her willingness to use deceit, Kate tells Mrs. Carruth: "I will feign what I do not feel, to accomplish my purpose. . . . Strategy must be met by strategy, and for your sakes, I will stoop to a brief deceit" (89). Although she calls such methods "distasteful" (89) and feels "a guilty sense of treachery" while misleading him (91), she also admits to "[t]aking a malicious pleasure" in her subterfuge (91). Typically, the virtuous and caring Kate condemns the forms of deception she practices. Thus, for instance, while Steele is called a "dishonorable spy and eavesdropper" (57) and while Kate upbraids him for this "dishonorable surveillance" (70), Kate herself eavesdrops on a conversation between the Carruth children, Steele, and his mother, "peeping out after they had passed" to catch her first ever glimpse of Steele (52).

One of Kate's most cunning forms of deception is to assume (feign) power-lessness precisely at the moment she assumes (seizes) power. In Alcott's writing, power circulates according to a finite economy. The loss of, abdication of, or submission to power yields an increase of power in another location; an increase of power requires a commensurate decrease of power elsewhere.[86] In the closing pages of "A Nurse's Story," Kate's loss of her power to calm patients (through magnetism) temporarily empowers the defeated and dying Steele. "My weakness seemed to give him strength," says Kate (113). But, before this final chapter, she consciously manipulates this power dynamic to trick Steele, assuming submission in order to assume control over him. In chapter 6, "Snow Versus Steele," she seemingly surrenders to him and his love. She admits coyly that "Snow melts" (96), averts her eyes so as to feign secret affection (while also guarding against his reading of her face and true intentions), acts "shy," and affects an "outward submission" (97). Now convinced that he can win Kate (gaining power) by humbling himself before the Carruths and honestly admitting his wrongs (relin-quishing power), Steele marches off to the Carruths only to discover that Kate had feigned her submission as a way to dupe him into surrendering his power over the

Carruths. Steele's climactic abdication of his power over the Carruths results not in an increase in his power over Kate, but instead in an increase in her power over him. Thus, in her exploration of humanitarian power/care, Alcott depicts the careprovider as sympathetic, devoted, kind, magnanimous but also exceptionally controlling and commanding. At every turn, Kate exercises power over patients and uses it against adversaries.

Patients, however, occupy a much different position in the conventional caring relationship. Care without sympathy in "A Nurse's Story" is unambiguous domination: patients are prisoners. Before becoming Kate's patient, Elinor is incarcerated in a room with "iron bars" (33) and "locked" doors (34). "To and fro she went, like a wild creature in its cage," says Kate. And, until he is rescued by Kate, the once mighty but now infirm Steele also behaves "like a caged panther" (111) in his room "which was a sadder prison than the darkest cell" (110).

Kate takes a much different approach to patients, however. Her power is gentle. During Kate's first day as Elinor's nurse, Elinor begins to behave not as a wild animal but as a child, that is, in the way in which Kate expects patients to act. Happy and proud with her accomplishments, Kate says, "She looked and spoke now like a little child, and watched me wistfully, still kneeling at my side" (36). Elinor is also, of course, "helpless" (45). Diagnosing the patient as childlike and helpless, Kate is then free to order the patient about, offer preachy advice, and speak for the patient. In one revealing sentence, Kate manages to do all three: "Now let us go and walk in the conservatory [a patronizing order], exercise is good for you [advice], and you are fond of being there [speaking for the patient, telling her what she feels and likes]" (38). The benevolent discourse that constructs patients as childlike and helpless allows Kate to justify and ennoble coercive action by defining it as "help."

Nevertheless, patients are not only "helpless children" under humanitarian care, according to Alcott's thriller, they are also the objects of the agents' gazes. Kate and the other careproviders in this tale like to look without being looked at. While in France, Kate and Harry take a tour of Dr. Maurice's private asylum. Delighted with their sightseeing jaunt, Kate recalls, "With the courtesy of his nation, the good doctor did the honors of his well-kept house, taking us into every room, and showing us every patient but one" (110). Not wanting to miss any of the scopophilic pleasures offered by the hospital, Kate insists on taking a look into the one forbidden room. "This omission excited my curiosity," says an excited Kate, "[and] I stole a hasty peep through the half-opened wicket in that closed door" (110). Thinking they may have found Steele after a ten-year separation following his collapse at Kate's hands, Dr. Maurice and Harry "look in" as well, and then Kate takes another look. Realizing that the object of their gaze is indeed Steele, Kate responds in typical humanitarian fashion: she aches to help him. Nevertheless, after years of avoiding Kate and the Carruths, Steele does not want to be the object of humanitarian pity or medical gazes. As Dr. Maurice explains to Kate and Harry, Steele "had an intense dread of becoming an object of pity or curiosity to strangers, and desired me to conceal his presence here, and let him live unknown" (111). But neither Steele's fear of pity nor his wish to live unwatched stops Kate. As soon as

Dr. Maurice finishes his few words, Kate enters Steele's room and says, "Robert! dear Robert! it is . . . Kate—the old Kate who tried to help you once, and will again, for she loves and pities you" (113). She makes him an object of pity and help, despite her knowledge that he has "an intense dread of becoming an object of pity."

Although Harry thinks that "she has saved him," Kate admits that it was "only for a little while" (114). Soon after being released into the care of Harry and Kate, Steele dies, and Kate observes, "His long suffering atoned for his deceit" (114). Thus, under the caring eyes of Harry and Kate, Steele dies a patient, helpless and powerless, a receiver of humanitarian pity, a mere shadow of his former "all-powerful" and deceitful self. Kate, on the other hand, lives on, an empowered humanitarian agent who does not apparently have to suffer or atone for her deception. According to Kate's narrative, suffering in disempowered patients is a sign of atonement for deceitfulness and sin, whereas the humanitarians' freedom from suffering indicates little, perhaps nothing more than their agency to help others, those who do suffer, those who are different from them.

Kate's sympathetic help is built on a relationship that empowers the careprovider and constructs others as disempowered patients. Kate not only parentalistically cares for patients, she seems indeed to create them. There are precious few scenes in which patients like Elinor and Steele manifest their insanity, their illness; they are in fact remarkably sane throughout most of the story. What transforms Elinor and Steele into patients is precisely their contact with the nurse. Kate's assumption of the nursing role certifies Elinor as a patient and marks the beginning of Elinor's final decline. Kate's power struggle with the ruthless Steele, including the humanitarian care she offers in the final chapter, not only subdues him, but transforms him into a patient so enfeebled that he needs permanent care. Like Elinor, Steele eventually dies under Kate's care. By construing others as patients, Kate creates for herself the role of careprovider, the source of her agency; without patients, she has neither the role nor the power that attends it.

"A Nurse's Story" moves beyond a simple protest against conventional humanitarian care and begins to examine humanitarianism as a practice of power. If readers tend to see the world as a place where "right" and "power" are alien to each other, as Steele thinks (41), then they would probably see Kate's exercise of power as a simple attempt at domination and her humanitarianism as deceptive cover for her will to power. If, on the other hand, readers agree with Kate and believe that those who hold power need only use it "magnanimously" (72), then they would hesitate to criticize the compassionate and self-sacrificing heroine and instead perhaps admire her powerful and benevolent humanitarian works. Regardless of how readers might want to configure power and humanitarian care, what Alcott insists upon in "A Nurse's Story" is the indissolubility of power and care. Kate is obviously sympathetic, caring, helpful; she is also deceptive, manipulative, and exhilarated by her ability to control others.

By not invoking the notion of a benevolence somehow removed from power, "A Nurse's Story" can begin its postwar critique of humanitarianism and its relationship to power. An understanding of the ways in which power circulates among patients and agents is critical—Alcott's writing would suggest—to constructing a less paternalistic, more egalitarian relationship among patients and providers. In this thriller, nursing as a caring practice is also undeniably an exercise of power in which not all players are equal. Humanitarianism is about control. And, just as agents such as Harry and Kate move successfully and energetically through life while patients such as Elinor and Steele grow weaker and sicker until eventually meeting an early demise, caring as a practice of power serves those who control it, not those who are controlled by it. Hence, humanitarianism becomes something to be scared of, not because might makes right nor because benevolence is always only a screen for domination, but simply because disempowered patients are acutely vulnerable. This is the horror of the story: patients without power, patients locked in a frighteningly unequal relationship with their careproviders. The remedy would be something more than patients helping patients. It would be patients having control over their own care.

Like Harriet Jacobs, Alcott used her Civil War–era writing as a tool for both advocating humanitarianism and analyzing inequitable patient/agent relationships within humanitarianism. Whereas John Brown had distrusted the role of language in philanthropic reform and insisted on the need for action, Alcott and Jacobs confidently employed language as an instrument that could fashion and incite an eccentric humanitarian action. In the sad and difficult months following the war, Whitman would find in language itself a basis for humanitarian action, a source for humanitarian comforting and consolation.

FIVE

WHITMAN AND THE HUMANITARIAN
POSSIBILITIES OF LILACS

Testimony for the dead is not driven by a desire to overcome death, but to prevent it from eroding the meaningfulness of life.

TIMOTHY F. MURPHY[1]

1865–66

In 1865 while Whitman was preparing *Drum-Taps* (1865) for publication in New York, John Wilkes Booth fatally wounded Lincoln at Ford's Theater in Washington. As the nation expressed its grief in public mourning, poems, sermons, speeches, and funeral parades, Whitman paid close attention to the country's bewilderment and the "strange mixture of horror, fury, [and] tenderness" which followed the "black, black, black" of Lincoln's death.[2] Although some volumes of *Drum-Taps* were bound and distributed, Whitman apparently realized that his new book needed a companion collection about Lincoln's death and the war's end. Postponing the release of *Drum-Taps*, Whitman began work on "a little book" (23), a collection of eighteen poems titled *Sequel to Drum-Taps (Since the Preceding Came from the Press.) When Lilacs Last in the Door-Yard Bloom'd. And Other Pieces* (1865–66).[3] More than any other group of poems by Whitman, *Lilacs and Other Pieces* is a response to a moment in history; this immediacy of relation to historical discourses and events makes the volume an uncommonly suggestive example of Whitman's dialogue with his culture.

Yet, somewhat surprisingly, there has been little critical commentary on *Lilacs and Other Pieces* as a "cluster" of poems.[4] Most critics have opted to examine these poems either individually or in relationship to the poems of *Drum-Taps*. While critics have offered interpretations of the "Other Pieces," including a few noteworthy discussions of "Chanting the Square Deific,"[5] "When Lilacs Last in the Door-yard Bloom'd" is by far the most discussed poem of the eighteen. Betsy Erkkila's treatment of "Lilacs" as well as the commentaries by Kerry Larson and M. Wynn Thomas are probably the most useful readings of the poem-in-its-culture; nevertheless, these critics accentuate the sociopolitical aspects of the poet and his poetry: Whitman as the political poet, Whitman as a national consensus builder, and Whitman as a justifier of the past in order to bring political-historical order to the present.[6] While these sociopolitical readings are illuminating, "Lilacs" and the other poems in this volume are not primarily focused on politics, but on grief, mourning, and humanitarian consolation.[7]

Without ignoring the relationship of grieving to politics and ideology, I want to suggest an approach to Lilacs and Other Pieces that examines the poems as a group and neither neglects the poetry's historical situation nor subordinates its primary thematic concern with humanitarian consolation and loss. In reading these poems as a group, I am not arguing that this cluster is somehow the best, most natural, or most artistic arrangement of these poems—a "great" edition later destroyed by Whitman's tinkering, revision, and scattering of the poems. Instead, I want to examine the complex significance of this particular juxtapositioning of poems within its cultural context. That his writings appear distinct or unconventional when compared to other selected discourses of sorrow and sympathy does not indicate that Whitman transcended his culture, but that he took up another position within it.

Read as one of the various cultural responses to the highly emotional events of 1865, Lilacs and Other Pieces becomes something more than a random assortment of poems on how Whitman felt about Lincoln's death and the war's end. In a year in which sections of the nation felt elated by the coming of peace, infuriated at their enemies, stunned by news of Lincoln's death, and profoundly saddened by memories of the more than 620,000 (360,000 federal and 260,000 rebel) soldiers who died in the war, Whitman's "little book" appeared as an attempt to provide consolation to the war's survivors, civilian and military. In contrast to the more coercive consolation practices of the era, however, Whitman offered an eccentric consolation.

Although it seems peculiar that this remarkable group of poems has been disregarded as a distinct clustering, it is important to remember that Lilacs and Other Pieces never appeared by itself. In October 1865 Whitman had its twenty-four pages bound with Drum-Taps in a simple cover with no printing except for the words "DRUM TAPS" on the front and back. In 1867 Lilacs and Other Pieces reappeared as an annex to some printings of the fourth edition of Leaves of Grass. And, although "Drum-Taps" survived as a cluster retaining many of its original poems in future versions of Leaves of Grass, Lilacs and Other Pieces dissolved as a grouping after 1867. By 1881 Whitman had scattered its eighteen poems throughout Leaves of Grass.

The original "little book," however, invites us to consider these poems as a separate group. Distinguishing itself from Drum-Taps and Leaves of Grass, Lilacs and Other Pieces has its own separate pagination, its own title on a different title page, a different printer and place of publication (Washington, not New York), and a year of publication (1865–66) that separates it from *Drum-Taps* (1865). Furthermore, the subject and mission of *Lilacs and Other Pieces* is different. While *Drum-Taps* focuses on the war and shows us a poet offering comfort as a nurse ("The hurt and the wounded I pacify with soothing hand / I sit by the restless all the dark night" [34]), *Lilacs and Other Pieces* centers on the uneasy peace following the war.[8]

Coming together in the few months between the printing of *Drum-Taps* in April and the publishing of its sequel in October,[9] these poems propose a more or less immediate response to the events and moods of 1865. Whitman's description of "O Captain! My Captain!" might well apply to the entire cluster: "it had certain emotional immediate reasons for being."[10] We can infer some of those "reasons" by examining the title and the positioning of the collection within the *Drum-Taps* volume. Although appended to *Drum-Taps, Lilacs and Other Pieces* is also a new beginning—but a tentative one. The unstable nature of this group of poems as a cluster (a separate book that exists only as a part of another book, a new beginning that is nonetheless a sequel) is suggestive of the historical moment hovering between war and peace, revenge and forgiveness, reestablished union and lingering divisions. The title, *Sequel to Drum-Taps (Since the Preceding Came from the Press.) When Lilacs Last in the Door-Yard Bloom'd. And Other Pieces,* provides a short description of what is to come: a major poem and some other, smaller poems. But, the word "Pieces" also gives us a hint of the fragmentation which follows. We see this fragmentation in the awkward, quadruply divided title, in the year of publication which splits itself with a hyphen (the split date joins the first year of peace to the final year of war, thus designating a transitional year, a year bridging war and peace), in the visions of debris which follow the bird's carol in "Lilacs," in the split voice of "O Me! O Life!," and in the dreamlike blending of bits of horror and beauty in "In Clouds Descending."

"Pieces" also conjures up the word "peaces" or peace—which gives us another hint about what follows. "Lilacs" and the other poems are attempts to talk about the newly born peace as well as offerings of peace to readers and to a nation in pieces. While "Lilacs" extends solace to those mourning Lincoln's death, other poems, like "Reconciliation," make peace by binding up the divisions in the nation, healing the fragmentation, and reconciling North and South, the living and the dead. These themes of peacemaking and healing find themselves worked out in the poem's closing rhythms:

> For my enemy is dead—a man divine as myself is dead;
> I look where he lies, white-faced and still, in the coffin—I draw near;
> I bend down and touch lightly with my lips the white face in the coffin. (23)

The first of these three lines is snapped into two pieces by the dash in the middle. The healing and reconciling process begins in the next line with the adding of the gentler commas and the shifting of the dash to near the end of the line: the dash is working itself out of the poem. The final line flows along in one unbroken piece (peace). This movement toward a peace among all the pieces of 1865 shapes *Lilacs and Other Pieces* and gives us a perspective on Whitman's attempt to rethink the possibilities for consolation. Before I examine Whitman's eccentric consolation, however, I want to survey briefly coercive consolation as a practice of nineteenth-century humanitarianism.

Coercive Consolation

Culminating in April 1865 with Lee's surrender and the assassination of Lincoln, the Civil War marked an unprecedented need for consolation in the United States. Following Lee's surrender, a climate of joy and relief prevailed in the North. A few days later, however, the assassination of Lincoln induced a violent swing in the mood, quickly restoring a painful awareness of the 620,000 who died in the war. The *New York Times* recorded this reversal with a headline proclaiming "The Songs of Victory Drowned in Sorrow"; in *Harper's Weekly* Thomas Nast represented the reawakened despair with an illustration of Victory weeping at the feet of Death (Figure 5.1); and millions of Americans ceased rejoicing and became participants in the elaborate public mourning of the President's death.[11] Never before had the need to mourn and to give and receive mournful sympathy been so intense and widespread in the United States.

The consolatory practices that appeared during and after the war were shaped within a culture stirred by a humanitarian sensibility sympathetically responsive to the suffering of others. In response to the grief produced by the war, middle- and upper-class Americans turned to a complex set of already established codes for mourning the dead, dealing with loss, and offering sympathy to the bereaved. For them, mourning customs included elaborate, fashionable, and expensive attire designed for various stages of mourning (First Mourning, Second Mourning, Ordinary Mourning, and Half Mourning); mourning jewelry, usually made of human hair; memorial pictures and photographs, especially of dead infants; black-bordered stationery and calling cards; and numerous other varieties of mourning paraphernalia.[12] According to Karen Halttunen, these mourning and consolation customs provided bourgeois men and women with an opportunity "to establish their respectability by demonstrating in outward social forms the deep sensibility of their private hearts." In mourning the dead and sympathizing with the bereaved, members and aspiring members of the bourgeoisie claimed for themselves a place among the genteel classes within the social hierarchy:

> Mid-nineteenth-century middle-class Americans were obsessed with mourning their dead because, in their sentimental scheme of social status, the capacity to experience deep grief demonstrated true gentility. For the same sentimental reasons, they were almost equally obsessed with the act of offering sympathy to those who mourned. . . . Sympathy, as well as bereavement, was cherished by Victorian Americans and cultivated as a mark of sensibility.[13]

This linking of social prestige with expressions of sentiment produced within the middle class an attack on the hypocrisy of formal mourning rituals. In his short story "Going Into Mourning" (1841), T. S. Arthur contrasts the true sentiments of

Figure 5.1. Thomas Nast, *Victory and Death*,
1865. *Harper's Weekly* 10 June 1865: 360-61.

Ellen and the obsessions with mourning dress characteristic of the middle-class Condys. At the end of the story, however, Ellen's true feelings have taught the Condys a valuable lesson about the importance of genuine sentiment and the vanity of hollow mourning rituals: "and each one respected her [Ellen] the more that she shunned all exterior manifestations of the real sorrow that they knew oppressed her spirits." The bourgeois critique of bourgeois mourning customs did not, however, lead to a relaxing of the social restrictions governing mourning. "[T]he sentimental critique of mourning ritual," Halttunen explains, "merely increased the complexity of the sentimental typology of grief and made mourning ritual the most elaborate expression of a dominant middle-class culture by the mid-nineteenth century."[14] Rather than a vehicle for the direct expression of "pure" emotions, mourning and consolation were a part of the cultural codes creating and regulating acceptable middle-class behavior.

The consolation literature of the era, religious in tone and substance, also participated in a consolatory humanitarianism that in its crusade against suffering sought a form of benevolent control. Nineteenth-century consolation literature offered to teach "troubled soul[s] to endure and hope" and to lead "weary spirit[s] to the Fountain of consolation." In her novel *The Gates Ajar* (1868), Elizabeth Stuart Phelps attempts to console the bereaved with Aunt Winifred's visions of a domestic heaven filled with reunions with loved ones, the beauties of earthly landscapes, and "homes, not unlike the homes of this world." Rev. F. R. Anspach describes in less vivid prose a similar universe, in which heaven is "the Christian's eternal home" and where "God, the father, is at the head of this family." In a book "designed to be a Companion for the sorrowing," Anspach's *The Sepulchres of Our Departed* (1854) offers consolation by emphasizing the resurrection of all Christian souls (chapter 13); the "Indestructibility of the Family Bond" (chapter 14); the doctrine of "future recognition," i.e., that identity persists after death and that those in heaven will recognize each other as they did upon earth (chapter 16); and the promise of heaven as home (chapter 18 and throughout).[15]

Nevertheless, the consolation in consolation literature comes only after the bereaved persons pledge themselves, implicitly or explicitly, to live in accordance with the doctrines, ideals, and sentiments outlined. Phelps indicates that the comfort offered in *The Gates Ajar* depends upon a concession to the authority of Winifred's domestic religion. In chapter 14 Dr. Bland's wife is fatally burned. In his despair Dr. Bland, a minister who earlier in the novel advocates an austere Calvinistic view of the afterlife, turns to Aunt Winifred, seeking solace in her talk about "some pleasant things about heaven." Burning his sermon book and thereby abandoning his bland, abstract Calvinism to accept Winifred's domestic religion, Dr. Bland finds consolation, which leads to a transformation in his life:

> Dr. Bland gave us a good sermon yesterday. There is an indescribable change in
> all his sermons. . . . A certain indefinable *humanness* softens his eyes and tones,
> and seems to be creeping into everything that he says.

But, to receive this transformative consolation, Dr. Bland must first adopt Winifred's belief system. Consolation literature does offer comfort to mourners, but the consolation has a price. In *The Crown of Thorns* (1860), E. H. Chapin tries to be clear about the obligations involved:

> Many come to religion for consolation who never apply to it for instruction, for sanctification, for obedience. Let us learn that we can claim its privileges only by performing its duties.

Even less-rigid consolationists who might urge their audience to abandon "ineffectual" notions of the "terrors" which follow death—Unitarians like Emerson, for example—hold the view that God grants "eternal happiness" as "the reward of obedience."[16]

Acting as the heralds of heaven and death, the writers of consolation literature used their books and sermons—their offerings of sympathy to the bereaved—to expand their influence among the living. In their "colonization of the afterlife" and in their tempting bribes of paradise for the dead and comfort for the sorrowful, consolationists made a compelling attempt to secure a type of domination.[17] Seeking control of the souls of readers, these writers tried to make their audiences an offer they couldn't refuse: join the faithful going to heaven, or face the often silent but fully present threat of eternal suffering. For readers already assured of the existence of heaven and hell, such offers did not in all likelihood present themselves as intimidating rhetorical gestures but as reaffirmations of cosmic truths. And, undoubtedly, believers expecting a future paradise found comfort in such doctrines. Nevertheless, in a religious culture filled with perennial revivals as well as increasing doubt and uncertainty, this literature used the afterlife as a tool for bolstering the faith of readers during a time of sorrow and loss and for instilling in them right beliefs, right conduct, and right sentiment.

Much of the domestic consolation literature produced shortly after Lincoln's death asks mourners to put their faith in God. Replying to the question "who shall bind the nation's wounds," an anonymous poet writes: "The voice that can with comfort sound / Is only that of God in heaven." Accordingly, Charles W. Reed counsels the nation to "Weep not" because "God doeth all things right." Having faith that God would do all things right, another poet simply prays that "Whate'er Thy purpose / Help us to be resigned to Thee."[18] The chief example of the domestic consolation literature that emerged during Reconstruction, Phelps's *The Gates Ajar,* begins with Mary Cabot's grief for her brother Roy who died in the war and also counsels faith in God and resignation to divine will as the remedy to grief. According to Phelps and others, only by obeying God's law can the bereaved receive God's comfort.

Another type of response to the suffering created by the war uses this discourse of religious consolation to direct attention to the nation. In a letter to Lydia Bixby upon the deaths of her sons, Lincoln writes:

> I feel how weak and fruitless must be any words of mine which should attempt to beguile you from the grief of a loss so overwhelming. But I cannot refrain from tendering to you the consolation that may be found in the thanks of the Republic they died to save.

> I pray that our Heavenly Father may assuage the anguish of your bereave-
> ment, and leave you only the cherished memory of the loved and lost, and the
> solemn pride that must be yours, to have laid so costly a sacrifice upon the altar
> of Freedom.[19]

Lincoln represents his own grief and his inability to offer any genuine consolation
by referring to the "weak and fruitless" nature of his words; but then he attempts
consolation by noting that they died for a worthy cause—the salvation of the
Republic—and that their deaths ought to be seen as "a sacrifice upon the altar of
Freedom." The language is religious, but the focus is the nation. Similarly, many of
the poetic responses to Lincoln's assassination represent his death as a sacrifice for
the greater glory of the United States. According to P. A. Hanaford, who sees
Lincoln as the "Martyred President," and the other poets of American Civil
Religion, the country ought to take solace in knowing that Lincoln and the Union
soldiers died for liberty. To accept the consolation offered by Lincoln or the poets
of Civil Religion, the bereaved must acknowledge that the cause of freedom or the
republic is more important than individual lives. I call this kind of consolation
"coercive" because it implicitly demands loyalty, patriotism, and obedience to
national ideals as the pre-condition for any offer of comfort, sympathy, or
understanding.

   In fact, most forms of consolation were exacting in their demands on the
bereaved. Those who specialized in "tendering" consolation usually sought more
than the mere amelioration of sorrow; they insisted explicitly or implicitly on
national loyalty, submission to God's will, a more rigid adherence to religious or
civic values, or acceptance of a certain system of religious belief. Consolation was
not free. In these discourses, we see not only 'the gentle hand of mournful
sympathy,' but also a will to direct behavior, exact obligations, and assign duties.
Approximately two-thirds of the way through his sermon on Lincoln's death, after
his injunction to grieve for Lincoln and the nation ("we ought to sorrow . . .
Humanity demands it"), Henry Darling begins his tendering of consolation by
asking, "Now what are some of these duties that the day imposes?"[20]

Lilacs

   By contrast, Whitman's offer of consolation begins not with a list of duties, but
with the odor of lilacs. Unlike *The Gates Ajar* or *The Crown of Thorns, Lilacs and Other
Pieces* was an eccentric response to the grief of the moment. Though distinct from the
predominant modes of consolation, these poems are nonetheless deeply rooted in
their culture. As a piece of humanitarian cultural work that responded to the
extensive outpouring of grief at the war's close, *Lilacs and Other Pieces* participated in
mourning the dead and sympathizing with the bereaved, while also reacting against
humanitarian practices that Whitman (following his experiences during the war)
and others clearly disliked. But, because he borrowed widely from his society's
discourses on death, grief, mourning, and consolation, it would be hyperbolic to
claim that his eccentric consolation represents somehow a transcendent triumph in
the era. In shaping a less coercive consolation, the poet turned to beliefs popular in

Transcendentalist, Unitarian, Universalist, and Spiritualist circles; he recycled ideas and sentiments found in writers like Emerson, William Cullen Bryant, T. S. Arthur, Henry Thoreau, and the British Romantics; and he introduced notions similar to those of ministers like Henry Ward Beecher, humanitarians like Clara Barton, and soldiers like William E. Vandemark and Lewis K. Brown.[21] While any one element of his consolation can be found elsewhere in the culture, Whitman managed in *Lilacs and Other Pieces* to constellate these elements in a distinctive manner. He revealed an eccentric articulation of emerging concerns, an articulation that offered to this culture at a key moment a consolation designed to elude the coercive tendencies of dominant mourning practices.

One of the most noticeable differences between Whitman's poetry and conventional consolation literature is the handling of the afterlife. Quite unlike Aunt Winifred narrating her tales of a domestic heaven, Whitman unhesitatingly rejects the bribe of a future paradise and the intimidation of the lake of fire: "the threat of what is call'd hell is little or nothing to me; / And the lure of what is call'd heaven is little or nothing to me" (19). Even in an explicitly theological poem like "Chanting the Square Deific," Whitman surpasses dominant eschatological views:

> Santa Spirita, breather, life,
> Beyond the light, lighter than light,
> Beyond the flames of hell—joyous, leaping easily above hell;
> Beyond Paradise—perfumed solely with mine own perfume. (16-7)

He does not, however, exclude the notion of an afterlife. Depending on how the poem is construed, "When Lilacs Last in the Door-Yard Bloom'd" can affirm the notion of immortality or remain completely silent about it.[22] Moreover, in "How Solemn, As One by One," Whitman unequivocally announces:

> O the bullet could never kill what you really are, dear friend,
> Nor the bayonet stab what you really are:
> . . . The soul! yourself I see, great as any, good as the best,
> Waiting secure and content, which the bullet could never kill,
> Nor the bayonet stab, O friend! (22)

These lines affirm the existence of a soul beyond death. Speaking directly to readers ("As I glance upward out of this page, studying you, dear friend, whoever you are") and to the souls of "the ranks returning" (22), the poet offers assurances that "what you really are" is "secure and content" despite the threat of physical extinction—assurances designed to offer consolation to readers dealing with death. But, in the context of *Lilacs and Other Pieces,* this personal immortality remains beyond "the threat of what is call'd hell" and "the lure of what is call'd heaven." Furthermore, the poet does not tie this notion of the soul to any morality or teleology: he just vaguely asserts it. The poem does not even define this "what you really are," except to suggest that it eludes death. Thus, Whitman offers his readers a notion of immortality designed to console, but carefully avoids linking it to any implied duty, obligation, or pregiven closed definition.

Whitman illustrates a similar delicacy in his poetic treatment of Lincoln and the war dead. Whereas Lincoln and the poets of Civil Religion pay their respects to the dead by extolling the sacrifice made to freedom and country, Whitman refuses to make rational or spiritual sense out of the war deaths or to attach to them a positive meaning. As Larson explains in his discussion of "Lilacs":

> To invoke a higher cause as justification for all those slain in battle was, as Whitman came to perceive during the fighting, to blaspheme rather than honor their memory. . . . The result is an awed capitulation to death's mastery rather than an effort to retrieve its meaningfulness for the social world.[23]

This "awed capitulation" to death is central to *Lilacs and Other Pieces*. Refusing to sing "mastery's rapturous verse," Whitman writes "a little book, containing night's darkness, and blood-dripping wounds, / And psalms of the dead" (23). Vanquished by the "mastering odor" of lilacs (8), by lovers ("the lovers I recklessly love—lo! how they master me" [17]), by war, and most of all by death, the poet sings not of mastery, but of being mastered. Like Nast's Victory weeping abjectly at the feet of Death (Figure 5.1), *Lilacs and Other Pieces* abandons celebrations of victory in order to weep with the mourners. The five-line triumph of "Race of Veterans" quickly gives way to the lamentation of "O Captain!":

> From fearful trip, the victor ship, comes in with object won:
>> Exult, O shores, and ring, O bells!
>>> But I, with silent tread,
>>>> Walk the spot my captain lies,
>>>>> Fallen cold and dead. (13)

Distancing himself from the exulting victors, Whitman focuses our attention on the dead.

Nast's tribute to Lincoln also shifts our focus from "Victory" to "Death." Yet, as Whitman works to create an eccentric consolation, Nast brings together many of the coercive elements of conventional consolation. For Whitman, death is the almighty democratic leveler; for Nast, however, Death's "mighty strength" restores society to its serene, "natural" (status quo), hierarchical order. At the top of the illustration, Nast presents a pair of domestic scenes in which a patriarch leads his family in religious devotions. The white father reads from the Bible, apparently trying to discern how Lincoln's death is God's will, while the rest of the group weeps—a sign of their true bourgeois feeling. The black family kneels together in prayer, thanking God for the "Saviour" who delivered them from slavery. In these sentimental vignettes Nast shows how meditation on death brings domestic order (the subordinate members of the family listen obediently to the father) and religious order (each family draws nearer to God as they seek consolation in their period of woe). Like Hanaford, Nast reiterates Lincoln's status as an instrument of God, as a messianic deliverer, by naming him "Our Martyred President," and thus reinforces the Christian interpretation of his death and its concomitant call for faith in God. Along the bottom of the illustration the theme is civil or secular. The chaotic energy of the "Victory" celebration—presented as a crowded urban street filled with the bustling excitement of individuals from various classes—yields in the face of "Death" to somber, well-ordered columns of military personnel in the state funeral of a great leader. Between these two frames, we see uncovered America, the daughter, weeping on the shoulder of Europe, the crowned Queen, the mother. The royalty theme is replayed in the major tondo in which Victory dressed as a knight kneels obediently to Death, a mighty King who stands majestically albeit gruesomely before his throne. Nast pays homage to Lincoln by showing how the martyr's death brings a serene (though unhappy) sense of harmony and order to this world: Death reminds each figure of his or her proper place in relationship to God, the family, and the state. Whitman, in contrast, honors Lincoln and the war dead not by celebrating their sacrifice or the fruits of their sacrifice in freedom, order, or renewed faith, but by singing of his love for them: "O my soldiers . . . My heart gives you love" (22). He commiserates with the bereaved not because their dead fought gloriously to secure victory, but because they are "loved so well" (12).

In addition to suggesting these somewhat unconventional perspectives on death, *Lilacs and Other Pieces* also provides a distinctive *process* for mourning the dead and for finding meaning in death. In contrast to the rigid codes governing the bourgeois mourning experience, the cyclical structures of *Lilacs and Other Pieces* set up a flexible, open-ended mourning process that depends not upon expensive mourning attire or obedience to social standards, but upon personal memories and poetry. Although these poems are a collection of lyrics and not a neatly ordered epic, *Lilacs and Other Pieces* does have a certain structural coherence. Its progressive cycles move from an initiating sorrow (grief, sadness, despair) which induces mourning to a moment of acceptance and reconciliation which yields a peaceful solace, and back to painful memories which begin the process over again. "When Lilacs Last in the Door-Yard Bloom'd" is the resonant center of the collection, containing the major ideas, themes, and moods that inform the rest of the poems: grief and fragmentation, the search for consolation or peace, affection for the dead soldiers, a refusal of traditional eschatological beliefs, an embrace of death and loss, and a use of polyvalent symbols and images. But "Lilacs" is also the beginning of the mourning process that is *Lilacs and Other Pieces*.

"Lilacs" begins in between mourning. "I mourn'd," the poet tells us, ". . . and yet shall mourn with ever-returning spring" (3). He presents mourning as a process that moves in cycles—it comes and it goes. Not statically constant, but "ever-returning," mourning reappears with the "perennial" lilacs, the metonymic fragrance that brings the poet back to memories of the original moment of grief.[24] The choppy rhythms of section 2 represent that grief. In the following four sections (3 to 6) the poet moves from representations of pure grief to expressions of mourning: the breaking of the lilac sprig (section 3), the bird's song (section 4), and the funeral (sections 5 and 6). The unfolding of mournful sentiments culminates in section 7 where the poet embraces death:

>   Nor for you, for one, alone;
> Blossoms and branches green to coffins all I bring:

> For fresh as the morning—thus would I chant a song for you,
>> O sane and sacred death.
>> All over bouquets of roses,
> O death! I cover you over with roses and early lilies;
> But mostly and now the lilac that blooms the first. (5)

The verses indicate that the lilacs are brought not just for the dead president nor the war dead, but for death itself. The recognition of death brings a peacefulness represented by the gentle, flowing phrases of section 8, which show a marked change from the fragmented, broken sobs of section 2.

Still, this acceptance of death is apparently incomplete. In section 7 the poet embraces the abstract concept, the personification of the idea of "sane and sacred death." The intellectual acceptance of "the sacred knowledge of death" (8) is not yet complemented by the memories of actual physical deaths, "the thought of death" (9). Although an intellectual appreciation of the knowledge of death is a part of the process that allows the mourner to remember the dead, the poet has not yet prepared himself to consciously reexperience those memories.

Before he can come to re-membered visions of the war dead, he will hear the bird's carol. In section 9 the poet tells the thrush, "I come presently" (6)—but instead he delays. He insists that he is "detain'd," first by "the lustrous star" (in section 9) and then by "the lilacs, with mastering odor" (section 13). On his way to the swamp where the thrush hides, the poet observes the nation and its landscapes and wonders how exactly he should mourn for the dead. In section 15 the poet joins hands with his companions (the knowledge of death and the thought of death) and finally makes his visit to "The gray-brown bird" (9) who sings his song of death in section 16.

This controlled seven-quatrained carol is an affirmation of the inevitability and peacefulness of death. Although it is certainly not Whitman's final word on death, the bird's song and its embrace of death prepare the poet to recall the painful memories of the war and its carnage:

> And I saw, as in noiseless dreams, hundreds of battle-flags;
> Borne through the smoke of the battles, and pierc'd with missiles, I saw them,
> And carried hither and yon through the smoke, and torn and bloody;
> And at last but a few shreds of the flags left on the staffs, (and all in silence,)
> And the staffs all splinter'd and broken.
> I saw battle-corpses, myriads of them,
> And the white skeletons of young men—I saw them;
> I saw the debris and debris of all dead soldiers;
> But I saw they were not as was thought;
> They themselves were fully at rest—they suffer'd not;
> The living remain'd and suffer'd—the mother suffer'd,
> And the wife and the child, and the musing comrade suffer'd,
> And the armies that remain'd suffer'd. (11)

Among all the fragments of battle and the "debris" of the dead soldiers, we find one consolatory reflection: the dead "themselves were fully at rest—they suffer'd not."

Whitman's emphasis, however, is on the horror that precedes this line and the suffering that follows it. Although learning to confront "the visions of armies . . . in noiseless dreams" is essential to the mourning process, Whitman emphasizes the difficulty of this confrontation by taking nine pages of mourning verse before the poet can embrace and relive the painful memories. Although the poet has traveled an important cycle in the mourning process, the grief work is not complete. In fact, according to *Lilacs and Other Pieces,* it is never complete, but perennial and incessant.

At the end of "Lilacs," the poet has not regained control through successfully completed grief work nor resigned himself to the advice of religious instruction, as Phelps, Chapin, or Nast would urge. Isolated from human society, in the dark, secluded swamp, "There in the fragrant pines, and the cedars dusk and dim," the poet holds on to his memories of the dead he "loved so well" (12).

Opening a new cycle in the mourning process, these memories return us to the original grief. The poet attempts to fend off this anguish preemptively by imagining his beloved soldiers as a "Race of Veterans," but the marching exultation of this second poem gives way to the grief of "O Captain!" Because of his memories of Lincoln and the associated memories of all the war dead, the poet cannot bring himself to celebrate the Union's victory. In "Spirit whose Work is Done," the poet asks the reminders of war to fade from his memories; but while remembering the sights and sounds of war, he suddenly embraces the "spirit of dreadful hours / . . . spirit of hours I knew":

> Touch my mouth, ere you depart—press my lips close!
> Leave me your pulses of rage! bequeath them to me! fill me with currents convulsive!
> Let them scorch and blister out of my chants, when you are gone;
> Let them identify you to the future in these songs. (14)

More than an acceptance of the idea of death and the fact of the war dead, this embrace signals a determined reception of the source of war and death.

In "Chanting the Square Deific," we move from this embrace to a spiritual vision in which such a dreadful spirit—represented in "Chanting" as the "warlike" Satan, the defiant third side of the quaternity—becomes a timeless component in the operation of the universe. "Chanting" marks a calm, thoughtful acceptance of the permanence and necessity of rebellion, death, loss, and separation. This theological vision brings a feeling of peaceful closure in the Santa Spirita who says "I the most solid, / Breathe my breath through these little songs" (17).

The images of music and breath carry the poet, temporarily content with the order of the universe, back to memories of his lover in "I heard you, Solemn-sweet Pipes of the Organ," which begins another, more intensely personal cycle in the mourning process. No longer held powerless by the images of the war, the poet remembers his lover: "Heart of my love!—you too I heard, murmuring low, through one of the wrists around my head; / Heard the pulse of you when all was still, ringing little bells last night under my ear" (17). Unfortunately, these memories bring a new kind of fearfulness and panic to the poet: "Not my enemies ever invade me—no harm to my pride from them I fear; / But the lovers I recklessly love—lo! how they master me!" (17). Brought by thoughts of his lovers to a "grovelling" (17) low point, the poet "reproaching" himself wonders in the next poem: "What good amid these, O me, O life?" (18). Out of nowhere, apparently, an "*Answer*" comes: "That you are here—that life exists, and identity; / That the powerful play goes on, and you will contribute a verse" (18). Like the bird's carol in "Lilacs," the consolation offered here should not be taken as Whitman's definitive solution to despair. Indeed, both appear in a voice clearly distinguished from the poet's own. Yet, both the thrush's song and the *Answer* accept and affirm what is inevitable and permanent: death in the former and life in the latter. These simple affirmations are not the conclusions to mourning. Rather they act to remove temporary obstacles blocking the mourning process: the reluctance to confront memories of the war dead in "Lilacs," the poet's "Utterly abject" (17) despair in this cycle. Not by giving lucid philosophical answers, but by simply affirming life and death, these two subpoems encourage the poet to stop dwelling on unanswerable questions (i.e., what is death? what is the meaning of life?). Within the culture, there were, of course, various answers to these questions, but such answers often took the form of religious dogma or socially restrictive imperatives. Whitman, however, takes an eccentric approach by including these two subpoems, which seem to say, "I answer that I cannot answer, you must find out for yourself,"[25] while maintaining all along the beauty of death and the continued existence of life.

Thus, in the next poem, the poet can move beyond "poverties, wincings, and sulky retreats" to a look at his "real self" (18). Attempting to avoid the guilt and self-reproach that could prolong grief work, Whitman maintains that the mourning process must include not only an acceptance of the inevitability of death, but also an acceptance of one's self without guilt or self-condemnation. The acknowledgment of his "real self," which might be seen as the sum of his multiple selves or as simply one aspect of his multitudinous self, allows the poet to come into a fuller recognition of his own character and his own dark qualities:

> I know I am restless, and make others so;
> I know my words are weapons, full of danger, full of death;
> . . .
> I confront peace, security, and all the settled laws, to unsettle them;
> I am more resolute because all have denied me, than I could ever have been had
> all accepted me;
> I heed not, and have never heeded, either experience, caution, majorities, nor
> ridicule. (19)

In "Chanting" the poet recognized and accepted the evil in the universe, and here in "As I Lay with My Head in Your Lap, Camerado" he accepts the evil within himself. His embrace of his dark qualities leads to a brief peace in which the poet can say to himself in the next poem: "This day, O soul, I give you a wondrous mirror; / Long in the dark, in tarnish and cloud it lay—But the cloud has pass'd, and the tarnish gone" (19).

The image of the cloud connects the peaceful end of one cycle to the return of memories in the next. The cloud that had passed returns and brings with it the nightmares of the war:

> In clouds descending, in midnight sleep, of many a face of anguish,
> Of the look at first of the mortally wounded—of that indescribable look;
> Of the dead on their backs, with arms extended wide,
>   I dream, I dream, I dream. (20)

What follows in this final cycle is not the convulsive despair of "O cruel hands that hold me powerless! O helpless soul of me! / O harsh surrounding cloud that will not free my soul" (3). Instead, the poet sadly reexperiences with a newly acquired composure the vivid, haunting images of the war: "the dead on their backs, with arms extended wide" (20); the "swarming ranks" of "An Army on the March" (20); and the death and burial of "Two veterans, son and father" in "Dirge for Two Veterans" (21). In "Two Veterans" the poet laments the two deaths, but seems consoled by the mourning process: "O strong dead-march, you please me! / O moon immense, with your silvery face you soothe me!" (22). In the next two poems, Whitman returns to themes previously presented. In "How Solemn, As One by One," the poet reasserts the notion of a real self, "what you really are," but now directs his thoughts not toward himself but to the returning soldiers. Repeating the call to embrace death, the poet announces in the ironically titled "Lo! Victress on the Peaks" that he will not gloatingly sing paeans to Victory, but instead chant "psalms of the dead" (23). The affirmative reminder of the existence of a soul in "How Solemn" and the focus on death in "Lo! Victress" bring the poet to the final moment of acceptance or inclusion in the collection—"Reconciliation" with his dead enemy. Although the poet takes comfort in the fact "that war, and all its deeds of carnage, must in time be utterly lost" and that the separations of the war have been bandaged by deaths and reconciliations, the mourning process is not over but continues forever as "the hands of the sisters Death and Night, incessantly softly wash again, and ever again, this soil'd world" (23). The collection's final moment of reconciliation gives way to the peaceful new beginning of "To the Leaven'd Soil They Trod," as the "soil'd world" of war and death transforms itself into the life-giving "leaven'd soil." Watching the soldiers return to "the wordless earth" (24), the poet asks not the former soldiers but the mute earth, "the witness of war and peace" (24), to confirm the significance of his songs.

Although Whitman projects no end to the mourning process, the movement through these cycles from "Lilacs" to "Leaven'd Soil" indicates a gradual amelioration of grief. Within this grief/mourning-to-reconciliation/peace-to-memories cycle, the key moment is the reconciliation or acceptance, the point at which the poet or the mourner embraces death, evil, or the sources of death, evil, separations, and loss, whether that source is located in the self, in another, an enemy, or in the structures of the universe. This is unusual, and seems even more so when compared to more widely accepted notions of the mourning process.[26] Rather than declaring the lost love object dead or promising a future reunion with family in heaven, Whitman urges a merging, not with the lost love object, but with the cause of loss—spiritual evil, rebelliousness, the South, the dark side of the self, and death itself. In Whitman's view, reconciliation to the source of death and loss accomplishes two things in the mourning process. First, it brings an intellectual awareness and spiritual understanding of what Donald Pease would call the "law of regeneration"[27]: all die; in death all is merged, averaged, composted, re-formed; and life begins again and again out of death. Second, and consequent to the understanding of the law of regeneration, reconciliation with the source of death and loss brings a peaceful consolation that allows the cyclical mourning process to continue to "incessantly softly wash again, and ever again," and provides mourners with a space in which to create a new beginning and a fresh meaning out of the debris of war and death.

Whitman's purpose in *Lilacs and Other Pieces* is not to cajole the bereaved out of their grief. It is not even to persuade them into an absolute acceptance of the law of regeneration, an idea that in *Lilacs and Other Pieces* serves only to facilitate the mourning process. Instead, his goal is to bring the bereaved to a place of new beginnings, to give to the bereaved the *process* and the *language* that will enable them to construct for themselves a meaning that makes sense of death and that lends value to their daily living. In the cyclical structure of *Lilacs and Other Pieces,* we find the *process* and in this cluster's suggestive poetry the *language.*

Part of the soothing beauty of the poems in *Lilacs and Other Pieces* is their provoking suggestiveness. In his 1865 review of *Drum-Taps,* William Dean Howells noticed this quality in Whitman's poetry: "the thought is as intangible as aroma; it is no more put up than atmosphere." Clearly disdainful of such an "unspeakably inartistic" method of writing poetry, Howells complained that Whitman "made you a partner of the poetical enterprise," when in Howells's opinion "no one wants to share the enterprise."[28] But, for me, Whitman's invitation to the reader to share in the process of creating poetic meaning (or put another way, Whitman's ability to evoke meanings and refusal to pin down the one meaning) is precisely the quality to be appreciated.

In a poem like "Lilacs," Whitman indicates his desire to avoid fixed meaning by generating a group of polyvalent symbols. Most commentators see a trinity of basic symbols: lilac, star, and bird. But the poet announces in the first section that the trinity brought to him by spring is lilac, star, and "thought of him I love" (3). What is this third part? Is it a symbol like lilacs and star? Or is it a symbol's referent? If a referent, to which of the symbols does it attach? Other critics have challenged the customary three-symbol view and added a fourth. James E. Miller sees the cloud as the fourth basic symbol, and George B. Hutchinson says it is the coffin.[29] Yet, Whitman also provides the swamp with its pines and cedars, the West and the western sky, the poet's two comrades (the knowledge of death and the thought of death), the funeral procession, the bird's song, and the poet's chant. Are these all symbols? They can all certainly suggest some type of meaning beyond their literal reference, and all of them in the context of the poem remain undecided, unfixed. Critics might try to pin down the significance of lilacs by arguing that they represent love. But, is it the love of a patriotic citizen for a great president? Or a powerful homoerotic attachment? Or a poetic idealization of love? If the heart-shaped lilacs represent love, they also suggest spring, life, the earthly realm, rebirth, cyclical time, a Christ figure (and thus consolation, redemption, and spiritual rebirth), a father figure, the cause of grief (because of the mnemonic association with a lost love), as well as an instrument of sensual consolation.[30] The lilacs can represent all of these meanings or none of them. Perhaps, the odor of lilacs is the personal and coincidental memory that Whitman attaches to Lincoln's death:

> I remember where I was stopping at the time, the season being advanced, there were many lilacs in full bloom. By one of those caprices that enter and give tinge to events without being at all a part of them, I find myself always reminded of the great tragedy of that day by the sight and odor of these blossoms. It never fails.[31]

Or perhaps, the lilacs are, for some readers, simply lilacs.

Regardless of what any particular reader makes of the lilacs in this poem, Whitman's use of the lilacs and the other polyvalent symbols is central to the consolatory possibilities of the poem. The polyvalent language of the poem invites bereaved readers to fill its images and symbols with their own meanings. If a mourner takes comfort in recognizing the lilacs as a sign of love for an apotheosized Lincoln, the poem graciously accepts that significance; if, on the other hand, such an interpretation might become painful and coercive rather than consoling and liberating, the lilacs are easily emptied of meaning, representing simply "lilacs" and offering themselves up again to be reshaped with new meanings.

Whitman also avoids the monovalent rhetoric of consolation literature by refusing to establish the significance of the deaths of Lincoln and the soldiers. In sections of *Lilacs and Other Pieces,* such as "In Clouds Descending," "An Army on the March," and section 18 of "Lilacs," Whitman presents vivid scenes of war and the war dead with frighteningly detailed descriptions, but with little commentary and no attempt to claim that their deaths served a great political or cosmic purpose. Although he insists throughout these twenty-four pages on singing of death, in places where a reader might expect some conclusive or significant remark on the meaning of death, Whitman is silent. In the final poem, he does not conclude, summarize, or give us the moral of the story; instead, he just departs, asking "the leaven'd soil of the general western world" to give confirmation to his tallies of war and death. But, "The average earth, the witness of war and peace, acknowledges mutely" (24). Thus, in asking the mute earth to bestow significance on these deaths, Whitman leaves us with more silence.

Even in "Chanting the Square Deific," a poem that George Fredrickson calls "Whitman's final word on the Civil War" and Larson sees as "Whitman's lone effort to enclose the war's significance,"[32] Whitman avoids any *explicit* reference to the Civil War or the war dead. Thus, for some critics, the poem has "little or nothing to do with the war." They read "Chanting" as Whitman's challenge to traditional Christianity, or as his solution to the problem of metaphysical evil, or as his effort to develop a new democratic religion.[33] Each of these interpretations glosses the four suggestively allegorical figures (Jehovah, Christ, Satan, and Santa Spirita) without correlating them to any wartime referent. Still, coming at the end of the war, "Chanting" is open to an interpretation that links the North to Jehovah and the South to Satan. In this reading "Chanting" recalls the Puritan predilection for seeing large metaphysical struggles being carried out or mirrored in earthly events; it makes sense of the confusion of temporal struggles by revealing the timeless, divine forces that move beneath them. This interpretation depends, of course, on the reader keying the spiritual figures in the poem to the particular events of the Civil War. Literally, the poem is completely silent about the war. "Chanting" becomes a frame for understanding the war or commenting on its significance only when the reader completes that commentary or understanding by construing the four godheads as representative of historical forces. If such a discernment of divine plan beneath the chaos of human history offers a feeling of security or comfort to the bereaved, then "Chanting" can accept that interpretation. But, if such an interpretation of Civil War events would create more pain or act as a coercive demand, then the poem can also be read as having "little or nothing to do with the war." "Chanting" is a remarkable poem not because it acts as Whitman's final word on the war or on God, but because its four evocative figures create a verbal space open to multiple possibilities, a space in which readers can fashion, refashion, or not fashion meaning or consolatory understanding.

Furthermore, the interpretation that suggests that "Chanting" is a Hegelian synthesizing of antagonistic forces is only one conception of a quite suggestive poem, a conception that ignores the fact that these antagonistic forces are not binary (thesis, antithesis) but quaternary, and that they are not fused into a fresh synthesis, but are left permanently irreducible and permanently in tension. Thus, even Whitman's attempt "to enclose the war's significance" is strikingly heterogeneous, open, unresolved.

Whitman's refusal to pin down meaning should not, however, be read as an absurdist gesture denying sense nor as an announcement of the impossibility of humanitarianism. Instead, *Lilacs and Other Pieces* suggests that if poetry is to offer humanitarian consolation in a less coercive manner, then the bereaved must interact with the poems in the creation of consolatory significance. In this respect *Lilacs and Other Pieces* tends to resemble what Barthes calls the "*writerly*"; it asks readers to become producers of textual meaning, whereas the more "*readerly*" consolation of Chapin or Nast treats the bereaved audience as idle consumers of relatively fixed meanings. *Lilacs and Other Pieces*' *writerly* quality thus reveals a paradoxical demand buried at the heart of this eccentric consolation: the poems require readers to actively construct their consolatory meanings, in order that readers might be freed from the demands of coercive consolation or what Barthes calls "the poor freedom either to accept or reject the text."[34] Such a consolatory project is not inconsistent with the "Suggestiveness" of Whitman's poetic project. In "A Backward Glance o'er Travel'd Roads," he explains:

> I round and finish little, if anything; and could not, consistently with my scheme.
> The reader will always have his or her part to do, just as much as I have had mine.
> I seek less to state or display any theme or thought, and more to bring you,

reader, into the atmosphere of the theme or thought—there to pursue your own flight.[35]

In *Lilacs and Other Pieces* Whitman uses these principles to shape the consolatory possibilities of his poetry to the needs of his culture.

By 1871, after the crisis of the moment had passed, Whitman began to retreat in some ways from his eccentric position of 1865–66 and to scatter, rewrite, and recluster these poems. His later writings return to more conventional notions of immortality. And, after refusing in *Lilacs and Other Pieces* to link the war deaths to any higher purpose, he celebrates in 1871 the "old cause," the "good cause," for which the "strange sad war, great war" was fought.[36] These shifts in attitude seem to indicate that the cultural work of *Lilacs and Other Pieces* was in many respects particular to the exigencies of 1865–66, when Death towered over prostrate mourners.

Moreover, in the United States in 1865 readers would have had no problems identifying "Lilacs" as an elegy to Lincoln, though the dead president was nowhere named in the poem. For later editions and future readers, however, the references might not have been so clear. Thus, Whitman later formed around "Lilacs" a cluster that explicitly names Lincoln, "President Lincoln's Burial Hymn" in 1871, "Memories of President Lincoln" in 1881. Whitman moved "Chanting" to a cluster named "Whispers of Heavenly Death," thus emphasizing its theological perspective on death, and deemphasizing its allegorical relation to the Civil War. He also made minor changes relating to the positioning of poems within clusters. For example, when Whitman moved "In Clouds Descending, in Midnight Sleep" from *Lilacs and Other Pieces* to its position near the end of "Noon to Starry Night," he deleted the phrase "In clouds descending." The phrase was a unifying symbol in *Lilacs and Other Pieces,* serving also as a transition metaphor linking "In Clouds Descending, in Midnight Sleep" to the poems preceding and following it. The deletion in 1871 gave increased emphasis to the phrase "midnight sleep," an image of central importance within the "Noon to Starry Night" cluster. While the changes show that Whitman took great care in organizing and editing the clusters, they also suggest that Whitman conceived of, wrote, and arranged *Lilacs and Other Pieces* as a response to the immediate needs of a culture in mourning. Whitman's *Lilacs and Other Pieces* gives us not only an insight into the grief of that culture but also an example of humanitarian cultural work that depends not upon coercion or obedience to an ideal, but upon poetic polyvalency and the imagination of readers in a democratic society.

ECCENTRIC BENEVOLENCE
AND ITS LIMITS

. . . knowledge must indeed present the fatally rectilinear succession of victory and defeat, but should also address itself to those things which were not embraced by this dynamic, which fell by the wayside —what might be called the waste products and blind spots that have escaped the dialectic.

THEODOR ADORNO[1]

Emancipation

In the mid-1860s, during the last stages of the war and the years following the war, while many in the United States mourned the dead soldiers and dead president, two issues captured humanitarian attention: (1) the status and well-being of four million newly freed black people, and (2) the survival of 300,000 Native Americans living in the United States and its territories. Since both concerns entailed histories of racism and racist oppression, humanitarians were attempting practically to help peoples who had for centuries suffered at the hands of whites and ideologically to redefine the relationships between a white-controlled nation and its African American and Native American inhabitants.

Emancipation, from almost every perspective, meant enormous social, economic, political, and cultural changes. Sensing an opportunity to participate decisively in the reshaping of black life, and recognizing an occasion to help millions of people who were eager not only for liberty but also for land, livelihoods, and learning, humanitarians from the North moved south and brought with them schoolbooks, Bibles, and their own middle-class values and perspectives. Other humanitarians stayed in the North and, hoping to extend the aims and aspirations of the antislavery struggle, lobbied for black suffrage, civil rights, and protection and education for the freedpeople.[2]

Humanitarianism itself was changing as well. The antislavery movement, for instance, had usually imagined itself in an antagonistic relationship to the U.S. government. During the 1860s, however, the Northern aid societies hoping to help freedpeople embraced the participation and direction of the federal government through the Freedmen's Bureau, just as the Sanitary Commission had coordinated its philanthropic activity through government agencies. Postbellum humanitarianism had become a joint venture, bringing together private organizations and state authority.

Of course, some structures, attitudes, and values remained more or less constant during this transition in humanitarian thought and practice. Benevolent workers committed to freedpeople's relief continued to hold to the distinction between themselves, helpers who wished to do good, and their patients, the degraded and childlike freedpeople. The distinction discouraged active self-reflection among humanitarians and encouraged the earnest paternalism with which teachers and philanthropists pursued their missions. As the schoolbooks, primers, and newspapers published for the freedpeople indicate, teachers from the North wanted to give lessons not only in reading, writing, and arithmetic but also in the evils of rum, tobacco, and laziness and the merit of washing, thrift, industry, tidy housekeeping, dignified religious worship, obedience, and doing good.[3] That the values and attitudes of white, middle-class, Protestant New England shaped these texts written and promulgated by white, middle-class, Protestant New Englanders is hardly surprising. Still, the virtually unquestioned assumption that their values ought to become an integral part of Southern black life suggests the directive quality of the help extended.[4]

Hoping to avoid any questioning of these values or the humanitarian knowledge and authority that advanced them, *The Freedman,* a combination textbook and newspaper published by the American Tract Society in Boston, told its black readers straight out, "you must believe what you are told by those who wish to do you good."[5] Since such orders were rather unpersuasive in themselves, and since black people capably resisted unwanted paternalistic moral instruction, humanitarians were often frustrated in their attempts to reshape the lives of the freedpeople. As one disconcerted Northern teacher observed, "What they desire is assistance without control." And because these humanitarians could not imagine "assistance without control," they found their benevolent efforts thwarted by the people whom they were trying to help.[6]

Despite the continuities between antebellum and postbellum conventional humanitarianism (the agent/patient opposition, the paternalistic formulation of assistance as control, the assumption that the humanitarians' values were or ought to be universal), humanitarian discourses and projects were always open to internal discontinuity. During periods of dramatic change or crisis, this internal discontinuity became more pronounced. The lack of accord or consensus or communicative understanding was often the result of the different interests and histories among patients and agents. Notions of self-help and definitions of freedom, for example, were ubiquitous in the discourse surrounding freedpeople's relief and education. Yet, as the rhetorical presence of African American voices (as agents and patients) in this discourse demonstrated, the meanings of such ideas were also contested and plural, and thus indications of the fragmentation within this discourse.

For most white humanitarians self-help signified the adoption of certain values associated with the middle class: individualism, self-discipline, cleanliness, thrift, benevolence, industry, sobriety, tidiness, good manners. Thus, according to the white-authored schoolbooks provided black Southerners, "freedom" did not mean the liberty for people "to do just as they please." Instead, "true freedom is to do right," where right was defined by a white, Protestant, middle-class ethic preoccupied with issues of cleanliness, sobriety, diligence, decorum, individual responsibility, etc.[7]

While there is no reason to suppose that values like industry and benevolence had no appeal among newly freed African Americans, long-standing black notions of self-help designated something distinct from the ideals of the North's white middle class. According to The Freedman's Torchlight, a Brooklyn-based newspaper authored and published by African Americans, self-help meant that "the black man is the better leader and teacher among his own people." Arguing for self-determination and the utility of having the black community, North and South, rather than white benevolent societies, direct assistance and education for the freedpeople, The Freedman's Torchlight maintained, "We ourselves must elevate our own race."[8] The use of double pronouns as the subject of this phrase ("We ourselves") and the double adjectives ("our own") to mark the phrase's object ("race"), which is identical to the subject, emphasized and reemphasized precisely who was to be the agent doing the helping, the elevation.

Echoing this emphasis on self-determination, Frederick Douglass defined self-help by its exclusion of white philanthropy. In answer to the question "What Shall Be Done with the Slaves if Emancipated?" Douglass wrote:

> Our answer is, do nothing with them; mind your business, and let them mind theirs. Your *doing* with them is their greatest misfortune. They have been undone by your doings, and all they now ask, and really have need of at your hands, is just to let them alone. They suffer by every interference, and succeed best by being let alone. . . . When you, our white fellow-countrymen, have attempted to do anything for us, it has generally been to deprive us of some right, power or privilege.[9]

Douglass urged black self-help because the history of white helping, the history of whites "doing" for blacks, was one of undoing, hindrance, and disempowerment. White philanthropy was not only unhelpful, according to Douglass, it was oppressive.

Douglass's sense of self-help was bound up with his idea of freedom. "No man can be truly free," Douglass held, "whose liberty is dependent upon the thought, feeling, and action of others, and who has himself no means in his own hands for guarding . . . and maintaining that liberty." Moreover, he grounded this definition of freedom-as-self-reliance in a skeptical estimation of philanthropy for those not in one's own group; he professed he knew of "no class of my fellow-men, however just, enlightened, and humane, which can be wisely and safely trusted absolutely with the liberties of any other class." For black humanitarians in the North, freedom was not obedience to rules, but rather the right to self-determination and the possession and enjoyment of the value of one's labor free from white interference. "The meaning of freedom," explained *The Freedman's Torchlight,* "is *to work for self*; to enjoy the fruits of one's own labor."[10]

As African Americans in the North advanced their own versions of self-help and freedom and as black humanitarians and teachers (like Harriet Jacobs and Charlotte Forten) moved south to work, the freedpeople were already practicing their own versions of freedom and self-help. They instructed themselves, built schools without the aid of white philanthropists, constructed and reconstructed their own African American communities in the South. As Jacqueline Jones has shown, for many African Americans, "relinquishing any control over neighborhood institutions was a high price to pay for northern philanthropy."[11] Thus, using their own notions of freedom and self-help, these communities redefined for themselves and their white friends what they believed ought to be the appropriate relationship between white humanitarians and Southern blacks. The *New Orleans Tribune,* an African American newspaper established in 1864, rearticulated the philanthropic relationship in these terms: "We need friends, it is true; but we do not need tutors. The age of guardianship is past forever. We now think for ourselves, and we shall act for ourselves."[12]

Despite such declarations of independence and despite the diverse and sometimes innovative nature of humanitarianism in the 1860s, the Euro-American friends of the freedpeople almost always relied on the controlling and condescending structures and assumptions that shaped conventional philanthropic discourse. Even progressives, like the veteran abolitionist Lydia Maria Child, did not forgo the benevolent paternalism that saturated the humanitarian perspective. In *The Freedmen's Book* (1865), a collection of poems and articles she edited for the encouragement and education of the freedpeople, Child took important steps toward moving past the role of guardian by devoting most of the textbook to biographies of distinguished black people (such as Benjamin Banneker, Toussaint L'Ouverture, Phillis Wheatley, James Forten, Frederick Douglass, and William and Ellen Craft among others) and to pieces authored by African Americans (such as Frances E. W. Harper, Douglass, Harriet Jacobs, Wheatley, George Horton, and Charlotte Forten among others). Yet, Child apparently could not resist dispensing some rather predictable, paternalistic instruction via a pair of articles written by herself. In "The Laws of Health," she lectured on the necessity of washing, the importance of clean water and fresh air, the foolishness of overeating, and the wisdom of cleaning one's teeth after every meal. "Advice from an Old Friend" extended these exhortations about cleanliness, urging the freedpeople to keep their houses tidy, their personal appearance neat, and their gardens well weeded. Using the customary list of racist labels applied to freed blacks, she warned them against being "vicious, lazy, and careless," "idle," "dirty," "slovenly," or "vulgar." Confident and encouraging, she asked them to dedicate themselves instead to a customary list of white middle-class values: sobriety, industry, honesty, cleanliness, respectful and polite manners, economy, diligence, thrift, and benevolence. She concluded her "Advice" by informing readers that "The Abolitionists did a great deal for you," and thus she exhorted them to be ever mindful of their putative debt to Northern philanthropy.[13]

Though progressive in its focus on black history, Child's textbook ultimately reinforced the conventional and condescending manner of regarding freed blacks as equals who were nevertheless practically or developmentally inferior, and hence in need of some parental advice, some benevolent tutelage from those, like Child, who "did a great deal for you." Although, according to her own words, she would have preferred to relate with blacks "as . . . if they were white" (that is, according to her conflation of equality and sameness, as if they were equals), Child typically spoke of black adults as if they were children. "I doubt whether we *can* treat our colored brethren *exactly* as we would if they were white, though it is desirable to do so," Child explained to Sarah Shaw in 1866. "But we have kept their minds in a state of infancy, and children *must* be treated with more patience and forbearance than grown people."[14]

Even eccentric humanitarians, like Alcott and Whitman who had imagined a humanitarianism that would move away from treating patients as deficient and helpless children, slipped back into conventional and coercive attitudes when the patients of the benevolent project were African American or Native American rather than white or predominantly white. Soon after her stint as a nurse for the Union army, Alcott had wanted to shift her benevolent attention to the freedpeople. And, as her representations of African Americans demonstrate, she shared the romantic racialist assumptions of the "two generations of abolitionists" from whom she descended, assumptions that often guided the North's philanthropic effort on behalf of the freedpeople. In *Hospital Sketches,* her autobiographical persona described African Americans as "obsequious, trickish, lazy and ignorant, yet kind-hearted, merry-tempered, quick to feel," and hence not exactly social or intellectual equals. Black people were in Alcott's writing more like "baby Africa," a bothersome but amusing child to be cared for.[15]

Whitman also thought black people were childlike, but he considered them intellectually "vacant," dirty, passive, biologically inferior, and like "the Injun" destined for extinction as well. And neither Alcott nor Whitman expressed much humanitarian concern about the suffering of North America's aboriginal peoples. During the war Whitman had visited "once or twice" the camps and hospitals for the war's black refugees, and in 1865 he served as a clerk in the Interior Department's Office of Indian Affairs. Yet, despite his demonstrated ability to think eccentrically and compassionately about helping, Whitman usually ignored the suffering of Native Americans and African Americans in the postemancipation United States. In *Drum-Taps* and *Lilacs and Other Pieces,* he made no reference to African Americans, slavery, or the freeing of slaves, even though both volumes were ostensibly devoted to the war and the period immediately following the war. Such a remarkable omission suggests an ignorance of or indifference to the significance of African Americans at this crucial moment in U.S. history and a disregard for the continued suffering and marginalization of black people after the war.[16]

In 1867, in an attempt to come to some understanding of the meaning of emancipation and the history of suffering that preceded it, Whitman wrote "Ethiopia Commenting," later retitled "Ethiopia Saluting the Colors." But the poet's picture of a "hardly human" freedwoman greeting Sherman's army and the Union flag was hardly an eccentric or progressive expansion in humanitarian thinking. The poem's speakers (the woman and a soldier marching with Sherman's army) sound much different from the Whitman persona found in other poems, and thus readers are unlikely to confuse the speakers with the poet himself. Nevertheless, the projection of these two voices lacks ironic force. Within a culture eager for black people to be grateful for their liberation at the hands of whites, the central action of the poem—the freedwoman's salutation of the flag and the army—would unambiguously stand for the thankfulness of a people freed by Union armies. And neither the use of terminal rhyme and regular stanzas nor the reproduction of popular racist images associated with black women would do much to upset the expectations of nineteenth-century poetry readers. Thus, "Ethiopia" could only function ultimately as a repetition of the culture's typically racist perception of black women, and as such was a manifestation of a racial shortsightedness in Whitman's humanitarian vision.[17]

Childlike: Lydia Maria Child, Analogy, and Infantilization in Humanitarian Indian Reform

While efforts to aid the freedpeople dominated humanitarian thought and action in the postwar United States, movements to adopt a more humane national policy toward Native Americans gained momentum as white America's preoccupation with the war ended. Although activists like Henry Whipple of Minnesota had agitated on behalf of Indians throughout the war, many more politicians and humanitarians previously absorbed by slavery and the war turned their attention during the second half of the 1860s to the suffering of Native Americans. In *An Appeal for the Indians* (1868) Child announced, "I think the time has now come when, without intermitting our vigilant watch over rights of black men, it is our duty to arouse the nation to a sense of its guilt concerning the red men." Veteran antislavery activists like Child and Wendell Phillips, who had for years struggled against racism and for social justice, readily dedicated or rededicated themselves to Indian reform, as did others with a philanthropic bent, such as George Stuart, former Chairman of the U.S. Christian Commission, and Vincent Colyer, a New Yorker with experience in antislavery work, poor relief, and freedpeople's assistance.[18]

Events in the West also led to a growing benevolent interest in the welfare of Native Americans. In August 1862, an uprising of the Santee Sioux garnered national attention. It generated vindictive calls for extermination of Indians as well as humanitarian pleas for reform of the "Indian System."[19] But, more than any other event in the first half of the decade, the U.S. army's heinous massacre of a sleeping Cheyenne village at Sand Creek (Colorado) in November 1864 provoked humanitarian outcries against the brutal treatment of Native Americans. Colonel

John Chivington, a former Methodist preacher and Sunday school teacher, led the vicious attack at Sand Creek, overseeing the grisly murders of infants, the scalpings, and the barbarous mutilations of victims' genitals. Reports of the horrifying torture and slaughter of defenseless Indians brought celebrations to the streets of Denver, but sparked protests and stirred outrage among humanitarians in the East, stimulating renewed interest in the reformation of Indian policy.[20]

White Americans living in the West thought differently about "the Indian problem." As white immigrants continued to stream westward in search of new homesteads, their dogged pursuit of land combined with the resistance of the Native inhabitants whose lands were being taken produced inevitable conflicts. For many whites, particularly those living in the West, the solution to these white-Indian conflicts was simple: extermination of Native Americans. When Senator James Doolittle led congressional investigators west in July 1865 "to learn all they deemed necessary to form a correct judgment of the true condition of the Indian tribes," they were met by raucous whites unpersuaded by nonviolent solutions to these conflicts. "Exterminate them! Exterminate them!" roared the mob at the Denver Opera House.[21] Western newspapers advocated genocide as well; the *Kansas Daily Tribune* editorialized:

> There can be no permanent, lasting peace on our frontiers till these devils are exterminated. Our eastern friends may be slightly shocked at such a sentiment, but a few year's residence in the West, and acquaintance with the continued history of their outrages upon the settlers and travelers of the West, has dispersed the romance with which these people are regarded in the East.[22]

Claiming that Eastern humanitarians had no authentic grasp on life in the West, Westerners offered genocide as the realistic solution, as the practical way to peace. This staggeringly immoral proposal emerged from a rather common pattern of non-humanitarian thinking that valorized difference to the point of dehumanization, to the point where North America's aboriginal peoples became simply "devils." Since, according to the logic of this metaphor, killing "devils" was comparable only to the eradication of religious evil and not at all comparable to murdering innocent people in order to take their land, this construction of extreme difference worked to legitimate a policy of mass murder.

Following a dramatic Sioux victory over a detachment of U.S. soldiers near Fort Phil Kearny (Wyoming) in 1866, calls for extermination spread, becoming louder and gaining greater national attention. "We must act with vindictive earnestness against the Sioux," railed General William Tecumseh Sherman, a soon-to-be member of a new Indian Peace Commission, "even to their extermination, men, women, and children. Nothing else will reach the root of this case."[23]

Humanitarian reformers, however, were not prepared to accept the extermination of Native peoples as necessary or practical, despite the idea's popularity among Westerners, expansionists, and the military. Humanitarians proposed instead an extension of the system of reservations; they demanded "civilization," Christianization, English language education, and instruction in white methods of farming for the Indians. For decades before the war, humanitarians had spoken against the policy of Indian removal, the forced dispossession and relocation of entire tribes to reservations in the West. In the 1830s, for instance, antislavery writers Child, Emerson, and Whittier had strongly opposed Cherokee removal. By the 1860s, however, humanitarians showed less resistance to the idea of reservations, apparently not appreciating the degree to which any reservation policy would entail dispossession and relocation by force, or perhaps realizing that reservations had become the lone alternative to genocide in white public discourse about Indian policy. In response to the proposal "that the tribes should be collected into some Territory, indicated by Congress," Child did not object to the notion of the reservation itself, but only to the suggestion that a white governor of such territories would be above corruption, "unless the Governor was subject to a great deal of careful overseeing."[24]

Presided over by Commissioner of Indian Affairs Nathaniel G. Taylor, a deeply religious humanitarian and ardent defender of Indian rights, the new Indian Peace Commission also advocated reservations as part of "the hitherto untried policy in connection with Indians of endeavoring to conquer by kindness"—a policy that was clearly more humane than genocidal calls for extermination but was nonetheless a program of conquest, "of endeavoring to conquer." Convinced that "civilization must not be arrested in its progress by a handful of savages," the commissioners' report championed what they considered a kinder, gentler version of Manifest Destiny:

> We earnestly desire the speedy settlement of all our Territories. None are more anxious than we to see their agricultural and mineral wealth developed by an industrious, thrifty, and enlightened population. And we fully recognize the fact that the Indian must not stand in the way.

The Taylor Commission Report supported reservations for practical, economic, and humanitarian reasons, but ultimately turned to a popular bottom-line logic and claimed that "it costs less to civilize than to kill."[25]

In an apparent coming together of federal policy and humanitarianism, reformers like Child embraced the Taylor Commission Report. "I welcomed this Report almost with tears of joy," wrote Child in her *Appeal for the Indians*. She disagreed with "a few particulars" in the report, objecting mostly to the use of force to compel Indians to abandon polygamy or their native languages. But in general she praised the report "which manifests something like a right spirit toward the poor Indians!"[26] The hesitations, however, evident in Child's use of qualifiers like "almost" and "something like," suggest an imprecise and uneasy lingering doubt about the commission's proposals, something more than disagreement over "a few particulars."

After decades of work in antislavery struggles, Child had learned to wield domestic-reform rhetoric with passion and authority and had developed stongly held beliefs about the unity of human nature and the ultimate spiritual equality of all peoples. She came to support reservations, education, and Christianity for Native peoples as an expression of those beliefs, as a continuation of the benevolent uplift she had advocated for decades for African Americans. The Indian Peace

Commission, on the other hand, a board composed of humanitarians as well as representatives from the military, proposed to "civilize" Native Americans as a more expedient, less expensive, and less objectionable method of subduing peoples who were resisting seizure of their lands by whites. Hence, while Child and the commission supported plans that were in practice similar, Child's deeply principled writing revealed some uneasiness about the commission's primary aim, subjugation of the Indians, just as it expressed uneasiness about the commission's willingness to advocate force.

Yet, the public discussion about white-Indian conflicts was never defined in a way that encouraged a wider debate about the morality or utility of an Indian assimilation policy, or even in a way that permitted active self-reflection. Instead, debate about the "Indian question" had been utterly narrowed to two positions: civilization or extermination, feed them or fight them, paternalistic subjugation or genocide. In defense of its plans for reservations, the Taylor Commission Report argued, "Aside from extermination this is the only alternative now left us." A year earlier Sen. Doolittle's committee had come to the same conclusion: "the reservation system . . . is the only alternative to their extermination."[27] In the 1860s most humanitarians could conceive of white-Indian relations solely in either/or terms: whites could either support a paternalistic humanitarian program and act as benevolent protectors or endorse the continued extermination of Native peoples.

Rejecting the racist belief that Native Americans were "*destined* to disappear before the white man" and the even more appalling notion that whites ought to hasten that extinction, Child argued the "humanitarian" position in this debate, aligning herself with Doolittle, Taylor, Sherman (ironically enough), and a host of other reformers, missionaries, politicians, and philanthropists.[28] Thus, while the U.S. Army continued to murder Native Americans who resisted confiscation of their lands or wandered from reservations, Child and other reformers constructed a humanitarian program that—however benevolent in its aspirations or preferable to genocide—resulted practically in the dispossession, confinement, impoverishment, and starvation of tens of thousands of Native Americans. Their program energetically attempted to obliterate Native languages and cultures; and the recipients of this humanitarian beneficence feared, resisted, and despised it.[29]

The foundations of this program were conventional philanthropic patterns of thought about those being helped. Portraying Native Americans as the helpless victims of a white onslaught, humanitarians highlighted pity as the proper affective basis for white-Indian relations and used stylized, racialist images to depict Native American patients. Images of Indian devils and savages circulated as a type of truth throughout nineteenth-century Euro-American society, as did the belief that Indians were a vanishing race. Rejecting these Indian-hating stereotypes and with them the notion that Native Americans were inherently or permanently inferior, humanitarian discourse advanced instead representations of Indians as noble primitives or children to be cared for.[30]

As a rhetorician realizing that how her society saw Native Americans would determine how it responded to discourses advocating differing solutions to the Indian question, Child took the issue of representation very seriously. "How *ought* we to view the peoples who are less advanced than ourselves?" asked Child, indicating an a priori disposition to regard Native peoples as comparatively "less advanced." Her answer, in conventional domestic-philanthropic fashion, empha-sized the childlike position of Native Americans: "Simply as younger members of the same great human family, who need to be protected, instructed, and encour-aged, till they are capable of appreciating and sharing all our advantages." Notions of whites as parents to Indian children permeated government discourse as well.[31]

Taking exception to their infantilization within white discourse, some Native Americans tried to reshape that discourse and its assumptions. Medicine Horse, for example, explained his objections in very clear terms for whites: "We are not children. We are men." So had Old Joseph, years earlier: "I am no child; I can think for myself."[32]

Despite Native American objections and despite the premise of inequality reproduced by the parent-child rhetoric, Child and other humanitarians used analogy—the comparison of Indians to children—as a way to urge whites to reform U.S. Indian policy and help Native Americans. Although her ideas ran counter to essentialist views of Indian inferiority and to aggressively racist views of difference associated with calls for extermination, Child's humanitarianism as-sumed that Native Americans were in fact inferior, not innately and unalterably but culturally and—like children—developmentally.

In Child's *Appeal,* this infantilization of Native peoples functioned, first of all, as a means for ignoring Native ideas about or solutions to white-Indian conflict. An enormous cultural-linguistic rift frustrated Indian-white communication. As Calvin Martin has put it, "Indian-White history is the process of two thought-worlds that at the time were more often than not mutually unintelligible. Surely this is the most poignant message of Indian-White relations: 500 years of talking past each other, of mutual incomprehension."[33] Though hardly effective, infantil-ization was and is a tactic for dealing with people one does not understand. By making the Indians infants (that is, in Latin, *infans,* literally "mute, speechless"), Child eliminated the white-Indian communication gap by abandoning white-Indian communication. According to the logic of Child's text, because the Indians were infants, without language, there was really no need for or possibility for dialogue with them. The Indians could not speak for themselves and were thus rendered helpless. Someone needed to speak for and protect the Indians. In the aggressively Indian-hating United States of the 1860s and in the profoundly difficult realm of white-Indian encounter, humanitarians like Child were eager to speak for the Indians.

By making Indians into children, Child's text also worked to minimize the perception of differences between white peoples and Native peoples. While nonhumanitarians built their calls for extermination around a valorization of difference, and while many Native Americans used arguments about the difference between white and Native cultures to oppose the reservation system, Child resolutely evaded an acknowledgment of difference, believing—as she had throughout her career—that a recognition of the essential unity and identity of the human species was the key to forming a just, humane, egalitarian society. Since difference was merely the result of varying social conditions, educations, and circumstances, difference could not be used as evidence of inherent inferiority nor as justification for slavery, racism, or genocide. Moreover, any intellectual, material, social, or cultural inequalities could eventually be modified or ameliorated by laws, social institutions, and education.[34] Working to reduce difference to an easily knowable sameness, Child used analogies comparing Indians to children as a mechanism for making unfamiliar and possibly threatening others seem familiar, safe, and recognizable. This analogy-making egalitarianism, everywhere underpinned by the conviction that an essential sameness or identity threads its way throughout the "great human family," was the core of the *Appeal*'s humanitarian argument: because they are like children, inferior only in a developmental way and similar in every essential way, Indians are capable of being and ought to be civilized, rather than murdered. Thus, Child maintained, "I know it is an almost universal opinion that Indians are incapable of civilization; but I see no rational ground for such an opinion. . . . I have no doubt that every nation and tribe on earth is capable of being softened and refined if brought under the right influences."[35]

In defense of this thesis, she offered a catalogue of the ways in which Indians were already civilized, commenting on Native Americans' trustworthiness, kindness, gratitude, modesty and respect for feminine modesty, respect for parents, affection for children and strong familial affection in general, "motherly dignity," "quiet decorum," sincerity in mourning, natural sentimentality, good manners, pastoral inclinations, and prayerfulness.[36] What is striking about Child's list of "natural" Indian virtues is how indistinguishable it is from the domestic-reform ideals of nineteenth-century New England's white, Christian middle class. By placing white humanitarians' ideological imaginary in a representational space she identified as Native identity and culture, Child continued her analogizing drive toward sameness. She wanted her readers to see how Indians were just like other people; and she wanted her readers to see themselves (or at least their collective ego ideal) mirrored in Native Americans. Such a move suggests a desire for identification rather than a will to power; but the homogenizing consequence of such analogy was to reinforce, for white people and Native peoples, a single standard of "civilization." Although she was saying that these virtues already resided within Native peoples, Child's main point was not that because the Indians are virtuous people white people should reform themselves. Her primary line of argument went something like: the Indians are already virtuous and civilized in ways like white people; any difference between them and us is purely developmental; therefore, we should support reservations as a way to reinforce these ideals, virtues, customs (this "civilization") in Native peoples. (White people would, of course, be left to their consciences and to the admonitions of wives and mothers in the effort to realize this domestic-philanthropic ideal.)

Within the context of Child's argument, then, the most basic function of infantilizing analogy was to naturalize the reservation system—to make it appear good, right, natural. Because, as Child believed, white people should speak for Native peoples and decide what is best for them; because Native peoples are basically the same as white people; because the only important difference between Indians and whites is an educational/developmental lack in the Indians; and because the Indians are civilizable and already have within them the virtues necessary for civilization, a system of reservations set up by white people for Indians would be the preferable means for continuing the process of civilization and assimilation. The logic of Child's infantilizing analogy suggested that sending the Indians off to live and learn in the reservations was as good, right, and natural as sending children off to kindergarten or boarding school. As this logic dominated her humanitarianism, it occluded Native American objections as well as consideration of the way in which this humanitarianism acted as a call for the systematic obliteration of Native cultures.

While her argument was a morally admirable stand against genocide, it could not imagine plural, viable American cultures and thus became a case for the benevolent eradication of Native American cultures. Child measured "civilization" according to the values of a white, middle-class, Christian domestic ideology, values she considered universal signs of civilization. She and other humanitarians tended to think of culture as a single, unitary achievement, as a "civilization," which they would generously bestow upon the not-yet-civilized but civilizable Indians. As Carolyn Karcher has explained,

> The evolutionary theory to which she subscribed (in common with virtually all progressive thinkers of her day) posited Euro-American "civilization" as the acme of development and the model for other cultures to emulate. It left no room for alternative models.[37]

The equality that Child imagined for Native peoples was their ability to become, through a cultural reeducation, the same as white people, to live their lives as whites and leave behind their own beliefs, languages, and cultural practices. She could not conceive of an alternative.

Such a vision of humanitarian "equality" terrified and depressed Native Americans. Big Eagle of the Santee Sioux had noted that "The whites were always trying to make the Indians give up their life and live like white men—go to farming, work hard, and do as they did—and the Indians did not know how to do that, and did not want to anyway." But humanitarians pushed forward with their assimilationist plans "to change the savage into a civilized man"; to "blot out" the cultural differences between Native Americans and "fuse them into one homogenous mass"; to teach English, white methods of farming, Christianity, and white customs of dress and appearance. (Whipple, for instance, insisted that a "hair cut" was the "first step in the change from barbarism to civilization.") Some Native peoples, like Big Bear of the Otoes, had explained to these whites who wanted to help that their scheme was imperious, oppressive, and futile: "you cannot make white men of us. That is one thing you can't do." Realizing what a white offer of help entailed, some Native Americans simply refused humanitarian assistance. "I do not need your help," Chief Joseph told U.S. agents, "we won't have any help from you."[38]

Tragically, for the Nez Perce and other American Indians, the government and the humanitarians continued to help. Under the Grant administration, the pro-gram for assimilation and civilization became the foundation of federal Indian policy. Managed by government agents and overseen by white missionaries and teachers, reservations functioned as the domestic-institutional space for the eradication of Native languages and cultures and the training of Indians in white cultural practices. They also functioned as a restraining institution, much like the asylum or the penitentiary, allowing the dominant classes to control or contain—by force when necessary—populations that did not obey or conform to sanctioned social practices or mainstream modes of living and being. The reservations reinforced a philanthropic relationship in which Native Americans became "help-less and ignorant wards" or "unlettered children of the wilderness," while white humanitarians took on the role of "guardian." Native Americans, as the patients of this oppressive and destructive humanitarianism, were denied a voice in decisions about their lives and cultures. As Christine Bolt has explained: "In tune with the coercive and paternalistic strain in the national reform tradition, neither the Indian office nor the philanthropists felt it was necessary to consult Indian opinion before making policy decisions and there was certainly no formal machinery for doing so."[39] Only outside this humanitarian relationship could they exercise their power or give voice to their own needs, interests, and ideals. Although Native Americans resisted the coercive imposition of white civilization, Sherman and his armies ruthlessly patrolled the West to ensure that no Indians strayed from the reservations and, accordingly, that none remained outside humanitarianism.[40]

Humanitarianism and Race after the War

As I have been arguing throughout this book, humanitarian discourses and practices in this era were internally fragmented, fluid, changeable, and sometimes open to progressive, radical, and eccentric innovations. Nevertheless, in the years following the war, a new paradigm with an emphasis on government sponsorship, discipline, institutions, efficiency, and order established itself as the dominant mode for thinking and acting philanthropically. With the establishment of a new paradigm, eccentricity and change in humanitarianism had reason to slow.[41]

Furthermore, as a survey of humanitarian efforts on behalf of Native Ameri-cans and freedpeople indicates, white responses to racial and cultural difference continued to constitute a considerable impasse to radical, progressive, or eccentric humanitarian thought among whites in the post–Civil War era, as it had in the antebellum United States. While this is not a case of *plus ça change, plus c'est la même chose,* the history of early postwar humanitarianism does suggest the imposing extent to which racism shaped the transformations within humanitari-anism in the 1860s and impeded certain radical or eccentric innovations in humanitarian thinking and practice. When patients of a particular domain of humanitarian practice were nonwhite, typical sets of racialist representations would then, almost invariably, participate in the construction of those patients as helpless, childlike, culturally or developmentally inferior, and unable to act or speak for themselves. Such representations served to reinforce, rather than transform, the agent/patient dyad. The hierarchical structure of the agent/patient relationship then called forth certain humanitarian practices which, when examined in light of their consequences, tended to suppress cultural differences, deny power and voice to patients, encourage paternalistic instruction as a benevolent act, and invite agents to act as guardians and tutors without regard to the objections of those being helped. Despite their professions of equality and their opposition to inegalitarian notions of difference, benevolent workers often enforced a type of inequality wherein equality could only signify sameness or identity. As an element and later a product of the postbellum philanthropic paradigm, this impasse in humanitarianism limited the ways in which benevolence was thought and practiced.

Hence, a humanitarian like Child—a progressive who held strong egalitarian and activist ideals, who tried to imagine black history and black writings as the cornerstone for education of the freedpeople, who expressed a discernible uneasiness about the coercive nature of Indian reform—would also lecture African Americans about the importance of clean hands and well-weeded gardens and champion the confinement of Native Americans to reservations where they would take lessons in Christianity and white culture. And eccentric humanitarians like Alcott and Whitman, who advocated a patient-centered humanitarianism when their patients were white (or typically white), would fall back on racist notions of inferiority when those being helped were Native peoples or African Americans.

Thoreau's Difference

Thoreau's place in any discussion of humanitarianism and Native Americans is tenuous. Although he spent memorable time with and was drawn to both humanitarian reformers like John Brown and American Indians like Joe Polis, he did not and could not identify himself with either group. He tended to take up the role of observer or anthropologist of both groups.[42]

His relationship to humanitarian reform politics was inconsistent, idiosyncratic, antagonistic. He outspokenly opposed the imperialistic Mexican War, refusing to pay his poll tax in protest of the war's antidemocratic, proslavery designs. A participant in Concord's antislavery activities and a regular reader of abolitionist newspapers such as Garrison's *Liberator,* Nathaniel Rogers's *Herald of Freedom,* and Horace Greeley's *New York Tribune,* Thoreau gave his antislavery radicalism its most powerful public expression in "Slavery in Massachusetts" and in his John Brown addresses.[43] Despite this commitment to abolitionism, he keenly criticized humanitarian reform movements throughout his career. Reformers should stop meddling, complaining, and telling others what to do, he suggested. Instead they should reform themselves. His insistence that they look inside and not out and reform their individual lives rather than society and its institutions became a central doctrine of his reform politics. He took very little interest in social reform projects per se (attempts "to make this [world] a good place to live in") or collective political action in general, admiring instead only the rare and revolutionary actions of extraordinary individuals like John Brown.[44]

Thoreau's participation in humanitarian reform politics was characteristically an expression of deeply held moral principles (centered on issues of individualism and integrity) and not a demonstration of philanthropic sympathy. He refused, for instance, to name sympathy for the enslaved among his reasons for opposing slavery. Even in his antislavery speeches, Thoreau scarcely discussed or even referred to black people. On the infrequency of his feelings of philanthropic sympathy, Thoreau wrote in his *Journal*:

> I have been conscious of a certain softness to which I am otherwise and commonly a stranger, in which the gates were loosened to some emotions; and if I were to become a confirmed invalid, I see how some sympathy with mankind or society might spring up. Yet what is my softness good for, even to tears. . . . The tears were merely a phenomenon of the bowels, and I felt that expression of my sympathy, so unusual with me, was something mean, and such as I should be ashamed to have the subject of it understand. I had a cold in my head withal, about those days. I found that I had some bowels, but then it was because my bowels were out of order. (11 November 1851)

James Goodwin has quoted this journal passage as proof of Thoreau's adherence to "a doctrine of individual nihilism." Though he overstates his case, Goodwin demonstrates the ways in which Thoreau's individualism was at odds with humanitarian reform movements and organized politics. Nevertheless, before dismissing Thoreau's work as the mere "dead end of radical individualism," as Goodwin does, we might want to rethink Thoreau's challenge to sympathetic humanitarian feeling here. Thoreau wondered what such sympathy was "good for," what its advantages and its consequences were, while also suggesting that such feelings were "mean." Given philanthropic sympathy's capacity to inflict suffering on those being helped or sympathized with, humanitarians would do well, it seems, to consider more carefully and more self-critically the value of such sympathy, the consequences of such sympathy, and indeed the possibility that a type of meanness typically enters into such soft, sympathetic feelings.[45]

Perhaps because of this distrust of conventional philanthropic sympathy, Thoreau's engagement with Indian reform was remote. While he did speak out in protest against slavery, he never made any plea for humanitarian consideration of Native Americans, nor did he outline any proposal for reform of U.S. Indian policy. He kept thousands of pages of notes about American Indian life and culture, but remained generally silent about the political and cultural oppression of American Indians.[46] As his Indian books and the numerous references in his journal and other writings indicate, Thoreau had a lifelong fascination with Native peoples and their cultures. While his extensive reading and notetaking on North American Indian tribes undoubtedly helped form his view on the subject, his personal encounters with American Indians, especially his 1857 journey with Joe Polis, were intense learning experiences that shaped in an uncommon way his perspective on Native Americans.

Hence, in order to designate the way in which Thoreau's point of view deviated from his society's conventional assumptions and attitudes, the way in which it moved to the margins of humanitarian reform but never quite escaped, the way in which it took shape from learning experiences atypical among whites, I call Thoreau's perspective on Native Americans and humanitarianism "eccentric." He remained never completely outside and never exactly inside humanitarian reform politics, although he moved along the edges of and was unquestionably influenced by the New England reform community. And while it is true that Euro-American culture's discursive production of Indians shaped what he knew and thought, he also learned about Native American cultures from people like Joe Aitteon and Joe Polis, American Indians who grew up in Indian and white cultures and who held perspectives on Native life much different from those of the white explorers, missionaries, and ethnographers whose books on North American Indians Thoreau had studied.[47] These personal contacts were the basis for a perspective that diverged, at times remarkably, from conventional ethnographic or popular or humanitarian views of Native Americans.

In 1862, in the midst of the Civil War and a crisis-driven transformation in humanitarian thought, Thoreau continued to revise his most significant piece of writing on American Indians, *The Maine Woods* (published 1864). Suffering from tuberculosis and growing steadily more ill, Thoreau had, much to his dismay, become a patient during this period of assembling and revising the *Maine Woods* manuscript. Thinking about this book even in his final moments, uttering "Moose" and "Indian" as his last words, Thoreau died on May 6, three months before the Santee Sioux uprising in Minnesota and the beginning of a widespread renewal in Indian reform efforts.[48] In the years of change immediately following Thoreau's death, even the most progressive elements of Euro-American humanitarianism would reach an impasse in developing a humanitarian relationship to Native Americans—an impasse that, as elaborated earlier, continued to rely on racialist notions of patient inferiority, conceived of helping as a form of paternalistic instruction, and imagined equality only in terms of identity. While he did not and could not completely step outside the racist beliefs of his community and his era, Thoreau's perspective on Indians and Indian-white relations envisioned a way through this impasse. Though not a direct intervention into Indian reform, *The Maine Woods* did provide humanitarians an alternative perspective on their work: it offered them an opportunity to rethink their representation of others, their notion of help, and their conception of the basis for equality.

As Robert Sattelmeyer has written, "Thoreau was a writer who participated fully if idiosyncratically in his age."[49] While he never transcended his age's racialism, in passages in *The Maine Woods* he did take important steps toward moving beyond the stereotypes by which most whites knew Indians. *The Maine Woods* begins, however, with these stereotypes. In the opening narrative, "Ktaadn," an account of an 1846 expedition to Maine first drafted that year and first published in 1848, Thoreau claims that "the Indian's history" is "the history of his extinction" (6), echoing racialist myths about the fated demise of this vanishing race and introducing such a claim with an image of a "woebegone" Indian carrying "a bundle of skins" and "an empty keg" (6).[50] Using standard vocabulary from nineteenth-century constructions of Indians as "savages," he describes various

Indians as "shabby" (6), "dull and greasy-looking," "sluggish," (9), "disposed to sulks and whims" (32), "sinister and slouching" (78). In the main white-Indian interaction in "Ktaadn," Louis Neptune and his companions, the Indian guides he hires, "delayed so long by a drunken frolic" (78), fail to rendezvous with Thoreau and his companions. These images confirm Thoreau in his belief that the Indians are a race whose "extinction" is imminent: they are unreliable, "degraded" (78), acutely vulnerable to white vices, and hence destined to disappear.[51] In "Ktaadn," Thoreau's "primeval, untamed, and forever untamable *Nature*" (69), this land that he later calls "exceedingly new" (81), is eternal, immutable, but its inhabitants, ill-adapted to contact with white culture, necessarily die off. "So he goes about his destiny, the red face of man" (79).

As the reader moves through *The Maine Woods,* however, it is the racialist generalizations that start to die off, not Native Americans. In "Chesuncook," the second narrative (first drafted in 1853, first published in 1858), the land is not so immutable and the American Indians not nearly the vanishing race they were in "Ktaadn." After discussing North America's expansive tracts of "primitive pine forest," Thoreau notes sadly: "But Maine, perhaps, will soon be where Massachusetts is. A good part of her territory is already as bare and common place as much of our neighborhood" (153). Deploring the too rapid and too devastating changes to the North American landscape, he bears witness to the fact that the land is not eternal, untamable, immutable, but rather all too vulnerable to human alterations. "The civilized man," Thoreau notes, "not only clears the land permanently to a great extent, and cultivates open fields, but he tames and cultivates to a certain extent the forest itself. By his mere presence, almost, he changes the nature of the trees as no other creature does" (151). In parts of "Chesuncook," moreover, Indians are no longer the soon-to-be-extinct inhabitants of this landscape. Instead, Thoreau presents his Penobscot guide, Joe Aitteon, as a person who is steady, reliable, adaptable, astutely aware of what he and his community must do to survive the incursions of white "civilization" into their lives, and hence not entirely poised to give way and die (see 107, 149). While his portrait of Aitteon takes him away from the vanishing race mythology, Thoreau elsewhere in "Chesuncook" succumbs to this mythology, remarking at one point: "What a coarse and imperfect use Indians and hunters make of Nature! No wonder that their race is so soon exterminated" (120). While the main point of this passage may indeed be, as Robert Sayre suggests, to wish the fate of Indians on to (white) hunters who exploitatively kill the majestic moose that so fascinate Thoreau, it stands nonetheless as another repetition of the vanishing race mythology that Euro-Americans used to construct their images of American Indians. Apparently, Thoreau's "Indians" were still primarily the product of racialist discourse.[52]

In "The Allegash and East Branch," however, Thoreau moves decidedly away from racialist myths about destined extinction. Uncomfortable with making any universalizable assertions about Native Americans or nature after this third trip to the Maine woods in 1857, he avoids conventional, stereotypical description. The wilderness that Thoreau once thought eternal now appears to be something of a discursive invention. Alluding satirically to Cotton Mather's rhetorical construction of the land inhabited by Indians, Thoreau writes: "Generally speaking, a howling wilderness does not howl: it is the imagination of the traveler that does the howling" (219).[53]

Although he had in previous narratives effortlessly reproduced and circulated the myth that Indians were a vanishing race, Thoreau now rejects that myth (for nothing in his "Allegash" observations makes it a warrantable belief) and instead represents Native Americans as living on rather than dying off. In the first paragraph of "Allegash" Thoreau encounters Molly Molasses, a Penobscot woman who lived to be over one hundred years old; her longevity is for Thoreau a particular that not only throws into question the certainty of Indian extinction but also serves as specific evidence that the Penobscots remain "extant as a tribe" (157). When Thoreau and his companion, Edward Hoar, arrive at Indian Island to begin their excursion, they find that "the Indians were nearly all gone, to the seaboard and to Massachusetts, partly on account of the small pox, of which they are very much afraid, having broken out in Oldtown" (157). The passage evokes the history of diseases, beginning with the European invasion, that devastated American Indian populations. The staggering depopulation of North American Indian tribes was, according to white racialist ideology, confirmation that the Indians' destiny was extinction, an argument that evaded the issue of white culpability by constructing these deaths as "destined." Thoreau, however, shows readers a community taking active measures to avoid extinction, despite the onslaught of whites and disease; the Penobscots in "Allegash" are not a race stoically resigned to destiny. Thus, at the beginning of this narrative, Thoreau raises the issue of Native American survival, without suggesting that Indians are fated to perish as a race.

Indeed, nowhere in "The Allegash and East Branch," by far the longest of the three *Maine Woods* narratives, does he repeat and reinforce the vanishing race myth. Thoreau's account of Joe Polis in fact contradicts that myth by offering up instead Polis's story of Indian survival. As Thoreau and Hoar follow Polis through the dense Maine forest, Polis recounts a story from his childhood, pointing out to them "where he had thus crept along day after day when he was a boy of ten, and in a starving condition" (279; see also 183-84). Trapped in the far north by an "unexpectedly early" (279) winter, Polis and two adult companions attempted to walk back to Oldtown, negotiating difficult terrain and wading at times through freezing, chin-deep waters. Having scarcely eaten (Polis did catch one otter that they shared) but having survived starvation and winter storms, the "very weak and emaciated" Polis arrived home: "he was very low, and did not expect to live" (279). But Polis did recover and even prospered. While perhaps explaining in part his reluctance to skip or delay meals (see 166, 261, 278), Polis's story of this scrape with starvation, retold here by Thoreau, also provides an alternative to Thoreau's previous anecdotes about Indian extinction (such as the Indian scrambling up the bank with an empty keg [6] or the mythic Indian who paddles away to meet "his destiny" [79]).

Moreover, the survival of Indians in Polis's story depends on the Indians themselves and not on the protection or guardianship of white humanitarians—

although a white teamster gives them as much food "as they could eat" (279) when they finally reach a town. In Polis's story, then, whites do not function in the two conventional roles that humanitarians had assigned whites in relation to Native Americans: whites are neither the superior race who constitute a threat to Indian life (the weather and the lack of food are the dangerous elements here), nor are they the benevolent protectors of threatened Native American lives. Instead, Polis's tale accords whites a different pair of roles: the provider of a meal—that is, a humanitarian of sorts (the teamster)—and the audience (Thoreau and Hoar).

While Polis's story helps move "Allegash" away from notions of Indian extinction, Thoreau's portrait of Polis takes the narrative beyond the stylized racialist images typically used by Euro-Americans to represent Native peoples. Unlike almost every other nineteenth-century Euro-American representation of American Indians, Joe Polis is complex, multidimensional. As a figure in Thoreau's writing, Polis is not simply the product of racist discourse, but rather the locus of multiple discourses. As a character, Joe Polis is, as Sayre puts it, "the most fully developed person (after the author himself) to appear anywhere in Thoreau's writing" (172). At times Thoreau's Polis conspicuously contradicts racialist images of Indians. Unlike the stern, taciturn, "roving and savage" Indian of savagism, Joe Polis loves "to play sometimes" (challenging Thoreau to a foot race at one point [286]), often talks on at great length (289), and owns a large white house, the only two-story house in town (157–58, 296–97).[54] In other passages, he behaves much as Thoreau expects Indians to behave. Baffled by white civil law (173–74) and white impertinence (289), Polis's skills are calling animals (206–207), hunting (162, 265–67), canoeing, and finding his way through the forests. He does, however, lose his way at times (276–77, 166). His other skills include making tea (206, 273) and potently sweet coffee (239) and making Sunday a day of rest (182, 193, 289–91)—in other words, talents that are not stereotypically "Indian." Thoreau hires Indian guides because, like an anthropologist, he wants to observe natives and study their ways (95). While his observation often confirms much of what he expects to find, Thoreau's study also produces Joe Polis—a Native American character who lies about having a pipe to keep a seedy drunk from using it (162–63), who sings songs (178–79), who accidentally spits on Thoreau's back (210), and who has an unfortunate run-in with Daniel Webster (252–53). Although an accumulation of specific and curious detail is not at all unusual in a Thoreauvian description, Thoreau makes such descriptions serve remarkable ends in "Allegash." The collection of contradictory, idiosyncratic minutiae that make up Polis as a character keeps Polis from being readily understood within the terms of Euro-American racialist knowledge or easily adapted to racialist representation.

As he moves beyond the racialist images associated with Indian reform discourse, Thoreau also rejects humanitarianism's paternalistic agent/patient dyad and constructs instead a relationship that rests on mutual helping, interdependence, and an acceptance of or regard for difference.

Most nineteenth-century humanitarians saw equality in terms of identity and homogeneity. Representing Indians as culturally disadvantaged, inferior in the way children are inferior to adults, humanitarians like Child believed that because Indians were the same as whites in terms of "human nature" or their "humanity," benevolent whites could lift up the Indians and teach them the value and virtue of "civilization"—conceived as a unitary achievement—"till they are capable of appreciating and sharing all our advantages."[55] The result was a program to eradicate Native American languages and cultural practices, replacing them with white "civilization." Intensely focused on the differences between Indians and whites, nonhumanitarian whites did not see Indians as part of Child's "same great human family" and could not imagine the equality that she had envisioned, and thus did not think a program of benevolent uplift wise, possible, or worthwhile.

Thoreau paid a great deal of attention to difference as well, but his was a difference with a difference. Thoreau begins his "Allegash" narrative by noting the "remoteness" that separates Indians and whites (158). Polis too comments several times on the "very distinct" "line of separation" between Thoreau and whites on the one hand and himself and Native peoples on the other. Thoreau observes that Polis never uses the pronoun "we" but, always mindful of the difference between them, says instead "you and I" (167). Reemphasizing the idea later, Polis reminds the author, "Great difference between me and white man" (185).

Although Thoreau and Polis both appreciate this "[g]reat difference," difference in Allegash is not a simple operation that neatly divides whites from Indians and Native American cultures from Euro-American cultures. Thoreau's portrait of Polis captures a person acculturated to certain traditionally Euro-American habits: Polis takes Sunday as a day of rest (182, 193, 289–91), lives in town in a big white house (157–58, 296–97), favors schools for Penobscot children (293), etc. Yet, as his recurring concern for difference suggests, Polis is also a Penobscot who, while identifying with aspects of white culture, always insists on his own alterity in relation to white culture. Both the humanitarian conception of a common identity and the nonhumanitarian distinction between "us" and inimical others are inadequate perspectives from which to understand Polis's identity, Thoreau's identity, and the relationship between Polis and Thoreau.

Thus, Thoreau takes careful note of Polis's accentuation of the differences *between* whites and Penobscots, and he also pays heed to diversity *within* Native American individuals, as his multidimensional portrait of Polis suggests. Thoreau is attentive to differences *among* Native Americans as well. He shows interest in historical differences, the differences between the present generation of Indians and their ancestors (107), political differences within the tribe (148–49, 293–94), differences in assimilation, and linguistic variations (320–25). This emphasis on difference is not that of nonhumanitarians, who use difference as evidence of the inferiority of the culture which is not theirs and as justification for exclusionary practices and worse. Instead, Thoreau shapes his emphasis on difference into a notion of equality that, moving beyond the impasse in humanitarian thought, will allow him to picture diverse people living together without hierarchy or homogenization.

As a writer distrustful of philanthropic sympathy, Thoreau has doubts about the virtue of benevolent uplift. Yet such doubts about helping others do not lead Thoreau in *The Maine Woods* to misanthropy and antisocial isolationism. The interdependence of Native Americans and European Americans, which Thoreau acknowledges in "Chesuncook" (108–109), develops later into a picture of Native Americans and whites living together subjectively and intimately. Near the end of "Chesuncook," for example, he gives readers an image of "two white men and four Indians" sleeping together "side by side" (142). He suggests this familiarity in a more idiosyncratic way in his account of Polis, when he writes: "Having resumed our seats in the canoe, I felt the Indian wiping my back, which he had accidently spat upon. He said it was a sign that I was going to be married" (210). Made even more peculiar by a consideration of Thoreau's disinclination toward marriage, this moment of awkward intimacy entails touching (a rare event in Thoreau's writing), some faint embarrassment and humor, the projection of Thoreau into a traditional intimate relationship, and the brief sharing of this "sign" of future intimacy.

Perhaps even more important than his picture of Indians and whites living together and sharing personal space is Thoreau's conviction that Native Americans and whites can and ought to be learning from each other. As mentioned earlier, Thoreau seeks out Indian guides because he wants to learn from them (95). Particularly interested in Penobscot names for birds, for example, Thoreau wants to learn Polis's language. Yet the learning relationship they agree upon is neither paternalistic (white humanitarian teaching civilization to childlike Indians) nor strictly anthropological (white observer recording native ways), but rather dialogic and mutual. "I told him that in this voyage I would tell him all I knew," writes Thoreau, "and he should tell me all he knew, to which he readily agreed" (168).[56] These are also the only conditions according to which Thoreau would teach his spiritual beliefs: "all that would tempt me to teach the Indian my religion would be his promise to teach me *his*" (182). Thoreau describes Polis as an excellent student, "very clever and quick to learn" (111). And in his contact with Native Americans, Thoreau himself proves to be a capable learner as well. As he shifts from typically racialist images of Indians in "Ktaadn" to his complex, detailed portrait of Polis in "Allegash," Thoreau broadens and reshapes his own and his readers' knowledge of Native Americans.

Moreover, Thoreau is exhilarated by what he learns from American Indians, especially Joe Polis. Just after the third trip, Thoreau wrote in a letter to his friend Harrison Blake:

> I have now returned from Maine, and think I have had a quite profitable journey, chiefly from associating with an intelligent Indian. Having returned I flatter myself that the world appears in some respects a little larger, and not as usual smaller and shallower for having extended my range. I have made a short excursion into the new world which the Indian dwells in or is. He begins where we leave off. . . . The Indian who can find his way so wonderfully in the woods possesses so much intelligence which the white man does not,—and it increases my own capacity as well as faith to observe it. I rejoice to find that intelligence flows in other channels than I knew.[57]

During his journey with Polis, Thoreau had opened himself up to new learning experiences and new ways of exchanging knowledge. His notion of "intelligence," unlike conventional humanitarian and nonhumanitarian conceptions of "civilization," had finally come to respect the diversity of mental culture in a world which seemed "a little larger" after Polis. Though only an initial step toward an antiracist practice, this recognition and celebration of "other channels" is the foundation of learning in *The Maine Woods*. This appreciation for (and indeed rejoicing over) difference enables Thoreau to imagine a Native American–European American relationship that encourages dialogic exchange, mutual learning, and mutual helping—a relationship that avoids one-way benevolent instruction and the assumptions of superiority and inferiority therein. The equality Thoreau postulates is not the leveling homogenization of conventional benevolence, but rather an equality based on difference and the possibility for dialogic learning that difference affords.

The Limits of Eccentricity

Thoreau's eccentric perspective on Indian-white relations could only deviate from his culture's racist thinking. He could not transcend it. While he takes important steps away from racialist representation, Thoreau does not entirely abandon such modes of language and thought, even in "Allegash." Responding to Polis's singing, for instance, Thoreau writes: "There was, indeed, a beautiful simplicity about it; nothing of the dark and savage, only the mild and infantile" (179). Despite Polis's profound influence on Thoreau's representation of Native peoples, the change in Thoreau's discourse is registered here as a shift from the "dark and savage" popular imagery to the benevolent racialism that preferred to see Indians as "mild and infantile." Even in his approach to difference, Thoreau sometimes slips back into dominant rhetorical constructions of difference. Commenting on Polis's conjecture that he'd make a poor hunter in New York City, Thoreau says, "He understood very well both his superiority and his inferiority to the whites" (197). The remark is, of course, part of Thoreau's attempt to appreciate the differences between Euro-Americans and Native Americans. Although he does not suggest that Indians are *generally* inferior, the conventional racialist categories of "superiority" and "inferiority" remain as a trace within Thoreau's rhetoric.[58]

Moreover, Thoreau's writing lacked a political practice that would translate his counterhegemonic vision into action—or, more specifically, a type of action that would struggle to halt the murder and abuse of Native Americans while also opposing the eradication of Native languages and cultural practices from which he felt whites had so much to learn. As a dissident writer eccentrically engaged with humanitarians and Native Americans, Thoreau began to think about Indian-white relations in a way that stood apart from the two dominant Euro-American views, extermination versus civilization. Yet, because of his disinclination for making a political intervention into the national debate on this issue (his unwillingness to shape his writing into an incitement to action or into a policy-making appeal), *The Maine Woods* became an eccentric but largely unnoticed humanitarian text. Even reformers as credentialed as Thomas Wentworth Higginson never made connections between *The Maine Woods* and Indian reform's humanitarian agenda, probably because Thoreau never encouraged readers to make such connections.

Reviewing *The Maine Woods* for the *Atlantic Monthly,* Higginson admired Thoreau's "minute observation" of Indians, but ultimately found "the table-talk of the aboriginal" to be "a bore." He had little else to say about Native Americans.[59]

Thoreau's weakness or failure was in a sense the opposite of Child's activism. Determined to make a convincing and practical intervention that would halt the killing and persecution of American Indians, Child shaped her *Appeal for the Indians* according to the dominant terms of the national debate, a strategy that led her to adopt a humanitarian position that had some not-so-humanitarian consequences for those being helped. Assiduously avoiding any such intervention and disregarding the dominant voices constructing the national debate, Thoreau's work was not prepared to make the kind of immediate political impact that Child aimed for. Nevertheless, the marginal, eccentric nature of Thoreau's humanitarian work—the feature that made *The Maine Woods* a more or less ignored voice in Indian reform in the 1860s—also laid the foundation for a vision that advocated neither death nor assimilation but rather a notion of an equality based on differences and the cultural possibilities therein.

In humanitarian Indian reform in the 1860s, activists like Child and dissidents like Thoreau never came together. An exchange between activists demanding a political practice and dissidents redefining the terms and meanings of the struggle might have incited further or different changes in philanthropic thinking and philanthropic approaches to the suffering of others. Despite the epistemic transformations in humanitarianism during this decade, Indian reform (like other conventional humanitarian movements) continued to lack an equitable and equity-making, meaningful and meaning-making dialogue between agents and patients. In a text as far removed from humanitarian policy-making as the East Branch of the Penobscot is from Washington, D.C., Thoreau had imagined what a dialogue between Native Americans and whites could sound like. Yet Thoreau's eccentricity was no panacea for what ailed philanthropy, and was in fact a part of the problem: limited by a disaffection for urging collective struggle, Thoreau could never translate his vision into political action.

Nevertheless, the limits of such eccentricity are no reason to ignore Thoreau in our contemporary consideration of philanthropy and its history. *The Maine Woods* reminds us that humanitarianism after the collapse of the antebellum paradigm lived on in a particular way only because the opportunity to realize another way, an eccentric way, was missed. Reread in a period characterized by calls for empowerment and for recognition of the diversity of cultural identities within society, but also by the AIDS crisis and a strengthening of the hierarchy separating humanitarian agencies from their patients, Thoreau's writing resonates with the yearnings for less homogenizing and less oppressive humanitarian options. In so doing, Thoreau's writing becomes newly illuminated by the eccentric tendencies in our own era; it also then becomes available for a new cultural work within the eccentric possibilities of our own era.

SEVEN

AFTERWORD: AIDS
AND UNCONVENTIONAL CARING

*The worst thing about being sick in America, Ethel, is you are booted out of the
parade. Americans have no use for the sick.*

ROY COHN IN TONY KUSHNER'S ANGELS IN AMERICA[1]

*Leading the 500,000 march participants were people with AIDS, some in wheel-
chairs pushed by their friends—a reminder that fighting AIDS is now a priority for
gay people and that first in the fight are people living with AIDS.*

DOUGLAS CRIMP AND ADAM ROLSTON'S ACCOUNT OF THE 1987 MARCH ON WASHINGTON[2]

AIDS and Cultural Criticism

From the beginning of this study, I have argued that during the Civil War a
crisis erupted in philanthropy, a crisis that dramatically changed humanitarian
discourses and practices and temporarily cleared a space for the formation of
eccentric approaches to humanitarian work. A similarly profound crisis is currently reshaping humanitarianism in the United States. The AIDS pandemic and
the coercive and inadequate humanitarian responses to it have produced suffering
of a devastating magnitude. Although some "experts" are incorrectly announcing
that the impact of AIDS on the United States will be minor because the disease is
confined to "marginalized" groups such as "homosexuals," IV-drug users, the poor,
African Americans, Latinos, the infants of HIV+ women, etc.,[3] the economic and
social costs of this disease in the United States and worldwide are already
staggering.

The dying and suffering produced by this pandemic are precipitating changes
in history, society, and subjectivity through changes in the economy and markets,
everyday habits and practices, sexuality and the representation of sexualities,
family structures, science, the medical industry, politics, language, and the media.
AIDS is also transforming the way we see our cultures, our histories, and our
literatures. Reading Whitman's verse on sexuality and death, for example, changes
in an era of AIDS, according to Michael Moon. AIDS has had a similar impact on

the way we read and write history, the way we watch and make movies, the way we teach and learn. AIDS has changed our cultures as well as the way we interpret our cultures.[4]

It is my hope, however, that we as readers and writers of history, literature, and culture will do more than be changed by AIDS. I hope that the teaching, reading, and writing of history, literature, and culture might change AIDS, might participate in the transformation of action directed against the suffering created by AIDS. I do not intend to be naive or hyperbolic in my estimation of the power that readers and writers, especially academic readers and writers, wield. Nor do I intend to let them or me off the hook by imagining that teachers, students, or scholars are peculiarly powerless to do anything. I am not arguing that cultural history and criticism are the best and most important tools to combat the suffering caused by AIDS and the variously oppressive responses to persons with AIDS (PWAs). There are certainly other powerful and more reliable tools available to AIDS activists and AIDS workers, including money, political advocacy, and caregiving. Still, my hope is that the writing and teaching of history, literature, and culture will be more effectively enlisted in the fight against AIDS.

In "AIDS & Theory," Daniel Harris has worried that ineffective decon-structionist tactics and postmodern academic criticism (characterized by Jacques Derrida's foray into discussions of nuclear disarmament) will "take precedence over things like the availability of hospital beds and experimental drugs" as priorities in AIDS activism. Labeling the move of intellectuals into AIDS activism as "careerist imperialism," Harris has attacked those in the university for having "redefined as intrinsically political the work they already perform as literary critics." If Harris's point is that AIDS activism needs a sense of priorities, then I agree with him, though I've met few AIDS workers who believe that a vigorous recuperation of Derrida is more important than increased federal funding for AIDS research or the implementation of a nondiscriminatory, single-payer national healthcare system. Likewise, if his point is that AIDS activism needs a realistic appraisal of what tools are effective and available, then again I agree. Academic readings and writings of history, literature, and culture are no substitute for direct political advocacy or organized caregiving. Moreover, a university position in postmodern cultural theory or any other academic office can hardly qualify one to speak meaningfully or effectively about AIDS. As Jan Zita Grover has remarked, "getting in contact with the actual lived experience of people who are dealing with the extraordinary complications of this—that is what entitles, empowers, some-body to have something profound to say about AIDS."[5]

Nevertheless, the belief that literary and cultural criticism is "intrinsically political" does not necessarily lead, as Harris thinks, to a blind and irresponsible exaggeration of the role that academics can play in AIDS activism. A belief in the political content/context of literary and cultural criticism ought to impress aca-demics with the need for social responsibility in their work. And such a sense of social responsibility could very well shape a critical writing that would contribute to the momentum, power, and persuasiveness of AIDS activism.[6] Moreover, how can feigning powerlessness—pretending that intellectuals are "utterly insular," utterly removed from society and power—productively benefit AIDS activism? Doesn't the Ivory Tower apology allow literary and cultural critics to excuse themselves from engagement in collective political action (like joining an AIDS advocacy organization) and everyday political practices (like making AIDS the topic for a writing assignment)? "Please don't ask us. We are too weak and insular to help anybody or to do anything political." Isn't the Ivory Tower position, in fact, more thoroughly "careerist," allowing academics to advance themselves professionally as they quietly reinforce the status quo?[7]

Hence, instead of proclaiming the social inutility of professors or abandoning the academy and its resources as powerless, I believe that those who work and teach in the university can and should see AIDS work as a field where they can make a contribution. What the AIDS crisis demands is humanitarian workers who can combine reformist activism (the persistent struggle to mitigate present suffering) with intellectual-political dissidence (the relentless, often subversive critique of oppressive systems of power and knowledge)—humanitarian workers who embrace both a Lydia Maria Child–like activism and a Henry Thoreau–like dissidence.[8] Cultural critics and university professors—like journalists, chefs, potters, aerobic instructors, secretaries, lawyers, carpenters—can lobby for increased funding, show up for demonstrations, and volunteer time to provide care and support for those most devastated by this epidemic. As long as we live in a society that refuses to provide medical and nursing care in a humane fashion, that clings to an obscene healthcare system that eludes democratic decision making at every level, then a great deal of philanthropic/volunteer care and support must be provided. To reject such volunteerism as a material and ideological part of an unjust capitalist healthcare system is intellectually coherent, but hardly useful to a person who is sick at this moment. Thus, I would urge contradiction: an energetic critique of such philanthropy and an equally energetic commitment to helping provide the care and support needed.

Moreover, those in the university can use their positions as teachers and scholars to urge a dissident critical analysis of institutional care; federal AIDS policy and funding; our collective social priorities as citizens of the United States and as citizens of the world; the discourses that represent AIDS and persons living with AIDS; and the homophobia, racism, sexism, and classism that have made a nondiscriminating virus much deadlier than it might have been. Given the current ideological orientation of the United States and the academy, and given the devastating physical reality of a disease that we barely understand, I do not expect that writing a book or giving a writing assignment or devising a suitably postmodern demonstration tactic will move us out of this present pain and into a world of perfect health. But because readers, students, and bystanders can and do learn from reading books, going to school, and listening to protestors, those in the university can participate in the processes of social change that might ameliorate the suffering within this pandemic and end the needless oppression of people who are sick.

Likewise, I hope my study of humanitarianism can make a contribution, however modest, to the fight against the suffering generated by AIDS and the responses to AIDS. Cultural critical writing cannot be a substitute for caregiving and direct advocacy, and I did not write this book so that it could take any kind of lead role in the formulation and organization of AIDS activism. As should be inferred from my previous six chapters, I believe persons living with HIV should be and are at the forefront of AIDS work. Nevertheless, what I have learned as an AIDS worker, from people living with AIDS as well as other volunteers and activists, has shaped my analysis of humanitarianism, the relationship between patients and agents, and the possibilities for change that open up in a period of social crisis. Those of us living in the age of AIDS—in a time so visibly marked by loss, grief, and anger, by the urgent need for new approaches to humanitarian work and by the politically imperative calls for "self-empowerment" among people living with HIV—have been positioned to look at cultural history in a new way. As Slavoj Žižek has observed: "Every historical rupture . . . changes retroactively the meaning of all tradition, restructures the narration of the past, makes it readable in another, new way."[9] I encounter necessarily a different cultural past than historians who wrote before me. The conditions of my own historical existence have prepared me to see new dimensions, new facts, new truths in the cultural history of philanthropy in the United States. Yet the awareness that my perception of history is itself historically constituted has led me neither to despair over the impossibility of finding transparent or unmistakable truth in the past nor to delight in the textual play that generates the fiction of "what really happened." Instead, I am reminded that historical writing always exists within history and never outside or apart from it, and that within its own historical context, historical writing aims to fashion not only a usable past but also an intelligible present. Such reminders raise fundamental questions about the function of histori- cal writing: What kind of past does a particular historiography render readable? What does such a past do in the present? How will such a past operate in the processes of social transformation that lead to the future?

This concern with the function of historical writing is what has brought me again and again to the "eccentric"—that is, the path not taken or what failed in history. In a discussion of Walter Benjamin's "Theses on the Philosophy of History" (1940), Žižek writes:

> By confining itself to "the way it really was," by conceiving history as a closed, homogeneous, rectilinear, continuous course of events, the traditional historio- graphic gaze is a priori, formally the gaze of "those who have won": it sees history as a closed continuity of "progression" leading to the reign of those who rule today. It leaves out of consideration what *failed* in history, what has to be denied so that the continuity of "what really happened" could establish itself. . . . In contrast to the triumphal procession of victors exhibited by official historiogra- phy, the oppressed class appropriates the past to itself in so far as it is "open," in so far as the "yearning for redemption" is already at work in it—that is to say, it appropriates the past in so far as the past already contains—in the form of what failed, of what was extirpated—the dimension of the future: "The past carries with it a temporal index by which it is referred to redemption." (Thesis II)[10]

My book has attempted to forgo "the traditional historiographic gaze," the narration of "what really happened" as the way "those who rule today" explain and justify the "progression" from the past to their current position of dominance. Instead, following Benjamin and Žižek, I have tried to develop an historiographical method that might, in its focus on the eccentric, reveal new, redemptive possibilities. Eccentric historiography appropriates the forgotten, left out, stifled aspects of our cultural history because they contain "in the form of what failed" a future far preferable to "the reign of those who rule today."

Hence, I hope that my writing will participate in the transformation of humanitarian action by urging a rethinking of the possibilities within humanitarianism. From the Good Samaritan to John Brown and Florence Nightingale to Mother Teresa, cultural-historical icons have always played a significant role in the construction of certain modes of humanitarian action, just as they have obstructed the development of other approaches. While shedding light on neglected portions of the cultural history of philanthropy in the United States (that is, the eccentric portions, the failed dimension of our cultural history), I have tried to participate in the recovery of and reshaping of certain cultural icons and selected conceptions of helping. My rereading of these cultural figures and alternative notions of helping has aimed to clarify the promise within a less coercive and more egalitarian humanitarianism.

The (Re)Emergence of Unconventional Care

Many of the humanitarian responses to AIDS have been appalling—cruel, humiliating, disempowering beyond what illness in itself could do. In 1983, the Shands Hospital in Gainesville, Florida, chartered a Learjet to fly a seriously ill patient to San Francisco, where he was abandoned at the offices of the San Francisco AIDS Foundation. During his stay at the privately run Shands, the twenty-seven-year-old man, diagnosed with a severe case of AIDS-related cryptosporidiosis, had run out of state Medicaid benefits. The hospital decided that moving the young man to the offices of a philanthropic foundation (not a hospital) on the other side of the country was the best financial solution to a difficult situation. When called upon to explain an action as disgraceful as "dumping" a dangerously ill patient, the Shands Hospital cited "humanitarian reasons." As outrageous as this one case and explanation might be, abandoning, ignoring, and turning away persons with AIDS-related illnesses have been common humanitarian responses to this disease.[11]

Even in hospitals less ruthless than the Shands, persons with AIDS regularly attest to being ignored, abused, mistreated, and humiliated. A 1992 survey released by the National Association of People with AIDS (NAPWA) has reported that Americans infected with HIV are a common target of abuse. PWAs have a more difficult time obtaining healthcare, and they are often discriminated against by physicians, nurses, and other humanitarian careproviders. Much of the problem is not the intentions, good or bad, of the hospitals and careproviders, but the gap between providers' power and knowledge and the knowledge and experiences of patients—a gap that seems to widen when patients are IV-drug users. "The way they treat you is the shits," one IV-drug-using woman living with AIDS has complained. "You don't feel good. You're afraid. Nobody wants to see you. . . . I'm tired of being put down and made to feel worse. . . . They take my dignity and squash it."[12]

Numerous others living with AIDS have also expressed feelings of indignity, anger, and frustration about the way the healthcare system administers (to) them. One PWA has grieved:

> The nurses are scared of me; the doctors wear masks and sometimes gloves. Even the priest doesn't seem too anxious to shake my hand. What the hell is this? I'm not a leper. Do they want to lock me up and shoot me? I've got no family, no friends. Where do I go? What do I do? God, this is horrible![13]

Attending this description of AIDSphobia among careproviders is confusion and perhaps even despair: Where does one go for help when the usual humanitarian workers seem more intent on maintaining distance and control than on mitigating pain?

Finding mistreatment in exactly the place where one had expected care has produced a PWA-authored literature of conspicuous irony, a literature that is both an account of and a response to such mistreatment. In "Isolation" (1991), for example, a poem about alienation within an AIDSphobic healthcare system, Tony J. Giordano writes:

> they wouldn't bring me the food
> the tray was left outside
> my room because they were
> afraid to come in, afraid
> of catching god knows what.
> the tray remained where it was
> until a masked nurse had the
> kindness to bring it into the
> room and finally uncover
> what was once food.[14]

In a poem remembering careproviders' refusal to carry food to patients with AIDS—their readiness to allow the food to rot rather than risk any proximity with the hospitalized speaker—Giordano's ironic use of the word "kindness" identifies this AIDSphobic conduct as obvious unkindness, thus highlighting the discrepancy between the not unreasonable expectation of humanitarian-medical attention and the experience of cold disregard.

Giordano's deployment of irony here is not subtle; it is arresting. Readers do not trip lightly over a suggestively witty perception of inconsistency; they smash into words that say the opposite of what they mean. To cite another example, Giordano writes:

> . . . . had to sleep.
> lulled by the endless silence.
> bed-bound. not able to move from

the prison bed, the lovely soft
bed, the island bed, the hated bed.[15]

Emphasizing the painful boredom of this lonely hospital stay, Giordano monoto-
nously repeats "bed," "bed," "bed," "bed," and amplifies that monotony with a
thick pattern of like consonants—the plosive *p/b* and *t/d* sounds, as well as the
slow, lingering line of *l* sounds. Amid this aural tedium, surrounded by images of
the bed as "hated," as a "prison," as an "island," and engulfed by the steady flow of
hard, thudding *d* sounds, the description of the bed as "lovely soft" is flagrantly
incongruous with the sense of the rest of the passage. In "Isolation," this obtrusive
irony arrests the reader's attention and then draws that attention to the
uncompassionate, callous mistreatment of people with AIDS-related illnesses.
Giordano never sees the hospital as a benevolent place; yet, with words like
"kindness" or "lovely soft / bed," he inserts a benevolent ideal into the poem, where
it sits awkwardly, inappropriately, painfully out of place, isolated from a context
where it would make (straightforward) sense. Thus, while emphasizing the
painfulness and isolation of being a patient, Giordano's conspicuous irony reminds readers of how extremely distant (not just slightly removed) a compassionate mode of care is from the speaker's actual experience of care.

In addition to medical or nursing mistreatment and neglect, conventional
humanitarianism has a number of representational practices that attempt to isolate
PWAs and squash the dignity of those who are sick. The most common are pity
rhetoric and images of people with AIDS as "victims." From the earliest years of the
pandemic, PWAs have actively fought the disempowering pity of the benevolent
and have consistently and clearly refused the label "victim." As one of the first
persons to speak publicly about living with the disease, Gary Walsh became the
target of "the gay community's maudlin fawning over AIDS patients." After a
person whom he had never met declared "I love you," Walsh—refusing the easy
and empty affection of this benevolent stranger—said, "If one more person says
they love me, I'll punch them in the mouth." At the founding of NAPWA in Denver
in 1983, a group of PWAs issued a founding statement, known as "The Denver
Principles," that immediately and unambiguously rejected disempowering humanitarian rhetoric. "The Denver Principles" begin:

> We condemn attempts to label us as "victims," which implies defeat, and we are
> only occasionally "patients," which implies passivity, helplessness, and depen-
> dence on the care of others.

Despite the early and continued opposition to representations of PWAs as
defeated, helpless, passive, and dependent, many benevolent discourses persis-
tently produce disempowering images of "AIDS victims" and "AIDS patients."[16]

One of the most popular and disempowering of these benevolent discourses
is found in New Age writing that attempts to construct PWAs not merely as victims
but as self-made victims. The New Age understanding of disease maintains that
sickness is mental or attitudinal in its origins; hence, Louise Hay always writes
"dis-ease," so as to emphasize that the problem is psychological and not physical.

In *A Return to Love* (1992), Marianne Williamson, a best-selling author of New Age self-help books and lecturer who regularly fashions herself a humanitarian AIDS activist, writes:

> It is not the body that gets sick, but the mind. "Health or sickness of the body depends entirely on how the mind perceives it, and the purpose the mind would use it for." It is not the body but the mind that is in need of healing, and the only healing is a return to love.
>
> Our bodies are merely blank canvases onto which we project our thoughts. Disease is loveless thinking materialized.[17]

Although she qualifies this assertion by saying that "loveless thinking" is "not necessarily" the direct cause of illness in a child or otherwise "innocent" person and that the "lovelessness" that exists in our collective "racial consciousness" explains the emergence of disease in such cases, Williamson does insist that we are responsible for our sickness. "Sickness is not a sign of God's judgment on us," she writes, "but of our judgment on ourselves." Likewise, Hay identifies the cause of AIDS as a "lack of love," implying that those who died from AIDS failed to love themselves adequately.[18] Again emphasizing how PWAs bring sickness on themselves but shifting that emphasis slightly away from "lovelessness" and toward personality, C. Norman Shealy and Caroline M. Myss locate the origin of AIDS in what they call "victim consciousness." According to their book *AIDS: Passageway to Transformation* (1987), a text that aims to identify "the type of personality that is most likely to attract AIDS," the "perception of oneself as so completely lacking in personal power that one continually fears being taken advantage of or hurt in some way," what Shealy and Myss call "victim consciousness," is "the core weakness within the personalities of AIDS patients." It is this victim consciousness "that act[s] as a magnet which attracts the HIV virus to such an individual."[19] Because sickness is self-created, people with AIDS are not simply "victims" in New Age humanitarian discourse, they are self-made victims: with their lack of (self) love or their want of positive attitude or their personality weaknesses, they (like a "magnet") bring AIDS (like a "judgment") upon themselves.

Although it differs in tone and intention from the religious right's belief that AIDS is God's punishment of gay men for their sin, this New Age etiology of AIDS is clearly another version of "blame the victim," the "humanitarian" version. New Age benevolence attempts to offer hope and comfort to people who have not, understandably, found much hope or comfort in the present healthcare system. Yet, this humanitarian support demands that PWAs accept blame for their disease. According to this type of humanitarianism, any failure to be well is a personal failure, the result of a bad attitude.

New Age teachings complement this dubious victimology with irresponsibly bad information about the treatment of AIDS and the transmission and prevention of HIV. Shealy, for example, lists nine preventive measures—such as a healthy diet, monogamy, positive imaging and affirmations, avoiding "'street' drugs," avoiding caffeine, tobacco, and alcohol, avoiding anal intercourse (without distinguishing between protected and unprotected sex, without noting that HIV is spread via other forms of unprotected intercourse), etc.—none of which will prevent the transmission of HIV. Because this doctor completely fails to mention the two most important things we can do to stop HIV transmission—don't share needles or hypodermic syringes, don't have unprotected sex—his list seems designed not so much to prevent the transmission of HIV as to create a regimen and control behavior.[20]

Moreover, New Age humanitarian work is positively detrimental to AIDS activism. Always urging PWAs to let go of their anger, New Agers preach the value of surrender, the importance of a proper, acquiescent attitude toward AIDS, God, and life. Upset by the anger among PWAs and AIDS workers, Hay and Williamson ask PWAs to love and embrace AIDS through visualizations in the form of letters to "Dear AIDS." Through such surrender, Williamson has found cause for hope:

> An epidemic such as AIDS is a collective heartbreak, pulling millions of people into its painful vortex. But this also means that it brings millions of people to their knees.

And people on their knees is, for Williamson, the only solution to the AIDS crisis.[21] Thus, accordingly, she feels no need to advocate healthcare reform, or needle-exchange programs, or more or better safer-sex education programs that include the distribution of condoms, or an activist movement that would fight AIDS as well as prejudice, violence, and discrimination against people with AIDS. Thus, shifting attention away from any useful medical, social, or political project to combat AIDS, New Age teachings have focused their attention on encouraging PWAs to accept responsibility for their illness and on stifling the anger that currently fuels so much AIDS activism.[22]

A more extreme example of the way in which humanitarian rhetoric can be used to justify controlling or disempowering action against people with AIDS is the work of William F. Buckley. In a 1986 *New York Times* article, Buckley argued that "everyone detected with AIDS should be tattooed in the upper fore-arm, to protect common-needle users, and on the buttocks, to prevent the victimization of other homosexuals." Although the forcible tattooing of a particular group has brought to mind not humanitarians but the Nazis who tattooed prisoners in concentration camps during the Holocaust, Buckley advocated his outrageously totalitarian idea for reasons that he articulated as philanthropic: he wanted to protect IV-drug users and gay men from possible infection. As common in the representation of AIDS as they were in Nazi propaganda, such philanthropic arguments have a specific public function: to justify the coercive control of particular groups and deny them agency.[23]

Buckley's plan to tattoo everybody with AIDS was notably different from most popular or conventional humanitarian responses to AIDS. His scheme went beyond the humanitarian mainstream: his designs were so plainly cruel that the pretense of benevolent concern for others was difficult to credit. Yet, in a moment of crisis, projects that are more coercive than usual can sometimes become plausible, as the presence of Buckley's article in the very mainstream *New York*

Times might suggest. One might also wonder how much the situation has changed since 1986, as Simon Watney has in his recent *Practices of Freedom* (1994):

> It would be difficult to exaggerate the impact of media sensationalism, stupidity, and malicious inhumanity, in drawing gay men together in those early years of the epidemic, as the targets of repeated insult and vilification, long before most of us had any direct experience of HIV or AIDS in our everyday lives. We saw the sick pilloried, and the worst abuse reserved for the most severely devastated communities. This situation has been modified subsequently but not, I think, substantially changed.[24]

Those who believe that this vilification has diminished or that the advocacy of totalitarian schemes for controlling PWAs has stopped should listen to Lou Sheldon of the Traditional Values Coalition or to J. Paul Emerson on San Francisco's Hot Talk KSFO-AM. Emerson, one of the station's conservative hosts, has been urging a quarantine of people who are HIV+.[25]

A crisis can also inspire less cruel and less coercive changes in humanitarianism. And the AIDS epidemic has been the occasion for the development of eccentric, patient-centered modes of humanitarian care. In the most unlikely of places, an enormous county hospital, resides one of the most famous examples of such an approach, the fifth-floor AIDS unit at the San Francisco General Hospital, originally known as Unit 5A and later called 5B. Created in July 1983 by patients and nurses who "disliked the hierarchical doctor-nurse-patient model that dominated hospitals," this inpatient unit has structured its caring practices around the principle that "AIDS patients staying at the hospital would be taught about their disease and would make many of their own medical decisions." The patient-centered approach to hospital care and the dislike for the hierarchical management of healthcare have led to innovations that have been described as "surprising," "unheard-of," "unorthodox," "controversial." Patients' rooms are often filled with things from home—artwork, dinnerware, bedding, and other personal belongings. Visitors can drop by any time. Patients, not the hospital, decide who counts as family and who has visiting privileges. For gay men and others whose families might not fit dominant definitions, the right to designate a family for themselves restores a power often denied them by a heterosexist society—the power to choose who will make critical decisions about patients and who will spend time with patients during their illness. Another innovation is the authority and autonomy given to patients and nurses in the management of the unit. In 1983, a nurse named Cliff Morrison consulted patients about the creation of the ward, and they expressed annoyance with the "arrogance" and "egos" of the hospital workers. "You don't listen to us. You never approach as humans." So, Morrison decided to create a place where careproviders would listen to patients. "Patients would have a louder voice in their own care," according to Morrison, "because they usually knew more about the intricacies of their often experimental medications than their doctors." It has been widely noted that people living with AIDS are often very knowledgeable about the disease and its treatments. They are sometimes better informed than nurses and doctors.[26] To deny people living with AIDS an important voice in the management of AIDS care, as Morrison realized, would be to exclude the group that knows—through education and personal experience—the most about this disease and the medical and nursing management of its complications.

From the beginning of the pandemic, people with AIDS have understood that they were uniquely prepared to become the leading voices in AIDS work. Thus, "The Denver Principles" recommend that persons with AIDS:

> Be involved at every level of AIDS decision making and specifically serve on the boards of directors of provider organizations.
>   Be included in all AIDS forums with equal credibility as other participants, to share their own experiences and knowledge.

Constructing an AIDS care that takes its direction from those living with HIV is not only empowering for PWAs, but also for careproviders who can thus learn from those most qualified to share experiences, information, and knowledge about AIDS. As Bobbi Campbell, one of the earliest PWA activists, always insisted: "people with AIDS are the *real* experts." PWAs are considered the experts in some AIDS organizations, and the line between patient and agent is productively erased. In his book on volunteering and Gay Men's Health Crisis (GMHC), Philip Kayal notes that the blurring of the patient/agent distinction, "where volunteers become clients and the clients become volunteers," has been a "significant feature of AIDS volunteerism," particularly at GMHC.[27]

Yet, it is not only the wish to share experience and expertise but also the particular political exigencies of the AIDS crisis that have led PWAs to demand a central role in decisions regarding the treatment of AIDS. The abuse of PWAs, the indifference to AIDS as a serious political and health issue, the profiteering of drug corporations, the inadequate and discriminatory nature of the U.S. healthcare system, and the use of AIDS to push a narrowly moralistic and viciously antigay cultural agenda have all made such demands essential to PWA survival. "It is therefore hardly surprising," from Watney's view, "to find people with AIDS organising politically in groups such as ACT UP and the 'People with AIDS Coalition' in order to collectively resist the consequences of the cultural agenda of AIDS." And the organized presence of PWAs as major players in their own care is working to change the nature and conception of humanitarian care. Phyllida Brown believes that the place of PWAs in AIDS care is "radically altering the way medical researchers and health officials think." She writes:

> The AIDS epidemic in the US has spawned a new breed of patients who expect to be involved in the political, scientific, and medical decisions surrounding their treatment. Led by people with HIV and AIDS, this approach has now spread to affect other groups, such as women with breast cancer.

Like cancer survivors, like PWAs, people with dystrophic illnesses also are demanding that humanitarianism change. Fronted by Jerry Lewis and an annual telethon for "Jerry's Kids," the Muscular Dystrophy Association (MDA) has a long history of some of the most demeaning infantilization of people with disabilities. Since the beginning of this decade, however, people with muscular dystrophy have objected with ever-increasing volume to the degrading philanthropy of Lewis and the MDA, calling for the right to be agents in their own lives and adding to the growing numbers in the disability rights movement.[28]

The development of a patient-centered humanitarian care cannot happen, however, without an activist politics. As so many PWAs and AIDS workers have pointed out, the entire arena in which AIDS is treated, researched, funded, represented, and discussed is highly politicized. Indeed, in the words of the playwright Larry Kramer, cofounder of GMHC and ACT UP (AIDS Coalition to Unleash Power), "THERE IS NOTHING IN THIS WHOLE AIDS MESS THAT IS NOT POLITICAL!" Kramer has many times insisted that AIDS workers must not be interested only in providing care for the sick (an immediate but in some ways relatively short-term approach to the amelioration of suffering) at the expense of political action (which might provide a more long-term solution to suffering). In his play *A Normal Heart* (1985), for example, Kramer's autobiographical character, Ned Weeks, complains:

> [T]hey only want to take care of patients—crisis counseling, support groups, home attendants . . . I know that's important, too. But I thought I was starting with a bunch of Ralph Naders and Green Berets, and the first instant they have to take a stand on a political issue and fight, almost in front of my eyes they turn into a bunch of nurses' aides.[29]

Kramer's purpose here is not to discount the necessity of caregiving but to highlight the importance of political action.

A number of AIDS workers have joined Kramer in recognizing how vital political advocacy and political action are to curing what ails our society in its mishandling of AIDS. Like John Brown and Harriet Jacobs, these twentieth-century activists and writer-activists have come to see political action as an indispensable part of humanitarian action. Writers like Paul Monette or James Robert Baker, for example, do not simply express grief or urge compassion; they articulate an unmistakable, visceral rage, prophesying a type of John Brown retaliatory political action in response to the coercive mistreatment of people with AIDS. Monette, for instance, responds to the scheme for forcibly tattooing PWAs by aggressively promising in his poem "Buckley" (1988): "ink and bleed me / name and number and I will dance on you." In Baker's novel *Tim and Pete* (1993), Pete, a rock singer and the ex-boyfriend of the narrator, vehemently lashes out at humanitarian AIDS workers, saying:

> I've had it with these fucking AIDS vultures like Louise Hay and Marianne Williamson. Hug a teddy bear, boys, and visualize Bambi, till you're too weak to cross the room, let alone pick up a gun. George Bush couldn't come up with a better containment plan.

Witnessing the way in which AIDS philanthropy subdues and disempowers PWAs by containing the anger that animates action, Pete despises this humanitarianism because it replaces political agency with enfeebling warm fuzzies. His fury about "these fucking AIDS vultures" and the entire AIDS crisis compels him to hope for a type of violent action that would end the violence against people with AIDS. He sings in one song:

> I'm sick of watching the wrong people die
> with a victim's whimper instead of a bang
> What I'd like to see
> What this country needs
> Is a Baader-Meinhof gang

Pete insists that his music is only "a catalog of fantasies a lot of people had but usually censored, a suppressed rage," yet his song inspires a group of queer, HIV+ artist-terrorists to act upon that rage. Although Pete himself, like Baker's novel, stops ambiguously short of advocating violence, both Pete and his author use their writing to imagine grief turned into rage and rage transfigured into action.[30]

Although the queer anarchoterrorist imaginary of Baker's novel differs—most obviously in its turn to violence—from ACT UP, both yearn to see "anger" made into "action," action that would end AIDS and the oppressive, criminal mistreatment of people with AIDS. ACT UP describes itself, in fact, as "a diverse, non-partisan group united in *anger* and committed to direct *action* to end the AIDS crisis." As their "zaps," graphic productions, and widely visible demonstrations illustrate, the members of ACT UP have been confrontational, innovative, unorthodox, eccentric (and nonviolent) in their choice of political means to end the AIDS crisis. More to the point, they have envisioned that political action as a process led and directed by people living with HIV. As Crimp and Rolston write in their account of ACT UP's first years of political activism: "first in the fight are people living with AIDS." ACT UP/Chicago has among its working groups a PISD Caucus, a People with Immune Systems Disorders Caucus. Just as the caucus's acronym suggests the anger that inspires ACT UP, PISD's self-description—"The front line troops of our activism"—suggests the caucus's role within ACT UP and ACT UP's commitment to an eccentric humanitarian-political action.[31]

Still, the angry members of ACT UP are hardly the only activists pledged to political action that accords a fundamental, leading role to PWAs. There are several political advocacy organizations run by and for people living with HIV disease, including NAPWA, the People with AIDS Coalition (PWA Coalition), the Body Positive, and The Committee of Ten Thousand ("an organization by, for, and of people infected with HIV through blood and blood products").[32] The AIDS crisis—particularly the government's unwillingness to respond and the main-stream media's insistence on disregarding, scapegoating, and pitying persons with AIDS—has forced PWAs to unite and fight politically for their survival. The result has been the unprecedented formation of eccentric humanitarian-political organizations led by those who would be the recipients of care. As George Annas, director of the Law, Medicine and Ethics Program at the Boston University School of Public Health, has observed, "There never was a politically savvy group of sick people before."[33]

Such a development in the history of humanitarian reform organizations has not been the result of a giant step forward in humankind's collective moral vision, as a humanist-progressivist historian might narrate. And it would be silly to see these PWA-led and inspired organizations as simply collaborating with those who would attempt to control individuals living with HIV. "Anger" and the emphasis on "self-empowerment" have led eccentric groups like ACT UP and the PWA Coalition into battles with federal agencies, local, state, and national governments, local direct services agencies, pharmaceutical companies, and the medical industry.[34] PWAs have resisted the benevolent control of kind and well-meaning volunteers as well as the more impersonal control exerted by the media, the FDA, Burroughs Wellcome, and the Department of Health and Human Services.

Products neither of pure benevolence nor of an insidious will to dominate, these eccentric groups are the result of a crisis in conventional forms of caring. Some eccentric organizations and practices emerged simply to fill a philanthropic void. Kayal quotes an early GMHC volunteer who remarked in 1983, "We started out just to find out who was supposed to be dealing with the problems [of AIDS sufferers]. Then we realized no one was: it would have to be us." The suffering spread by a pandemic along with the avoidable suffering inflicted by the coercive responses to persons living with AIDS led other humanitarians to recognize the inadequacy of the usual solutions to suffering, particularly solutions that depend on a hierarchical agent/patient model. The San Francisco General Hospital was probably the first institution, according to Randy Shilts, "to realize that the old way that hospitals cared for their patients needed to be changed if the institution was going to be able to cope with this horrible new disease." Eccentric care is neither an attempt to control better through the mask of benevolence nor a product of a morally advanced consciousness, but instead the historical result of a crisis demanding new approaches. Such a crisis permits accidents and eccentric approaches to play an intensified role in dealing with the new suffering. The "innovation" and "flexibility" that characterized the eccentric care of the fifth floor occurred, according to Paul Volberding, director of the San Francisco General Hospital AIDS Clinic, "mostly because we didn't know what we were doing. We didn't know what we were supposed to do. We didn't follow the usual rules." As the spontaneous, ad hoc formation of ACT UP in March 1987 suggests, accident can play a crucial part in the history of humanitarian-political groups.[35] Nevertheless, deliberate, planned, and direct action is indispensable to progressive social change. Although accidents and the fissures created by social crisis can create the opportunity for eccentric humanitarianism, the effectiveness of eccentric humanitarianism requires a commitment to action and a commitment to self-empowerment.

Like the eccentric benevolence of the nineteenth-century, eccentric AIDS work looks to ameliorate suffering by listening to and empowering those who suffer. By juxtaposing certain modes of AIDS work with the Civil War–era benevolence of Jacobs and Alcott and others, I am drawing only an indirect connection between practical abolitionism and ACTing UP, between Walt Whitman and Cliff Morrison. More importantly I have aimed to identify and illustrate an unconventional model for care and suggest the political commitments and historical conditions necessary for its realization. Eccentric benevolence, whether inspired by Harriet Wilson's *Our Nig* or the NAPWA's "Denver Principles," opens up the possibility of a humanitarian work that is both more effective and less cruel to those who suffer. Studying, teaching, learning, and advocating this eccentric possibility will, I hope, persuade us to practice the possibility.

NOTES

1. An Introduction to Eccentric Benevolence

1. Anne Sexton, "One-Eye, Two-Eyes, Three-Eyes," *The Complete Poems* (Boston: Houghton Mifflin, 1981) 260.

2. David L. Kirp, "AIDS in Our Time—I: After the Band Stopped Playing," *The Nation* 4 July 1994: 15, 17. See also John Nguyet Erni, *Unstable Frontiers: Technomedicine and the Cultural Politics of "Curing" AIDS* (Minneapolis: U of Minnesota P, 1994). Erni suggests that the obsessive focus on "curing" AIDS, the framing of AIDS discourses in terms of a curability/incurability binary, has hampered advances in and attention to *caring* for persons living with AIDS.

3. For more on the conservative implications of traditional, realist historiography, see Hayden White, *Metahistory: The Historical Imagination in Nineteenth-Century Europe* (Baltimore: Johns Hopkins UP, 1973) 163-90.

4. Walter Benjamin, "Theses on the Philosophy of History," *Illuminations,* ed. Hannah Arendt (New York: Schocken Books, 1969) 256. Further references to Benjamin's "Theses" are noted parenthetically in the text.

5. "Reform Schools and Houses of Reformation," *New York Times* 25 Aug. 1859: 4.

6. For the best account of the changes within humanitarianism during the 1850s and 1860s, see Lori D. Ginzberg, *Women and the Work of Benevolence: Morality, Politics, and Class in the Nineteenth-Century United States* (New Haven: Yale UP, 1990) esp. 98-213. Also helpful are Robert H. Bremner, *The Public Good: Philanthropy and Welfare in the Civil War Era* (New York: Knopf, 1980); and George M. Fredrickson, *The Inner Civil War: Northern Intellectuals and the Crisis of the Union* (New York: Harper & Row, 1965).

For more on romantic, moral suasionist approaches to philanthropy and their decline, see John L. Thomas, "Romantic Reform in America, 1815-1865," *American Quarterly* 17, no. 4 (Winter 1965): 656-81; Ronald G. Walters, *American Reformers 1815-1860* (New York: Hill and Wang, 1978); and Ginzberg 11-132.

7. Alan Trachtenberg, *The Incorporation of America: Culture and Society in the Gilded Age* (New York: Hill and Wang, 1982) 3-4.

8. By focusing on the Civil War era, I am pulled toward certain movements and practices, such as antislavery, war relief, freedpeople's relief, mourning, and U.S. Indian policy reform. Likewise, I do not discuss important nineteenth-century humanitarian reform movements, such as temperance and prostitution reform, that experienced a dip in interest and activity during the Civil War. For more on these two movements and their Civil War–era decline, see Barbara Meil Hobson, *Uneasy Virtue: The Politics of Prostitution and the American Reform Tradition* (New York: Basic Books, 1987) esp. 45; and Barbara Leslie Epstein, *The Politics of Domesticity: Women, Evangelism, and Temperance in Nineteenth-Century America* (Middletown: Wesleyan UP, 1981) esp. 93.

9. In addition to its usual sense of someone who receives medical treatment (a definition that is important in my fourth chapter), I use the word "patient" to designate a person who undergoes some type of action, someone who is acted upon, someone who is helped. A "patient" is the opposite of an "agent," who causes something to happen, who effects some

type of action. "Patient" suggests passivity and identifies a person as an object rather than a subject. I use this term with its condescending implications not because receivers of humanitarian care were in fact passive sites for philanthropic action but because mainstream humanitarianism often treated people as if they were "patients."

Although my project, like Susan A. Ostrander and Paul G. Schervish's, is to understand philanthropy as a social relation, my terms and focus are significantly different from theirs. Moving away from an exclusive focus on donors, Ostrander and Schervish examine philanthropy as a relationship between "donors" (individuals who support and endow philanthropic organizations) and "recipients" (the philanthropic agencies themselves). Yet, in organizing this theory of philanthropy along a donor-recipient axis, they tend to ignore those who are helped by philanthropy—that is, the "beneficiaries" or "patients." Shifting my analysis away from the donor-recipient axis, I examine philanthropy as a social relation among "patients" and "agents," whether those agents are donors, organizations, individuals, or even the patients themselves. See Susan A. Ostrander and Paul G. Schervish, "Giving and Getting: Philanthropy as a Social Relation," *Critical Issues in American Philanthropy,* ed. Jon Van Til (San Francisco: Jossey-Bass, 1990) 67-98.

10. Harriet E. Wilson, *Our Nig; or Sketches from the Life of a Free Black, In A Two-Story White House, North. Showing That Slavery's Shadows Fall Even There,* intro. Henry Louis Gates, Jr. (1859; New York: Vintage, 1983). Quotations from *Our Nig* are noted parenthetically in the text.

The best secondary source for information about Wilson's life is Barbara A. White, "'Our Nig' and the She-Devil: New Information about Harriet Wilson and the 'Bellmont' Family," *American Literature* 65, no. 1 (Mar. 1993): 19-52. See also Eric Gardner, "'This Attempt of Their Sister': Harriet Wilson's *Our Nig* from Printer to Readers," *New England Quarterly* 64, no. 2 (June 1993): 226-46; Beth Maclay Doriani, "Black Womanhood in Nineteenth-Century America: Subversion and Self-Construction in Two Women's Autobiographies," *American Quarterly* 43, no. 2 (June 1991): 199-222; and Henry Louis Gates, Jr., "Harriet E. Adams Wilson," *Afro-American Writers before the Harlem Renaissance,* ed. Trudier Harris, Dictionary of Literary Biography 50 (Detroit: Gale, 1986) 268-71.

11. For what is an excellent analysis of nineteenth-century sentimental writing and its "designs" on readers (that is, its cultural-political, often humanitarian, aims), see Jane Tompkins, *Sensational Designs: The Cultural Work of American Fiction 1790-1860* (New York: Oxford UP, 1985).

12. Maria Susanna Cummins, *The Lamplighter,* ed. Nina Baym (1854; New Brunswick: Rutgers UP, 1988) 15, 22.

13. Although Wilson's critical attitude toward humanitarianism has not so far been the object of much attention, Barbara White's study of Wilson's life has suggested that "a critique of abolitionists' racism was more central to Wilson's story than previously supposed" (38).

14. See Deborah Carlin, "'What Methods Have Brought Blessing': Discourse of Reform in Philanthropic Literature," *The (Other) American Traditions: Nineteenth-Century Women Writers,* ed. Joyce W. Warren (New Brunswick: Rutgers UP, 1993) 203-25.

15. John Ernest, "Economies of Identity: Harriet E. Wilson's *Our Nig,*" *PMLA* 109, no. 3 (May 1994): 434.

16. See, for instance, the fundamental significance attached to "discipline" in three recent but vastly different histories of humanitarian reform in the nineteenth century: Michel Foucault, *Discipline and Punish: The Birth of the Prison,* trans. Alan Sheridan (New York: Pantheon, 1978); Bremner, *The Public Good*; and Ginzberg. Note also that between 1859 and 1983, Wilson's novel "received almost no commentary" (Gates, "Harriet Wilson" 269).

17. I am using "humanitarianism" in a broad, nonderogatory sense to refer to movements, institutions, principles, and practices that promote the welfare of human beings by reducing pain and suffering, giving aid and care to those who suffer, and eliminating the causes of suffering. Such projects include relief work, caring practices, and political

activism. Moreover, I have come to see "humanitarianism" as that specific mode of "philanthropy" concerned with the suffering of others.

Throughout this study, I use the terms "benevolence," "reform," and "philanthropy" to talk about humanitarianism, and the words "reformer," "philanthropist," and "humanitarian" to refer to those who practice humanitarianism. During the nineteenth century (when the word became common), "humanitarianism" was synonymous with "benevolence," just as "humanitarian" was synonymous with "philanthropist." In his *American Dictionary of the English Language* (1828), Noah Webster defined "benevolence" as "an act of kindness; good done; charity given." "Reform" meant "to change from bad to good," and "philanthropy" was "benevolence towards the whole human family." Like these three overlapping terms, "humanitarianism" is also about doing "good" to and for others. "Humanitarianism" is, to use Robert Payton's definition of philanthropy, "voluntary action for the public good," when that "good" stands for the amelioration or elimination of suffering.

In the nineteenth century, projects that described themselves as reform, moral reform, social reform, charity, benevolence, philanthropy, humanitarianism, or some more specific designation (like abolitionism) constantly intersected and overlapped. In some historical discussions, one might want to make strict distinctions among these various terms. For my purposes, however, I am interested in actors from the aggregate, and not, for instance, in whether these actors were technically philanthropists or reformers. In *The Eighteenth Presidency!* (1856), when he mentioned "the flowing fire of the humanitarianism of the new world," Whitman brought together diverse concerns—the reform of government, moral reform, and the elimination of suffering (by ending slavery and the oppression of the working classes). I use "humanitarianism" in a similarly capacious manner.

See the entries on "benevolence," "philanthropy," and "reform" in Noah Webster, *An American Dictionary of the English Language,* 2 vols. (1828; New York: Johnson Reprint, 1970); the entries on "benevolence," "humanitarianism," "philanthropy," and "reform" in Noah Webster, *An American Dictionary of the English Language,* rev. ed. (1859; Springfield, MA: George and Charles Merriam, 1861); the entry on "humanitarianism" in the *Oxford English Dictionary*; and Walt Whitman, *The Eighteenth Presidency!,* ed. Edward F. Grier (1856; Lawrence: UP of Kansas, 1956) 29. For Payton's definition of philanthropy, see Robert L. Payton, *Philanthropy: Voluntary Action for the Public Good* (New York: ACE/ Macmillan, 1988). On the overlapping nature of nineteenth-century humanitarian reform movements, see Walters, *American Reformers.*

18. David Owen, *English Philanthropy 1660–1960* (Cambridge: Harvard UP, 1964) 11, 68; Bremner, *Public Good* xvii; Russel B. Nye, *William Lloyd Garrison and the Humanitarian Reformers* (Boston: Little Brown, 1955) 3. See also F. J. Klingberg, *Antislavery Movement in England* (New Haven: Yale UP, 1926). For examples of neo-abolitionist history, see James M. McPherson, *The Struggle for Equality: Abolitionists and the Negro in the Civil War and Reconstruction* (Princeton: Princeton UP, 1964); and the essays in Martin Duberman, ed., *The Antislavery Vanguard: New Essays on the Abolitionists* (Princeton: Princeton UP, 1965).

19. Owen 37, 38. Even a historian like Bremner, who wants to adopt a questioning attitude toward benevolence, relies primarily on texts of dominant humanitarians and maintains a humanist adherence to notions of "altruism" and "human nature."

20. Despite this attack, humanist approaches are still common. See, to mention three recent examples in the scholarship on the nineteenth-century United States, Deborah Pickman Clifford, *Crusader for Freedom: A Life of Lydia Maria Child* (Boston: Beacon Press, 1992); Charles Schlaifer and Lucy Freeman, *Heart's Work: Civil War Heroine and Champion of the Mentally Ill, Dorothea Lynde Dix* (New York: Paragon House, 1991); and Dorothy Sterling's important and much-needed biography of Abby Kelley, *Ahead of Her Time: Abby Kelley and the Politics of Antislavery* (New York: Norton, 1991).

21. Jacques Lacan, *Ecrits,* trans. Alan Sheridan (New York: Norton, 1977), 7.

22. What is called "social control" theory has actually generated histories that are quite different from each other. For a highly selective list of works written in this mode, see Clifford S. Griffin, *Their Brothers' Keepers: Moral Stewardship in the United States, 1800–1865*

(New Brunswick: Rutgers UP, 1960); Michael B. Katz, *The Irony of Early School Reform* (Cambridge: MIT Press, 1968); Anthony M. Platt, *The Child-Savers: The Invention of Delinquency* (Chicago: U of Chicago P, 1969); Frances Fox Piven and Richard A. Cloward, *Regulating the Poor: The Functions of Public Welfare* (New York: Pantheon, 1971); Jacques Donzelot, *The Policing of Families,* trans. Robert Hurley (New York: Pantheon, 1979); Foucault, *Discipline and Punish*; Michel Foucault, *The Birth of the Clinic: An Archaeology of Medical Perception,* trans. A. M. Sheridan Smith (New York: Pantheon, 1973); Michel Foucault, *Madness and Civilization: A History of Insanity in the Age of Reason,* trans. Richard Howard (New York: Pantheon, 1965); David J. Rothman, *The Discovery of the Asylum: Social Order and Disorder in the New Republic* (Boston: Little, Brown, 1971); William Graebner, *A History of Retirement: The Meaning and Function of an American Institution, 1885-1978* (New Haven: Yale UP, 1981); Barbara M. Brenzel, *Daughters of the State: A Social Portrait of the First Reform School for Girls in North America, 1856–1905* (Cambridge: MIT Press, 1983); and Linda Gordon, *Heroes of Their Own Lives: The Politics and History of Family Violence* (New York: Penguin, 1988). For an analysis of the social control approach to history, see Lois W. Banner, "Religious Benevolence as Social Control: A Critique of an Interpretation," *Journal of American History* 60, no. 1 (June 1973): 23-41; William A. Muraskin, "The Social-Control Theory in American History: A Critique," *Journal of Social History* 9, no. 4 (June 1976): 557-569; David J. Rothman, "Social Control: The Uses and Abuses of the Concept in the History of Incarceration," *Rice University Studies* 67, no. 1 (Winter 1981): 9-20; and Linda Gordon, "Family Violence, Feminism, and Social Control," *Feminist Studies* 12, no. 3 (Fall 1986): 453-478.

There are some historians who have combined aspects of social control and humanist historiography rather than embrace one or the other. See, for example, Lawrence J. Friedman, *Gregarious Saints: Self and Community in American Abolitionism, 1830–1870* (Cambridge: Cambridge UP, 1982); and Walters, *American Reformers*. Some scholars have been working to transcend both approaches. See Thomas L. Haskell, "Capitalism and the Origins of the Humanitarian Sensibility," *American Historical Review* 90, nos. 2 and 3 (Apr. and June 1985): 339-61, 547-66; and Gordon, *Heroes*.

23. Foucault, *Discipline and Punish* 82. Foucault is in my view a dramatic example of a social control perspective: his work illustrates not merely how regimes of power-knowledge "control" us, but more specifically how they utterly constitute our subjectivity. In literary and cultural studies, Foucault has been put to divergent uses; some accord well with the notion of Foucault-as-social-control-historian, and some revise or subvert that view. Within certain strains of new historicism, Foucauldian historiography shapes a view of literature and culture that is pessimistic about the possibilities for ameliorative social change. Walter Benn Michaels, for example— tired of questions about the oppositional capacity of representations and the "endless theorizing" about the relationship between texts and reality—disparages attempts to evaluate literary texts as acts of cultural criticism or incitements to social change:

> Like the question of whether Dreiser liked or disliked capitalism, these questions seem to me to posit a space outside the culture in order then to interrogate the relations between that space (here defined as literary) and the culture. . . . the only relation literature as such has to culture is that it is part of it. (*The Gold Standard and the Logic of Naturalism: American Literature at the Turn of the Century* [Berkeley: U of California P, 1987] 27)

Michaels's notion of "culture" (in which literature has no critical capacity because its only relation to culture is its docile status as an uncritical "part") seems dystopically absolute and unnecessarily scornful of the oppositional agency of cultural productions.

Judith Butler's interpretation of Foucault, on the other hand, deploys Foucault to theorize agency and the possibilities of social change via representation. Her version of Foucault, her thinking about the control that cultural systems exert in the production of our identities *and* the possibilities for subversion and agency within those systems, is for me a compelling and useful modification of Foucault. See Judith Butler, *Gender Trouble: Feminism and the Subversion of Identity* (New York: Routledge, 1990).

24. For another view of humanitarianism that endeavors to avoid these social control and liberal-humanist extremes, see Haskell, "Capitalism and the Origins of the Humanitarian Sensibility." Although my focus, methods, and conclusions are much different, I am indebted to Haskell's analysis of nineteenth-century humanitarians and twentieth-century historians.

25. Battling the pessimism of social control historians, Bremner has insisted, "The question is not whether dominant groups will seek to control the behavior of others, but how the control is exercised and to what ends it is directed" (*Public Good* xviii). If humanitarians use their power to control others in a way that is beneficent rather than malevolent or repressive, such a deployment of power should not arouse suspicions about philanthropy or serve as a reason to deplore humanitarian projects. In a similar fashion, Robert Payton is hopeful about the relationship between power and benevolent work: "The philanthropic is a restraint on self-interest, selfishness, acquisitiveness, greed. The philanthropic is also a bridle on power" (45).

26. For a clear example of a social control position on power, see Clifford S. Griffin, "Religious Benevolence as Social Control, 1815–1860," *Mississippi Valley Historical Review* 44, no. 3 (Dec. 1957): 423-44; and Griffin, *Their Brothers' Keepers*. Griffin sees social control of the difficult classes as the goal of the middle-class religious humanitarians who founded numerous benevolent societies to distribute Bibles and tracts, promote temperance, and aid the poor.

27. For the best introduction to Foucault's notion of power, see Michel Foucault, *The History of Sexuality. Volume 1: An Introduction,* trans. Robert Hurley (New York: Pantheon, 1978). For his discussions of humanitarian reform, see *Discipline and Punish, The Birth of the Clinic,* and *Madness and Civilization.*

28. There are important exceptions. In Linda Gordon's *Heroes of Their Own Lives* and in *Regulating the Poor* by Frances Fox Piven and Richard A. Cloward, for example, the patients of humanitarian projects play an active, central role in the narrative. While acknowledging her debt to social control historiography, Gordon is also critical of social control explanations that depict "the flow of initiative going in only one direction: from top to bottom, from professionals to clients, from elite to subordinate" ("Family Violence, Feminism, and Social Control" 471).

29. See Gordon, *Heroes*; Ginzberg; Epstein; Mary P. Ryan, *Cradle of the Middle Class: The Family in Oneida County, New York, 1790-1865* (Cambridge: Cambridge UP, 1981); and Mary P. Ryan, *Women in Public: Between Banners and Ballots, 1825-1880* (Baltimore: Johns Hopkins UP, 1990). See also the essays collected in *The Power of Culture: Critical Essays in American History,* ed. Richard Wightman Fox and T. J. Jackson Lears (Chicago: U of Chicago P, 1993); and in *The New Cultural History,* ed. Lynn Hunt (Berkeley: U of California P, 1989), including especially Thomas W. Laqueur, "Bodies, Details, and the Humanitarian Narrative," 176-204.

30. As Raymond Williams has written, "*no mode of production and therefore no dominant social order and therefore no dominant culture ever in reality includes or exhausts all human practice, human energy, and human intention*" (125, the emphasis is his). Similarly, in their Introduction to *Culture/Power/History,* Nicholas B. Dirks, Geoff Eley, and Sherry B. Ortner argue, "Power never totally suppresses resistance, nor ever fully destroys the multiple subjects who resist" (11). I mention Gramsci, Butler, and bell hooks along with Williams and Dirks, Eley, and Ortner to suggest the array of cultural critics who have maintained complex views of culture that imagine the possibilities for resistance and social change grounded in the struggles, contradictions, subversions, or inconsistencies in culture itself. Such thinkers avoid both an ahistorical concept of agency as well as a social control view of history in which culture possesses such a high degree of internal unity as to proscribe contradiction, subversion, eccentricity, or counterhegemonic struggle. See Williams, *Marxism and Literature* (New York: Oxford UP, 1977); Dirks, Eley, and Ortner, Introduc-

tion, *Culture/Power/History: A Reader in Contemporary Social Theory,* ed. Dirks, Eley, and Ortner (Princeton: Princeton UP, 1994) 3-45; Antonio Gramsci, *An Antonio Gramsci Reader: Selected Writings, 1916-1935,* ed. David Forgacs (New York: Schocken Books, 1988); Butler; and bell hooks, *Yearning: Race, Gender, and Cultural Politics* (Boston: South End Press, 1990).

31. For a survey of Clara Barton's work during the Civil War, see Elizabeth Brown Pryor, *Clara Barton: Professional Angel* (Philadelphia: U of Pennsylvania P, 1987) 73-133. See also Stephen B. Oates, *A Woman of Valor: Clara Barton and the Civil War* (New York: Free Press, 1994).

32. Michel de Certeau, *The Practice of Everyday Life,* trans. Steven Rendall (Berkeley: U of California P, 1984) xvii.

2. Dangerous Philanthropy

1. Muriel Rukeyser, "The Soul and Body of John Brown," *Poetry* 46, no. 3 (June 1940): 115.

2. Frederick Douglass, *Life and Times of Frederick Douglass* (1892; London: Collier Books, 1962) 317-320.

3. For an account of the raid on Harpers Ferry, see Stephen B. Oates, *To Purge This Land With Blood: A Biography of John Brown,* 2nd ed. (Amherst: U of Massachusetts P, 1984) 290-306.

4. Mrs. J. C. Swayze, *Ossawattomie Brown: or, The Insurrection at Harpers' Ferry* (New York: Samuel French, 1859) 25. Further references to Swayze's play are noted by page number in the text.

5. Franklin B. Sanborn, "Dirge," *Echoes of Harper's Ferry,* ed. James Redpath (Boston: Thayer and Eldridge, 1860) 454; A. Bronson Alcott, "Sonnet XXIV, Addressed to John Brown, Harper's Ferry," *A John Brown Reader,* ed. Louis Ruchames (New York: Abelard-Schuman, 1959) 281; William Ellery Channing, "The Martyr's Sacrifice" originally published as "The Burial of John Brown" (1860), rpt. in *John Brown and the Heroes of Harper's Ferry* (Boston: Cupples, Upham and Company, 1886) 125; Rev. J. T. Powers, "Freedom," *Liberator* 13 Apr. 1860: 60; Justitia, "Elba," *Liberator* 10 Feb. 1860: 24.

6. M. D. Conway, "Excalibur," *The Dial* 1, no. 1 (Jan. 1860): 47.

7. Robert M. De Witt, *The Life, Trial, and Execution of Capt. John Brown* (New York: Robert M. De Witt, 1859; Miami: Mnemosyne, 1969) 45.

8. De Witt 48, 47; John Brown, letter to Mary Brown and children, 8 Nov. 1859, in F. B. Sanborn, *The Life and Letters of John Brown, Liberator of Kansas, and Martyr of Virginia* (1885; New York: Negro Universities P, 1969) 586.

9. For more on Cheever, see Robert M. York, *George B. Cheever, Religious and Social Reformer 1807-1890,* University of Maine Studies, 2nd ser., 69 (Orono: U of Maine P, 1955). For more on Cheever's strong preference for "Old Testament truth" (iv) and "the incorruptible, eternal Word of God" (64), see George B. Cheever *God Against Slavery: And the Freedom and Duty of the Pulpit to Rebuke It, as a Sin Against God* (New York: Joseph H. Ladd, 1857; New York: Negro Universities P, 1969).

10. Rev. George B. Cheever, "The Example and the Method of Emancipation by the Constitution of Our Country, and the Word of God," 24 Nov. 1859, in *Echoes* 157. Further references to this sermon are noted by page number in the text.

11. "Practical Abolitionism," *New York Times* 28 Oct. 1859: 4; John Brown qtd. in James Redpath, "Reminiscences of the Insurrectionists," *Liberator* 28 Oct. 1859: 169; John Brown qtd. in William Lloyd Garrison, "The Criticism of Garrison," *Echoes* 307. See also Sanborn, *John Brown* 131; and Oates 272. For an example of Brown's preference for "men of action" over "men who have the gift of eloquence," see Oates 240. For Brown's position on the futility of moral suasion, see his interview with Vallandigham and Mason in De Witt 48.

12. Radical nonresistants in antislavery humanitarianism had claimed for years that the U.S. Constitution was a proslavery document. In perhaps the most famous expression of

this position, William Lloyd Garrison burned a copy of the Constitution at an antislavery meeting in 1854. During the burning, he condemned the document as "a covenant with death, and an agreement with hell." See William Lloyd Garrison et al., "The Meeting at Framingham," *Liberator* 21 July 1854: 106. See also [Wendell Phillips], *The Constitution a Pro-Slavery Compact* (New York: American Anti-Slavery Society, 1856).

13. John Brown, letter to Theodore Parker, 2 Feb. 1858, in Sanborn, *John Brown* 435; De Witt 48; Garrison, *Echoes* 307.

14. See John R. McKivigan, *The War against Proslavery Religion: Abolitionism and the Northern Churches, 1830-1865* (Ithaca: Cornell UP, 1984) 156.

15. Rev. Edwin M. Wheelock, sermon, 27 Nov. 1859, in *Echoes* 187-88.

16. Henry D. Thoreau, "A Plea for Captain John Brown," *Reform Papers,* ed. Wendell Glick (Princeton: Princeton UP, 1973) 133.

17. Redpath, Preface, *Echoes* 6-7.

18. Sanborn, *John Brown* 131; Garrison, *Echoes* 307.

19. John R. McKivigan, "James Redpath, John Brown, and Abolitionist Advocacy of Slave Insurrection," *Civil War History* 37, no. 4 (Dec. 1991): 313.

20. See Thoreau, "Plea" 137-38; McKivigan, "Redpath"; Redpath, *Echoes* 9; James Redpath, *The Roving Editor; or Talks with Slaves in the Southern States* (New York: A. B. Burdick, 1859) vii; and Lydia Maria Child, *Correspondence between Lydia Maria Child and Gov. Wise and Mrs. Mason of Virginia* (Boston: American Anti-Slavery Society, 1860) 8.

In advocating this "new" antislavery action, Redpath faced a problem that had never troubled the nonresistants: How does someone make a slave insurrection happen? What methods should antislavery folks deploy to enact such an upheaval? John Brown had, of course, left Redpath with one example: Harpers Ferry. But, in 1859 and 1860, common sense seemed to argue against an exact repetition of the John Brown method; Harpers Ferry had failed to start any rebellion among slaves and Brown himself was hanged. Hence, apparently unsatisfied with other means or uncertain of how else to act, Redpath turned to the oldest, most popular, and most often used weapon in the antislavery arsenal— language. His writing, he hoped, would incite the kind of action he had imagined. See Redpath's Preface to *Echoes* 5-6.

21. Wendell Phillips, "The Puritan Principle and John Brown," *Speeches, Lectures, and Letters,* 2nd ser. (Boston: Lee and Shepard, 1891) 301; Wendell Phillips, "Harper's Ferry" originally titled "The Lesson of the Hour," *Speeches, Lectures, and Letters,* 1st ser. (Boston: James Redpath, 1863; Boston: Lee and Shepard, 1891) 263. Further references to these two speeches are noted parenthetically in the text.

22. A facsimile of the Brown document appears opposite page 554 in Oswald Garrison Villard, *John Brown, 1800-1859: A Biography Fifty Years After* (1910; New York: Knopf, 1943); Wendell Phillips, "Burial of John Brown," *Speeches,* 1st ser., 292. Further references to "Burial of John Brown" are noted parenthetically in the text.

23. Herman Melville, "The Portent," *Battle-Pieces and Aspects of the War,* ed. Sidney Kaplan (1866; Amherst: U of Massachussetts P, 1972) 11. See also Kent Ljungquist, "'Meteor of the War': Melville, Thoreau, and Whitman Respond to John Brown," *American Literature* 61, no. 4 (Dec. 1989): 674-80.

24. See James Brewer Stewart, *Holy Warriors: The Abolitionists and American Slavery* (New York: Hill and Wang, 1976) 124-77.

25. For more on the Pottawatomie Massacre, see Oates 126-37.

26. John Greenleaf Whittier, letter to Lydia Maria Child, 21 Oct. 1859, in *The Letters of John Greenleaf Whittier,* ed. John B. Pickard, 3 vols. (Cambridge: Harvard UP, 1975) 2:435-36.

27. John Greenleaf Whittier, letter to Elizabeth Lloyd Howell, 6 Nov. 1859, in *Letters* 2:438; Henry Ward Beecher, sermon, 30 Oct. 1859, in *Echoes* 261-62. Although Whittier and Beecher shared a similar response to Harpers Ferry, Beecher was not a pacifist. Indeed, during Bleeding Kansas, he had endorsed the use of violence in service of the antislavery cause.

28. John G. Whittier, "Brown of Osawatomie," in *Echoes* 304.

29. Lydia Maria Child, letter to Sarah Blake (Sturgis) Shaw, 4 Nov. 1859, in *The Collected Correspondence of Lydia Maria Child, 1817–1880,* ed. Patricia G. Holland and Milton Meltzer (Millwood, NY: KTO Microform, 1979) card 41/letter 1131; Child, letter to John Brown, 26 Oct. 1859, in *Correspondence Between Child and Wise and Mason* 14; James Freeman Clarke, "Causes and Consequences of the Affair at Harper's Ferry," 6 Nov. 1859, in *Echoes* 317.

30. Clarke 330.

31. Ingleby Scott, "Representative Men: The Puritan Militant, John Brown," *Once A Week* 2, no. 31 (28 Jan. 1860): 107. See Michael Meyer, "Thoreau's Rescue of John Brown from History," *Studies in the American Renaissance/1980,* ed. Joel Myerson (Boston: Twayne, 1980) 301-16; James Redpath, *The Public Life of Captain John Brown* (Boston: Thayer & Eldridge, 1860) 115-19.

32. Clarke 323-24.

33. "The Harper's Ferry Rebellion," *New York Times* 20 Oct. 1859: 1; "The Virginia Rebellion," *New York Times* 22 Oct. 1859: 1; "The Virginia Rebellion," *New York Times* 28 Oct. 1859: 1-2; "Who is Responsible?" *Liberator* 28 Oct. 1859: 169.

34. Sanborn, *John Brown* 560-61; De Witt 94. Commenting on Brown's courtroom speech, Oates says, "It is hard to tell whether Brown was coolly and deliberately lying for the benefit of his Northern sympathizers or whether he was confused or simply so excited, so carried away with his own drama, that he actually believed what he was telling the court" (326).

35. "The Negro Insurrection," *New York Times* 20 Oct. 1859: 4. For a twentieth-century historian's account of Brown's "mental disease," see Allan Nevins, *The Emergence of Lincoln,* 2 vols. (New York: Scribner's, 1950) 2:5-27, 70-97.

36. "The Negro Insurrection" 4. See Oates 299; De Witt 64-65; and John Brown, letter to Heman Humphrey, 25 Nov. 1859, in Sanborn, *John Brown* 603.

37. Ralph Waldo Emerson, *The Journals and Miscellaneous Notebooks of Ralph Waldo Emerson,* ed. William H. Gilman et al., 16 vols. (Cambridge: Harvard UP, 1960-82) 14:334; Rev. Leonard Bacon, "The Moral of Harper's Ferry, " *The New Englander* 17, no. 4 (Nov. 1859): 1071.

38. Julia Ward Howe, *Reminiscences, 1819–1899* (1899; New York: Negro Universities P, 1969) 256. Brown did not, of course, watch "Border Ruffians" kill two of his sons. When Martin White murdered one of Brown's sons, Frederick, at Osawatomie in August 1856, Brown was not present and could not have witnessed the shooting.

39. Conway 48. For Thoreau's censure of allegations that Brown was mad, see "Plea" 122-28. See also Bacon 1066-78, esp. 1071-76.

40. See Oates 221.

41. Theodore Parker, letter to Francis Jackson, 24 Nov. 1859, in *Echoes* 74; Douglass, *Life and Times* 275. See also Jeffrey Rossbach, *Ambivalent Conspirators: John Brown, The Secret Six, and a Theory of Slave Violence* (Philadelphia: U of Pennsylvania P, 1982); and David W. Blight, *Frederick Douglass' Civil War: Keeping Faith in Jubilee* (Baton Rouge: Louisiana State UP, 1989) 95-99.

42. William Lloyd Garrison, "The Tragedy at Harper's Ferry," *Liberator* 28 Oct. 1859: 170; Garrison, "Speech of Wm. Lloyd Garrison," *Liberator* 16 Dec. 1859: 198; Ednah Dow Cheney, *Reminiscences of Ednah Dow Cheney* (Boston: Lee & Shepard, 1902) 83. See Garrison, "The Criticism of Garrison," in *Echoes* 305-309. See also George M. Fredrickson, *The Inner Civil War: Northern Intellectuals and the Crisis of the Union* (New York: Harper & Row, 1965) 41-42.

43. Harriet Tubman qtd. in *Reminiscences of Ednah Dow Cheney* 81-82; Harvey C. Jackson, broadside, 7 Dec. 1859, rpt. in *Blacks on John Brown,* ed. Benjamin Quarles (Urbana: U of Illinois P, 1972) 33.

44. J. S. Martin, "Speech of Rev. J. S. Martin," *Liberator* 9 Dec. 1859: 194; John S. Rock, speech, 5 Mar. 1860, in *The Black Abolitionist Papers,* ed. C. Peter Ripley, 5 vols. (Chapel

Hill: U of North Carolina P, 1985–92) 5:59; George Lawrence, Jr., editorial, 27 Apr. 1861, in *Black Abolitionist Papers* 5:112.

45. ["ladies of New York, Brooklyn, and Williamsburgh"], letter to Mary Brown, 23 Nov. 1859, in *Blacks on John Brown* 16-19; William Lambert, resolutions, 2 Dec. 1859, in *Black Abolitionist Papers* 5:53; H. O. W. and others, letter to John Brown, 17 Nov. 1859, in *Echoes* 391; Quarles, Introduction, *Blacks on John Brown* ix; Frederick Douglass, *John Brown* (Dover, NH: Morning Star Job Printing House, 1881) 9. For Frederick Douglass's unequivocal defense of "the John Brown way" of opposing slavery, see Frederick Douglass, "John Brown's Contribution to the Abolition Movement: An Address Delivered in Boston, Massachusetts, on 3 December 1860," *The Frederick Douglass Papers*, ed. John W. Blassingame, 4 vols., (New Haven: Yale UP, 1978-91) 3:412-20. See also, M. J. S. T., letter to John Brown, 26 Nov. 1859, in *Echoes* 419.

Adopting the view of these nineteenth-century African American activists, important twentieth-century historians have continued to see John Brown as a humanitarian dedicated to antiracist egalitarianism. In the Preface to his biography of John Brown, W. E. B. Du Bois writes: "John Brown worked not simply for the Black Man—he worked with them, and he was a companion of their daily life, knew their faults and virtues, and felt as few white Americans have felt, the bitter tragedy of their lot." More recently Herbert Aptheker has argued: "Among white participants in the movement, Brown was extraordinary—perhaps unique—in the completeness with which he, his wife, Mary Brown, and their children shed concepts and feelings of white supremacy." See W. E. B. Du Bois, *John Brown* (1909; Millwood: Kraus, 1973); and Herbert Aptheker, *Abolitionism: A Revolutionary Movement* (Boston: Twayne, 1989) 123. See also Benjamin Quarles, *Allies for Freedom: Blacks and John Brown* (New York: Oxford UP, 1974). For more on John Brown as a symbol of "black rather than white achievement" (307), see William E. Cain, "Violence, Revolution, and the Cost of Freedom: John Brown and W. E. B. Du Bois," *boundary 2* 17, no. 1 (Summer 1990): 305-30.

46. [Henry S. Olcott], "From another correspondent, Harper's Ferry, Dec. 3," *New York Tribune* 5 Dec. 1859, excerpted in Cecil D. Eby, Jr., "Whittier's 'Brown of Ossawatomie,'" *New England Quarterly* 33, no. 4 (Dec. 1960): 456.

47. John Brown, letter to Mrs. George L. Stearns, 29 Nov. 1859, in Sanborn, *John Brown* 610-11. There is a facsimile of this letter opposite page 611 in Sanborn, *John Brown*.

48. Channing 128.

49. See De Witt 10-14.

50. For the interview and trial speech, see De Witt 44-49, 94-95.

51. First written in 1848 for the black antislavery newspaper the *Ram's Horn*, "Sambo's Mistakes" is reprinted in Villard 659-661. "Words of Advice," an 1851 text addressed to the League of Gileadites, a black abolitionist organization, is reprinted in Sanborn, *John Brown* 124-26. Quotations are taken from these texts as they are reprinted in Villard and Sanborn.

52. Oates 59; Quarles, Introduction, *Blacks on John Brown* x.

53. Redpath, *Roving Editor* iv.

54. Thomas Hamilton, "Mistakes of the South," editorial, *Weekly Anglo-African,* 5 Nov. 1859, in *Black Abolitionist Papers* 5:39.

55. L. Maria Child, letter to Harriet Jacobs, 13 Aug. 1860, letter 11 in Harriet A. Jacobs, *Incidents in the Life of a Slave Girl,* ed. L. Maria Child, new edition ed. Jean Fagan Yellin (Boston: For the Author, 1861; Cambridge: Harvard UP, 1987) 244. References to *Incidents* are noted parenthetically in the text.

56. Bruce Mills, *Cultural Reformations: Lydia Maria Child and the Literature of Reform* (Athens: U of Georgia P, 1994) 129, 113, 114.

57. Harriet Jacobs, letter to Amy Post, 8 Nov. 1860, in Dorothy Sterling, ed., *We Are Your Sisters: Black Women in the Nineteenth Century* (New York: Norton, 1984) 83; Jacobs, letter to Post, 8 Oct. 1860, letter 13 in *Incidents* 247. Commenting on the November 8th letter, Alice A. Deck writes, "Jacobs' sarcastic reference to her own small ideas indicates her confidence in her integrity as a writer, and an unwillingness completely to surrender her

manuscript to an editor without being consulted on any changes." See Alice A. Deck, "Whose Book Is This?: Authorial Versus Editorial Control of Harriet Brent Jacobs' *Incidents in the Life of a Slave Girl: Written By Herself*," *Women's Studies International Forum* 10, no. 1 (1987): 40.

58. Child, letter to Shaw, 4 Nov. 1859, *Collected Correspondence of Child* card 41/letter 1131.

59. John S. Jacobs, in the *Anti-Slavery Standard* 10 Oct. 1859, qtd. in Quarles, *Allies for Freedom* 71.

60. Child, *Correspondence Between Child and Wise and Mason* 14. For another view of Child's editing of Jacobs's text—one that emphasizes the "sensitivity" that Child showed Jacobs—see Carolyn L. Karcher, *The First Woman in the Republic: A Cultural Biography of Lydia Maria Child* (Durham: Duke UP, 1994) 436.

3. Harriet Jacobs and the Subversion of Style

1. Judith Butler, *Gender Trouble: Feminism and the Subversion of Identity* (New York: Routledge, 1990) 147.

2. See Harriet A. Jacobs, *Incidents in the Life of a Slave Girl*, ed. L. Maria Child, new edition ed. Jean Fagan Yellin (Boston: For the Author, 1861; Cambridge: Harvard UP, 1987) 159-160, 227, 282n3, 283n4. References to *Incidents* are designated parenthetically in the text. I refer to the author of *Incidents* as Harriet Jacobs and to the text's protagonist as Linda Brent, the pseudonym Jacobs uses in her autobiography.

3. I borrow this term from Judith Butler's *Gender Trouble.*

4. See P. J. Staudenraus, *The African Colonization Movement, 1816-1865* (New York: Columbia UP, 1961); and George M. Fredrickson, *The Black Image in the White Mind: The Debate on Afro-American Destiny, 1817-1914* (1971; Middletown: Wesleyan UP, 1987) 6-21, 145-52. Although my focus is on white-led colonization schemes as an example of coercive humanitarianism, there were important black-led emigration plans. Although black opposition to white colonization schemes prevailed throughout the century, in the 1850s, after the passage of the Fugitive Slave Law, some African Americans began to reconsider the possibilities of emigration. Under the leadership of black nationalists like Martin Delany and Henry Highland Garnet, African Americans began to plan black-led and black-organized emigration to Canada, Haiti, the Niger Valley, and other places. See Benjamin Quarles, *Black Abolitionists* (New York: Oxford UP, 1969) 215-22; and Jane H. Pease and William H. Pease, *They Who Would Be Free: Blacks' Search for Freedom, 1830-1861* (1974; Urbana and Chicago: U of Illinois P, 1990) 251-278.

5. Thomas Jefferson, letter to Jared Sparks, 4 Feb. 1824, in *Writings*, ed. Merrill D. Peterson (New York: Library of America, 1984) 1484-85.

6. Abraham Lincoln, "Address on Colonization to a Committee of Colored Men, Washington, D.C.," *Speeches and Writings, 1859-1865*, ed. Don E. Fehrenbacher (New York: Library of America, 1989) 354-55.

7. See Harriet Beecher Stowe, *Uncle Tom's Cabin*, ed. Elizabeth Ammons (1852; New York: Norton, 1994). References to *Uncle Tom's Cabin* are noted parenthetically in the text. For an analysis of the response of black abolitionists to *Uncle Tom's Cabin*, see Quarles, *Black Abolitionists* 220-21; and Marva Banks, "*Uncle Tom's Cabin* and the Antebellum Black Response," *Readers in History: Nineteenth-Century American Literature and the Contexts of Response*, ed. James L. Machor (Baltimore: Johns Hopkins UP, 1993) 209-27. Although most were skeptical of Stowe's colonization ideas, black readers and leaders were not uniformly critical of Stowe. Robert Levine has shown that while some African American antislavery activists like William Wilson and Martin Delany criticized the novel and its politics, Frederick Douglass hoped that white sympathy might help their cause. Thus, he creatively appropriated Stowe's novel. By printing the praises of Stowe's novel in the pages of his newspaper, "Douglass sought to make *Uncle Tom's Cabin* do the cultural work that he

wanted it to do" (88). See Robert S. Levine, "*Uncle Tom's Cabin* in *Frederick Douglass' Paper*: An Analysis of Reception," *American Literature* 64, no. 1 (Mar. 1992): 71-93. Nevertheless, Douglass also spoke pejoratively of Uncle Tom at times, and *Frederick Douglass' Paper* did print negative evaluations of Stowe's novel. See Frederick Douglass, "Colored Men's Rights in this Republic: An Address Delivered in New York, New York on 14 May 1857," *The Frederick Douglass Papers,* ed. John W. Blassingame, 4 vols. (New Haven: Yale UP, 1978–1991) 3:148; and George T. Downing, "Letter from George T. Downing," *Frederick Douglass' Paper* 22 Dec. 1854: [third page of issue].

8. Theodore S. Wright, "From the Friend of Man / Speech of a Colored Brother / Delivered at the late meeting of the N.Y. State Anti-Slavery Society at Utica," *Liberator* 13 Oct. 1837: 165; David Walker, *David Walker's Appeal,* ed. Charles M. Wiltse (1829; New York: Hill and Wang, 1965) 55; George T. Downing, "The Corrector Corrected," *Frederick Douglass' Paper* 18 May 1855: [second page of issue]. See also Quarles, *Black Abolitionists* 1-22; and Pease and Pease, *They Who Would Be Free* 17-28. For the protests of black abolitionists to colonization, see, for example, Walker 45-78; and Maria W. Stewart, *Maria W. Stewart: America's First Black Woman Political Writer: Essays and Speeches,* ed. Marilyn Richardson (Bloomington: Indiana UP, 1987) 46-47, 61. See also the objections of white abolitionists, including William Lloyd Garrison, *Thoughts on African Colonization* (Boston: Garrison and Knapp, 1832); John Greenleaf Whittier, *Justice and Expediency* (1833), rpt. in *The Writings of John Greenleaf Whittier,* 7 vols. (Boston: Houghton Mifflin, 1889) 7:14-25; and L. Maria Child, *An Appeal in Favor of that Class of Americans Called Africans* (New York: John S. Taylor, 1836; New York: Arno, 1968) 123-47.

9. I distinguish here between racism as a behavior ("racism") and racism as an ideology ("racialism"). I rely on the more common "racism" to designate both. I borrow this distinction between racism and racialism from Tzvetan Todorov. See Tzvetan Todorov, *Nous et les autres: La réflexion française sur la diversité humaine* (Paris: Seuil, 1989) 113.

For analyses of racism in the antislavery movements, see William H. Pease and Jane H. Pease, "Antislavery Ambivalence: Immediatism, Expediency, Race," *American Quarterly* 17, no. 4 (Winter 1965): 682-95; Fredrickson, *Black Image* 1-42, 97-129; Pease and Pease, *They Who Would Be Free*; Robert L. Allen and Pamela P. Allen, *Reluctant Reformers: Racism and Social Reform Movements in the United States* (Washington, D.C.: Howard UP, 1974) 11-48; Lawrence J. Friedman, *Gregarious Saints: Self and Community in American Abolitionism, 1830–1870* (Cambridge: Cambridge UP, 1982) 161-95; and R. J. M. Blackett, *Building an Antislavery Wall: Black Americans in the Atlantic Abolitionist Movement* (Baton Rouge: Louisiana State UP, 1983). On the racism faced by black women in antislavery reform, see Shirley J. Yee, *Black Women Abolitionists: A Study in Activism, 1828-60* (Knoxville: U of Tennessee Press, 1992) 35-36.

10. James Redpath, *The Roving Editor; or Talks with Slaves in the Southern States* (New York: A. B. Burdick, 1859) iv.

There were, of course, abolitionists who explicitly rejected racialism and espoused instead a doctrine of racial equality. They insisted on what Child called "the identity of the *human* type" (*Appeal* 148), the essential unity (and hence equality) of the human species. To support their ideas about the unity and equality of the various races, and to combat the endless pronouncements about the innate physical and mental inferiority of negroes, they turned to environmentalist explanations of race and the perceived differences between the races. Against claims that "the Negroes are a different race from the whites, and may be enslaved, because they are inferior in intellectual capacity," John G. Fee confidently asserted his environmentalist view:

> There is no one position more clearly established by facts than this: *the intellectual capacity of an individual, or a people, depends, in a great degree, upon the state of society in which they live,*—the amount of liberty which they enjoy, the facilities for acquiring knowledge;—the peculiar circumstances with which they are surrounded. (*An Anti-Slavery Manual* [Maysville, KY: Herald Office, 1848; New York: Arno, 1969] 206)

Likewise, countering an essentialism in racialist thinking, Child argued, "the present degraded condition of that unfortunate race is produced by artificial causes, not by the laws of nature" (*Appeal* 148). This attention to environmental factors allowed abolitionists to rebut racialist claims by returning the focus of the debate to the cruel treatment of slaves. Environmentalism provided the grounds for a belief in human equality and for a refusal of "scientific" arguments about racial difference and black inferiority.

Yet, as Ronald Walters has demonstrated, "environmentalism was neither clearly articulated nor consistently upheld" in the antislavery movement. Despite efforts (by abolitionists such as Wendell Phillips, for instance) to counter the various racialist discourses of the period, antislavery activists were often equivocal or confusing in their statements on race and equality. Some antislavery humanitarians unequivocally embraced the racialism of their era, in some instances becoming an important site for the production of racialist discourse. See Ronald G. Walters, *The Antislavery Appeal: American Abolitionism after 1830* (Baltimore: Johns Hopkins UP, 1976) 63. On Phillips's rejection of racialism, see James Brewer Stewart, *Wendell Phillips: Liberty's Hero* (Baton Rouge: Louisiana State UP, 1986) 104-06; and Wendell Phillips, "Toussaint L'Ouverture," *Speeches, Lectures, and Letters* (Boston: Lee and Shepard, 1863; New York: Negro Universities P, 1968) 468-94, esp. 468-69.

11. See Ronald T. Takaki, *Iron Cages: Race and Culture in Nineteenth-Century America* (New York: Knopf, 1979) 109-28; and Fredrickson, *Black Image* 52-58.

12. Several other passages also illustrate Jacobs's awareness of the pervasiveness of racialist analogies that emphasized the not-quite-human nature of black people:

> These God-breathing machines are no more, in the sight of their masters, than the cotton they plant, or the horses they tend. (8)

> They regard such children as property, as marketable as the pigs on the plantation. (36)

> [Masters] look upon [slaves'] suffering with less pity than they would bestow on those of a horse or a dog. (92)

Not unrelated to these perceptions of black people as animal-like were the attempts in biology, zoology, and ethnology to "document" and interpret differences (physical, intellectual, moral) among humans. Samuel G. Morton's "empirical" study on American Indian skulls, *Crania Americana* (1839), the encyclopedia of racist ideas in *Types of Mankind* (1854, edited by Josiah C. Nott and George R. Gliddon), Louis Agassiz's theory of the plural origins of the human species, and later Count Joseph Arthur de Gobineau's influential four-volume *Essai sur l'inégalité des races humaines* (1854, American edition and translation 1856) stimulated a great deal of "scientific" work on as well as popular interest in the origins, diversity, and classificatory order of human races. In the writings of Andrew Jackson Davis, a spiritualist who mixed heretical Swedenborgianism with scientific discourse and a progressivist theory of history, for example, there is a distinct ranking of the development of human races from the lowest to the highest: Negro, Aborig-American, Malay-Mongolian, Caucasian, Anglo-American. In the late 1840s, it is interesting to note, Davis became a persuasive presence in the household of abolitionists Angelina Grimké and Theodore Weld. For a discussion of scientific racialism in the United States, see William Stanton, *The Leopard's Spots: Scientific Attitudes toward Race in America* (Chicago: U of Chicago P, 1960); Fredrickson, *Black Image* 71-96; and Reginald Horsman, *Race and Manifest Destiny: The Origins of American Racial Anglo-Saxonism* (Cambridge: Harvard UP, 1981). See also Andrew Jackson Davis, *The Magic Staff; An Autobiography* (1857; New York: A.J. Davis, 1874) 374; Robert W. Delp, "Andrew Jackson Davis: Prophet of American Spiritualism," *Journal of American History* 54, no. 1 (June 1967): 43-56; and Robert H. Abzug, *Passionate Liberator: Theodore Dwight Weld and the Dilemma of Reform* (New York: Oxford UP, 1980) 249-53.

13. See Fredrickson, *Black Image* 97-129; and David Levin, *History as Romantic Art: Bancroft, Prescott, Motley, and Parkman* (Stanford: Stanford UP, 1959).

14. See Thomas Graham, "Harriet Beecher Stowe and the Question of Race," *New England Quarterly* 46, no. 4 (Dec. 1973): 614-22.

15. Elizabeth Cady Stanton, "To the Women of the State of New York," *Frederick Douglass' Paper* 22 Dec. 1854: [front page].

16. Angelina E. Grimké, letter to Sarah Douglass, 3 Apr. 1837, in *The Public Years of Sarah and Angelina Grimké: Selected Writings, 1835–1839*, ed. Larry Ceplair (New York: Columbia UP, 1989) 127. For more on Grimké's antiracist efforts, see Gerda Lerner, "The Grimké Sisters and the Struggle Against Race Prejudice," *Journal of Negro History* 48, no. 4 (Oct. 1963): 277-291.

17. Jane and William Pease have also noted the condescension in Angelina Grimké's letters to Sarah Douglass. According to Pease and Pease, "in a display of tactlessness as gargantuan as it was overbearing," Grimké wrote Douglass: "May the Lord lift you from the dung hill and set you among princes." See Pease and Pease, "Antislavery Ambivalence" 692-93. See also Angelina Grimké, letter to Sarah Douglass, 22 Feb. 1837, in *Letters of Theodore Dwight Weld, Angelina Grimké Weld, and Sarah Grimké, 1822–1844*, ed. Gilbert H. Barnes and Dwight L. Dumond, 2 vols. (New York: D. Appleton-Century Company, 1934) 1:365.

18. In *We Are Your Sisters: Black Women in the Nineteenth Century*, ed. Dorothy Sterling (New York: Norton, 1984) 255.

19. Friedman 167; Garrison qtd. in Waldo E. Martin, *The Mind of Frederick Douglass* (Chapel Hill: U of North Carolina P, 1984) 46. For more on paternalism within the antislavery movement, see Leon F. Litwack, *North of Slavery: The Negro in the Free States, 1790–1860* (Chicago: U of Chicago P, 1961) 214-46.

20. See Lincoln, "Address on Colonization" 356. See also the four articles signed S. T. U., "What Can the Free Colored People Do for Themselves," *Liberator* 11 Feb. 1832, 18 Feb. 1832, 25 Feb. 1832, 3 Mar. 1832: 21, 26, 29-30, 33-34.

21. Harriet Beecher Stowe, letter to Wendell Phillips, [1854], in *Wendell and Ann Phillips: The Community of Reform, 1840–1880*, ed. Irving H. Bartlett (New York: Norton, 1981) 71; Sarah Grimké, "Address to the Free Colored People of the United States," *Selected Writings* 132-33; S. T. U., "What Can the Free Colored People Do For Themselves? No. IV" 34.

22. The *Oxford English Dictionary* defines "altruize" in precisely this way: "To change into someone else." The etymological source of "altruize" is "altruism," the principle of unselfish concern for the welfare of others. Although my neologism suggests a direct link between altruism and altruizm (the words share the same pronunciation), altruism (Auguste Comte's coinage from the 1850s) and altruizm (my word) are not identical: altruism denotes an ethical principle; altruizm specifies an affective process, although, in some cases, altruizm might be a symptom of an exaggerated sense of altruism.

My introduction of the term "altruizm" indicates perhaps my methodological debt to social control theorists and historians, particularly Foucault. Later in this chapter, I hope to offset and redirect this term's social control element by discussing Jacobs's resistance to altruizm in antislavery discourse.

23. Walt Whitman, *Leaves of Grass*, ed. Harold W. Blodgett and Sculley Bradley (1891–92; New York: New York UP, 1965) 66-67.

24. For an example of exhortations to "feel" for the slaves, see [William Lloyd Garrison], "What Shall Be Done?" *Liberator* 30 July 1831: 121. Child's request appears in a letter to Wendell Phillips, 2 July 1860, in *Wendell and Ann Phillips* 68.

25. Ethiop [William Wilson], "From Our Brooklyn Correspondent," *Frederick Douglass' Paper* 22 Apr. 1852: [third page of issue].

26. Agnes Mary Grant, letter to Wendell Phillips, 9 Dec. 1859, in *Wendell and Ann Phillips* 75-76.

27. [Harriet Jacobs], "Letter From a Fugitive Slave," *New York Tribune* 21 June 1853: 6. For reprintings of this letter, see Harriet A. Jacobs, letter to Horace Greeley, 19 June 1853,

in *Black Abolitionist Papers,* ed. C. Peter Ripley, 5 vols. (Chapel Hill: U of North Carolina P, 1985-92) 4:164-69; or Jean Fagan Yellin, "*Legacy* Profile: Harriet Ann Jacobs (c. 1817–1897)," *Legacy* 5, no. 2 (Fall 1988): 60-61.

28. Frederick Douglass qtd. in "National Council of the Colored People," *Frederick Douglass' Paper* 18 May 1855: [front page]; Frederick Douglass, "These Questions Cannot Be Answered by the White Race: An Address Delivered in New York, New York on 11 May 1855," *Papers* 3:87. See Pease and Pease, *They Who Would Be Free* 3-16.

29. Douglass qtd. in "National Council."

30. William Whipper qtd. in Carleton Mabee, *Black Freedom: The Nonviolent Abolitionists from 1830 through the Civil War* (New York: Macmillan, 1970) 106. See also Richard P. McCormick, "William Whipper: Moral Reformer," *Pennsylvania History* 43, no. 1 (Jan. 1976): 23-46.

31. See Robert B. Stepto, "Distrust of the Reader in Afro-American Narratives," *Reconstructing American Literary History,* ed. Sacvan Bercovitch (Cambridge: Harvard UP, 1986) 300-22, esp. 304.

32. Frederick Douglass, *Narrative of the Life of Frederick Douglass, An American Slave,* ed. Houston A. Baker, Jr. (1845; New York: Penguin, 1982) 144.

33. Frances Smith Foster has also identified the "discourse of distrust" as an important element in Jacobs's style. See Frances Smith Foster, "Harriet Jacobs's *Incidents* and the 'Careless Daughters' (and Sons) Who Read It," *The (Other) American Traditions: Nineteenth-Century Women Writers,* ed. Joyce W. Warren (New Brunswick: Rutgers UP, 1993) 100-105.

34. In 1859 the Phillips and Sampson & Co. agreed to publish *Incidents* if Stowe or Nathaniel Parker Willis (Jacobs's boss, Mr. Bruce in *Incidents*) would write the preface. But, because of her personal and professional conflict with Stowe and because of Willis's "proslavery" sympathies, Jacobs could ask neither for a preface. Thayer & Eldridge agreed to publish *Incidents* in 1860, if Jacobs "could obtain a Preface from Mrs. Child." Although neither publisher ever issued her book (both firms went bankrupt), their insistence on a preface written by a notable white person indicates the importance of such a convention for marketing the book to a primarily white readership. See Harriet Jacobs, letter to Amy Post, 8 Oct. [1860], letter 13 in *Incidents* 246-47. See also Harriet Jacobs, letter to Amy Post, [1852?], letter 4 in *Incidents* 231-33.

35. In attempting to understand *Incidents* as a document of antislavery humanitarianism, we need to see Jacobs's "self" as the result of these discursive choices, rather than as an expression of some genuine core identity that exists prior to or apart from discourse. Prior to 1981, this borrowing from and revision of other discourses led some commentators to doubt the authenticity of Jacobs's autobiography. Because of its literary nature, John W. Blassingame considered *Incidents* "fictional or largely fictional." In *The Slave Community* (1972, rev. ed. 1979) he wrote that *Incidents* "is not credible" because the work "is too orderly" and "too melodramatic." When he wrote that statement, however, Blassingame did not have the benefit of Jean Fagan Yellin's formidable research verifying with external evidence Jacobs's authorship and the historical authenticity of her narrative. Since the first publication of Yellin's findings in 1981, scholars have welcomed Jacobs's *Incidents* as an authentic slave narrative "Written by Herself," and Blassingame was among the first to acknowledge the significance of Yellin's work. Nevertheless, in their eagerness to embrace the truthfulness of Jacobs's tale, some post-Yellin critics tend to ignore the discursive nature of the "self" constructed in *Incidents.* Thomas Doherty, for example, has argued that Jacobs's presentation of self is remarkable in its straightforwardness, candor, and lack of disguise. "She wears no mask," Doherty writes of Jacobs, "she is only herself." What this position fails to realize is that the "self" of *Incidents* is a discursive "self" constructed for a particular audience and for specific rhetorical purposes. See John W. Blassingame, *The Slave Community: Plantation Life in the Antebellum South,* rev. ed. (New York: Oxford UP, 1979) 372-73; Jean Fagan Yellin, "Written By Herself: Harriet Jacobs' Slave Narrative," *American Literature* 53, no. 3 (1981): 479-86; and Thomas Doherty, "Harriet Jacobs' Narrative Strategies: *Incidents in the Life of a Slave Girl,*" *Southern Literary Journal* 19, no. 1 (Fall 1986): 87. See also Henry Louis Gates, Jr.,

"To Be Raped, Bred or Abused," rev. of *Incidents in the Life of A Slave Girl*, edited by Jean Fagan Yellin, *New York Times Book Review* 22 Nov. 1987: 12.

36. Henry Louis Gates, Jr., *The Signifying Monkey: A Theory of Afro-American Literary Criticism* (New York: Oxford UP, 1988) 80, 90.

37. Claudia Mitchell Kernan and Geneva Smitherman qtd. in *The Signifying Monkey* 80, 94. See Claudia Mitchell-Kernan, "Signifying as a Form of Verbal Art," *Mother Wit from the Laughing Barrel: Readings in the Interpretation of Afro-American Folklore,* ed. Alan Dundes (Englewood Cliffs: Prentice-Hall, 1973) 310-28; and Geneva Smitherman, *Talkin and Testifyin: The Language of Black America* (Boston: Houghton Mifflin, 1977).

38. Andrew Jackson, *Narrative and Writings of Andrew Jackson, of Kentucky* (Syracuse: Daily and Weekly Star Office, 1847; Miami: Mnemosyne, 1969) 15. See chapter 1, "Mystery of Market Speech and Prayer Meeting," of Frances E. W. Harper's *Iola Leroy, or Shadows Uplifted,* intro. by Frances Smith Foster (Philadelphia: Garrigues Brothers, 1892; New York: Oxford UP, 1988) 7-14.

39. See Gates, *The Signifying Monkey* 68.

40. For a discussion of motivated and unmotivated Signifyin(g), see Gates, *The Signifying Monkey* xxvi–xxvii, 94, 121-24.

41. Theodore S. Wright, "Speech of Rev. T. S. Wright at the N. E. A. S. Convention," *Liberator* 25 June 1836: 101.

42. See Monrose C. Gwin, "Green-eyed Monsters of the Slavocracy: Jealous Mistresses in Two Slave Narratives," *Conjuring: Black Women, Fiction, and Literary Tradition,* ed. Marjorie Pryse and Hortense J. Spillers (Bloomington: Indiana UP, 1985) 39-52.

43. In a discussion of sentimental and gothic literature's effects on the bodies of readers, Karen Sánchez-Eppler makes a similar point about Jacobs, one well worth repeating:

> Jacobs's narrative—despite frequent evocations of sentimental literary conventions from flowers and graves to motherhood, and equally frequent recourse to gothic "dungeons" and the suspense of sustained and repeated threats—leaves the bodies of its readers remarkably untouched. The story Jacobs tells is as horrible as Stowe's; it clearly hopes to make its readers angry and ashamed, but rarely, if ever, does it make them gasp or weep. . . . the text's assumptions about its readers' bodily experiences disallow comprehension of or identification with Linda's choices.

Sánchez-Eppler's analysis underscores the significance of Jacobs's antisentimental designs within her sentimental narrative. See Karen Sánchez-Eppler, *Touching Liberty: Abolition, Feminism, and the Politics of the Body* (Berkeley: U of California P, 1993) 135. See also Dana D. Nelson, *The Word in Black and White: Reading "Race" in American Literature, 1638–1867* (New York: Oxford UP, 1992) 131-45.

44. Harriet Jacobs, letter to Amy Post, 9 Oct. [1853], letter 7 in *Incidents* 236.

45. Frederick Douglass, "Suppose You Yourselves Were Black: An Address Delivered in New York, New York, on 10 May 1848," *Papers* 2:128-29.

46. Sojourner Truth qtd. in Jean Fagan Yellin, *Women and Sisters: The Antislavery Feminists in American Culture* (New Haven: Yale UP, 1989) 80-81; Stewart 49; Sarah H. Bradford, *Scenes in the Life of Harriet Tubman* (Auburn: W. J. Moses, 1869; New York: Arno, 1971) 24-36; Frederick Douglass, *My Bondage and My Freedom* (New York: Miller, Orton & Mulligan, 1855) 92-95; Josephine Brown, *Biography of an American Bondsman* (Boston: R. F. Walcutt, 1856), rpt. in *Two Biographies by African-American Women,* intro. by William L. Andrews (New York: Oxford UP, 1991) 77. See also William Craft, *Running a Thousand Miles for Freedom; or The Escape of William and Ellen Craft from Slavery* (London: William Tweedie, 1860; Miami: Mnemosyne, 1969).

47. For an analysis of Jacobs's "ambivalence" toward Mrs. Bruce's arrangements, see William L. Andrews, *To Tell a Free Story: The First Century of Afro-American Autobiography, 1760–1865* (Urbana: U of Illinois P, 1986) 260-63.

48. Harriet Jacobs, letter to Amy Post, Mar. [1854], letter 8 in *Incidents* 237-38. Louisa is Jacobs's daughter.

49. In the nineteenth century there was a long and diverse tradition of African American resistance to philanthropic social control. See, for instance, John L. Rury, "Philanthropy, Self-Help, and Social Control: The New York Manumission Society and Free Blacks, 1785–1810," *Phylon* 46, no. 3 (Sept. 1985): 231-41.

50. Frederick Douglass, "Self-Help: An Address Delivered in New York, New York, on 7 May 1849," *Papers* 2:168-70.

51. Douglass, "Advice to Black Youth: An Address Delivered in New York, New York, on 1 February 1855," *Papers* 3:3-4; Douglass qtd. in "National Council."

52. Douglass, "Advice to Black Youth" 3.

53. For the *New England Anti-Slavery Almanac* quotation, see Charles T. Davis and Henry Louis Gates, Jr., eds., *The Slave's Narrative* (New York: Oxford UP, 1985) iv. For the Stowe quotation, see Stowe, letter to Phillips, in *Wendell and Ann Phillips* 71.

54. Frances Foster, "'In Respect to Females . . .': Differences in the Portrayals of Women by Male and Female Narrators," *Black American Literature Forum* 15, no. 1 (Summer 1981): 66.

55. As one ex-slave recalled: "she [her mistress] scolded me . . . [so] I sassed her." See *We Are Your Sisters* 57; and Joanne M. Braxton, *Black Women Writing Autobiography: A Tradition Within a Tradition* (Philadelphia: Temple UP, 1989) 30-32. See also bell hooks, "Talking Back," *Talking Back: Thinking Feminist, Thinking Black* (Boston: South End Press, 1989) 5-9.

56. William Andrews has used the verbal encounters of Linda and Flint to make a fascinating point about the dialogic negotiation of power in *Incidents*: "power, as Jacobs shows us, is negotiated through speech acts, through dialogue in which the woman constantly matches wits with the man to define a margin of option for herself." In the autobiographies of Jacobs, Frederick Douglass, and J. D. Green, according to Andrews, "the master-slave relationship was not monologic, but rather dialogic." He sees her talking back as a part of the "dialogic verbal jousts" or "dialogic negotiations" between slave and master. See Andrews, *To Tell a Free Story* 265-91.

57. Aunt Martha and Benny (Linda's son) also sass Flint. See *Incidents* 82, 116-17.

58. Yellin, *Women and Sisters* 95.

59. Linda [Harriet Jacobs], "Life Among the Contrabands," *Liberator* 3 Sept. 1862: 144.

60. H[arriet] Jacobs and L[ouisa] Jacobs, letter to Lydia Maria Child, 26 Mar. 1864, in *The Collected Correspondence of Lydia Maria Child, 1817–1880*, ed. Patricia G. Holland and Milton Meltzer (Millwood, NY: KTO Microform, 1979) card 58/letter 1552. This letter was published in the *National Anti-Slavery Standard* on 16 Apr. 1864.

61. Harriet Jacobs, letter to Lydia Maria Child, 18 Mar. 1863, in *The Black Abolitionist Papers*, ed. C. Peter Ripley, 5 vols. (Chapel Hill: U of North Carolina P, 1985–1992) 5:194. This letter was printed in the *Liberator* on 10 Apr. 1863. In other Civil War letters, Jacobs used a similar approach to criticize the coercive actions of Northern humanitarians. See Jacobs, letter to Child, 26 Mar. 1864, in *Collected Correspondence of Child*, card 58/letter 1552; and Harriet Jacobs, letter to Hannah Stevenson, 1 Mar. [1864], in *We Are Your Sisters* 247-48.

62. Jacobs, letter to Stevenson, 1 Mar. [1864], in *We Are Your Sisters* 247-48. Jacobs also narrated this story in her 26 Mar. 1864 letter to Child.

4. Suffering beyond Description

1. Emily Dickinson, *The Complete Poems of Emily Dickinson*, ed. Thomas H. Johnson (Boston: Little Brown, 1960) 323.

2. Cornelia Hancock, *South After Gettysburg: Letters of Cornelia Hancock from the Army of the Potomac, 1863–1865*, ed. Henrietta Stratton Jaquette (Philadelphia: U of Pennsylvania P, 1937) 90, 85. See Elaine Scarry, *The Body in Pain: The Making and Unmaking of the World* (New York: Oxford UP, 1985) 121-24; and Walt Whitman, *Prose Works*, ed. Floyd Stovall, 2 vols. (New York: New York UP, 1963–64) 1:115.

3. Hancock 4-5.

4. Linus Pierpont Brockett, *The Philanthropic Results of the War in America* (New York: Wynkoop, Hallenbeck, & Thomas, 1864) 150. Twentieth-century historians have also emphasized the number and diversity of philanthropic activities occasioned by the war. As Robert Bremner has written, "The Civil War was so vast and terrible that there was room for a variety of charitable enterprises" (80). See Robert H. Bremner, "Philanthropic Rivalries in the Civil War," *Social Casework* 49 (Feb. 1968): 77-81.

5. Henry J. Bigelow, "Insensibility during Surgical Operations Produced by Inhalation" (1846), *Medical America in the Nineteenth Century: Readings from the Literature*, ed. Gert H. Brieger (Baltimore: Johns Hopkins UP, 1972) 175. Bigelow's article was originally published in the *Boston Medical and Surgical Journal* 35 (1846): 309-17. For the Stevens quotation, see Martin S. Pernick, *A Calculus of Suffering: Pain, Professionalism, and Anesthesia in Nineteenth-Century America* (New York: Columbia UP, 1985) 115.

6. For discussions of the differences between the Christian Commission and the United States Sanitary Commission, see Lori D. Ginzberg, *Women and the Work of Benevolence: Morality, Politics, and Class in the Nineteenth-Century United States* (New Haven: Yale UP, 1990) 133-73; Robert H. Bremner, *American Philanthropy*, 2nd ed. (Chicago: U of Chicago P, 1988) 72-81; Robert H. Bremner, *The Public Good: Philanthropy and Welfare in the Civil War Era* (New York: Knopf, 1980) 54-71; Bremner, "Philanthropic Rivalries in the Civil War" 77-81; George M. Fredrickson, *The Inner Civil War* (New York: Harper & Row, 1965) 98-112; and William Quentin Maxwell, *Lincoln's Fifth Wheel: The Political History of the United States Sanitary Commission* (New York: Longmans, Green & Co., 1956) 191-93.

7. Henry W. Bellows, "The Sanitary Commission," *North American Review* 98 (Jan. 1864) 153; Fredrickson, *Inner Civil War* 98; Hancock 117.

8. George Templeton Strong, *The Diary of George Templeton Strong*, ed. Allan Nevins and Milton Halsey Thomas, 4 vols. (New York: Macmillan, 1952) 3:274-75. For Olmsted's description of himself as a "growler," see Bremner, *Public Good* 41.

9. Charles J. Stillé, *History of the United States Sanitary Commission* (Philadelphia: J. B. Lippincott & Co., 1866) 92, 34; Mary A. Livermore, *My Story of the War* (Hartford: A. D. Worthington and Company, 1887) 124.

10. Strong 3:253; Bellows qtd. in Ginzberg 154; Brockett, *Philanthropic Results of War* 35; Katharine Prescott Wormeley, *The Cruel Side of War* (1888; Boston: Roberts Brothers, 1898) 7-8, 102. See also Bellows, "The Sanitary Commission" 153-54.

11. Stillé 104-105, 177; L[inus] P[ierpont] Brockett and Mary C. Vaughan, *Woman's Work in the Civil War: A Record of Heroism, Patriotism, and Patience* (Philadelphia: Zeigler, McCurdy & Co., 1867) 106; Strong 3:589. In his diary Strong calls Dix a "philanthropic lunatic." See Strong 3:165.

12. Christian Commission *Second Annual Report* qtd. in Fredrickson, *Inner Civil War* 107; "Instructions to Delegates of the Christian Commission" (1862), Thomas Biggs Harned Collection of the Papers of Walt Whitman, Library of Congress, container 2; Andrew B. Cross, *The War and the Christian Commission* (Baltimore [?]: n.p., 1865) 49.

13. Walt Whitman, *Notebooks and Unpublished Prose Manuscripts*, ed. Edward F. Grier, 6 vols. (New York: New York UP, 1984) 2:596; "Instructions to Delegates of the Christian Commission," Harned Collection, container 2; Whitman, *Prose Works* 1:51-52. Whitman included the "Instructions to Delegates of the Christian Commission" in a notebook stamped with the words "CHRISTIAN COMMISSION" in gold lettering. This notebook is now located in the Harned Collection of the Papers of Walt Whitman, Library of Congress, container 2. Although the "Instructions" have not been reprinted, the other contents of that notebook are in Whitman, *Notebooks and Unpublished Prose Manuscripts* 2:602-10.

14. Walt Whitman, *The Correspondence*, ed. Edwin Haviland Miller, 6 vols. (New York: New York UP, 1961–1977) 110-11. For more on the issue of paying humanitarian workers, see Ginzberg 162-67; Bremner, *The Public Good* 57-62; Fredrickson, *Inner Civil War* 106-107; and Maxwell 266.

15. See Bremner, "Philanthropic Rivalries in the Civil War," 79.

16. See Alan Trachtenberg, *The Incorporation of America: Culture and Society in the Gilded Age* (New York: Hill and Wang, 1982).

17. Strong 3:507, 188, 274; Bremner, *Public Good* 45. See also Maxwell 93-115.

18. Brockett and Vaughan, *Woman's Work in the Civil War* 172-76; Maxwell 301; Elizabeth Brown Pryor, *Clara Barton: Professional Angel* (Philadelphia: U of Pennsylvania P, 1987) 87-133; Ann Douglas Wood, "The War Within a War: Women Nurses in the Union Army," *Civil War History* 18, no. 3 (Sept. 1972): 210-11. See also Stephen B. Oates, *A Woman of Valor: Clara Barton and the Civil War* (New York: Free Press, 1994).

19. Brockett, *Philanthropic Results of War* 28, 90, 140, 91.

20. Horace Traubel, ms. diary (unpublished *With Walt Whitman in Camden*), 25 Aug. 1891, Horace L. and Anne Montgomerie Traubel Papers, Library of Congress, container 130; Whitman, *Notebooks and Unpublished Prose Manuscripts* 2:588. For a discussion of Whitman's motivations for his hospital work, see Lewis Hyde, *The Gift: Imagination and the Erotic Life of Property* (New York: Vintage, 1983) 204-11.

21. Esther Hill Hawks, *A Woman Doctor's Civil War: Esther Hill Hawks' Diary,* ed. Gerald Schwartz (Columbia: U of South Carolina P, 1984) 68; Wormeley, *Cruel Side of War* 28; Annie K. Kyle qtd. in Anne L. Austin, *History of Nursing Source Book* (New York: Putnam's, 1957) 426.

22. Louisa May Alcott, *The Journals of Louisa May Alcott,* ed. Joel Myerson and Daniel Shealy (Boston: Little, Brown, 1989) 95, 105, 115. In *Hospital Sketches* (1863), Alcott's autobiographical persona, Tribulation Periwinkle, also expresses the wish to be a man. For a compelling discussion of the function of this wish and the multiply gendered narrative voice in *Hospital Sketches,* see Jane E. Schultz, "Embattled Care: Narrative Authority in Louisa May Alcott's *Hospital Sketches,*" *Legacy* 9, no. 2 (Fall 1992): 104-18. References to L. M. Alcott, *Hospital Sketches* (Boston: James Redpath, 1863) will be noted parenthetically in the text.

23. Lizzie R. Torrey, *The Ideal of Womanhood, or Words to the Women of America* (1857; Boston: Wentworth, Hewes, & Co., 1859) 158, 37, 23-24.

24. See Alcott, *Journals* 113-14; and Alcott, *Hospital Sketches* 54-65.

25. Hancock 115, 116.

26. Cross 7; Whitman, *Notebooks and Unpublished Prose Manuscripts* 2:655; Whitman, *Correspondence* 1:159. Whitman's certificate of appointment as a Christian Commission delegate is in The Charles E. Feinberg Collection of the Papers of Walt Whitman, Library of Congress, container 45. See also Whitman, *Correspondence* 1:111.

27. For more on Alcott's service on behalf of the Sanitary, see Sarah Elbert, *A Hunger for Home: Louisa May Alcott's Place in American Culture* (New Brunswick: Rutgers UP, 1987) 151-52.

28. See, for example, the very similar catalogs of individual suffering in the Sanitary Commission's *Narrative of Privations and Sufferings of United States Officers & Soldiers while Prisoners of War in the Hands of Rebel Authorities* (Boston: Littell's Living Age, 1864) and in Cross's *The War and the Christian Commission.* To stir up jingoistic anger against the the South and its "designedly inflicted" (*Narrative* 23) atrocities and to laud Northern benevolence, both texts contrast the mistreatment of Union soldiers in Southern prisons (detailed in lengthy and graphic inventories) with the benevolent care of suffering soldiers, Union and Confederate, provided by Northern humanitarians.

29. Stillé 61; Henry Wadsworth Longfellow, "Santa Filomena," *Atlantic Monthly* 1, no. 1 (Nov. 1857): 22-23. In *The Philanthropic Results of the War in America,* Brockett recalled, "There was a strong impulse on the part of many of the younger ladies to devote themselves to the work of nursing the sick and wounded; the noble deeds of Florence Nightingale had surrounded her with a halo of saintliness which they would give life itself to win" (33). That same year, the *New York Herald* declared in an editorial on women working in hospitals, "All our women are Florence Nightingales." See *New York Herald,* 5 Apr. 1864, qtd. in Mary Elizabeth Massey, *Bonnet Brigades* (New York: Knopf, 1966) 43.

30. "Instructions to Delegates of the Christian Commission," Harned Collection, Library of Congress, container 2.

31. Bellows, "The Sanitary Commission" 180-81. Emphasis added.

32. Charles E. Rosenberg, "Florence Nightingale on Contagion: The Hospital as Moral Universe," *Healing and History: Essays for George Rosen*, ed. Charles E. Rosenberg (New York: Science History Publications, 1979): 116-36; Florence Nightingale, *Notes on Nursing: What It Is and What It Is Not* (1860; New York: Churchill Livingston, 1969); Stillé 436-50; Alfred Post and Wm. H. Van Buren, *Report on Military Hygiene and Therapeutics* (Washington: M'Gill & Witherow [?], 1862); Freeman J. Bumstead, *Venereal Diseases* (Washington: M'Gill & Witherow, 1862) 3.

33. Brockett, *Philanthropic Results of War* 97; *Armory Square Hospital Gazette* 6 Jan. 1864: 4; Cross 7; *Armory Square Hospital Gazette* 3 Feb. 1864: 1, 3; Hannah Ropes, *Civil War Nurse: The Diary and Letters of Hannah Ropes*, ed. John R. Brumgardt (Knoxville: U of Tennessee P, 1980) 96-97. Copies of the *Armory Square Hospital Gazette* are located in the Harned Collection, Library of Congress, container 4.

34. W. W. Lyle, *Lights and Shadows of Army Life: or, Pen Pictures from the Battlefield, the Camp, and the Hospital* (Cincinnati: R. W. Carroll, 1865) 54-55.

35. Cross 49.

36. Katharine Prescott Wormeley, *The United States Sanitary Commission: A Sketch of its Purposes and its Work* (Boston: Little, Brown and Company, 1863) 253-54.

37. Ann Douglas Wood, "Women Nurses in the Union Army" 208-209. See also Kristie Ross, "Arranging a Doll's House: Refined Women as Union Nurses," in *Divided Houses: Gender and the Civil War*, ed. Catherine Clinton and Nina Silber (New York: Oxford UP, 1992) 97-113.

38. Gerald F. Linderman, *Embattled Courage: The Experience of Combat in the American Civil War* (New York: Free Press, 1987) 26.

39. Ropes 53; Emily Parson qtd. in Ann Douglas Wood, "Women Nurses in the Union Army" 201; Alcott, *Journals* 114; Hawks 49; Ropes 95, 98.

The language portraying patients as children was and still is a convention in medical and humanitarian discourse. Even contemporary medical ethicists concerned with the paternalistic and sometimes coercive nature of patient-physician relations—well-known physician-ethicists like Eric J. Cassell, for instance—sometimes depict patients as helpless children. In *The Healer's Art* Cassell writes:

> There is one time in our lives, common to us all, when we are in a state of helplessness: infancy. The infant has a muddled nervous system, a seeming inability to communicate, a tiny world, and useless appendages. Infancy is a frightening state—if not to the infant, then in retrospect. The sick have much in common with the infant. The significance of this comparison becomes apparent when one sees the face of someone who is clear-minded but very sick as he lies surrounded by the smelly mess of his illness.

As this passage indicates contemporary medical-humanitarian discourse remains quite attached to representations of patients as childlike, helpless, and unable to communicate. See Eric J. Cassell, *The Healer's Art* (Cambridge: MIT Press, 1985): 45.

40. Linderman 30.

41. William Howell Reed, *Hospital Life in the Army of the Potomac* (Boston: William V. Spencer, 1866) 66.

42. Walt Whitman, "The Great Army of the Sick," *New York Times* 26 Feb. 1863: 2.

43. See Hancock 6.

44. Ropes 67; Brockett and Vaughan, *Woman's Work in the Civil War* 578-80; Livermore 189; Ann Douglas Wood, "Women Nurses in the Union Army" 200-203; Ropes 53; Lyle 72.

45. Wormeley, *The Cruel Side of War* 99; Reed 65; Cross 39.

46. Benton H. Wilson, letter to Walt Whitman, 11 Nov. 1865, in *Drum Beats: Walt Whitman's Civil War Boy Lovers*, ed. Charley Shively (San Francisco: Gay Sunshine Press, 1989) 213; *The Civil War Diary of Allen Morgan Geer, Twentieth Regiment, Illinois Volunteers*, ed. Mary Ann Andersen (Denver: Robert C. Appleman, 1977) 111, 129. See the letters of soldiers to Whitman collected in Charley Shively's invaluable *Drum Beats*.

47. Maxwell 148.

48. For an excellent analysis of staffing problems, supply shortages, corruption, and bureaucratic inhumanity in Civil War hospitals, see Jane E. Schultz, "The Inhospitable Hospital: Gender and Professionalism in Civil War Medicine," *Signs* 17, no. 2 (Winter 1992): 363-92.

49. *Armory Square Hospital Gazette* 6 Jan. 1864: 1; Whitman, *Correspondence* 1:63, 127, 205, 231. See also George Worthington Adams, *Doctors in Blue: The Medical History of the Union Army in the Civil War* (New York: Henry Schuman, 1952) 54-55; and Mary Denis Maher, *To Bind Up the Wounds: Catholic Sister Nurses in the U.S. Civil War* (Westport: Greenwood Press, 1989) 47.

50. William E. Vandemark, letter to Walt Whitman, 16 Dec. 1863, in *Drum Beats* 207; Bell Irvin Wiley, *Billy Yank: The Common Soldier of the Union* (Indianapolis: Bobbs-Merrill, 1952) 132, 394n131; Ropes 69.

51. Ropes 73; Wiley, *Billy Yank* 131; Whitman, *Prose Works* 1:84-85. For Whitman on "incompetency" in the hospitals, see Whitman in Austin, *History of Nursing* 415. From patients' perspectives, among the most detested results of such inefficiency were meals. When hospitals provided an adequate quantity of food, it was usually unpalatable, poorly prepared, and unhealthy. See Ropes 107; Hancock 24; Wiley, *Billy Yank* 127-28; Wormeley *Sanitary Commission* 242-43; and Alcott, *Hospital Sketches* 68-69.

52. Hancock 40. See also Alcott, *Hospital Sketches* 74; Livermore 127; and Joseph T. Glatthaar, *Forged in Battle: The Civil War Alliance of Black Soldiers and White Officers* (New York: Free Press, 1990) 189.

53. Whitman, *Notebooks and Unpublished Prose Manuscripts* 2:664; Whitman, *Correspondence* 1:205; Ropes 79. See also Ropes 55, 69, 107-108.

54. Linderman 23. See also Frank Wilkeson, *Recollections of a Private Soldier in the Army of the Potomac* (New York and London: G. P. Putnam's Sons, 1886) 149-50.

55. Glatthaar 187-95. "As a result of such woeful and discriminatory medical care," Glatthaar has noted, "nine times as many black troops died from disease as on the battlefield, and compared to white volunteers, two and one-half times as many black soldiers per one thousand died of disease" (194-95).

56. William D. F. Landon, "Prock's Letters from Camp, Battlefield and Hospital," *Indiana Magazine of History* 34 (1938): 96. See also Wiley, *Billy Yank* 149.

57. Hancock 19, 40; Whitman qtd. in Austin, *History of Nursing* 415; Lewis K. Brown, letter to Walt Whitman, 5 Nov. 1863, in *Drum Beats* 121. Brown finished his letter by saying, "you have give me more than all of the rest put together. . so you are the relief association that I (as well as all the rest of the boys) like best."

58. Whitman, *Correspondence* 1:205.

59. Louisa May Alcott, *The Selected Letters of Louisa May Alcott,* ed. Joel Myerson and Daniel Shealy (Boston: Little, Brown, 1987) 94.

60. For accounts of Alcott's illness, see Alcott, *Hospital Sketches* 66-71, 83-85; Alcott, *Journals* 111, 113-17; and Martha Saxton, *Louisa May: A Modern Biography of Louisa May Alcott* (Boston: Houghton Mifflin, 1977) 251-68.

61. Alcott, *Journals* 116. The cancellation is Alcott's.

62. Alcott, *Journals* 118.

63. Louisa M. Alcott, *Work: A Story of Experience* (Boston: Roberts Brothers, 1873) 93. This quotation is taken from chapter 5, "Companion," which is a reworking of Alcott's serialized thriller "A Nurse's Story" (1865–66). I discuss "A Nurse's Story" at length later in this chapter.

64. Louisa M. Alcott, "A Hospital Christmas," *Hospital Sketches and Camp and Fireside Stories* (Boston: Roberts Brothers, 1869) 322, 325. See also Schultz, "Embattled Care."

65. Whitman, *Correspondence* 1:237. See Shively in *Drum Beats* 61-70; Justin Kaplan, *Walt Whitman: A Life* (New York: Simon & Schuster, 1980) 295-97; and Whitman, *Correspondence* 1:223-43.

66. See Whitman, *Correspondence* 1:111; Whitman, *Prose Works* 1:73-74; the letters in *Drum Beats* 121, 207, 211; Whitman, *Correspondence* 1:159.

67. Whitman, *Correspondence* 1:81-82; Walt Whitman, *Leaves of Grass,* Comprehensive Reader's Edition, ed. Harold W. Blodgett and Sculley Bradley (New York: New York UP, 1965) 67. See also Whitman, *Notebooks and Unpublished Prose Manuscripts* 2:594. For a fascinating approach to Whitman's writing, one that examines the correspondence between body and text as well as the uncertain boundary between Whitman and the wounded soldiers he cared for, see Mark Maslan, "Whitman's 'Strange Hand': Body as Text in *Drum-Taps*," *English Literary History* 58, no. 4 (Winter 1991): 935-55.

68. Whitman, *Correspondence* 1:171; Whitman, *Notebooks and Unpublished Prose Manuscripts* 2:579-80. See also his notes toward a book about Civil War hospitals, then tentatively titled "Hours in Our Military Hospitals," in Whitman, *Notebooks and Unpublished Prose Manuscripts* 2:575-99. See also Horace Traubel, *With Walt Whitman in Camden,* vol. 4 (Philadelphia: U of Pennsylvania P, 1953) 415-18.

69. Quotations from "The Dresser" are from Walt Whitman, *Drum-Taps (1865) and Sequel to Drum-Taps (1865-6): A Facsimile Reproduction,* ed. F. De Wolfe Miller (Gainesville: Scholars' Facsimiles & Reprints, 1959) 31-34.

70. Nineteenth-century critics who admired Whitman's poetry defended *Drum-Taps* on precisely these grounds. John Burroughs wrote in an 1866 review, "the beautiful benevolence he has shown during the war in nourishing the sick and wounded soldiers, and his great love and humanity as exhibited in this little volume, entitle him, on grounds of justice alone, to more respect and consideration than he has hitherto received at the hands of his countrymen" (606). Burroughs's appraisal of *Drum-Taps* was inseparable from his tribute to Whitman's humanitarianism: "he went among them purely in the spirit of love. . . . Many soldiers can be found who aver that he saved their lives out and out" (610). See John Burroughs, "Walt Whitman and His 'Drum-Taps,'" *Galaxy* 2 (1 Dec. 1866): 606-15.

71. Whitman, *Correspondence* 1:100. See also Whitman, *Correspondence* 1:230; and Whitman, "Great Army of the Sick," 2.

72. Kerry C. Larson, *Whitman's Drama of Consensus* (Chicago: U of Chicago P, 1988) 221.

73. This metonymic practice was and still is a familiar convention. In *Hospital Sketches,* Alcott recounts the injured sergeant who delights in "the fashion of calling his neighbors by their afflictions instead of their names." Seeing this practice as a source of "perfect good humor and much enjoyment" among the soldiers, Tribulation Periwinkle shares some of their dialogue with readers:

> "Hallo, old Fits is off again!" "How are you, Rheumatiz?" "Will you trade apples, Ribs?" "I say, Miss P., may I give Typus a drink of this?" "Look here, No Toes, lend us a stamp, there's a good feller." (94)

For another perspective on Whitman's representation of patients, including the role of metonymy, see Robert Leigh Davis, "Wound-Dressers and House Calls: Medical Representations in Whitman and Williams," *Walt Whitman Quarterly Review* 6, no. 3 (Winter 1989): 133-39.

74. Quotations from "A March in the Ranks Hard-Prest, and the Road Unknown" are taken from Whitman, *Drum-Taps* 44-45. See also Betsy Erkkila's discussion of this poem in *Whitman the Political Poet* (New York: Oxford UP, 1989) 223-25. She too has called the humanitarian act represented in this poem "meaningless," writing "the gesture is only temporary, perhaps meaningless" (224).

75. See Walt Whitman, *Leaves of Grass: A Textual Variorum of the Printed Poems,* ed. Sculley Bradley, Harold W. Blodgett, Arthur Golden, William White, 3 vols. (New York: New York UP, 1980) 2:494, line 16.

76. The irregular spelling was later corrected. See Whitman, *Leaves of Grass: Variorum* 2:494, line 12.

77. Timothy Sweet, *Traces of War: Poetry, Photography, and the Crisis of the Union* (Baltimore: Johns Hopkins UP, 1990) 42-43.

78. See Louisa May Alcott, "A Nurse's Story," *Freaks of Genius: Unknown Thrillers of Louisa May Alcott,* ed. Daniel Shealy (Westport: Greenwood Press, 1991). References are noted parenthetically in the text.

In a discussion of Alcott's *Work,* the 1873 novel that absorbed an abridged and rewritten version of "A Nurse's Story," Glenn Hendler has also explored the limits of sympathetic identification and the efforts to "bring the helpers and the helped into truer relations with each other" (Alcott's *Work* qtd. by Hendler 699). According to Hendler's analysis of Alcott and the sentimental novel as a genre, the danger in sympathy is its threat to individual identity: the sympathizer risks a loss of self by sympathetically identifying with another. In *Work,* Alcott tries (unsuccessfully) to work through the difficult contradiction between sympathy and individuality by transforming sympathetic identification into the basis for a feminist subjectivity, a new form of "collective public femininity" (703). See Glenn Hendler, "The Limits of Sympathy: Louisa May Alcott and the Sentimental Novel," *American Literary History* 3, no. 4 (Winter 1991): 685-706. My examination of the limits of sympathetic identification, in this chapter and others, tracks not the risks for sympathizers, "the helpers," but rather the dangers of a rhetorically performed sympathetic identification for patients, "the helped," the targets of sympathy.

79. See Madeleine B. Stern, Introduction, *Freaks of Genius* 19. See also Ednah D. Cheney, *Louisa May Alcott: Her Life, Letters, and Journals* (Boston: Roberts Brothers, 1889) 111.

80. Alcott, *Journals* 139, 141. My characterization of Anna Weld derives from Alcott, *Journals* 150, 145, 148n39, and 142. In her Introduction to *Freaks of Genius,* Stern first identified Anna Weld as a character source for Alcott's Elinor Carruth. See Stern, Introduction, *Freaks of Genius* 6. See also Saxton 285-91.

81. Saxton 258.

82. Although the title would suggest that the story's focus is the nurse, Kate Snow, Alcott referred to the thriller as "The Carruths," the family name of the afflicted Elinor. See Stern, Introduction, *Freaks of Genius* 5, 23n15.

83. See Madeleine B. Stern, Introduction, *Louisa May Alcott: Selected Fiction,* ed. Daniel Shealy, Madeleine B. Stern, and Joel Myerson (Boston: Little, Brown, 1990) xviii; Stern, Introduction, *Freaks of Genius* 4; Karen Halttunen, "The Domestic Drama of Louisa May Alcott," *Feminist Studies* 10, no. 2 (Summer 1984): 240; Alfred Habegger, "Precocious Incest: First Novels by Louisa May Alcott and Henry James," *Massachusetts Review* 26, nos. 2 and 3 (Summer-Autumn 1985) 238-39; and Elbert 174. For Alcott's description of her illness and the delirium and dreams that followed, see Alcott, *Journals* 116-17. On Alcott's "double literary life," see Ann Douglas, Introduction, *Little Women* (New York: NAL, 1983) vii–xxvii, esp. vii.

84. "[A] blood & thunder tale" and "the lurid style" are phrases Alcott used to describe her sensation fiction. See Alcott, *Letters* 79; and Alcott qtd. in LaSalle Corbell Pickett, "[Louisa Alcott's 'Natural Ambition' for the 'Lurid Style' Disclosed in a Conversation]," in *Critical Essays on Louisa May Alcott,* ed. Madeleine B. Stern (Boston: G.K. Hall, 1984) 42.

In articulating humanitarian thinking and themes via the thriller, Alcott's work was not at all unusual within nineteenth-century American culture. Recently, literary and cultural historians have persuasively revealed a fascinating network of connections between humanitarian reform in the United States and the gothic horror style in writing. See Karen Halttunen, "Early American Murder Narratives: The Birth of Horror," *The Power of Culture: Critical Essays in American History,* ed. Richard Wightman Fox and T. J. Jackson Lears (Chicago: U of Chicago P, 1993) 67-101; Karen Halttunen, "Gothic Imagination and Social Reform: The Haunted Houses of Lyman Beecher, Henry Ward Beecher, and Harriet Beecher Stowe," *New Essays on "Uncle Tom's Cabin,"* ed. Eric J. Sundquist (Cambridge: Cambridge UP, 1986): 107-34; and David S. Reynolds, *Beneath the American Renaissance: The Subversive Imagination in the Age of Emerson and Melville* (New York: Knopf, 1988) esp. 54-91.

85. Ann Douglas, "Mysteries of Louisa May Alcott," *Critical Essays on Louisa May Alcott* 236.

86. This is true within much of Alcott's writing. In "Psyche's Art" (1868), for example, Psyche Dean's submissive decision to give up her study of art to take care of her family results ultimately in an increase in her artistic powers. See Louisa May Alcott, "Psyche's Art" (1868), in *Alternative Alcott,* ed. Elaine Showalter (New Brunswick: Rutgers UP, 1988) 207-26, esp. the references to Psyche's "power" 220, 225.

5. Whitman and the Humanitarian Possibilities of Lilacs

1. Timothy F. Murphy, "Testimony," *Writing AIDS: Gay Literature, Language, and Analysis,* ed. Timothy F. Murphy and Suzanne Poirier (New York: Columbia UP, 1993) 316.

2. Walt Whitman, *Notebooks and Unpublished Prose Manuscripts,* ed. Edward F. Grier, 6 vols. (New York: New York UP, 1984) 2:762.

3. Walt Whitman, *Sequel to Drum-Taps (Since the Preceding Came from the Press.) When Lilacs Last in the Door-Yard Bloom'd. And Other Pieces* (Washington, D.C., 1865–66), rpt. in *Drum-Taps (1865) and Sequel to Drum-Taps (1865–6),* ed. F. DeWolfe Miller (Gainesville: Scholars' Facsimiles & Reprints, 1959). References to *Lilacs and Other Pieces* and *Drum-Taps* are noted in the text by page number.

4. In his introduction to the facsimile reprinting of *Drum-Taps (1865) and Sequel to Drum-Taps (1865–6),* F. DeWolfe Miller presents a detailed account of the publishing history of *Lilacs and Other Pieces,* but offers no critical examination of the poems. Quoting from Miller's edition, Betsy Erkkila devotes chapter 9 of *Whitman the Political Poet* to a political-historical analysis of the sequel, but examines only the two most famous pieces, "O Captain! My Captain!" and "When Lilacs Last in the Door-Yard Bloom'd." In her discussion of *Drum-Taps* she looks at a few of the sixteen other poems but (like other critics) ignores *Lilacs and Other Pieces* as an arrangement of poems. See F. DeWolfe Miller, Introduction, *Drum-Taps (1865) and Sequel to Drum-Taps (1865–6)*; and Betsy Erkkila, *Whitman the Political Poet* (New York: Oxford UP, 1989).

5. See George L. Sixbey, "'Chanting the Square Deific': A Study in Whitman's Religion," *American Literature* 9, no. 2 (May 1937): 171-95; C. Carroll Hollis, *Language and Style in Leaves of Grass* (Baton Rouge: Louisiana State UP 1983) 148-53; and Kerry C. Larson, *Whitman's Drama of Consensus* (Chicago: U of Chicago P, 1988) 226-29.

6. See Erkkila 226-37; Larson 231-44; and M. Wynn Thomas, *The Lunar Light of Whitman's Poetry* (Cambridge: Harvard UP, 1987) 239-51. See also Timothy Sweet, *Traces of War: Poetry, Photography, and the Crisis of the Union* (Baltimore: Johns Hopkins UP, 1990) 67-77; Allen Grossmann, "The Poetics of Union in Whitman and Lincoln: An Inquiry toward the Relationship of Art and Policy," *The American Renaissance Reconsidered,* ed. Walter Benn Michaels and Donald E. Pease (Baltimore: Johns Hopkins UP, 1985) 183-208; and Thomas Parkinson, "'When Lilacs Last in the Door-Yard Bloom'd' and the American Civil Religion," *Southern Review* 19, no. 1 (Jan. 1983): 1-16. Two recent critics, George B. Hutchinson and David Kuebrich, have examined "Lilacs" in its historical context without focusing on its sociopolitical meanings. Taking an anthropological perspective informed by the work of Victor Turner, Hutchinson sees Whitman as a literary shamanist with a clear sense of the social and religious function of poetry. Whitman in "Lilacs" is a shaman escorting the dead to their final resting place and the poem itself a ritual bestowing "sacred significance" (162) on the war. Kuebrich's perspective is cultural and theological, and his discussion of the cultural and religious responses to Lincoln's death as a context for understanding the religious work of "Lilacs" is informative. He does not, however, examine any of the poems in *Lilacs and Other Pieces* besides the title poem; for a book concerned with "Walt Whitman's New American Religion," the absence of any comment on "Chanting the Square Deific" seems very odd. See George B. Hutchinson, *The Ecstatic Whitman: Literary Shamanism and the Crisis of the Union* (Columbus: Ohio State UP, 1986) 136-69; and David

Kuebrich, *Minor Prophecy: Walt Whitman's New American Religion* (Bloomington: Indiana UP, 1989) 119-29.

7. These central concerns in "Lilacs" have, of course, been explored by other critics—critics not particularly concerned with questions about history—some focusing on its elegiac form, others using Freudian or New Critical approaches. For a discussion of "Lilacs" and the elegiac tradition, see Richard P. Adams, "Whitman's 'Lilacs' and the Tradition of Pastoral Elegy," *PMLA* 72, no. 3 (June 1957): 479-87. Adams's article on Whitman's use of the conventions of pastoral elegy, the first systematic analysis of the relation of "Lilacs" to the pastoral elegy, is important, but ought to be read as only one voice in a debate which includes Richard Chase, *Walt Whitman Reconsidered* (New York: William Sloan, 1955) 140-45; Charles Clay Doyle, "Poetry and Pastoral: A Dimension of Whitman's 'Lilacs,'" *Walt Whitman Review* 15, no. 4 (Dec. 1969): 242-45; Ellen S. Goodman, "'Lilacs' and the Pastoral Elegy Reconsidered," *Books at Brown* 24 (1971): 119-33; and Evelyn J. Hinz, "Whitman's 'Lilacs': The Power of Elegy," *Bucknell Review* 20, no. 2 (Fall 1972): 35-54. In "Whitman's 'Lilacs' and the Grammars of Time," *PMLA* 97, no. 1 (Jan. 1982): 31-38, Mutlu Konuk Blasing proposes a startling revision of this perspective and challenges many of the assumptions about Whitman's use of traditions and conventions. For an analysis of "Lilacs" through a Freudian grid, see Jeffrey Steele, "Poetic Grief-Work in Whitman's 'Lilacs,'" *Walt Whitman Quarterly Review* 2, no.3 (Winter 1985): 10-16; and Mark Edmundson, "'Lilacs': Walt Whitman's American Elegy," *Nineteenth-Century Literature* 44, no. 4 (Mar. 1990): 465-91. For important New Critical examinations of "Lilacs," see F. O. Matthiessen, *American Renaissance: Art and Expression in the Age of Emerson and Whitman* (New York: Oxford UP, 1941) 618-23; Charles Feidelson, Jr., *Symbolism and American Literature* (Chicago: U of Chicago P, 1953) 21-25; and James E. Miller, Jr., *A Critical Guide to Leaves of Grass* (Chicago: U of Chicago P, 1957) 111-19.

8. This collection also invites consideration as a cluster because of the highly regarded quality of the poems. Although he examines only "Chanting the Square Deific," George L. Sixbey notes the significance of *Lilacs and Other Pieces* as a separate publication: "[A]mong the eighteen pieces included in the *Sequel to Drum-Taps* are several which have become almost universally known and admired. As he hurried this little volume through the press in Washington, possibly even before *Drum-Taps* had appeared in New York, it seems likely that Whitman attached some special importance to the poems it contained. . . . That Whitman attached special importance to the poems in the *Sequel* is shown by their peculiarly serious message and somber tone, and by their separate publication in a special volume" (172-73). In his introduction to *Drum-Taps and Sequel to Drum-Taps,* supporting his thesis that Whitman's book "was the most important volume that Whitman published" and "the greatest book of war lyrics ever written by a single author," F. DeWolfe Miller cites three poems ("Lilacs," "O Captain! My Captain!" and "Chanting the Square Deific"), all of which belong to *Lilacs and Other Pieces* (viii). "Lilacs" and "O Captain" are probably the best-known Whitman poems, but this attention to "Lilacs" and "O Captain" should not blind us to the significance of the other poems: the compelling theological revisioning of the Civil War in "Chanting the Square Deific," the remarkable weaving of "Calamus" themes and *Drum-Taps* setting in "As I Lay with My Head in Your Lap, Camerado," and the shocking but beautiful penultimate piece—"Reconciliation"—a poem highly regarded for its "delicacy" and the beauty of its well-made rhythms. See James Wright, "The Delicacy of Walt Whitman," *Walt Whitman: The Measure of His Song,* ed. Jim Perlman, Ed Folsom, and Dan Campion (Minneapolis: Holy Cow, 1981) 161-76.

9. Whitman did not, however, write all eighteen poems during that half-year. "I heard you, Solemn-sweet Pipes of the Organ" originally appeared in a slightly longer version as "Little Bells Last Night" in the *New York Leader* 12 October 1861. Produced before Peter Eckler had begun printing *Drum-Taps* in April 1865, a premature advertisement for *Drum-Taps* listed: "Spirit with muttering voice" (probably an early version of "Spirit whose Work is Done"), "As I lay with my head in your lap, camerado," "Reconciliation," "I dream, I dream, I dream" (undoubtedly an early title for "In Clouds Descending, in Midnight

Sleep"), and "Race of weapon'd men" (perhaps a primitive version of "Race of Veterans"—if so, the change from "weapon'd men" to "Veterans" is telling). Thus, presumably, at least five or six of the poems were written before April 1865. Nevertheless, the bulk of these verses took shape in the months following war's end. See footnote to "I Heard You Solemn-Sweet Pipes of the Organ," in Walt Whitman, *Leaves of Grass*, ed. Harold W. Blodgett and Sculley Bradley (New York: New York UP, 1965) 110. For a facsimile reprinting of this premature *Drum-Taps* advertisement, see F. DeWolfe Miller xxxii–xxxiii.

10. Walt Whitman qtd. in Horace Traubel, *With Walt Whitman in Camden,* vol. 2 (New York: Mitchell Kennerly, 1915) 333. Although I believe this observation sheds some light on the immediacy of the collection's response to the emotional events of 1865, Whitman made this comment in a conversation with Traubel in which they were damning "O Captain" with faint praise. Whitman said: "The thing that tantalizes me most is not its rhythmic imperfection or its imperfection as a ballad or rhymed poem (it is damned bad in all that, I do believe) but the fact that my enemies and some of my friends who half doubt me, look upon it as a concession made to the philistines—that makes me mad. I come back to the conviction that it had certain emotional immediate reasons for being: that's the best I can say for it myself."

11. *New York Times* 16 Apr. 1865: 1; Thomas Nast, *Victory and Death, Harper's Weekly* 10 June 1865: 360-61. The public mourning of Lincoln's death included a cross-country funeral parade, a multitude of sermons and poems on Lincoln, the wearing of mourning clothes and badges, Lincoln memorabilia, and much more. For an analysis of the shift in national mood, see Thomas Reed Turner, *Beware the People Weeping: Public Opinion and the Assassination of Abraham Lincoln* (Baton Rouge: Louisiana State UP, 1982) 18-52, 65-89. For a nineteenth-century account of Lincoln's funeral, see William T. Coggeshall, *Lincoln Memorial: The Journeys of Abraham Lincoln* (Columbus: The Ohio State Journal, 1865); for an examination of Lincoln's funeral parade within a history of American parades, see Mary Ryan, "The American Parade: Representations of the Nineteenth-Century Social Order," *The New Cultural History,* ed. Lynn Hunt (Berkeley: U of California P, 1989), 132, 141-144. For poems dedicated to Lincoln's memory, see *Poetical Tributes to the Memory of Abraham Lincoln* (Philadelphia: J. B. Lippincott & Co., 1865); and P. A. Hanaford, *Our Martyred President* (Boston: B.B. Russell and Company, 1865). For sermons, see *Our Martyr President, Abraham Lincoln: Lincoln Memorial Addresses* (1865; New York: Abingdon Press, 1915).

12. I specify upper and middle classes because many of the customs that I discuss were expensive, and thus not generally practiced by poorer classes. The scholarship on mourning and death in nineteenth-century America is considerable. For the best discussion of mourning customs, see Karen Halttunen, *Confidence Men and Painted Women: A Study of Middle Class Culture in America, 1830–1870* (New Haven: Yale UP, 1982) 124-52; but see also Martha V. Pike, "In Memory Of: Artifacts Relating to Mourning in Nineteenth-Century America," *Rituals and Ceremonies in Popular Culture,* ed. Ray B. Browne (Bowling Green: Bowling Green UP, 1980) 296-315; and Lou Taylor, *Mourning Dress: A Costume and Social History* (London: Allen, 1983). For discussions of American attitudes toward death, see James J. Farrell, *Inventing the American Way of Death, 1830–1920* (Philadelphia: Temple UP, 1980); and the essays collected in *Death in America,* ed. David E. Stannard (Philadelphia: U of Pennsylvania P, 1975), and in *Passing: The Vision of Death in America,* ed. Charles O. Jackson (Westport: Greenwood Press, 1977). For the perspective of a social scientist on nineteenth-century grief, see Paul C. Rosenblatt, *Bitter, Bitter Tears: Nineteenth-Century Diarists and Twentieth-Century Grief Theories* (Minneapolis: U of Minnesota P, 1983). On the rise of the rural cemetery movement, see Thomas Bender, "The 'Rural' Cemetery Movement: Urban Travail and the Appeal of Nature," *New England Quarterly* 47, no. 2 (June 1974): 196-211; Stanley French, "The Cemetery as Cultural Institution: The Establishment of Mount Auburn and the 'Rural Cemetery' Movement," *Death in America* 69-91; and Ann Douglas, *The Feminization of American Culture* (New York: Knopf, 1977) 208-213. On the development of funeral undertaking as a profession, see Robert Habenstein and

William M. Lamers, *The History of American Funeral Directing* (Milwaukee: National Funeral Directors Association, 1955) 225-50. For scholarship on the responses of nineteenth-century writers to death, see Daniel Aaron, "The Etiquette of Grief: A Literary Generation's Response to Death," *Prospects* 4 (1979): 197-213; Sharon Cameron, "Representing Grief: Emerson's 'Experience,'" *Representations* 15 (Summer 1986): 15-41; J. Gerald Kennedy, *Poe, Death, and the Life of Writing* (New Haven: Yale UP, 1987); and Neal L. Tolchin, *Mourning, Gender, and Creativity in the Art of Herman Melville* (New Haven: Yale UP, 1988).

13. Halttunen, *Confidence Men* 144-45.

14. T. S. Arthur, "Going Into Mourning," *Godey's Lady's Book* Oct. 1841: 174; Halttunen, *Confidence Men* 125.

15. E. H. Chapin, *The Crown of Thorns. A Token for the Sorrowing* (Boston: Universalist Publishing House, 1860) vi; Elizabeth Stuart Phelps, *The Gates Ajar,* ed. Helen Sootin Smith (1868; Cambridge: Harvard UP, 1964) 94; F. R. Anspach, *The Sepulchres of Our Departed* (Philadelphia: Lindsay & Blakiston, 1854) 369, 335, viii.

16. Phelps 144, 147; Chapin 218; Ralph Waldo Emerson, *The Complete Sermons of Ralph Waldo Emerson,* ed. Albert J. von Frank et al., 4 vols. (Columbia: U of Missouri P, 1989) 1:309-10.

17. Douglas, *Feminization* 220.

18. *Poetical Tributes* 132, 176, 110.

19. Abraham Lincoln, *Speeches and Writings, 1859–65,* ed. Don E. Fehrenbacher (New York: Library of America, 1989) 644.

20. Henry Darling, *Grief and Duty. A Discourse* (Albany: S. R. Gray, 1865) 7, 17.

21. Although this chapter is not a study of *Lilacs and Other Pieces'* literary and intellectual sources, I do want to suggest a few of the correspondences between these poems and the discourses on death, grief, mourning, and consolation in nineteenth-century culture. In ways similar to *Lilacs and Other Pieces,* British Romantic poetry, Bryant's "Thanatopsis," and rural cemeteries all made explicit connections between death and nature. (See Bender; French; and Douglas, *Feminization* 208-13.) Like Whitman, various consolationists were strongly attached to the notion of "process" in consolation discourse. (See, for example, Emerson, *Sermons* 1:310-11.) Universalists and Spiritualists rejected the doctrine of eternal damnation. (See, for instance, B. F. Foster and J. H. Lozier, *Theological Discussions on Universalism and Endless Punishment* [Indianapolis: B. F. Foster, 1867].) Arthur and Beecher each criticized rigid, formal mourning customs. (See Farrell 81-82.) Barton, Thoreau, and numerous soldiers, to name only a few, launched attacks on coercive humanitarianism. And by offering his consolation in verse, Whitman participated in a widespread, highly conventional practice: the use of poems to console the bereaved.

22. In recent scholarship there is an interesting debate on this issue. For arguments supporting the affirmation of immortality in "When Lilacs Last in the Door-Yard Bloom'd," see Kuebrich 119-29; and James E. Miller 111. For contrary arguments, see Adams 486; Blasing 37-38; Chase 144; Larson 233-43; and Steele 10-11.

23. Larson 240.

24. See Walt Whitman, *Prose Works 1892,* ed. Floyd Stovall, 2 vols. (New York: New York UP) 2:503.

25. Whitman, *Leaves of Grass* 84.

26. Although the opinion was unpopular in the months after Lincoln's assassination, Whitman's call for reconciliation with the South was not unheard of. See, for example, Stephen H. Tyng, in *Our Martyr President* 40-59; and Herman Melville, "Supplement," *Battle-Pieces and Aspects of the War,* ed. Sidney Kaplan (1866; Amherst: U of Massachusetts P, 1972) 259-272. Instead, what is so striking is Whitman's conception of the mourning process. Perhaps I can clarify Whitman's distinctive approach to mourning by a brief look at two widely accepted "solutions" to grief in the nineteenth and twentieth centuries. Most analyses of grief and mourning begin with the assumption that human beings grieve because they are affected by the loss of someone who is significant or beloved. According

to Freud, grief is the clinging to the lost love object. The end of grief is the freeing of the libido from its desire for the lost object. Thus, the conclusion of successful mourning is declaring the lost love object dead. Phelps offers the opposite solution to grief: she consoles the bereaved with promises of a future reunion with their loved ones who are living a peaceful existence in heaven. See Phelps; and Sigmund Freud, "Mourning and Melancholia," *The Standard Edition of the Complete Psychological Works of Sigmund Freud,* ed. and trans. James Strachey, 24 vols. (London: Hogarth, 1953-74) 14:237-58. See also the important revisions of Freud's insights, Melanie Klein, "Mourning and its Relationship to Manic Depressive States," *International Journal of Psychoanalysis* 21 (1940): 125-53; and Julia Kristeva, *Black Sun: Depression and Melancholia* (New York: Columbia UP, 1989) 1-30.

27. See Donald E. Pease, *Visionary Compacts: American Renaissance Writings in Cultural Context* (Madison: U of Wisconsin P, 1987) 123-31, 138-42.

28. W[illiam] D[ean] Howells, rev. of *Drum-Taps,* by Walt Whitman, *The Round Table* 11 Nov. 1865: 147.

29. See James E. Miller 117-19; and Hutchinson 149-69.

30. See James E. Miller 119, 113; and W. P. Elledge, "Whitman's 'Lilacs' as Romantic Narrative," *Walt Whitman Review* 12, no. 3 (Sept. 1966): 59-67.

31. Whitman, *Prose Works* 2:503.

32. George M. Fredrickson, *The Inner Civil War: Northern Intellectuals and the Crisis of the Union* (New York: Harper & Row, 1965) 96; Larson 226.

33. Gay Wilson Allen, *The Solitary Singer: A Critical Biography of Walt Whitman* (1955; Chicago: U of Chicago P, 1985) 358. See R. F. Fleissner, "Whitman as Heretic?" *American Notes and Queries* 9, no. 10 (June 1971): 153; Lester Goodson, "Whitman and the Problem of Evil," *Walt Whitman Review* 16, no. 2 (June 1970): 45-50; and Allen 358-59.

34. Roland Barthes, *S/Z,* trans. Richard Miller (New York: Hill and Wang, 1974) 4.

35. Whitman, *Leaves of Grass* 570.

36. Whitman, *Leaves of Grass* 4.

6. Eccentric Benevolence and Its Limits

1. Theodor Adorno, *Minima Moralia,* trans. E. F. N. Jephcott (London: Verso, 1974) 152.

2. On the changes wrought by emancipation, see Leon F. Litwack, *Been in the Storm So Long: The Aftermath of Slavery* (New York: Knopf, 1979); and Eric Foner, *Reconstruction: America's Unfinished Revolution* (New York: Harper & Row, 1988). On Northern teachers and philanthropists in the South during Reconstruction, see Joe M. Richardson, *Christian Reconstruction: The American Missionary Association and Southern Blacks, 1861–1890* (Athens: U of Georgia P, 1986); Robert C. Morris, *Reading, 'Riting, and Reconstruction: The Education of Freedmen in the South, 1861–1870* (Chicago: U of Chicago P, 1981); Ronald E. Butchart, *Northern Schools, Southern Blacks, and Reconstruction: Freedmen's Education, 1862–1875* (Westport: Greenwood Press, 1980); Jacqueline Jones, *Soldiers of Light and Love: Northern Teachers and Georgia Blacks, 1865–1873* (Chapel Hill: U of North Carolina P, 1980); and Carl R. Osthaus, *Freedmen, Philanthropy, and Fraud: A History of the Freedmen's Savings Bank* (Urbana: U of Illinois P, 1976).

3. See, for example, the articles published in *The Freedman,* Jan. 1864 to Mar. 1869. All located issues of *The Freedman* are reprinted in *Freedmen's Schools and Textbooks: 3,* ed. Robert C. Morris (New York: AMS Press, 1980).

4. In his study of the American Missionary Association, Joe M. Richardson has written, "the association assumed that the more quickly blacks conformed to white standards the sooner artificial racial barriers would be dismantled. Teachers were often paternalistic and sometimes arrogant in their assumptions of cultural superiority, but their intent was egalitarian" (138).

5. "The Hospital," *The Freedman* May 1864: 17.

6. Qtd. in Eric Foner, *Reconstruction: America's Unfinished Revolution* (New York: Harper

& Row, 1988) 99. For a discussion of the paternalistic nature of the American Missionary Association's assistance and the black community's resistance to such paternalism, see Joe M. Richardson 237-55.

7. "Freedom," *The Freedman* Aug. 1865: 30. For more on white definitions of self-help in philanthropic discourse during Reconstruction, see Litwack 379-81; and Jones 138-39.

8. "An Appeal," *The Freedman's Torchlight* Dec. 1864: 3. This initial issue of *The Freedman's Torchlight,* the only one located, is reprinted in *Freedman's Schools and Textbooks: 3.*

9. Frederick Douglass, "What Shall Be Done with the Slaves if Emancipated?" *Douglass' Monthly* Jan. 1862, rpt. in *The Life and Writings of Frederick Douglass,* ed. Philip S. Foner, 4 vols. (New York: International Publishers, 1952) 3:189.

10. Frederick Douglass, qtd. in Waldo E. Martin, *The Mind of Frederick Douglass* (Chapel Hill: U of North Carolina P, 1984) 68; "Address to Our Southern Brethren," *The Freedman's Torchlight* Dec. 1864: 2.

11. Jones 4. See also Charlotte L. Forten, *The Journals of Charlotte Forten Grimké,* ed. Brenda Stevenson (New York: Oxford UP, 1988); Litwack; and Foner, *Reconstruction* 77-123.

12. *New Orleans Tribune* 1 Feb. 1865, qtd. in Litwack 513.

13. L. Maria Child, *The Freedmen's Book* (Boston: Ticknor and Fields, 1865) 246-50, 269-76.

14. Lydia Maria Child, letter to Sarah Blake (Sturgis) Shaw, 8 Apr. 1866, in *The Collected Correspondence of Lydia Maria Child, 1817–1880,* ed. Patricia G. Holland and Milton Meltzer (Millwood, NY: KTO Microform, 1979), card 64.

15. Louisa May Alcott, *The Selected Letters of Louisa May Alcott,* ed. Joel Myerson and Daniel Shealy (Boston: Little, Brown, 1987) 96; L. M. Alcott, *Hospital Sketches* (Boston: James Redpath, 1863) 82, 80. Poor health prevented Alcott from returning to nursing and traveling south to work with the freedpeople.

16. See Horace Traubel, ms. diary (unpublished *With Walt Whitman in Camden*), 25 Aug. 1891, Horace L. and Anne Montgomerie Traubel Papers, Library of Congress, container 130; Horace Traubel, *With Walt Whitman in Camden,* vol. 2 (New York: D. Appleton & Company, 1908) 283; Walt Whitman, *The Correspondence,* ed. Edwin Haviland Miller, 6 vols. (New York: New York UP, 1961–77) 1:115; Walt Whitman, "An Indian Bureau Reminiscence," *Prose Works 1892,* ed. Floyd Stovall, 2 vols. (New York: New York UP, 1963–64) 2:577-80; and Horace Traubel, *With Walt Whitman in Camden,* vol. 3 (New York: Mitchell Kennerly, 1914) 468-77.

On Whitman's attitudes about race, see Betsy Erkkila, *Whitman the Political Poet* (New York: Oxford UP, 1989) 121-28, 240-42; Ed Folsom, *Walt Whitman's Native Representations* (New York: Cambridge UP, 1994) 55-98; Justin Kaplan, *Walt Whitman: A Life* (New York: Simon & Schuster, 1980) 132-33, 291-92; and Michael Moon, *Disseminating Whitman: Revision and Corporeality in "Leaves of Grass"* (Cambridge: Harvard UP, 1991) 80-87. Although he abhorred slavery, Whitman usually held to conservative, commonplace racist ideas after the war and, for awhile, opposed black suffrage. Still, as recent critics have shown, portions of Whitman's writings also absorbed and reproduced nineteenth-century antiracist discourse. Furthermore, to pigeonhole his writings as uniformly "racist" is to ignore both the changes in his thought across time and his constant incorporation of multiple and contradictory discourses on numerous issues, including slavery and race. On Whitman's blending of liberating and coercive, antiracist and racist discourses, see the discussions of "The Sleepers" and "I Sing the Body Electric" in Moon, *Disseminating Whitman* 80-87; and Erkkila 117-128. On the evolution of Whitman's attitudes on slavery and race and their cultural context, see Martin Klammer, *Whitman, Slavery, and the Emergence of "Leaves of Grass"* (University Park: Pennsylvania State UP, 1995). On Whitman's opposition to the enfranchisement of African Americans, see Kaplan 344; and Jerome Loving, *Walt Whitman's Champion: William Douglas O'Connor* (College Station: Texas A&M Press, 1978) 94-102; but also Erkkila 284. On Whitman's attitude toward Native Americans, "a contradictory but characteristically American mix of disdain and admiration, of desires to absorb natives and find his antecedents in them fused with desires to distance himself from them" (68-69), see Folsom 55-98. See also George B. Hutchinson, "Whitman and the Black Poet: Kelly Miller's Speech to the Walt Whitman Fellowship," *American Literature* 61, no. 1 (Mar. 1989): 46-58; and Maurice Kenny, "Whitman's Indifference to Indians," *The Continuing Presence of Walt Whitman: The Life After the Life,* ed. Robert K. Martin (Iowa City: U of Iowa P, 1992) 28-38.

17. Walt Whitman, "Ethiopia Saluting the Colors," *Leaves of Grass,* ed. Harold W. Blodgett and Sculley Bradley (New York: New York UP, 1965) 318.

18. Henry B. Whipple, "The Indian System," *North American Review* 99 (Oct. 1864): 449-64; Lydia Maria Child, *An Appeal for the Indians,* rpt. in *Hobomok and Other Writings on Indians,* ed. Carolyn L. Karcher (New Brunswick: Rutgers UP, 1986) 225; Robert W. Mardock, "The Anti-Slavery Humanitarians and Indian Policy Reform," *Western Humanities Review* 12, no. 2 (Spring 1958): 131-46; Robert Winston Mardock, *The Reformers and the American Indian* (Columbia: U of Missouri P, 1971) 8-66; Linda K. Kerber, "The Abolitionist Perception of the Indian," *Journal of American History* 62, no. 2 (Sept. 1975): 271-95.

19. Whipple 449-64. For more on the 1862 Santee Sioux uprising and its historical background, see C. M. Oehler, *The Great Sioux Uprising* (New York: Oxford UP, 1959); Roy W. Meyer, *History of the Santee Sioux: United States Indian Policy on Trial* (Lincoln: U of Nebraska P, 1968); Kenneth Carley, *The Sioux Uprising of 1862,* 2nd ed. (St. Paul: Minnesota Historical Society, 1976); Robert M. Utley, *The Indian Frontier of the American West, 1846–90* (Albuquerque: U of New Mexico P, 1984) 76-81; and Francis Paul Prucha, *The Great Father: The United States Government and the American Indians,* 2 vols. (Lincoln: U of Nebraska P, 1984) 1:437-47.

20. For more on Sand Creek and responses to it, see Helen Hunt Jackson, *A Century of Dishonor* (New York: Harper and Brothers, 1881) 343-58; Stan Hoig, *The Sand Creek Massacre* (Norman: U of Oklahoma P, 1961); Dee Brown, *Bury My Heart at Wounded Knee: An Indian History of the American West* (1970; New York: Bantam, 1972) 67-98; *The Sand Creek Massacre: A Documentary History,* intro. by John M. Carroll (New York: Sol Lewis, 1973); Utley 86-93; Prucha, *Great Father* 1:457-61; and Duane Schultz, *Month of the Freezing Moon: The Sand Creek Massacre, November 1864* (New York: St. Martin's, 1990).

21. "Report of the Doolittle Committee," 26 Jan. 1867, *Documents of United States Indian Policy,* ed. Francis Paul Prucha, 2nd ed. (Lincoln: U of Nebraska P, 1990) 102; Utley 102.

22. *Kansas Daily Tribune* 10 July 1866, qtd. in Mardock, *Reformers and the American Indian* 22.

23. W. T. Sherman, telegram to U. S. Grant, 28 Dec. 1866, rpt. in *The American Indian and the United States: A Documentary History,* ed. Wilcomb E. Washburn, 4 vols. (New York: Random House, 1973) 3:1509.

24. Child, *Appeal for the Indians* 219. For more on humanitarian opposition to Cherokee Removal, see Ralph Waldo Emerson, "Letter to Martin Van Buren, President of the United States: A Protest Against the Removal of the Cherokee Indians from the State of Georgia," 23 Apr. 1838, *The Complete Works of Ralph Waldo Emerson,* 12 vols. (Boston: Houghton Mifflin, 1903–1904) 11:89-96; Carolyn L. Karcher, *The First Woman in the Republic: A Cultural Biography of Lydia Maria Child* (Durham: Duke UP, 1994) 86-100; and Kerber 272-74.

25. "Report of Indian Peace Commissioners," 7 Jan. 1868, *House Executive Documents,* 40th Congress, 2nd session, executive document no. 97, serial 1337: 4, 7, 15. See also William E. Unrau, "Nathaniel Green Taylor, 1867–69," *The Commissioners of Indian Affairs, 1824–1977,* ed. Robert M. Kvasnicka and Herman J. Viola (Lincoln: U of Nebraska P, 1979) 115-22.

26. Child, *Appeal for the Indians* 216, 219. For a discussion of Child's *An Appeal for the Indians,* its historical limitations and "its humanitarian spirit" (555), see Karcher, *First Woman* 552-56.

27. "Report of Indian Peace Commissioners" 18; "Report of the Doolittle Committee"

104. See Mardock, *Reformers and the American Indian* 19-29, 85-106. For a discussion of the rhetoric and imagery of this debate in nineteenth-century writing and art, see Lucy Maddox, *Removals: Nineteenth-Century American Literature and the Politics of Indian Affairs* (New York: Oxford UP, 1991) 15-49.

28. Child, *Appeal for the Indians* 231. Sherman and the other generals on the Indian Peace Commission did not approve of the final report, but they agreed to sign it anyway. Sherman thought that since the military officers had been outvoted, they had to sign the report. In any case, Sherman believed that the Peace Commission might be a useful way "to kill time which will do more to settle the Indians than anything we can do." See Prucha, *Great Father* 1:492n22; and Sherman qtd. in Robert G. Athearn, *William Tecumseh Sherman and the Settlement of the West* (Norman: U of Oklahoma P, 1956) 210-11.

29. See the stories of Native Americans testifying to the degrading, unlivable conditions on reservations in the 1860s, in *Native American Testimony: A Chronicle of Indian-White Relations from Prophecy to the Present, 1492–1992,* ed. Peter Nabokov (New York: Viking, 1991) 193-202. See also William T. Hagan, "Indian Policy after the Civil War: The Reservation Experience," *American Indian Policy: Indiana Historical Society Lectures, 1970–71* (Indianapolis: Indiana Historical Society, 1971) 20-36; William T. Hagan, "The Reservation Policy: Too Little and Too Late," *Indian-White Relations: A Persistent Paradox,* ed. Jane F. Smith and Robert M. Kvasnicka (Washington, DC: Howard UP 1976) 157-69; Ronald T. Takaki, *Iron Cages: Race and Culture in Nineteenth-Century America* (New York: Knopf, 1979) 171-93; Prucha, *Great Father* 1:566-76; Christine Bolt, *American Indian Policy and American Reform: Case Studies of the Campaign to Assimilate the American Indians* (London: Allen & Unwin, 1987) 81-85.

30. See "Report of Indian Peace Commissioners" 16; Child, *Appeal for the Indians* 221-25. For studies of the representation of Native Americans in white discourse, see Robert F. Berkhofer, Jr., *The White Man's Indian: Images of the American Indian from Columbus to the Present* (New York: Vintage, 1979); Roy Harvey Pearce, *Savagism and Civilization: A Study of the Indian and the American Mind* (1953; Baltimore: Johns Hopkins UP, 1965); Richard Slotkin, *Regeneration through Violence: The Mythology of the American Frontier, 1600–1860* (Middletown: Wesleyan UP, 1973). On the role of scientific racialism in the production of these images, see Reginald Horsman, "Scientific Racism and the American Indian in the Mid-Nineteenth Century," *American Quarterly* 27, no. 2 (May 1975): 152-68; but see also Francis Paul Prucha, "Scientific Racism and Indian Policy," *Indian Policy in the United States: Historical Essays* (Lincoln: U of Nebraska P, 1981) 180-97. See also Reginald Horsman, *Race and Manifest Destiny: The Origins of American Racial Anglo-Saxonism* (Cambridge: Harvard UP, 1981).

31. Child, *Appeal for the Indians* 220. In a typical example of the government's infantilization of Native Americans, the Southern Treaty Commission condescendingly announced to Native Americans living in the Indian Territory, "the President is willing to hear his erring children." See "Report of the President of the Southern Treaty Commission," 30 Oct. 1865, *Documents of United States Indian Policy* 97. For an account of Indians as children in government discourse, see Prucha, *Great Father* passim. For a discussion of the infantilization of Native peoples in literature, see Maddox 89-130, esp. 101-103.

32. *Native American Testimony* 137, 131.

33. Calvin Martin, "The Metaphysics of Writing Indian-White History," *The American Indian and the Problem of History,* ed. Calvin Martin (New York: Oxford UP, 1987) 33.

34. For a characteristic sampling of Child's profession of such ideas, see L. Maria Child, *An Appeal in Favor of that Class of Americans Called Africans* (New York: John S. Taylor, 1836; New York: Arno, 1968) 148; L. Maria Child, "The Patriarchal Institution" (New York: American Anti-Slavery Society, 1860) 49, rpt. in *Anti-Slavery Tracts,* series 2 (Westport: Negro Universities P, 1970); and L. Maria Child, "Letter from L. Maria Child," *The National Standard* 27 Aug. 1870: 4.

35. Child, *Appeal for the Indians* 220, 225.

36. Child, *Appeal for the Indians* 227-31.

37. Karcher, *First Woman* 555.

38. Big Eagle qtd. in Dee Brown 38; "Report of the Doolittle Committee" 104; "Report of Indian Peace Commissioners" 17; Whipple 454; *Native American Testimony* 139, 132.

39. "Indian Commissioner Parker on the Treaty System: Extract from the *Annual Report of the Commissioner of Indian Affairs*," 23 Dec. 1869, *Documents of United States Indian Policy* 135; "Indian Commissioner Taylor on Transfer of the Indian Bureau," 23 Nov. 1868, *Documents of United States Indian Policy* 121; Bolt 69. See also George W. Manypenny, *Our Indian Wards* (Cincinnati: Robert Clarke, 1880) vii–xxvi; and Bolt 81-85.

On the implementation of the humanitarians' policy during the Grant presidency, see "President Grant's Peace Policy: Extract from Grant's Second Annual Message to Congress," 5 Dec. 1870, *Documents of United States Indian Policy* 135; Mardock, *Reformers and the American Indian* 30-149; Clyde A. Milner II, *With Good Intentions: Quaker Work among the Pawnees, Otos, and Omahas in the 1870s* (Lincoln: U of Nebraska P, 1982) 1-26; Robert H. Keller, *American Protestantism and United States Indian Policy, 1869–82* (Lincoln: U of Nebraska P, 1983); Prucha, *Great Father* 1:479-606; and Utley 129-55.

40. It is important to note that the humanitarian program was always backed up by the threat of force, should the Indians decide to resist being "civilized" by their humanitarian "friends." Sherman described Grant's peace policy as a "double process of *peace* within their reservation and war *without*." See Sherman qtd. in Milner 2.

41. As Louis Gerteis has written, for example, "As far as blacks were concerned, the Freedmen's Bureau hardly represented a bright beginning. Rather, it marked a discouraging end to the variety of alternatives which the Civil War seemed to make possible" (188). See Louis S. Gerteis, *From Contraband to Freedman: Federal Policy Toward Southern Blacks, 1861–1865* (Westport: Greenwood Press, 1973).

42. At Thoreau's funeral in 1862, Emerson named John Brown and Joe Polis along with Walt Whitman as the three people who had the most significant impact on Thoreau during the last years of his life. See Robert F. Sayre, *Thoreau and the American Indians* (Princeton: Princeton UP, 1977) 184. For Thoreau's anthropological view of Native Americans, see the selections from Thoreau's Indian books in *The Indians of Thoreau: Selections from the Indian Notebooks*, ed. Richard F. Fleck (Albuquerque: Hummingbird Press, 1974). For more on Thoreau's Indian books, see William L. Howarth, *The Literary Manuscripts of Henry David Thoreau* (Columbus: Ohio State UP, 1974) xxii–xxviii, 294-301; Lawrence Willson, "From Thoreau's Indian Manuscripts," *Emerson Society Quarterly* 11, no. 2 (2nd quarter 1958): 52-55; and Sayre 101-22, 217-220. For his anthropological view of humanitarian reformers, see Henry D. Thoreau, "Reform and the Reformers," *Reform Papers,* ed. Wendell Glick (Princeton: Princeton UP, 1973) 181-97. See also Lawrence Willson, "Thoreau: Student of Anthropology," *American Anthropologist* 61, no. 2 (Apr. 1959): 279-89.

43. See Henry D. Thoreau, *Reform Papers,* especially "Resistance to Civil Government" 63-90; "Slavery in Massachusetts" 91-109; "A Plea for Captain John Brown" 111-138; "Martyrdom of John Brown" 139-43; and "The Last Days of John Brown" 145-153. On Thoreau's reading of antislavery newspapers, see Robert Sattelmeyer, *Thoreau's Reading: A Study in Intellectual History with Bibliographical Catalogue* (Princeton: Princeton UP, 1988) 51; and Henry D. Thoreau, "Herald of Freedom," *Reform Papers* 49-57. For more on Thoreau and antislavery, see Michael Meyer, "Thoreau's Rescue of John Brown from History," *Studies in the American Renaissance/1980,* ed. Joel Myerson (Boston: Twayne, 1980) 301-16; Michael Meyer, "Thoreau and Black Emigration," *American Literature* 53, no. 3 (Nov. 1981): 380-96; and Wendell Glick, "Thoreau and Radical Abolitionism," diss., Northwestern U, 1950.

44. Thoreau, "Resistance to Civil Government" 74. In "Reform and the Reformers" Thoreau says, "The great benefactors of their race have been single and singular and not masses of men" (186). He echoed this distrust of collective political action in "Resistance to Civil Government," writing, "There is but little virtue in the action of masses of men" (70). See Thoreau, "Reform and the Reformers," 181-97; Henry D. Thoreau, "Paradise (To Be) Regained," *Reform Papers* 20; and Thoreau's addresses on John Brown, *Reform Papers*

111-53. Although his defense of individualism and his criticism of society were marked and forceful, it would be inaccurate to see Thoreau as completely antisociety or antireform. See Robert D. Richardson, Jr., *Henry Thoreau: A Life of the Mind* (Berkeley: U of California P, 1986) 31-34.

45. Henry David Thoreau, *Journal,* ed. Bradford Torrey and Francis H. Allen, 14 vols. (Boston: Houghton Mifflin, 1906) 3:106; James Goodwin, "Thoreau and John Brown: Transcendental Politics," *Emerson Society Quarterly* 25, no. 3 (3rd quarter 1979): 162, 156, 167.

46. See Sayre 24-25.

47. For a thoughtful examination of Joe Polis's position at the crossing of Penobscot and Euro-American cultures, I am grateful to Stan Tag's "Crossing the River: Joe Polis and the Penobscot Indians," unpublished paper, 1989. On Thoreau's reading in the history of North American Indian cultures, see Sattelmeyer 99-110. For more on the influence of Joe Aitteon and Joe Polis on Thoreau's thinking, see Sayre xiii, 155-93, 203-204, 212-15; D. M. Murray, "Thoreau's Indians and His Developing Art of Characterization," *Emerson Society Quarterly* 21, no. 4 (4th quarter 1975): 222-29; Bette S. Weidman, "Thoreau and Indians," *Thoreau Journal Quarterly* 5 (Oct. 1973): 4-10. See also Philip F. Gura, "Thoreau's Maine Woods Indians: More Representative Men," *American Literature* 49, no. 3 (Nov. 1977): 366-84.

48. See Walter Harding, *The Days of Henry Thoreau* (1965; Princeton: Princeton UP, 1992) 441-66; and Robert D. Richardson, Jr., 385-89. On *The Maine Woods,* Sayre writes: "From the standpoint of Thoreau's Indian education, it is, unquestionably, his most important book, 'the book about Indians' which he *did* write" (155).

49. Sattelmeyer x.

50. Henry D. Thoreau, *The Maine Woods,* ed. Joseph J. Moldenhauer (Boston: Ticknor and Fields, 1864; Princeton: Princeton UP, 1972). References to *The Maine Woods* are noted parenthetically in the text.

51. The moral force of Thoreau's disapproval of the Indians' "drunken frolic" collapses, however, when a mere two sentences later in this same paragraph Thoreau and his other white companions head to Tom Fowler's house to drink beer (and frolic perhaps) before continuing downstream.

52. But, then again, whether we see Thoreau moving away from or remaining indebted to these racialist notions of the vanishing race depends on how we read Thoreau's ambiguous language. The full paragraph, which follows a moose-hunting scene, reads:

> This afternoon's experience suggested to me how base or coarse are the motives which commonly carry men into the wilderness. The explorers, and lumberers generally, are all hirelings, paid so much a day for their labor, and as such, they have no more love for wild nature, than wood-sawyers have for forests. Other white men and Indians who come here are for the most part hunters, whose object is to slay as many moose and other wild animals as possible. But, pray, could not one spend some weeks or years in the solitude of this vast wilderness with other employments than these—employments perfectly sweet and innocent and ennobling? For one that comes with a pencil to sketch or sing, a thousand come with an axe or rifle. What a coarse and imperfect use Indians and hunters make of nature! No wonder that their race is so soon exterminated. I already and for weeks afterward felt my nature the coarser for this part of my woodland experience, and was reminded that our life should be lived tenderly and daintily as one would pluck a flower. (119-20)

If the "race . . . so soon to be exterminated" is the race of hunters and Indians, as in Sayre's reading, then Thoreau indeed continues to rely on his society's racialist mythology. Although it seems odd that Thoreau would refer to Indians (like Joe Aitteon) and hunters (like "Our Nimrod" [110], his white companion George Thatcher) as if they belonged to the same race, in the singular, Sayre's reading does make sense grammatically: "Indians and hunters" is the most appropriate antecedent to the pronoun "their." But, if "race" refers to the moose being slaughtered, then Thoreau's purpose is to describe the dangerously exploitative way in which humans are "permanently" altering wild lands and wildlife (a crucial theme throughout "Chesuncook"), and thus the sentence does not refer to the extermination of Indians and thus does not reproduce this particular racialist myth. I bring attention to the ambiguity of this passage precisely because it illustrates my sense of how "Chesuncook" seems to waver between reproducing racialist representations of Native Americans and refusing them. See Sayre 169.

53. See also Thoreau's earlier nonironic use of "the howling wilderness" in "Ktaadn" (82-83).

54. The "roving and savage" description is from "Instructions to the Board of Indian Commissioners," 1869, *Documents of United States Indian Policy* 129. See also Mary Sherwood, "The Joe Polis Property," *Thoreau Journal Quarterly* 10 (July 1978): 11.

55. Child, *Appeal for the Indians* 220.

56. As usual, Thoreau was a meticulous student. See Thoreau's "A List of Indian Words" in Appendix, *The Maine Woods* 320-25.

57. Henry David Thoreau, letter to H. G. Otis Blake, 18 Aug. 1857, *The Correspondence of Henry David Thoreau,* ed. Walter Harding and Carl Bode (New York: New York UP, 1958) 491-92.

58. Lucy Maddox has also used Thoreau's "dark and savage"/"mild and infantile" comment to locate *The Maine Woods* within the conventional, racist rhetoric of nineteenth-century debates about U.S. Indian policy (Maddox 157). Nevertheless, while Maddox and I both want to acknowledge the considerable influence these debates had on shaping Thoreau's language, Maddox exaggerates the case by claiming that Thoreau is "fully persuaded that there is no alternative to the future extinction of the Indians" (158) and by suggesting that Thoreau's only interest in Polis is in using him to make the Indian past "intelligible" to white readers (157). As I argued earlier, Thoreau in *The Maine Woods* begins to imagine a story of Indian survival rather than extinction; and, the complex and idiosyncratic portrait of Polis makes Polis much more than a mere, stereotypical "representative of the Indian past" (157). Recognizing the ways in which dominant cultural scripts determine Thoreau's language should not blind us to the ways that Thoreau deviated from or subversively improvised upon those dominant scripts.

59. [Thomas Wentworth Higginson], rev. of *The Maine Woods,* by Henry D. Thoreau, *Atlantic Monthly* Sept. 1864: 386.

7. Afterword: AIDS and Unconventional Caring

1. Tony Kushner, *Angels in America, Part Two: Perestroika* (New York: Theatre Communications Group, 1994) 62.

2. Douglas Crimp and Adam Rolston, *AIDS demo graphics* (Seattle: Bay Press, 1990) 37.

3. "Research Group Says AIDS Epidemic Will Have Little Effect on U.S.," *New York Times* 5 Feb. 1993: A7. Data from the Centers for Disease Control and Prevention indicate that this conclusion is dangerously false. See Pamela M. Walsh, "Growing AIDS Epidemic Becomes More Diverse," *Boston Globe* 7 Feb. 1995: 32.

4. See Michael Moon, "Rereading Whitman under Pressure of AIDS: His Sex Radicalism and Ours," *The Continuing Presence of Walt Whitman: The Life After the Life,* ed. Robert K. Martin (Iowa City: U of Iowa P, 1992) 53-66; Dorothy Nelkin, David P. Willis, and Scott V. Parris, eds., *A Disease of Society: Cultural and Institutional Responses to AIDS* (New York: Cambridge UP, 1991); Elizabeth Fee and Daniel M. Fox, eds., *AIDS: The Burdens of History* (Berkeley: U of California P, 1988); Douglas Crimp, ed., *AIDS: Cultural Analysis, Cultural Activism* (Cambridge: MIT Press, 1988); Michael Bronski, "Movies, Death, and AIDS" *Z Magazine* Nov. 1992: 64-66; and Peter M. Bowen, "AIDS 101," *Writing AIDS: Gay Literature, Language, and Analysis,* ed. Timothy F. Murphy and Suzanne Poirier (New York: Columbia UP, 1993) 140-60. For more on AIDS and literature, see the essays collected in *Writing*

AIDS; Emmanuel S. Nelson, *AIDS: The Literary Response* (New York: Twayne, 1993); and Judith Laurence Pastore, ed., *Confronting AIDS through Literature: The Responsibilities of Representation* (Champaign-Urbana: U of Illinois P, 1993).

5. Daniel Harris, "AIDS & Theory," *Lingua Franca* June 1991: 18-19; Jan Zita Grover, "AIDS, Keywords, and Cultural Work," *Cultural Studies*, ed. Lawrence Grossberg, Cary Nelson, Paula A. Treichler (New York: Routledge, 1992) 237.

6. Indeed, it has. See the cultural criticism in Crimp, ed., *AIDS: Cultural Analysis, Cultural Activism*; Cindy Patton, *Inventing AIDS* (New York: Routledge, 1990); Catherine Saalfield and Ray Navarro, "Not Just Black and White: AIDS, Media, and People of Color," *PWA Coalition Newsline* May 1991: 15-19; Paula A. Treichler, "AIDS, HIV, and the Cultural Constructions of Reality," *Social Analysis in the Time of AIDS*, ed. Gilbert Herdt and Shirley Lindenbaum (Newbury Park, CA: Sage, 1992) 65-98; Simon Watney, *Policing Desire: Pornography, AIDS, and the Media*, 2nd ed. (Minneapolis: U of Minnesota P, 1989); and Simon Watney, *Practices of Freedom: Selected Writings on HIV/AIDS* (Durham: Duke UP, 1994).

7. The "utterly insular" and "careerist" charges are from Harris, "AIDS & Theory" 19. University professors can be and are often insular and careerist. But, this is not true of everyone who teaches in universities, and it is not an inevitable or natural fact of being a professor.

8. The efforts of PWAs like the late Michael Callen, activist intellectuals like Simon Watney (a former university professor), or AIDS workers like Jan Zita Grover epitomize such an approach to humanitarian work.

9. Slavoj Žižek, *The Sublime Object of Ideology* (London: Verso, 1989) 56.

10. Žižek 138. See also Walter Benjamin, "Theses on the Philosophy of History," *Illuminations*, ed. Hannah Arendt, trans. Harry Zohn (1968; New York: Schocken Books, 1985) 253-64.

11. See Randy Shilts, *And the Band Played On: Politics, People, and the AIDS Epidemic* (New York: St. Martin's, 1987) 374-75.

12. "Abuse of AIDS Patients," *Washington Post* 18 Oct. 1992: A22; "HIV-Infected Persons Say Health-Care Workers Discriminate," *American Journal of Hospital Pharmacy* 50, no. 1 (Jan. 1993): 28-32; Carol Pogash, *As Real As It Gets: The Life of a Hospital at the Center of the AIDS Epidemic* (New York: Birch Lane, 1992) 177. See also Robert J. Blendon and Karen Donelan, "Discrimination against People with AIDS," *New England Journal of Medicine* 319 (13 Oct. 1988): 1022-26; Peter Conrad, "The Social Meaning of AIDS," *Social Policy* 17 (Summer 1986): 51-65; Reneé C. Fox, Linda H. Aiken, and Carla M. Messikomer, "The Culture of Caring: AIDS and the Nursing Profession," in *Disease of Society* 137; Charles Perrow and Mauro F. Guillén, *The AIDS Disaster: The Failure of Organizations in New York and the Nation* (New Haven: Yale UP, 1990) 146-47; and Pogash 173-79.

13. Quoted in Arthur Kleinman, *The Illness Narratives: Suffering, Healing, and the Human Condition* (New York: Basic Books, 1988) 163.

14. Tony J. Giordano, "Isolation," in *Unending Dialogue: Voices from an AIDS Poetry Workshop,* by Rachel Hadas, with Charles Barber, Glenn Besco, Dan Conner, Tony J. Giordano, Kevin Imbusch, Glen Philip Kramer, Raul Martinez-Avila, and James Turcotte (Boston: Faber and Faber, 1991) 24. See also the other PWA-authored poems in *Unending Dialogue*, esp. Conner, "People Come Out of the Woodwork" 28-29; Turcotte, "Fall Sonnets" 36; Giordano, "Saturday Night" 56; Besco, "Tuesday in Holy Week, 1990, Dark Grey Day in Peekskill, NY" 77-78; and Barber, "Fairy Book Lines" 79-81.

15. Giordano, "Isolation" 24.

16. Shilts, *And the Band Played On* 362; "The Denver Principles," rpt. in the ACT UP/New York Women and AIDS Book Group, *Women, AIDS, and Activism* (Boston: South End Press, 1990) 239. See also Lew Katoff, "Working in an AIDS Organization," *PWA Coalition Newsline* June 1991: 20. For analyses of the typically repressive and disempowering representation of people with AIDS, see Crimp, ed., *AIDS: Cultural Analysis, Cultural Activism*; Douglas Crimp, "Portraits of People with AIDS," *Cultural Studies* 117-33; Sander

L. Gilman, *Disease and Representation: Images of Illness from Madness to AIDS* (Ithaca: Cornell UP, 1988) 245-72; Patton, *Inventing AIDS*; and Susan Sontag, *AIDS and Its Metaphors* (New York: Farrar, Straus and Giroux, 1989). (Sontag's book ought to be read alongside D. A. Miller, "Sontag's Urbanity," *The Lesbian and Gay Studies Reader,* ed. Henry Abelove, Michèle Aina Barale, and David M. Halperin [New York: Routledge, 1993] 212-20.) See also Edmund White's comments in an interview in *Life Sentences: Writers, Artists, and AIDS,* ed. Thomas Avena (San Francisco: Mercury House, 1994) 244-46.

17. Marianne Williamson, *A Return to Love: Reflections on the Principles of "A Course in Miracles"* (New York: HarperCollins, 1992) 196-97. The quotation within this passage is from *A Course in Miracles,* an important New Age scripture described by Williamson as "a self-study program of spiritual psychotherapy" (xv). For Hay's New Age account of AIDS, see Louise L. Hay, *The AIDS Book: Creating a Positive Approach* (Santa Monica: Hay House, 1988), esp. Part I, "Understanding the Dis-Ease of AIDS" 9-50.

Both Williamson and Hay have made careers from humanitarian AIDS work. Although Williamson has not devoted an entire book to the subject of AIDS, *A Return to Love* has a considerable amount to say about AIDS, sickness, and healing. Furthermore, about half of her book-jacket biography reads:

> Ms. Williamson is the Founder and Chairman of the Los Angeles and Manhattan Centers for the Living, non-profit organizations that provide free non-medical services to people living with life-challenging illnesses and grief. The L.A. Center's Project Angel Food prepares and delivers hot meals seven days a week to hundreds of home-bound people with AIDS.

Clearly, Williamson wants to be thought of as a humanitarian AIDS worker—and that is how I approach her writing.

18. Williamson 197, 198; Hay, Chapter 3 ("A Dis-Ease of Lack of Love"), 29-39.

19. C. Norman Shealy and Caroline M. Myss, *AIDS: Passageway to Transformation* (Walpole, NH: Stillpoint, 1987) 20, 37, 36, 54.

20. See Shealy and Myss 80-85.

21. Williamson 206. For Williamson on the value of "surrender," see Chapter 4, 45-54. For discussions on the need to eliminate anger, see Williamson 81-85; and Hay 89-92. For the "Dear AIDS" letters, see Williamson 209-16; and Hay 30-31.

22. Similar arguments about New Age philanthropy have been made by people living with AIDS. See Scott Tucker, "New Age vs. New Rage," *Z Magazine* Sept. 1992: 50-51; and the interviews with the Reverend Steven Pieters and "Lela," in Michael Callen, *Surviving AIDS* (New York: HarperCollins, 1990) 81-89 and 124-32.

23. William F. Buckley, "Identify All the Carriers," *New York Times* 18 March 1986: A27. Since then, Buckley has reluctantly but formally withdrawn his proposal that people with AIDS be tattooed. See *On the Firing Line: The Public Life of Our Public Figures* (New York: Random House, 1989) 212.

24. Watney, *Practices of Freedom* xiii.

25. John Tierney, "A San Francisco Talk Show Takes Right-Wing Radio to a New Dimension," *New York Times* 14 Feb. 1995: A10.

26. My account of the inpatient AIDS unit at the San Francisco General Hospital is taken primarily from Shilts, *And the Band Played On* 354-57, 394-96; and Pogash 101-12, esp. 104-105. The quotations are from these two texts. For more on the innovation in AIDS care at San Francisco General Hospital's AIDS unit, see Morrison's article, "Establishing a Therapeutic Environment: Institutional Resources," *The Person with AIDS: Nursing Perspectives,* ed. Jerry D. Durham and Felissa L. Cohen (New York: Springer, 1987) 110-24. See also Fox, Aiken, and Messikomer 134; and Ed Wolf, "A Week on Ward 5A," *The AIDS Reader: Social, Political, and Ethical Issues,* ed. Nancy McKenzie (New York: Meridian, 1991) 527-33. On the knowledge of PWAs and their active roles in their own healthcare, see, for example, Pogash 162; *Partners in Care: The patient/physician partnership,* spec. issue of

Positively Aware Spring 1993: 1-32, esp. Machelle H. Allen and Janet Mitchell, "Bridging the Gap Between People of Color and Their Physicians: How to Build a Partnership" 19; and *Now That You Know: Living Healthy with HIV. Part 2: Understanding HIV,* prod. and dir. Randall Neece, Kaiser Permanente, 1991.

My brief focus on Unit 5B is intended only as an example. There are also other AIDS organizations—such as the Gay Men's Health Crisis (GMHC) or the Association for Drug Abuse Prevention and Treatment (ADAPT)—committed to an eccentric approach to humanitarian work. For more on GMHC, see Philip M. Kayal, *Bearing Witness: Gay Men's Health Crisis and the Politics of AIDS* (Boulder: Westview, 1993); Lewis Katoff and Susan Ince, "Supporting People with AIDS: The GMHC Model," *AIDS Reader* 543-76; and Suzanne C. Ouellette Kobasa, "AIDS Volunteering: Links to the Past and Future Prospects," *Disease of Society* 172-88. For more on ADAPT, see Perrow and Guillén 117-26.

27. "The Denver Principles" 240; Bobbi Campell qtd. by Michael Callen, *Surviving Aids* 73; Kayal 9.

28. Watney, *Practices of Freedom* 30; Phyllida Brown, "How AIDS made patients act up," *New Scientist* 134 (6 June 1992) 21. For more on the objections to the MDA's infantilizing philanthropy and the patient-centered activism of people with dystrophic illnesses, see Leslie Bennetts, "Jerry vs. the Kids," *Vanity Fair* Sept. 1993: 82-98.

29. Larry Kramer, *Reports from the Holocaust: The Making of an AIDS Activist* (New York: St. Martin's, 1989) 110; Larry Kramer, *The Normal Heart* (New York: Plume, 1985) 79.

30. Paul Monette, "Buckley," *Poets for Life: Seventy-Six Poets Respond to AIDS,* ed. Michael Klein (New York: Persea, 1989) 170; James Robert Baker, *Tim and Pete* (New York: Simon & Schuster, 1993) 143, 131, 130.

31. Crimp and Rolston, *AIDS demo graphics* 37; "How to Join ACT UP/Chicago," *ACT UP News: AIDS Activist News* Summer 1992: 3. ACT UP's self-description appears in *AIDS demo graphics* 13 (emphasis added). While ACT UP's commitment to eccentric action is evidence of the reemergence of unconventional humanitarianism, all is not well with ACT UP. Most of ACT UP's 79 chapters are still vital and active, but the anger that "united" ACT UP has also created organizational instability. Such instability can be one of the risks of an eccentric approach. See "Battle Fatigue," *The New Yorker* 9 Nov. 1992: 39-40; and Sally Chew, "What's Going Down With ACT UP," *Out* Nov. 1993: 72-75, 130-37.

32. These organizations are easily contacted at the following addresses: National Association of People with AIDS, 1413 K Street N.W., Washington, DC 20005; People with AIDS Coalition, 31 West 26th Street, New York, NY 10010; Body Positive, 208 West 13th Street, New York, NY 10011; and The Committee of Ten Thousand, c/o The Packard Manse, 583 Plain Street, Stoughton, MA 02072.

33. Gina Kolata, "Advocates' Tactics on AIDS Issues Provoking Warnings of a Backlash," *New York Times* 11 March 1990, sec 2: 5.

34. See Crimp and Rolston, *AIDS demo graphics*; and Callen, *Surviving AIDS* esp. 8-9.

35. Kayal 15; Randy Shilts, Foreword, *As Real As It Gets,* by Carol Pogash x; Pogash 16; Kramer, "The Beginning of ACTing UP," *Reports* 127-9; Crimp and Rolston, *AIDS demo graphics* 26.

INDEX

Abbott, E. G., 95

Abolition. *See* Antislavery

ACT UP, 167-70, 208n31

Adorno, Theodor, 134

African Americans: and Stowe, 3, 48, 52, 53-54, 56, 57, 59, 64, 65-66, 67, 69, 73, 182-83n7, 186n34; and conventional humanitarianism, 5-9, 40-44, 46-48, 49-76, 134-39, 146-47, 199n4, 203n41; and eccentric humanitarianism, 5-10, 12, 15, 16, 17-19, 38-40, 45-46, 46-48, 50-51, 64-76, 135-37, 171, 203n41; and John Brown, 17-19, 19-20, 38-48, 181n45; setbacks in 1850s, 45-46; and Child, 46-48, 57, 61, 137-38, 141, 147, 183-84n10, 186n34; and Civil War, 91, 96; and Nast, 124; and Louisa May Alcott, 138, 147, 200n15; and Whitman, 138-39, 147, 200-201n16; and Thoreau, 148. *See also* Antislavery; Douglass, Frederick; Emigration; Freedpeople; Humanitarians, African American; Jacobs, Harriet; Wilson, Harriet

Agassiz, Louis, 184n12

Agency, 12, 13, 14, 49, 176-77n23; and Harriet Jacobs, 73-75. *See also* Patients as agents

Agent, humanitarian. *See* Patient-agent opposition

AIDS: as humanitarian crisis, 1, 156, 157, 159; and humanitarianism, 157-71, 173n2, 206n8, 208n31; and cultural criticism, 157-61; and literature, 157-58, 162-65, 168-71, 207n17

Aitteon, Joe, 149, 150, 204n52

Alcott, Bronson, 19, 99-100

Alcott, Louisa May, 75, 170, 194n84; as a patient, 15, 99-101, 108-109; as a nurse, 79, 85-87, 91, 98-101, 108; and patients in Civil War, 79, 86-87, 98-101, 193n73; postwar representations of patients, 107-14; and African Americans, 138, 147, 200n15

—*works by:* "A Hospital Christmas," 101; *Hospital Sketches,* 86-87, 98-101, 108, 138, 193n73; *Little Women,* 86, 100, 101; "A Nurse's Story," 107-14, 194n78; *Work,* 100-101, 194n78

Altruizm, 56-58, 185n22; and Stowe, 57, 65-66, 67; and Harriet Jacobs, 65-67, 68, 70, 185n22; and Whitman, 57, 65, 101-105

American Colonization Society, 52

American Indians. *See* Native Americans

American Medical Association, 78

American Missionary Association, 199n4

American Red Cross, 83

American Tract Society, 135

Andrews, William, 188n56

Annas, George, 169

Anspach, F. R.: *The Sepulchres of Our Departed,* 120

Antislavery, 3, 5, 6, 7, 8, 9, 10, 15, 17-76, 134-35, 137, 138, 139, 141, 144, 147, 148, 174n13, 175n17, 178-79n12, 179n20, 179n27, 182-83n7, 183-84n10, 184n12

Aptheker, Herbert, 181n45

Armory Square Hospital, 94

Armory Square Hospital Gazette, 89, 94

Army Medical Bureau, 80, 83

Arthur, T. S., 123, 198n21; "Going into Mourning," 118-20

Atlantic Monthly, 156

Bacon, Leonard, 35, 36

Baker, James Robert: *Tim and Pete,* 168-69

Banneker, Benjamin, 137

Barthes, Roland, 132

Barton, Clara, 15, 83, 123, 198n21

Beauregard, Pierre Gustave Toutant, 38

Beecher, Henry Ward, 26, 31-32, 123, 179n27, 198n21

Bellows, Henry, 80, 87

Benevolence. *See* Humanitarianism

Benevolent rhetoric, 51-52, 65, 67-68, 70, 81

Benjamin, Walter: "Theses on the Philosophy of History," 2, 16, 160, 161

Bickerdyke, Mary Ann, 83

Big Bear, 145

Big Eagle, 145

Bigelow, Henry J., 78

Bixby, Lydia, 121

Blake, Harrison, 154

Blassingame, John W., 186n35

Bleeding Kansas, 30, 33, 34, 35, 36, 179n27, 180n38

Bliss, Mrs. (mesmerist), 108

Body Positive, 169

Bolt, Christine, 146

Booth, John Wilkes, 115

Braxton, Joanne, 73

Bremner, Robert H., 10-11, 175n19, 177n25; *The Public Good: Philanthropy and Welfare in the Civil War Era,* 10

British Sanitary Commission, 88

Self-help, 9, 10, 56, 62, 71-75, 76, 135-37
Self-reliance. *See* Self-help
Sentimentalism, 3, 5-7, 9, 41, 62, 65, 70, 82, 87-88, 144, 187n43
Sexton, Anne, 1
Shands Hospital, 161
Shaw, Robert, 76
Shaw, Sarah, 138
Shealy, C. Norman: *AIDS: Passageway to Transformation,* 164
Sheldon, Lou, 166
Sherman, William Tecumseh, 83, 139, 140, 142, 146, 202n28, 203n40
Shilts, Randy, 170
Signifyin(g), 63-65, 70, 73-75
Sioux, 140
Sixbey, George L., 196n8
Slave narratives, 73. *See also* Douglass, Frederick; Jacobs, Harriet
Slavery. *See* Antislavery; Emancipation
Smitherman, Geneva, 63
"Songs of Victory Drowned in Sorrow" (*New York Times* article), 118
Sparks, Jared, 51
Stanton, Elizabeth Cady, 54
Stearns, Mary, 40
Stepto, Robert, 60
Stern, Madeleine B., 107, 108
Stevens, Alexander H., 78
Stewart, Maria W., 70
Stillé, Charles J., 79, 80
Stowe, Harriet Beecher: *Uncle Tom's Cabin,* 3, 48, 52, 53-54, 57, 59, 64, 67, 69, 182-83n7; and African Americans, 3, 48, 52, 53-54, 56, 57, 59, 64, 65-66, 67, 69, 73, 182-83n7, 186n34
Strong, George Templeton, 79, 80, 83
Stuart, George, 139
Swayze, Mrs. J. C.: *Ossawattomie Brown,* 19, 33, 34, 36-37, 44
Sweet, Timothy, 106
Sympathy, 6, 27, 35, 36, 37, 39, 72, 79, 80, 81, 87, 103-107, 118, 148, 194n78. *See also* Altruizm

Takaki, Ronald T., 53
Taylor Commission Report, 141-42
Taylor, Nathaniel G., 141-42
Thatcher, George, 204n52
Thayer & Eldridge, 186n34
Thomas, M. Wynn, 116
Thoreau, Henry David, 123, 159, 198n21; and John Brown, 26, 27, 33, 36, 147, 203n42; and antislavery, 27, 147-48; and Native Americans, 147-56, 203n42, 204n51, 204-205n52, 205n58; and collective politics, 147-49, 155-56, 203-204n44; and African Americans, 148; compared to Child, 156
—*works by:* "The Allegash and the East Branch," 150-55; "Chesuncook," 150, 154, 204-205n52; *Journal,* 148; "Ktaadn," 149-50, 154;

The Maine Woods, 149-56, 205n58; "A Plea for Captain John Brown," 26, 27, 147; "Reform and Reformers," 203n44; "Resistance to Civil Government," 203n44; "Slavery in Massachusetts," 147
Torrey, Lizzie R.: *The Ideal of Womanhood,* 85
Toussaint-Louverture, 137
Trachtenberg, Alan, 4, 82
Traditional Values Coalition, 166
Traubel, Horace, 84, 197n10
Truth, Sojourner, 37, 70
Tubman, Harriet, 38, 70
Turner, Nat, 39, 46, 47
Turner, Victor, 195n6

Union Hotel Hospital, 86, 99, 108
United States Colored Troops, 96
United States Sanitary Commission, 4, 79-82, 83-88 *passim,* 89-90, 91, 93, 135

Vallandigham, Clement L., 20, 44
Vandemark, William E., 94, 123
Vanderpool, Dr. (Union doctor), 77-78, 98
Vesey, Denmark, 39, 46
Violence (issue for humanitarians), 17-19, 21-46, 168-69
Volberding, Paul, 170
Voyeurism, 97, 110-12

Walker, David, 52
Walsh, Gary, 163
Walters, Ronald, 184n10
Warner, Susan: *The Wide, Wide World,* 5, 64
Watney, Simon, 167, 206n8; *Practices of Freedom,* 166
Webster, Daniel, 152
Weekly Anglo-African, 39, 46
Weld, Anna, 108
Weld, Theodore, 184n12
Wesley, John, 10-11
Western Sanitary Commission, 83
Wheately, Phillis, 137
Wheelock, Edwin M., 26, 27, 28
Whipper, William, 60
Whipple, Henry, 139, 145
White, Barbara A., 174n13
White, Martin, 180n38
Whitman, Walt, 77, 157, 170, 203n42; and postwar mourning, 15, 114, 115-18, 122-33, 198-99n26; as hospital volunteer, 16, 79, 81-82, 84, 86, 93-98, 101-102, 193n70; and patients in Civil War, 79, 81, 84, 86, 92, 93-98, 101-107, 193n70; as patient, 101; and African Americans, 138-39, 147, 200-201n16; and Native Americans, 138, 147, 200-201n16
—*works by:* "Ah Poverties, Wincings, and Sulky Retreats," 128; "An Army on the March," 129, 131; "As I Lay with My Head in Your Lap, Camerado," 128, 196n8, 196n9; "A Backward Glance o'er Travel'd Roads," 132-33; "Cala-

Gregory Eiselein is Assistant Professor of English
and a faculty member in the Program in
Cultural Studies at Kansas State University.